WITHDRAWN

JAN 1 8 2008

D1605117

WITHDRAWN

JAN 1 8 2008

APPIAN

Wars of the Romans in Iberia

Iberike

With an Introduction, Translation and Commentary by

J.S. Richardson

DG
207
.A64
I23
2000
c.2

ARIS & PHILLIPS LTD – WARMINSTER – ENGLAND

© J.S. RICHARDSON 2000. All rights reserved. No part of this book may be reproduced or utilized in any form or by any electronic, mechanical or other means, now known or hereafter invented, including photocopying or recording, or in any information storage or retrieval system without permission in writing from the publishers.

ISBNs   0 85668 719 7   Cloth
               0 85668 720 0   limp

British Library Cataloguing-in-Publication Data
A catalogue record of this book is available from the British Library

Printed and published in England by Aris & Phillips Ltd, Warminster, Wiltshire BA12 8PQ

For Patricia

sine qua non

Contents

Preface

Until recently, Appian was regarded by those interested in the history of Rome as an inferior writer who happened to have written about some matters on which we were otherwise very poorly informed. The position was well put to me as a young researcher by a senior colleague, who told me that the real question about such historians as Appian and Diodorus Siculus was whether they thought at all, or were simply repositories for earlier writers. It is not surprising that the only edition and commentary on the whole of Appian's surviving works remains that of Schweighäuser, published in three volumes in Leipzig in 1785. Schweighäuser was a remarkable scholar, who combined great erudition with hard work and shrewd common sense to make major contributions to the study of the writings of the ancient historians, especially Polybius and Appian, but his interests, as with most of his contemporaries, were primarily philological. It is only in the latter half of the twentieth century that interest in Appian has revived, especially under the influence of Emilio Gabba in Italy and Kai Brodersen in Germany. In the last decade, the *Iberike* (here translated as *The Wars of the Romans in Iberia*) has benefited from the work of Paul Goukowski and Christoph Leidl, who have shown far more clearly the historical and historiographical, as well as the philological, interest of the book.

During the same period, we have come to have a far clearer understanding of the history of the period and the area which Appian describes here, through the contributions both of scholars in Spain and Portugal and of those interested in the growth of Roman power in the third and second centuries BC throughout the world, and by the discovery and interpretation of new epigraphic and archaeological evidence. The intention of this volume is to bring together for the use of English-speaking readers these various strands of recent work in a new version of the text, an English translation, and a commentary, explaining in particular matters of historical and historiographical interest. Appian's *Iberike* is not only a major source for the history of Roman Iberia and of the growth of Roman imperialism in a vital period but a work which reveals that its author did indeed think about what he wrote, and did so interestingly and intelligently.

I take this opportunity to express my thanks to the many friends and colleagues (too many, indeed for me to be able to name them all) who have helped me in the writing of this book. In particular, among my colleagues, present and past, in Edinburgh, I would mention Ed Bispham, Fritz Gregor Herrmann, Geoffrey Lewis and Karen Stears; and among those from elsewhere, Kai Brodersen, Michael Crawford, Carlotta Dionisotti, Christoph Leidl and Malcolm Willcock. Still more is owed to a number of patient research students who have kept me thinking about Roman Spain when I was engaged in quite other matters, in particular Lisa Bligh, Paul Erdkamp, Bertrand Goffaux and Benedict Lowe; and more still to my wife, to whom I dedicate this book.

Edinburgh 2000   John Richardson

v

Short Bibliography and Abbreviations

Astin, A. E., *Scipio Aemilianus* (Oxford 1967) [= Astin, *Scipio Aemilianus*]

Astin, A. E., Walbank, F. W., Frederiksen, M. W. and Oglivie, R. M., *Cambridge Ancient History*, vol. VIII, *Rome and the Mediterranean to 133 BC* (2nd edition, Cambridge 1989) [= *CAH* VIII^2]

Brodersen, K., 'Appian und sein Werk', *ANRW* II.34.1 (Berlin and New York 1993), pp. 339-363 [=Brodersen]

Broughton, T. R. S., *The Magistrates of the Roman Republic*, 3 vols (New York 1951 and 1986) [= Broughton, *MRR*]

Brunt, P. A., *Italian Manpower, 25 BC - AD 14* (Oxford 1971) [= Brunt, *Italian Manpower*]

Crawford, M. H., *Roman Republican Coinage* (Cambridge 1974) [=Crawford, *RRC*]

Famerie, É., *Le latin et le grec d'Appien: conribution à l'étude du lexique d'un historien grec de Rome* (Paris 1998) [=Famerie, *Le latin et le grec*]

Gómez Espelosín, F. J., 'Appian's *Iberike*. Aims and attitudes of a Greek historian of Rome', *ANRW* II.34.1 (Berlin and New York 1993), pp. 403-27 [= Gómez]

Goukowsky, P., *Appien, Histoire Romaine, tome VI, L'Ibérique* (*Collections de Universités de France*, Paris 1997) [= Goukowsky, *Appien*]

Harrison, R. J., *Spain at the dawn of history: Iberians, Phoenicians and Greeks* (London 1988) [= Harrison, *Spain*]

Hornblower, S. and Spawforth, A. (edd), *Oxford Classical Dictionary* (3rd edition, Oxford 1996) [= *OCD*^{3}]

Janni, P., *La mappa e il periplo* (Rome 1984) [= Janni, *La mappa*]

Keay, S.J., *Roman Spain* (London 1988) [= Keay, *Roman Spain*]

Klotz, A., *Appians Darstellung des zweiten punischen Kreig* (Paderborn 1936) [= Klotz]

Lazenby, J., *Hannibal's War* (Warminster 1978) [= Lazenby, *Hannibal's War*]

Leidl, C., *Appians Darstellung des 2. punischen Krieges in Spanien (Iberike c.1-38 §1-158a)* (*Münchener Arbeiten zur alten Geschichte* Bd. 11, 1996) [= Leidl]

Mendelssohn, L., *Appiani Historia Romana*, 2 vols (Leipzig 1879 and 1881) [=Mendelssohn]

Mommsen, Th., *Römisches Staatsrecht*, 3 vols (Leipzig 1887-9) [= Mommsen, *StR*]

Richardson, J. S., *Hispaniae: Spain and the development of Roman imperialism, 218-82 BC* (Cambridge 1986) [= Richardson, *Hispaniae*]

Richardson, J. S., *The Romans in Spain* (Oxford 1996) [= Richardson, *The Romans in Spain*]

Schweighäuser, J., *Appiani Alexandrini Romanorum Historiarum quae supersunt*, 3 vols (Leipzig 1785) [= Schweighäuser, *Appian*]

Schweighäuser, J., *Polybii Megalopolitani Historiarum quae supersunt*, 8 vols (Leipzig 1789-1795) [= Schweighäuser, *Polybius*]

Schulten, A., *Fontes Hispaniae Antiquae*, vols 3 and 4 (Barcelona 1935 and 1937) [= Schulten, *FHA*]

Schulten, A., *Numantia*, 4 vols (Munich 1914-31) [= Schulten, *Numantia*]

Schwartz, Ed., *Appianus*, in Pauly-Wissowa, *RE* II (1896), 215-237 [Schwartz]

Scullard, H. H., *Scipio Africanus in the second Punic war* (Cambridge 1930)

Scullard, H. H., *Scipio Africanus: soldier and politician* (London 1970) [= Scullard, *Scipio*]

Simon, H. *Roms Kriege in Spanien, 154-133 v. Chr.* (Frankfurt am Main 1962) [= Simon, *Roms Kriege*]

Viereck, P. and Roos, A.G., *Appiani Historia Romana*, vol. 1 (corrected edition with additions by E. Gabba, Leipzig 1962) [= Viereck-Roos]

Walbank, F. W., *A Historical Commentary on Polybius*, 3 vols (Oxford 1957, 1967 and 1979) [= Walbank, *Historical Commentary*]

Walsh, P. G. *Livy, book XL* (Warminster 1996) [= Walsh, *Livy XL*]

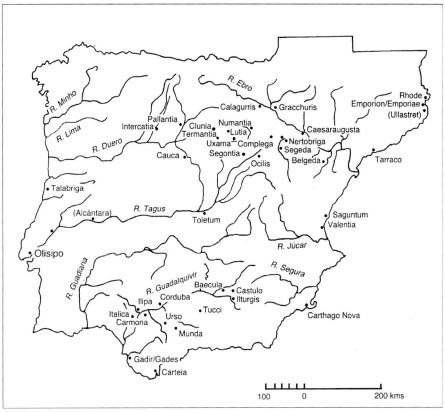

Map 1: Places to illustrate Appian's Iberike.

Map 2: Approximate extent of the provinces.

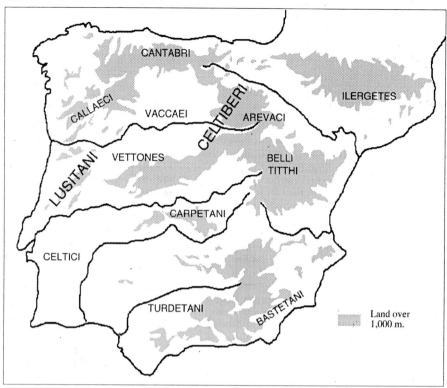

Map 3: Some tribes mentioned by Appian.

Introduction

Appian's *Wars of the Romans in Iberia* (usually known as the *Iberike*) is one of the twenty-four books of his *Roman History*, an ambitious attempt to chronicle the whole of the Roman empire, as being the largest and longest lasting of all times. His work has survived only in fragments, though several of these, including the *Iberike*, comprise complete books. One of the results of this has been that Appian has mostly been treated as a source of historical information and as a means of access to the lost works of earlier historians rather than as a historian in his own right. He is certainly useful to the modern writer on ancient history, and in some cases (such as periods of the last century of the Roman republic, recorded in the five books of the *Civil Wars*, or indeed the *Iberike* itself) provides the only continuous narrative of important sections of Roman history to have come down to us. In the case of the present work, Appian not only gives a reasonably coherent account of the Roman wars in Spain and Portugal from their arrival at the beginning of the Hannibalic wars in 218 BC down to the capture of the Celtiberian city of Numantia in 133 BC, but has the only continuous account of the crucial events of the last two decades of that period.

But if Appian is a useful source of historical data, he was also, at least in his own conception, an historian himself, with his own idea of how the history of Rome and its empire should be written. He was also very much a man of his own times, whose understanding of how the Roman empire come to be was shaped by his own experience of it, as an official of the imperial system as it was in the second century AD. The *Iberike* is not, any more than any other historical work from the ancient world, simply a mirror reflecting without distortion the events it describes. It is therefore essential, even for those who wish to use Appian mostly as a source of information, to understand who it is that is providing this data and the attitudes and opinions that he brought to the writing of his work.

The author

The writer of this work is known to us only from the autobiographical remarks he makes in the course of his own writings and from the correspondence of his friend, the famous orator and literary figure M. Cornelius Fronto. At the end of the preface to the whole collection of writings that make up his *Roman History*, he announces himself as "Appian of Alexandria, who, reached the first rank in my own native land and acted as an advocate before the emperors at Rome, and whom they thought worthy to be made their procurator", and adds that, for those who wish to know more, he has written a account of these matters (*praef.* 15.62). Of this last, nothing survives. As Fronto's letter about Appian is to the emperor Antoninus Pius, asking for the third time for the appointment of his friend as an imperial procurator (Fronto, *ep. ad Anton.* 9), it is not unreasonable to assume that it was on the recommendation of Fronto that Appian achieved the position of which he is evidently proud. Internal dating suggests that the *praefatio* was written in about AD 150, since he states that nine hundred years have passed since the beginning of the Roman state (*praef.* 9.34) and, in another place (*praef.* 6.22-7.24), that it is nearly two hundred since the institution of the monarchy, which he associates with Julius Caesar. Fronto, in his letter to Antoninus Pius, says that his friend is already old and is seeking the procuratorship for the dignity that it will bring to his old age, not out of ambition or because he wants the procurator's stipend. This suggests that he was born in the last years of the first century, and probably died in the 160s. It is quite likely that his procuratorship was honorary rather than active.[1]

Appian appears to have been born in Egypt, and probably in Alexandria, after the reign of Vespasian (as may be inferred from a note at *Syr.* 50.252). He was present in Alexandria during the troubles with the Jews in the reign of Trajan in AD 115-117.[2] When he came to Rome, perhaps in the reign of Hadrian, he practised as an advocate, and was a friend of Fronto and a member of the same literary group. Fronto writes of their *vetus consuetudo et studiorum usus prope quotidianus* ('long familiarity and almost daily collaboration in study'), which may be exaggeration but surely indicates a closeness in literary endeavour (Fronto, *ep. ad Anton.* 9.2). In addition to Fronto's letter, two letters in Greek have survived in the collection of Fronto's correspondence, one from Appian and one from Fronto, which attest their association and mention a favour which Fronto has done for Appian.[3] This indicates that not only was he a member of the equestrian order (which would be necessary for him to hold the office of procurator), but also associated with the most significant figures in the literary world of his time.[4]

Appian's *Roman History*

The Wars of the Romans in Iberia is the sixth book of Appian's *Roman History*. He explains in the preface to the work as a whole that he intends to deal with the history of the Romans by writing of their dealings with the various peoples and regions, to show how contact first took place, the progress of the wars and of diplomatic relations, the establishment of areas within the Roman empire and the arrangements which brought about the present situation (*praef.* 12.45-48). This emerges from an appreciation both of the geographical spread of Roman power in his own day (he begins his preface with an account of the nations under Roman control and of the boundaries between them: *praef.* 1.1-5.18) and of the length of time that the process had taken (*praef.* 6.19-11.44). He is aware that the whole of his history will not fit neatly into such a scheme, and therefore will write his first three books on the expansion in Italy (book 1 on Rome under the kings; book 2 on the wars against Italians, except for the Samnites, who are dealt with in book 3). The remaining books, he says, will be named according to the people with whom the Romans were fighting (Celts, Sicilians, Iberians, Hannibal, the Carthaginians, the Macedonians and so forth), arranged in order according to the time when the Romans began to wage war against them. He will then write about the civil wars, arranged under the names of the generals who were most involved in each (these are the five books of the *Civil Wars*), and at the end, an account of how Egypt came under the Romans and the Romans themselves established a monarchy (*praef.* 14.53-60). It is noteworthy that Appian, as a native of Alexandria, sees the incorporation of his own country into the empire as the climax of his work. It was not, however, the end. He himself states that a final book will set out the military and administrative details of the empire as it was in his time (*praef.* 15.61). No trace of this book has survived among the fragments of Appian's history, and, more surprisingly, it is not mentioned by Photius, the ninth-century patriarch of Constantinople, who listed, in his record of books he had read, the names of Appian's works. Photius does, however, add a book called *Hecatontaetia* ('The Hundred Years'), which appears to be about the emperors down to Trajan, and wars in Dacia and Arabia, making twenty-four in all.[5] Appian himself mentions a book about the wars fought by the emperors after the war in Egypt (*Illyr.* 30.87), which may be a reference to the *Hecatontaetia*.

The structure of the *Wars in Iberia*

Despite his wish to present a full account of the major events in Rome's involvement in Iberia (*Ib.* 101.438; cf. *praef.* 13.49-50), Appian's account is based on three major sections: the conflict with Carthage (3.9-38.157); the war with the Lusitanians (56.234-75.321); and the Celtiberian wars (44.180-55.233 and 76.322-98.427), framed by a brief preface on the geography and early history of Iberia (1.1-2.8) and an epilogue, bringing the account from the fall of Numantia down to the reign of Augustus (99.428-102.444). A short bridge passage between the first two sections links the end of the Hannibalic war with the first set of wars in Celtiberia (39.158-43.179). The arrangement is thus not strictly chronological, in that the sections on the Lusitanian and Celtiberian wars overlap with one another, the section on the Lusitanians (and in particular on the campaigns led by the great Lusitanian hero, Viriathus) (56.234-75.321) being inserted into the account of the Celtiberian wars; and the Lusitanian section itself is interrupted by the insertion of a section on the campaigns of D Iunius Brutus in the north-west of the peninsula (71.301-73.310: Appian himself apologises at 73.310 for this digression, allegedly inspired by a comparison between the bandit tactics of Viriathus and of the Callaeci). From the point of view of the structure of the work, this has the advantage of setting at the beginning and end of the work two large sections, which each has as its central character a member of the Scipio family: P. Scipio, the later Africanus, who expelled the Carthaginians from Iberia, and so brought to an end the opening conflict between Rome and Carthage; and his adoptive grandson, P. Scipio Aemilianus, who, by destroying Numantia, concluded the last major struggle between Romans and Iberians. These two individuals, whose similarities to one another are marked in Appian's account (as in the emphasis on the youth of each: 18.68 and 84.364), thus form an inner frame to the overall account of Rome's conquest of the peninsula.[6]

Appian as a historian

It is evident from the structure of the *Wars in Iberia* that Appian took care over the writing of his history as a piece of literature, and this will become clear again from a consideration of his style. There are, however, other questions which relate to the writing of history which require consideration before attempting to evaluate his work.

Writing in the second century AD about events three hundred years earlier, Appian was evidently dependant on earlier writers for the material of his history, and much scholarly endeavour over the past two centuries has gone into the identification of these sources. So far as the *Wars in Iberia* is concerned, Appian mentions in the preface to the *Roman History* that he has read about the Punic wars (including events in Spain) in the many Greek and Roman historians who had written about them (*praef.* 12.45-6), but does not give the names of any of these writers. Otherwise, he refers explicitly to only one historian in the course of the *Wars in Iberia*, that being Rutilius Rufus, whom he calls 'Rutilius Rufus, who wrote a history of these exploits' (38.382), and describes as serving with Scipio Aemilianus in Celtiberia (see below, *ad loc.*).

It is clear that the sources Appian has used for his account of the events of the second Punic War include neither of the two major writers that have survived to our times, Polybius and Livy.[7] This has usually been ascribed to the use by Appian of one or more of the historians on whom Livy drew, in addition to Polybius, for his version, and in particular the so-called Roman annalists, who wrote in the late second and early first centuries BC. Those whom Livy seems to have used most are L. Coelius Antipater, who wrote a history of the Hannibalic war in the period after the death of C. Gracchus in 121, and two slightly later writers, Claudius Quadrigarius and Valerius Antias.[8] Attempts have been made to identify which of these historians provided Appian with the information on which he has based his account, but the evidence is sufficiently unclear that it is probably best to conclude, with Scullard, that, though Coelius is a more likely candidate than Antias, identification of Appian's Latin source, assuming that he had one, is not possible.[9]

For the later period, Appian had available a monograph which Polybius wrote on the Numantine war (mentioned by Cicero, *ad fam.* 5.12.2), and the history which the Stoic philosopher and polymath, Posidonius, wrote in the first century BC. It has been argued[10] that Appian used Polybius for the period of the Lusitanian and Numantine wars, perhaps with Posidonius as an intermediary. On closer investigation, the differences between Appian and the surviving fragments of Polybius make this unlikely.[11] It is highly probable that Appian has read and used Polybius, but has not used him as his only or even primary source. It may be that he used Rutilius Rufus, as he mentions him as a historian of the events he is narrating, but again there is no reason to assume that Rutilius is his only source. As with the earlier period, it is better to admit our uncertainty than to put too much weight on speculation. It is worth noting, however, that the section on Scipio Aemilianus is made up of series of anecdotes, strung together to form a narrative, and it may be that this points to Appian's use of a biographically focused source, such as Rutilius' work seems to have been.[12]

Appian's value as a historian depends, of course, not only on the sources he used, but the use he made of them. As already noted, Appian was very conscious of his rôle as a historian, which was for an ancient writer primarily a literary rather than a scientific or academic notion. The view that Appian's value lies mostly in the information he transmits has led to his own contribution being neglected until relatively recently. This not only underestimates his aspirations but also his achievements. As we have seen, he took considerable care over the division of his narrative (even if the section on Iunius Brutus interrupts the chronological and narrative flow of the Lusitanian wars), and on a smaller scale also he writes in a clear and vivid style. His portrait of Scipio Africanus as a charismatic and divinely inspired leader, beginning with his address to the people and senate in Rome when he is chosen as commander in Spain (18.69) and continuing through his capture of New Carthage (see commentary on 20 76) and the battle of Carmona (25.96) is not original but gives a sharply drawn picture of a heroic and distinctive character; and his contrasting account of Scipio Aemilianus as an austere but equally effective general (85.367-87.380; 95.41-97.423), modified as it is by Appian's own sympathy for the plight of the Numantines (97.420-423), provides a striking antithesis. Although his prose style is generally straightforward, he occasionally uses unexpected forms, breaking into the historic present (as at 26.102) in a dramatic section of his account, and introducing elements of direct speech into a passage of indirect discourse (as for example at 61.259).[13]

Although as an historical writer Appian has more to be said for him than has always been acknowledged, he does have faults as a historian in the modern sense. Most notable of these is his cavalier attitude to geography. It is true (as argued by Gómez, pp. 405-6) that geography was not a primary concern to ancient historiographers, and some of the mistakes that Appian makes are no more than the common currency of his time (thus his belief on the proximity of the Iberian peninsula to Britain (1.3) is shared by others). In some cases, however, his errors are unique, and some of these (in particular the relative positions of Saguntum, New Carthage and the river Ebro, at 6.24, 7.25, 10.36, 12.47 and 76.320) are of considerable importance for the understanding of the history of the events in Iberia, not just its geography. These mistakes are sufficiently serious to suggest that other apparent oddities (such as his identification of Tartessus with Carpessus (2.7 and 63.267) and his belief (at 6.24) that the river Ebro cuts the peninsula in half and flows into the northern sea) may be errors of his own. It is not unfair to judge, even in the context of the ancient world, that Appian is 'ignorantissimo de geografia'.[14]

The other technical requirement of an historian is mastery of chronology. Here Appian does somewhat better than with his geography. On three occasions he uses the Olympiad system to fix significant stages in his history: at the beginning of the Hannibalic war (4.14: 'about the 140th Olympiad'); at the end of the war, which he reckons to be the beginning of full Roman control (28.152: 'shortly before the 144th Olympiad'); and at the outbreak of the 'rebellions' which were to lead to the settlement by Ti. Gracchus in the 170s (42.171: 'four Olympiads later (*sc.* than the campaigns of Cato), about the 150th'). He also occasionally uses synchronisms with other events, again to mark significant stages (39.158: the beginning of the Iberian 'rebellions' after the Hannibalic war; and 99.429-30, to explain Roman inaction in Iberia, caused by the Cimbric invasions and the slave war in Sicily). Although causing some confusion in the second section of his work through the interleaving of the Celtiberian and Lusitanian wars (exacerbated by the insertion of the passage about Brutus), Appian does carry out the promise he has made in the preface to the *Roman History* to give enough chronology for the reader to place the most important events (*praef.* 13.50).

So far as his attitudes to the history he relates are concerned, he is by no means uncritical of the Romans. The Scipio brothers are represented as equally effective in their diplomatic relations with the Iberians as they are in their military exploits (15.59, as opposed to the picture of Hannibal as cruel and deceitful, at, for instance, 10.38-9 and 12.47). Scipio Africanus is presented in a similar light (24.93). The Roman commanders of the mid-second century are presented in a much less favourable light. Both Lucullus and Galba are described as greedy (51.215; 54.230; 60.255), and Appian issues a general condemnation of those who at this time 'sought the command for glory or gain or the honour of a triumph, not for the benefit of the city' (80.349). Not surprisingly the generals responsible for the disastrous defeats in the war against Numantia are given harsh treatment (Pompeius: 76.322-79.344; Mancinus: 79.345-80.348 and 83.358-361; Lepidus Porcina 80.348-

82.357), but also those who were more successful, such as Caepio, who finally disposed of Viriathus (74.311-75.321), and even Scipio Aemilianus (see above) are shown as brutal or at least grimly ruthless. On the other hand he expresses real admiration for the Iberians, who on several occasions he depicts as prepared to commit mass suicide rather than lose their prized freedom (12.44-6; 25.135-6; 71.302; 72.305-6; 77.327; 97.419). To an extent, the contrast between the noble savages and the ignoble and treacherous Romans of the second part of his account is reminiscent of the picture which Tacitus had given at the end of the previous century of the inhabitants of Germany in his *Germania*.

There is another aspect of Appian's view of the wars in Iberia in which he also reflects the period in which he is writing. His picture of the Roman empire is that of the mid-second century. Although he recognises that the reason the Romans went to Iberia in the first place was to deal with the threat of Hannibal, he regards this as a struggle between Rome and Carthage for the possession of the peninsula (4.13), and his description of the sending of regular magistrates to the area at the end of the First Punic war, ignoring the hesitation shown at the time by the senate about continuing the Roman presence there at all (38.152 and commentary *ad loc.*), is clearly meant to represent the beginning of the *provinciae* there as part of an organised and administered empire. This is why he describes all the wars with the local peoples as rebellions against Roman authority (so 38.157; 39.158; 42.171). In reality, the Roman picture of their *provinciae* in the third and second centuries BC was much more as areas to which they sent commanders with armies in order to impose their political will by military means than as organised parts of an empire in the sense that Appian knew it some three hundred years later.[15] It may well be that is part of the reason for his disgust at the way in which the mid-second century commanders behaved themselves towards peoples for whom Appian, with his second-century AD outlook, felt they had a responsibility which in the second century BC was only just beginning to be recognised. This would explain, for instance, the cutting remark he makes about Galba, that he 'paid back treachery with treachery, imitating barbarians in a way that was unworthy of the Romans' (61.253). Appian writes with an intelligent and thoughtful appreciation of the problems of empire, but from a standpoint which belongs to his own time, rather than that about which he writes. The picture of the Roman empire with which he begins the preface to the *Roman History* (*praef.* 1.1) is that which is implicit in his narrative of the much earlier stages of it growth.[16]

The establishment of the text

The primary basis for the text of the *Iberike* is an eleventh century manuscript in the Vatican, Vat. gr. 141 (**V**), which also includes the books on the Hannibalic war and the Libyan wars, and is bound in with a twelfth century manuscript of the Preface

and an epitome of the Celtic wars.[17] Not only is this by far the earliest manuscript of
Appian, but all other extant manuscripts have been shown to derive from it.[18] The
earliest and most useful of these is the fifteenth century manuscript, Laurentianus
LXX 26 (**M**), which[19] is valuable for establishing the text at points where **V** has been
altered by a later hand, sometimes to the extent that its readings are unclear.[20]

Two papyri from Dura-Europos have been recognised as containing fragments of
Appian, one of which is from *Iberike* 4.16[21], but this offers no assistance in the
establishment of the text.

The first printed edition of the *Iberike*, by Henri Étienne in Geneva in 1557, which
he reprinted in his folio edition of the whole of the *Roman History* in 1592, was
based on another apograph of **V**, probably the sixteenth century manuscript in
Leiden (Leid. BPG 110)[22], and his text is of no independent value for a modern
editor. When he is referred to in the *apparatus criticus* (Steph.) to this edition, it is
for his emendations only.   Two translations appeared before Étienne's *editio
princeps*, one in Italian, added (along with the *Annibaike*) to the edition of the
translation of the rest of the *Roman History* by Alessandro Bracchio published by
the Aldine press in Venice in 1545, and one in Latin, translated by Caelius Secundus
Curio as part of the version of Appian by Gelenius, published by Froben in Basle in
1554.   These two translations have several major differences from **V** and its
apographs, and are closely connected.[23] It is uncertain, however, whether their
differences from the manuscript tradition derive solely from the tendency of
humanist scholars to fill out their texts with their own emendations and alterations[24],
or whether they had any independent manuscript evidence. It is safer to believe the
former.

The only other sources for the text of the *Iberike* are the sections of the work
included in the collection of extracts from classical historians, compiled in the mid-
tenth century at the behest of the Byzantine emperor, Constantine VII
Porphyrogenitus (referred to in the *apparatus criticus* as 'Exc.'); and the citations by
the lexicon, probably of approximately the same date, known as the Suda.[25]

The first major achievement in the establishment of the text of the *Iberike* after the
editio princeps was the splendid three edition of Johannes Schweighäuser, *Appiani
Alexandrini Romanorum Historiarum quae supersunt*, (Leipzig 1785), which
included what was, until the very end of the twentieth century, the last edition and
commentary on the work to be published. Schweighäuser had the disadvantage of
not seeing **V** for himself, relying on a far from accurate collation of the manuscript
made for him by G. Spalletti[26], but his work on the relation of the manuscripts to one
another was fundamental.   It was only with the Teubner edition of Ludwig
Mendelssohn[27] that a further advance was made, with the recognition of **V** as the
manuscript on which both **M** and Étienne's codex (as that stage still unidentified)
had been based, enabling Mendelssohn to produce what has properly been called the

first true critical edition. Further revision was undertaken by P. Viereck and A. G. Roos for the Teubner edition of 1939, reissued with corrections and additional notes by Emilio Gabba in 1962. Two recent editions have appeared, one of the section of the *Iberike* on the Hannibalic war[28] and one of the whole of the *Iberike*.[29] In each case, the editor has undertaken a careful re-reading of **V**, and in the latter case of **M** also.

This edition and commentary

The only translation into English of the *Wars in Iberia* is that by Horace White in the Loeb Classical Library series[30], which includes occasional brief notes and lacks an *apparatus criticus*. Kai Brodersen provided short notes to Otto Veh's translation into German[31]; and much fuller commentaries have appeared recently in the editions of Leidl and Goukowsky. The intention of this edition is to provide a text and *apparatus*, combined with a translation and commentary which will make the work accessible to those interested in Appian, both as a source for an important and fascinating period of Rome's involvement in the Iberian peninsula and as a historiographer in his own right. For this reason, the commentary in mostly concerned with historical and historiographical matters, and notes on linguistic and textual points are largely confined to those for which clarification is necessary to enable the reader to understand the meaning and significance of the text as a history. It is hoped thereby that this work will contribute to the recent revival of interest both in the Roman period in Iberia and in Appian as a historian.

[1] See H.-G. Pflaum, *Les procurateurs equestres sous le Haut Empire* (Paris 1950), pp. 200-205.

[2] *bell. civ.* 2.90.380 and fr. 19 (in Viereck and Roos' Teubner edition (second ed., Leipzig 1962), pp. 534-5).

[3] In M. P. J. van den Hout, *M. Cornelii Frontonis Epistulae* (Leipzig 1988), pp.242-8.

[4] See E. Champlin, *Fronto and Antonine Rome* (Princeton and London 1980).

[5] See the discussion in E. Gabba, *Appiani Bellorum Civilium liber primus* (2nd edition, Firenze 1967), pp. XI-XIV.

[6] See Gómez, pp. 407-12.

[7] See commentary on 4.14-15, 7.27-29, 10.36, 11.43, 13.51, 15.57, 19.74, 20.76, 25.96 for differences between their accounts.

[8] On whom see P. G. Walsh, *Livy: his historical aims and methods* (Cambridge 1961), ch. 5; E. Badian, 'The early historians', in T. A. Dorey, *Latin Historians* (London 1966), pp. 1-38, at pp. 15-22.

[9] H. H. Scullard, *Scipio Africanus in the second Punic War* (Cambridge 1932), pp. 1-2 and p. 26.

[10] Notably by A. Schulten, 'Polybius und Posidonius über Iberien und die iberische Kriege', *Hermes* 46 (1911), pp. 568-607.

[11] A. Sancho Royo, 'Consideraciones en torno al testimonio Apiano y Diodoro para las guerras celtibero-lusitanas', in *Actas del VI Congreso de Estudios Clásicos* (Sevilla 1981) 2, pp. 19-27; Richardson, *Hispaniae*, pp. 194-8.

[12] Goukowsky, *Appien*, p. 81 n. 488; E. Badian, *art. cit.*, pp. 23-25.

[13] On the 'sobriety' of Appian's Greek, see the recent study by Étienne Famerie, *Le latin et le grec d'Appien* (Paris 1998).

[14] P. Janni, *la mappa e il periplo:cartografia antica e spazio odologico* (Rome 1984), p. 114.

[15] Richardson, *Hispaniae* and, for the same phenomenon in the eastern Mediterranean, P. Derow, 'Polybius, Rome and the East', *Journal of Roman Studies* 69 (1979), pp. 1-15.

[16] See, for instance, commentary on 99.428.

[17] Goukowsky, pp. XLIII-XLIX for an account of this manuscript. I am particularly to Michael Crawford for help in obtaining a microfilm of this manuscript.

[18] Mendelssohn vol. 1, pp. XV-XVII; M. R. Dilts, 'Manuscripts of Appian's Iberica and Annibaica', in D. Harlfinger (ed.), *ΦΙΛΟΦΡΟΝΗΜΑ, Festschrift für Martin Sicherl* (Paderborn 1990), pp. 37-42.

[19] As Goukowsky, pp. XLIX-L, has pointed out.

[20] For a brief exposition of the manuscript tradition of Appian's work and the history of the establishment of the text, see K. Brodersen, 'Appian und sein Werk', *ANRW* II.34.1 (Berlin and New York 1993), pp. 339-363, at pp. 344-352.

[21] Th. F. Brunner, 'Two papyri of Appian from Dura Europos', *Greek, Roman and Byzantine Studies* 25 (1984), pp. 171-175.

[22] Famerie, *Le latin et le grec*, p. 45.

[23] As has been shown by Christoph Leidl, 'Appian in 16. Jahrhundert: Italienische und Lateinische Übersetzungen der *Iberike*', *Athenaeum* 85 (1997), pp. 155-192.

[24] So Leidl, *art. cit.* pp. 189-190.

[25] For a full exposition of the passages in these works which relate to the *Iberike*, see Goukowsky, pp. LII-LVII.

[26] Schweighäuser, *Appian*, vol. 1, pp. XXV-XXVIII.

[27] *Appiani Historia Romana*, 2 vols (Leipzig 1879 and 1881).

[28] Christoph Leidl, *Appians Darstellung des 2. punischen Krieges in Spanien (Iberike c.1-38 §1-158a)* (*Münchener Arbeiten zur alten Geschichte* Bd. 11, 1996). I am most grateful to Dr. Leidl for his generous assistance at various points in the composition of the present work.

[29] Paul Goukowsky, *Appien, Histoire Romaine, tome VI, L'Ibérique* (*Collections de Universités de France*, Paris 1997).

[30] *Appian's Roman History*, vol. 1, first published in 1912.

[31] *Appian von Alexandria: Römische Geschichte* (2 vols) (Stuttgart 1987).

APPIAN

THE WARS OF THE ROMANS IN IBERIA
'IBHPIKH

ΑΠΠΙΑΝΟΥ
ΡΩΜΑΙΚΩΝ ΙΒΗΡΙΚΗ

1 (1) Ὄρος ἐστὶ Πυρήνη διῆκον ἀπὸ τῆς Τυρρηνικῆς θαλάσσης ἐπὶ τὸν βόρειον ὠκεανόν, οἰκοῦσι δ᾽ αὐτοῦ πρὸς μὲν ἕω Κελτοί, ὅσοι Γαλάται τε καὶ Γάλλοι νῦν προσαγορεύονται, πρὸς δὲ δύσεων Ἴβηρές τε καὶ Κελτίβηρες, ἀρχόμενοι μὲν ἀπὸ τοῦ Τυρρηνικοῦ πελάγους, περιιόντες δ᾽ ἐν κύκλῳ διὰ τῶν Ἡρακλείων στηλῶν ἐπὶ τὸν βόρειον ὠκεανόν. οὕτως ἐστὶν ἡ Ἰβηρία περίκλυστος, ὅτι μὴ τῇ Πυρήνῃ μόνῃ, μεγίστῳ τῶν Εὐρωπαίων ὀρῶν καὶ ἰθυτάτῳ σχεδὸν ἁπάντων. (2) τοῦ δὲ περίπλου τοῦδε τὸ μὲν Τυρρηνικὸν πέλαγος διαπλέουσιν ἐπὶ τὰς στήλας τὰς Ἡρακλείους, τὸν δ᾽ ἑσπέριον καὶ τὸν βόρειον ὠκεανὸν οὐ περῶσιν, ὅτι μὴ πορθμεύεσθαι μόνον ἐπὶ Βρεττανούς, καὶ τοῦτο ταῖς ἀμπώτεσι τοῦ πελάγους συμφερόμενοι. (3) ἔστι δ᾽ αὐτοῖς ὁ διάπλους ἥμισυ ἡμέρας, καὶ τὰ λοιπὰ οὔτε Ῥωμαῖοι οὔτε τὰ ἔθνη τὰ ὑπὸ Ῥωμαίοις πειρῶνται τοῦδε τοῦ ὠκεανοῦ. (4) μέγεθος δὲ τῆς Ἰβηρίας, τῆς Ἰσπανίας νῦν ὑπό τινων ἀντὶ Ἰβηρίας λεγομένης, ἐστὶ πολὺ καὶ ἄπιστον ὡς ἐν χώρᾳ μιᾷ, ὅπου τὸ πλάτος μυρίους σταδίους ἀριθμοῦσι, καὶ ἔστιν αὐτῇ τὸ πλάτος ἀντὶ μήκους. ἔθνη τε πολλὰ καὶ πολυώνυμα αὐτὴν οἰκεῖ, καὶ ποταμοὶ πολλοὶ ῥέουσι ναυσίποροι.

2 (5) οἵ τινες δ᾽ αὐτὴν οἰκῆσαι πρῶτοι νομίζονται καὶ οἳ μετ᾽ ἐκείνους κατέσχον, οὐ πάνυ μοι ταῦτα φροντίζειν ἀρέσκει, μόνα τὰ Ῥωμαίων συγγράφοντι, πλὴν ὅτι Κελτοί μοι δοκοῦσί ποτε, τὴν Πυρήνην ὑπερβάντες, αὐτοῖς συνοικῆσαι, ὅθεν ἄρα καὶ τὸ Κελτιβήρων ὄνομα ἐρρύη. (6) δοκοῦσι δέ μοι καὶ Φοίνικες, ἐς Ἰβηρίαν ἐκ πολλοῦ θαμινὰ ἐπ᾽ ἐμπορίᾳ διαπλέοντες, οἰκῆσαί τινα τῆς Ἰβηρίας Ἕλληνές τε ὁμοίως, ἐς Ταρτησσὸν καὶ Ἀργανθώνιον Ταρτησσοῦ βασιλέα πλέοντες, ἐμμεῖναι καὶ τῶνδέ τινες ἐν Ἰβηρίᾳ. (7) ἡ γὰρ Ἀργανθωνίου βασιλεία ἐν Ἴβηρσιν ἦν, καὶ Ταρτησσός μοι δοκεῖ τότε εἶναι πόλις ἐπὶ θαλάσσης, ἣ νῦν Καρπησσὸς ὀνομάζεται. (8) τό τε τοῦ Ἡρακλέους ἱερὸν τὸ ἐν στήλαις Φοίνικές μοι δοκοῦσιν ἱδρύσασθαι· καὶ θρησκεύεται νῦν ἔτι φοινικικῶς, ὅ τε θεὸς αὐτοῖς οὐχ ὁ Θηβαῖός ἐστιν, ἀλλ᾽ ὁ Τυρίων.

3 (9) ταῦτα μὲν δὴ τοῖς παλαιολογοῦσιν μεθείσθω· τὴν δὲ γῆν τήνδε εὐδαίμονα οὖσαν καὶ μεγάλων ἀγαθῶν γέμουσαν Καρχηδόνιοι πρὸ Ῥωμαίων ἤρξαντο πολυπραγμονεῖν καὶ μέρος αὐτῆς τὸ μὲν εἶχον ἤδη, τὸ δ᾽ ἐπόρθουν, μέχρι Ῥωμαῖοι σφᾶς ἐκβαλόντες, (10) ἃ μὲν εἶχον οἱ Καρχηδόνιοι τῆς Ἰβηρίας, ἔσχον αὐτίκα, τὰ δὲ λοιπὰ σὺν χρόνῳ πολλῷ

APPIAN
THE WARS OF THE ROMANS IN IBERIA

1 (1) The Pyrenean range of mountains stretches from the Tyrrhenian sea to the northern ocean. The eastern side is occupied by the Celts, who are now generally called Galatians or Gauls, the western by Iberians and Celtiberians, beginning from the Tyrrhenian sea and running round in a circle through the Pillars of Herakles to the northern ocean. Thus Iberia is surrounded by the sea, except for the part cut off by the Pyrenees, the largest of the European mountains and almost the steepest of any. (2) Of this circuit, they sail through the Tyrrhenian sea as far as the Pillars of Herakles, but they do not cross the western or the northern ocean, except to cross to the Britons, taking advantage of the sea-tides. (3) This crossing takes half a day, and for the rest neither the Romans nor any of the peoples subject to the Romans risk this ocean. (4) The size of Iberia, or Hispania as some now call it rather than Iberia, is unbelievably large for one country, for they reckon it to be ten thousand *stadia* in breadth, and its length to be the same as its breadth. Many peoples of many different names live there, and many navigable rivers flow though it.

2 (5) I do not intend to consider who it is that are believed to have occupied it first and who came after them, since I am writing only about matters concerning the Romans. I do think, however, that the Celts crossed the Pyrenees at some time in the past, and lived with those who were already there, and so came to be called Celtiberians. (6) I also think that the Phoenicians from early times frequently sailed to Iberia for trade and lived in part of Iberia; and similarly some of the Greeks, who sailed to Tartessus and Arganthonius, king of Tartessus, also stayed in Iberia. (7) The kingdom of Arganthonius was among the Iberians and Tartessus seems to me to have been the name of the city by the sea which now is called Carpessus. (8) I think the Phoenicians established the temple of Herakles which is at the Pillars, and even now the religious rite there is Phoenician and the god is not the Herakles of Thebes but the Tyrian Herakles.

3 (9) But let us leave these matters to the antiquarians. This blessed land, overflowing with good things, the Carthaginians began to interfere with before the Romans. Part of it they held already, and part they ravaged, before the Romans expelled them. (10) They immediately took that part of Iberia which the Carthaginians held, but the rest they gained over a long period of time and with

καὶ πόνῳ λαμβανόμενά τε ὑπὸ σφῶν καὶ πολλάκις ἀφιστάμενα χειρωσάμενοι διεῖλον ἐς τρία καὶ στρατηγοὺς ἐς αὐτὰ πέμπουσι τρεῖς. (11) ὅπως δὲ εἷλον ἕκαστα καὶ ὅπως Καρχηδονίοις τε περὶ αὐτῶν καὶ μετὰ Καρχηδονίους Ἴβηρσι καὶ Κελτίβηρσιν ἐπολέμησαν, δηλώσει τόδε τὸ βιβλίον, μοῖραν μὲν ἐς Καρχηδονίους τὴν πρώτην ἔχον· (12) ὅτι δὲ καὶ τοῦτο περὶ Ἰβηρίας ἦν, ἀνάγκη μοι συνενεγκεῖν ἐς τὴν Ἰβηρικὴν συγγραφὴν ἐγένετο, ᾧ λόγῳ καὶ τὰ περὶ Σικελίας Ῥωμαίοις καὶ Καρχηδονίοις ἐς ἀλλήλους γενόμενα, ἀρξάμενα Ῥωμαίοις τῆς ἐς Σικελίαν παρόδου τε καὶ ἀρχῆς, ἐς τὴν Σικελικὴν συνενήνεκται γραφήν.

4 (13) πρὸς γὰρ δὴ Καρχηδονίους Ῥωμαίοις πρῶτος ἐγένετο πόλεμος ἔκδημος περὶ Σικελίας ἐν αὐτῇ Σικελίᾳ καὶ δεύτερος ὅδε περὶ Ἰβηρίας ἐν Ἰβηρίᾳ, ἐν ᾧ καὶ ἐς τὴν ἀλλήλων μεγάλοις στρατοῖς διαπλέοντες οἳ μὲν τὴν Ἰταλίαν, οἳ δὲ τὴν Λιβύην ἐπόρθουν. (14) ἤρξαντο δ᾽ αὐτοῦ μεθ᾽ ἑκατὸν καὶ τεσσαράκοντα ὀλυμπιάδας μάλιστα, ὅτε τὰς σπονδὰς ἔλυσαν, αἳ ἐπὶ τῷ Σικελικῷ πολέμῳ σφίσιν ἦσαν γενόμεναι. ἔλυσαν δ᾽ ἐκ τοιᾶσδε προφάσεως. (15) Ἀμίλχαρ ὁ Βάρκας ἐπίκλησιν, ὅτε περ ἐν Σικελίᾳ Καρχηδονίων ἐστρατήγει, Κελτοῖς τότε μισθοφοροῦσίν οἱ καὶ Λιβύων τοῖς συμμαχοῦσιν πολλὰς δωρεὰς ὑπέσχητο δώσειν, ἅς, ἐπειδὴ ἐπανῆλθεν ἐς Λιβύην, ἀπαιτούντων ἐκείνων ὁ Λιβυκὸς Καρχηδονίοις ἐξῆπτο πόλεμος, ἐν ᾧ πολλὰ μὲν πρὸς αὐτῶν Λιβύων ἔπαθον οἱ Καρχηδόνιοι, Σαρδόνα δὲ Ῥωμαίοις ἔδοσαν ποινὴν ὧν ἐς τοὺς ἐμπόρους αὐτῶν ἡμαρτήκεσαν ἐν τῷδε τῷ Λιβυκῷ πολέμῳ. (16) ὑπαγόντων οὖν ἐπὶ τοῖσδε τὸν Βάρκαν τῶν ἐχθρῶν ἐς κρίσιν, ὡς αἴτιον τῇ πατρίδι τοσῶνδε συμφορῶν γενόμενον, θεραπεύσας ὁ Βάρκας τοὺς πολιτευομένους, ὧν ἦν δημοκοπικώτατος Ἀσρούβας, ὁ τὴν αὐτοῦ Βάρκα θυγατέρα ἔχων, τάς τε δίκας διεκρούετο καὶ Νομάδων τινὸς κινήματος γενομένου στρατηγὸς ἔπραξεν ἐπ᾽ αὐτοὺς αἱρεθῆναι μετὰ Ἄννωνος τοῦ Μεγάλου λεγομένου, ἔτι τὰς εὐθύνας τῆς προτέρας στρατηγίας ὀφείλων.

5 (17) παυομένου δὲ τοῦ πολέμου καὶ Ἄννωνος ἐπὶ διαβολαῖς ἐς Καρχηδόνα μεταπέμπτου γενομένου, μόνος ὢν ἐπὶ τῷ στρατῷ καὶ τὸν κηδεστὴν Ἀσρούβαν ἔχων οἱ συνόντα, διῆλθεν ἐπὶ Γάδειρα καὶ τὸν πορθμὸν ἐς Ἰβηρίαν περάσας ἐλεηλάτει τὰ Ἰβήρων οὐδὲν ἀδικούντων, ἀφορμὴν αὑτῷ ποιούμενος ἀποδημίας τε καὶ ἔργων καὶ δημοκοπίας (18) (ὅσα γὰρ λάβοι, διῄρει καὶ τὰ μὲν ἐς τὸν στρατὸν ἀνάλισκεν, ἵνα προθυμότερον αὐτῷ συναδικοῖεν, τὰ δ᾽ ἐς αὐτὴν ἔπεμπε Καρχηδόνα, τὰ δὲ τοῖς ὑπὲρ αὐτοῦ πολιτευομένοις διεδίδου), (19) μέχρι Ἰβήρων αὐτὸν οἵ τε βασιλεῖς συστάντες οἱ κατὰ μέρος καὶ ὅσοι ἄλλοι δυνατοί, κτείνουσιν

---

14 δ᾽ αὐτοῦ V: δὲ αὐτοῦ Steph. **15** δὲ in V suprascr. a m. 2: om. M **19** αὐτὸν V: αὐτῶν M et corr. in V

much labour, and subdued it despite frequent revolts. They have divided it into three parts and send three praetors out to them. (11) How they gained these, how they fought for them with the Carthaginians, the Iberians and the Celtiberians, this book will show. The first part relates to the Carthaginians; (12) and because the war with the Carthaginians also involved Iberia, I have to bring that into my history of Iberia, in the same way that the interaction of the Romans and the Carthaginians over Sicily, beginning with the Roman invasion and control of Sicily, were brought into my history of Sicily.

4 (13) The first external war which the Romans fought was against the Carthaginians for Sicily and was fought in Sicily itself; and this second war was fought for Iberia in Iberia, in the course of which the two sides sailed to invade each other's territory with large forces and laid waste, the one Italy and the other Libya. (14) They began to fight in about the one hundred and fortieth Olympiad, when they broke the treaty which they had made after the Sicilian war. The reason given for the breaking of the treaty was as follows. (15) When Hamilcar, whose surname was Barca, commanded the Carthaginians in Sicily, he promised to give large rewards to the Celts who were serving as mercenaries and to his Libyan allies. They demanded these rewards when he returned to Libya, which was the cause of the outbreak of the Libyan war against the Carthaginians. In this war the Carthaginians suffered severely at the hands of the Libyans themselves, and surrendered Sardinia to the Romans as a recompense for wrongs they had committed against their merchants in the course of this Libyan war. (16) When Barca's enemies brought a prosecution against him because of these events, as having been the cause of such great disasters to his native land, he won over the leading politicians, of whom the most popular was Hasdrubal, who was married to Barca's daughter. So he evaded the lawsuits, and, when a disturbance broke out among the Numidians, managed to be chosen as commander against them, along with Hanno, who was called 'the Great', even though he had not yet rendered his accounts for his earlier generalship.

5 (17) At the end of the war Hanno was recalled to Carthage to answer accusations against him. Barca, now in sole charge of the army and having with him his son-in-law, Hasdrubal, went over to Gades and, having the crossed the straits into Iberia, plundered the possessions of the Iberians, who were doing him no wrong. So he provided himself with an opportunity for being away from Carthage, and also for winning popularity by his actions; (18) for everything that he seized, he divided up, and gave one third to the army, to make them more enthusiastic collaborators in his wrong-doing; one third he sent to Carthage itself; and one third he distributed to his political allies. (19) This continued until the kings of various of the Iberians and

ὧδε· ξύλων ἁμάξας ἄγοντες, αἷς βοῦς ὑπέζευξαν, εἵποντο ταῖς ἁμάξαις ὡπλισμένοι. (20) τοῖς δὲ Λίβυσιν ἰδοῦσιν εὐθὺς μὲν ἐνέπιπτεν γέλως, οὐ συνιεῖσι τοῦ στρατηγήματος· ὡς δ' ἐν χερσὶν ἐγένοντο, οἱ μὲν Ἴβηρες αὐταῖς βουσὶν ἐξῆψαν τὰς ἁμάξας καὶ ἐξώτρυναν ἐς τοὺς πολεμίους, τὸ δὲ πῦρ σκιδναμένων τῶν βοῶν πάντη φερόμενον ἐτάρασσε τοὺς Λίβυας. (21) καὶ τῆς τάξεως διαλυθείσης οἱ μὲν Ἴβηρες αὐτοῖς ἐπιδραμόντες αὐτόν τε τὸν Βάρκαν καὶ πολὺ πλῆθος ἀμυνομένων ἐπ' αὐτῷ διέφθειραν.

6 (22) οἱ δὲ Καρχηδόνιοι, τοῖς κέρδεσιν ἤδη τοῖς ἐξ Ἰβηρίας ἀρεσκόμενοι, στρατιὰν ἄλλην ἔπεμπον ἐς Ἰβηρίαν καὶ στρατηγὸν ἁπάντων ἀπέφηναν Ἀσρούβαν, τὸν τοῦ Βάρκα κηδεστήν, ὄντα ἐν Ἰβηρίᾳ. (23) ὁ δὲ Ἀννίβαν, τὸν οὐ πολὺ ὕστερον ἀοίδιμον ἐπὶ στρατηγίαις παῖδά τε ὄντα τοῦ Βάρκα καὶ τῆς γυναικός οἱ γιγνόμενον ἀδελφόν, ἔχων ἐν Ἰβηρίᾳ, νέον ὄντα καὶ φιλοπόλεμον καὶ ἀρέσκοντα τῷ στρατῷ, ὑποστράτηγον ἀπέφηνε. (24) καὶ τῆς τ' Ἰβηρίας τὰ πολλὰ πειθοῖ προσήγετο, πιθανὸς ὢν ὁμιλῆσαι, ἔς τε τὰ βίας δεόμενα τῷ μειρακίῳ χρώμενος προῆλθεν ἀπὸ τῆς ἑσπερίου θαλάσσης ἐς τὸ μεσόγεων ἐπὶ Ἴβηρα ποταμόν, ὃς μέσην που μάλιστα τέμνων τὴν Ἰβηρίαν καὶ τῆς Πυρήνης ἀφεστὼς ὁδὸν ἡμερῶν πέντε ἐξίησιν ἐς τὸν βόρειον ὠκεανόν.

7 (25) Ζακανθαῖοι δέ, ἄποικοι Ζακυνθίων, ἐν μέσῳ τῆς τε Πυρήνης καὶ τοῦ ποταμοῦ τοῦ Ἴβηρος ὄντες, καὶ ὅσοι ἄλλοι Ἕλληνες περί τε τὸ καλούμενον Ἐμπόριον καὶ εἴ πη τῆς Ἰβηρίας ᾤκουν ἀλλαχοῦ, δείσαντες ὑπὲρ σφῶν ἐπρέσβευον ἐς Ῥώμην. (26) καὶ ἡ σύγκλητος οὐκ ἐθέλουσα τὰ Καρχηδονίων ἐπαίρεσθαι πρέσβεις ἐς Καρχηδόνα ἔπεμπε. (27) καὶ συνέβησαν ἀμφότεροι ὅρον εἶναι Καρχηδονίοις τῆς ἀρχῆς τῆς ἐν Ἰβηρίᾳ τὸν Ἴβηρα ποταμὸν καὶ μήτε Ῥωμαίους τοῖς πέραν τοῦδε τοῦ ποταμοῦ πόλεμον ἐκφέρειν, Καρχηδονίων ὑπηκόοις οὖσι, μήτε Καρχηδονίους ἐπὶ πολέμῳ τὸν Ἴβηρα διαβαίνειν, Ζακανθαίους δὲ καὶ τοὺς ἄλλους ἐν Ἰβηρίᾳ Ἕλληνας αὐτονόμους καὶ ἐλευθέρους εἶναι. καὶ τάδε ταῖς συνθήκαις ταῖς Ῥωμαίων καὶ Καρχηδονίων προσεγράφη.

8 (28) Ἀσρούβαν δ' ἐπὶ τοῖσδε Ἰβηρίαν τὴν ὑπὸ Καρχηδονίοις καθιστάμενον ἀνὴρ δοῦλος, οὗ τὸν δεσπότην ὠμῶς διεφθάρκει, λαθὼν ἐν κυνηγεσίοις ἀναιρεῖ. (29) καὶ τόνδε μὲν Ἀννίβας ἐλεγχθέντα δεινῶς αἰκισάμενος διέφθειρε· ἡ στρατιὰ δὲ τὸν Ἀννίβαν, καίπερ ὄντα κομιδῇ νέον, ἀρέσκοντα δ' ἰσχυρῶς, στρατηγὸν ἀπέδειξαν αὐτῶν· καὶ ἡ Καρχηδονίων βουλὴ συνέθετο. (30) ὅσοι δὲ τοῦ Βάρκα διαπολιτευταὶ τὴν Βάρκα τε καὶ Ἀσρούβα δύναμιν ἐδεδοίκεσαν, ὡς ἔμαθον αὐτοὺς

---

22 ὄντα ἐν Ἰβηρίᾳ om. Exc.   24 βόρειον VM: ἑσπέριον Exc.   29 δὲ add. V m. 2   30 διαπολιτευταὶ Steph.: διαπολῖται VM Exc.

some other powerful men united against him, and killed him in this way. They brought up wagons loaded with wood, to which they had yoked oxen, and followed the carts in full armour. (20) When the Libyans saw this, they burst out laughing, because they did not see the stratagem that was being used; but when they were at close quarters, the Iberians set fire to the wagons with the oxen still yoked to them, and drove them against the enemy. As the oxen scattered in all directions, the fire was carried with them and confused the Libyans. (21) Once their ranks had been broken, the Iberians fell upon them and killed Barca and a large number of men who were defending him.

6 (22) The Carthaginians, who were by now delighted with the gains they were receiving from Iberia, sent another army to Iberia and appointed Hasdrubal, Barca's son-in-law, who was already in Iberia , as overall commander. (23) He had with him Hannibal, soon to become famous for his military exploits, who was Barca's son and the brother of Hasdrubal's wife. This young man, keen on war and popular with the army, he appointed as his second-in-command. (24) Hasdrubal won over most of Iberia by persuasion, and, through being plausible in conversation, and using the younger man for those occasions when force was needed, he advanced inland from the western sea as far as the river Ebro, which cuts Iberia approximately in half and flows into the northern sea, five days journey from the Pyrenees.

7 (25) The Saguntines, colonists from the Zakynthians and situated half way between the Pyrenees and the river Ebro, and the other Greeks, both those who lived in the region of the town called Emporion and those elsewhere in Iberia, fearing for their safety, sent an embassy to Rome. (26) The senate did not wish the Carthaginians to become more powerful, and sent ambassadors to Carthage. (27) The two sides agreed that the boundary for the Carthaginians of their empire in Iberia should be the river Ebro; that the Romans should not wage war against those beyond this river, who were subjects of the Carthaginians; that the Carthaginians should not cross the Ebro under arms; and that the Saguntines and the other Greeks in Iberia were to be autonomous and free. These points were added to the treaty between the Romans and the Carthaginians.

8 (28) While Hasdrubal was setting in order that part of Iberia which was under the control of the Carthaginians on the basis of these agreements, a slave, whose master Hasdrubal had cruelly put to death, surprised him while hunting and killed him. (29) Hannibal captured this man and put him to death with terrible tortures. The army then declared Hannibal to be their commander, since, although he was very young, he was extremely popular with them. The Carthaginian council confirmed this appointment. (30) But Barca's political opponents, who had been afraid of the power of Barca and Hasdrubal, on learning that they were dead, despised Hannibal because of his youth, and prosecuted their friends and supporters on the same charges that

τεθνεῶτας, Ἀννίβα κατεφρόνουν ὡς νέου καὶ τοὺς ἐκείνων φίλους τε καὶ στασιώτας ἐδίωκον ἐπὶ τοῖς ἐκείνων ἐγκλήμασιν. (31) ὅ τε δῆμος ἅμα τοῖς κατηγοροῦσιν ἐγίγνετο, μνησικακῶν τοῖς διωκομένοις τῆς βαρύτητος τῆς ἐπὶ Βάρκα τε καὶ Ἀσρούβα· καὶ τὰς δωρεὰς ἐκέλευον αὐτούς, ὅσας μεγάλας Ἀσρούβας τε καὶ Βάρκας αὐτοῖς ἐπεπόμφεσαν, ἐς τὸ κοινὸν ἐσενεγκεῖν ὡς ἐκ τῶν πολεμίων πεπορισμένας. (32) οἱ δ᾽ ἐπέστελλον τῷ Ἀννίβᾳ, σφίσιν τε ἐπικουρεῖν δεόμενοι καὶ διδάσκοντες, ὅτι καὶ αὐτὸς ἔσοιτο τοῖς πατρῴοις ἐχθροῖς εὐκαταφρόνητος, εἰ τοὺς ἐν τῇ πατρίδι συνεργεῖν αὐτῷ δυναμένους ὑπερίδοι.

9 (33) ὁ δὲ καὶ ταῦτα προεώρα καὶ τὰς ἐκείνων δίκας ἀρχὴν ἐφ᾽ ἑαυτὸν οὖσαν ἐπιβουλῆς· οὐδ᾽ ἠξίου τὴν ἔχθραν, ὥσπερ ὁ πατὴρ καὶ ὁ κηδεστής, ἐσαεὶ καὶ μετὰ φόβου διαφέρειν οὐδ᾽ ἐπὶ τῷ Καρχηδονίων κουφόνῳ μέχρι παντὸς εἶναι, ῥᾳδίως ἐς εὐεργέτας πρὸς ἀχαριστίαν τρεπομένων. (34) ἐλέγετο δὲ καὶ παῖς ὢν ἔτι ὑπὸ τοῦ πατρὸς ὀρκωθῆναι ἐπὶ ἐμπύρων ἄσπειστος ἐχθρὸς ἔσεσθαι Ῥωμαίοις, ὅτε ἐς πολιτείαν παρέλθοι. διὰ δὴ ταῦτ᾽ ἐπενόει, μεγάλοις καὶ χρονίοις πράγμασι τὴν πατρίδα περιβαλὼν καὶ καταστήσας ἐς ἀσχολίας καὶ φόβους, τὸ ἑαυτοῦ καὶ τὰ τῶν φίλων ἐν ἀδεεῖ θέσθαι. (35) Λιβύην μὲν οὖν εὐσταθοῦσαν ἑώρα καὶ Ἰβήρων, ὅσα ὑπήκοα ἦν· εἰ δὲ πρὸς Ῥωμαίους πόλεμον αὖθις ἀναρριπίσειεν, οὗ μάλιστα ἐπεθύμει, ἐδόκει Καρχηδονίους μὲν ἐν φροντίσι καὶ φόβοις ἔσεσθαι μακροῖς, αὐτὸς δέ, εἴτε κατορθώσειεν, ἐπὶ κλέους ἀθανάτου γενήσεσθαι, τὴν πατρίδα τῆς οἰκουμένης γῆς ἄρχουσαν ἀποφήνας (οὐ γὰρ εἶναί τινας ἀντιμάχους αὐτοῖς ἔτι ἐπὶ Ῥωμαίοις), εἴτε καὶ πταίσειε, μεγάλην καὶ ὣς τὸ ἐγχείρημα αὐτῷ δόξαν οἴσειν.

10 (36) ἀρχὴν δ᾽ ὑπολαμβάνων ἔσεσθαι λαμπράν, εἰ τὸν Ἴβηρα διαβαίη, Τορβολήτας, οἳ γείτονές εἰσι Ζακανθαίων, ἀνέπεισε τῶν Ζακανθαίων παρὰ οἱ καταβοᾶν ὡς τήν τε χώραν αὐτῶν ἐπιτρεχόντων καὶ πολλὰ σφᾶς ἄλλα ἀδικούντων. (37) οἱ δ᾽ ἐπείθοντο. καὶ πρέσβεις αὐτῶν ὁ Ἀννίβας ἐς Καρχηδόνα ἔπεμπεν αὐτός τε ἐν ἀπορρήτοις ἔγραφε Ῥωμαίους τὴν ὑπὸ Καρχηδονίοις Ἰβηρίαν ἀναπείθειν ἀπὸ Καρχηδονίων ἀφίστασθαι καὶ Ζακανθαίους Ῥωμαίοις ταῦτα συμπράσσειν. ὅλως τε τῆς ἀπάτης οὐ μεθίει πολλὰ τοιαῦτα ἐπιστέλλων, ἕως ἡ βουλὴ προσέταξεν αὐτῷ πράσσειν ἐς Ζακανθαίους, ὅ τι δοκιμάσειεν. (38) ὁ δ᾽ ἐπεὶ τῆς ἀφορμῆς ἐλάβετο, Τορβολήτας αὖθις ἔπραξεν ἐντυχεῖν οἱ κατὰ τῶν Ζακανθαίων καὶ Ζακανθαίων μετεπέμπετο πρέσβεις. οἱ δὲ ἀφίκοντο μέν, κελεύοντος δὲ τοῦ Ἀννίβου λέγειν ἑκατέρους ἐφ᾽ ἑαυτοῦ, περὶ ὧν διαφέρονται, Ῥωμαίοις ἔφασαν ἐπιτρέψειν τὴν δίκην. (39) ὁ μὲν δὴ ταῦτ᾽ εἰπόντας ἀπέπεμπεν ἀπὸ τοῦ στρατοπέδου καὶ τῆς ἐπιούσης νυκτὸς παντὶ τῷ στρατῷ τὸν

---

31 ἐπεπόμφεσαν Exc.: ἐπεπομφεισαν VM   33 ἀρχὴν <τῆς> Viereck-Roos   36 ἀνέπεισε τῶν Ζακανθαίων Exc.: om. VM

they had brought against them before. (31) The people sided with the prosecutors, remembering with resentment that those who were now being accused had caused them such difficulties in the time of Barca and Hasdrubal, and they demanded that they return to the public treasury the great gifts which Hasdrubal and Barca had sent to them, since they were booty taken from the enemy. (32) The accused then sent messages to Hannibal, asking him to help them and informing him that, if he neglected those who were able to support him at home, he also would be despised by those who had been his father's enemies.

9 (33) He had foreseen these developments, and also that their prosecution was the beginning of a conspiracy against himself. He decided that he would not endure being in perpetual fear of hostility of this sort, as his father and his brother-in-law had, nor for ever be faced with the inconstancy of the Carthaginians, who were likely to repay benefits done to them with ingratitude. (34) It was said also that while he was still a boy his father had him swear an oath on the sacrificial victims on the altar that he would be implacably hostile to the Romans when he was of an age to take part in the business of the state. For these reasons he thought that if he could involve his country in major and long-lasting enterprises, and keep it busy and afraid of failure, he would free his and his friends' affairs from threats. (35) He saw that Libya and those parts of Iberia which were subject to Carthage were stable; but that if he were to stir up the war against the Romans again (something which he very much wanted), the Carthaginians would have much to think about and be afraid of for a long time; and that he, if he were successful, would gain immortal fame, having made his country the ruler of the world (for they would have no rivals once the Romans were defeated); and, even if he failed, so great an attempt would bring him great glory.

10 (36) He decided that it would make an outstanding start if he crossed the Ebro, and so persuaded the Torboletae, who are neighbours of the Saguntines, to complain to him about the Saguntines, on the grounds that they were overrunning their territory and doing them many other wrongs. (37) They were persuaded by him, and Hannibal sent ambassadors from them to Carthage. Moreover he himself wrote secretly to say that the Romans were persuading that part of Iberia which was under Carthaginian control to rebel against the Carthaginians, and that the Saguntines were co-operating with the Romans in this. He kept on with this deception, sending many such messages, until the council instructed him to take such action against the Saguntines as he saw fit. (38) Once he had the opportunity, he got the Torboletae to complain to him again about the Saguntines, and summoned ambassadors from the Saguntines. On their arrival, Hannibal ordered each of them to explain the matters about which they disagreed, but they said that they would submit the dispute to the Romans. (39) Once they had said this, he dismissed them from his camp, and on the following night crossed the Ebro with his entire army, plundered their territory and

Ἴβηρα διαβὰς τὴν χώραν ἐπόρθει καὶ τῇ πόλει μηχανήματα ἐφίστη. ἑλεῖν δ' οὐ δυνάμενος ἀπετάφρευε καὶ περιετείχιζε καὶ φρούρια πολλὰ περιθεὶς ἐκ διαστημάτων ἐπεφοίτα.

11 (40) Ζακανθαῖοι δὲ αἰφνιδίῳ καὶ ἀκαταγγέλτῳ συμπεσόντες ἐπρέσβευον ἐς Ῥώμην. καὶ ἡ σύγκλητος αὐτοῖς συνέπεμπε πρέσβεις, οἳ πρῶτον μὲν Ἀννίβαν ἔμελλον ὑπομνήσειν τῶν συγκειμένων, οὐ πειθομένου δὲ ἐς Καρχηδόνα πλευσεῖσθαι κατ' αὐτοῦ. (41) τούτοις τοῖς πρέσβεσι πλεύσασιν ἐς Ἰβηρίαν καὶ ἐς τὸ στρατόπεδον ἀπὸ θαλάσσης ἀναβαίνουσιν ὁ Ἀννίβας ἀπηγόρευσε μὴ προσιέναι. καὶ οἱ μὲν ἀπέπλευσαν ἐπὶ Καρχηδόνος σὺν τοῖς πρέσβεσιν τοῖς Ζακανθαίων καὶ τῶν συνθηκῶν ἀνεμίμνησκον αὐτούς· Καρχηδόνιοι δὲ ἠτιῶντο τοὺς Ζακανθαίους πολλὰ τοὺς ὑπηκόους σφῶν ἀδικεῖν. (42) καὶ Ζακανθαίων οἱ πρέσβεις ἐς δίκην αὐτοὺς προυκαλοῦντο ἐπὶ Ῥωμαίων κριτῶν· οἱ δ' οὐκ ἔφασαν χρῄζειν δίκης, ἀμύνεσθαι δυνάμενοι. (43) ὧν ἐς Ῥώμην ἀπαγγελθέντων, οἱ μὲν ἐκέλευον ἤδη συμμαχεῖν τοῖς Ζακανθαίοις, οἱ δ' ἐπεῖχον ἔτι, λέγοντες οὐ συμμάχους αὐτοὺς ἐν ταῖς συνθήκαις σφῶν, ἀλλ' αὐτονόμους καὶ ἐλευθέρους ἀναγεγράφθαι, ἐλευθέρους δὲ ἔτι καὶ τοὺς πολιορκουμένους εἶναι. καὶ ἐκράτησεν ἡ γνώμη.

12 (44) Ζακανθαῖοι δέ, ἐπειδὴ τὰ Ῥωμαίων ἀπέγνωσαν καὶ ὁ λιμὸς σφᾶς ἐπίεζε καὶ Ἀννίβας περιεκάθητο συνεχῶς (εὐδαίμονα γὰρ καὶ πολύχρυσον ἀκούων εἶναι τὴν πόλιν οὐκ ἀνίει τῆς πολιορκίας), τὸν μὲν χρυσὸν καὶ ἄργυρον, ὅσος ἦν δημόσιός τε καὶ ἰδιωτικός, ἀπὸ κηρύγματος ἐς τὴν ἀγορὰν συνήνεγκαν καὶ μολύβδῳ καὶ χαλκῷ συνεχώνευσαν, ὡς ἀχρεῖον Ἀννίβᾳ γενέσθαι, (45) αὐτοὶ δ', ἐν χερσὶν ἑλόμενοί τι παθεῖν μᾶλλον ἢ ὑπὸ τοῦ λιμοῦ, ἐξέδραμον ἔτι νυκτὸς ἐπὶ τὰ φρούρια τὰ τῶν Λιβύων, ἀναπαυομένων ἔτι καὶ οὐδὲν τοιοῦτον [δ'] ὑπονοούντων· ὅθεν αὐτοὺς ἀνισταμένους τε ἐξ εὐνῆς καὶ σὺν θορύβῳ μόλις ὁπλιζομένους, ἔστι δ' οὓς ἤδη καὶ μαχομένους, διέφθειρον. μακροῦ δὲ τοῦ ἀγῶνος γενομένου, Λιβύων μὲν ἀπώλοντο πολλοί, Ζακανθαῖοι δὲ πάντες. (46) αἱ δὲ γυναῖκες, ἀπὸ τοῦ τείχους ὁρῶσαι τὸ τέλος τῶν ἀνδρῶν, αἱ μὲν ἐρρίπτουν ἑαυτὰς κατὰ τῶν τεγῶν, αἱ δ' ἀνήρτων, αἱ δὲ καὶ τὰ τέκνα προκατέσφαζον. καὶ τοῦτο τέλος ἦν Ζακανθαίοις, πόλει τε μεγάλῃ καὶ δυνατῇ γενομένῃ. (47) Ἀννίβας δ', ὡς ἔμαθε περὶ τοῦ χρυσοῦ, τοὺς μὲν ὑπολοίπους καὶ ἔτι ἡβῶντας αὐτῶν αἰκιζόμενος διέφθειρεν ὑπὸ ὀργῆς, τὴν δὲ πόλιν ὁρῶν ἐπιθάλασσόν τε καὶ Καρχηδόνος οὐ μακρὰν καὶ χώρας ἄρχουσαν ἀγαθῆς ᾤκιζεν αὖθις καὶ Καρχηδονίων ἄποικον ἀπέφαινεν· ἣν νῦν οἶμαι Καρχηδόνα καλεῖσθαι τὴν Σπαρταγενήν.

---

40 αἰφνιδίῳ καὶ ἀκαταγγέλτῳ VM: αἰφνιδίῳ κακῷ καὶ ἀκαταγγέλτῳ Exc. συμπεσόντες M Exc.: ἐμπεσόντες V ἐς Καρχηδόνα Exc.: om. VM **47** Σπαρταγενήν VM: Σπαρταγενῆ Schweig.

brought up siege weapons against the city. When he was unable to capture it, he encircled it with a trench and, setting a large number of guard-posts round it at intervals, attacked the city.

11 (40) Under the impact of this sudden and unannounced onslaught, the Saguntines sent an embassy to Rome. The senate sent ambassadors with them, whom they instructed first to remind Hannibal of their agreements, but, should he not obey, to sail to Carthage to complain about him. (41) When these ambassadors sailed to Iberia and were proceeding from the sea to the camp, Hannibal forbade them to approach. They then sailed to Carthage with the Saguntine ambassadors, and reminded them of the treaty. The Carthaginians in turn accused the Saguntines of committing many injustices against their subjects. (42) The ambassadors of the Saguntines challenged them to take the matter to arbitration before Roman assessors, but they said that they had no need of a court, as they were able to defend themselves. (43) When this was reported at Rome, some urged that they should support their Saguntine allies; but others held back, arguing that they were not allies according to the treaty, but were written in as autonomous and free, and that those under siege were still free. This was the opinion which prevailed.

12 (44) When the Saguntines realised that they would get no help from the Romans and were worn out with hunger and Hannibal was maintaining the blockade continuously (for he heard that the city was wealthy and rich in gold, and so did not relax the siege), they brought their gold and silver, both that belonging to the people and what was in private ownership, down to the market-place following a public announcement and mixed it with molten lead and bronze, to make it useless to Hannibal; (45) for themselves, preferring to suffer anything rather than to die of hunger, they charged out during the night against the Libyan guard-posts, while the Libyans were asleep and not expecting anything of the sort, as a result of which they killed some of them as they were getting out of bed and arming themselves with difficulty in the confusion, and some others already engaged in the battle. The fight went on for a long time, with many Libyans being killed, and all the Saguntines. (46) As for the women, having seen from the city-walls the deaths of their menfolk, some threw themselves from the roofs of their houses, some hanged themselves and some killed their children first. This was the end of the Saguntines, a great and powerful city. (47) When Hannibal learned about the gold, he tortured all the adult survivors to death in his fury; and, seeing that the city was on the sea, no great distance from Carthage and controlled good land, he colonised it again and made it a colony of the Carthaginians; and now it is called, I believe, Spartarian Carthage.

13 (48) Ῥωμαῖοι δὲ πρέσβεις ἐς Καρχηδόνα ἔπεμπον, οἷς εἴρητο ἐξαιτεῖν παρὰ Καρχηδονίων Ἀννίβαν ὡς ἐς τὰς συνθήκας ἁμαρτόντα, εἰ μὴ κοινὸν ἡγοῦνται τὸ ἔργον· ἢν δὲ μὴ διδῶσιν, εὐθέως αὐτοῖς πόλεμον προαγορεύειν. (49) καὶ οἳ μὲν ἔπραξαν ὧδε καὶ τὸν πόλεμον αὐτοῖς, οὐκ ἐκδιδοῦσι τὸν Ἀννίβαν, ἐπήγγειλαν· λέγεται δ᾽ οὕτω γενέσθαι. ὁ μὲν πρεσβευτὴς αὐτοῖς γελώμενος ἔφη, τὸν κόλπον ἐπιδεικνύς· "ἐνταῦθ᾽ ὑμῖν, ὦ Καρχηδόνιοι, καὶ τὴν εἰρήνην καὶ τὸν πόλεμον φέρω· ὑμεῖς δ᾽, ὁπότερα αἱρεῖσθε, λάβετε". (50) οἳ δ᾽ ἔφασαν· "σὺ μὲν οὖν, ἃ βούλει, δίδου". προτείναντος δὲ τὸν πόλεμον ἐξεβόησαν ὁμοῦ πάντες· "δεχόμεθα". καὶ εὐθὺς ἐπέστελλον τῷ Ἀννίβᾳ πᾶσαν ἤδη τὴν Ἰβηρίαν ἀδεῶς ἐπιτρέχειν ὡς τῶν σπονδῶν λελυμένων. (51) ὁ μὲν δὴ τὰ ἔθνη τὰ ἀγχοῦ πάντα ἐπιὼν ὑπήγετο, ἢ πείθων ἢ δεδιττόμενος ἢ καταστρεφόμενος, καὶ στρατιὰν πολλὴν συνέλεγεν, τὴν μὲν χρείαν οὐχ ὑποδεικνύς, ἐς δὲ τὴν Ἰταλίαν ἐπινοῶν ἐμβαλεῖν, (52) Γαλάταις τε διεπρεσβεύετο καὶ τὰς διόδους τῶν Ἀλπείων ὀρῶν κατεσκέπτετο καὶ διῆλθεν, Ἀσρούβαν τὸν ἀδελφὸν ἐν Ἰβηρίᾳ «καταλιπών.»

14 (53) «οἱ δὲ Ῥωμαῖοι προορῶντες πρὸς Καρχηδονίους ἐν Ἰβηρίᾳ» σφίσι καὶ Λιβύῃ τὸν πόλεμον ἔσεσθαι (οὐ γὰρ δὴ μὴ Λίβυές ποτε ἐς τὴν Ἰταλίαν ἐσβάλωσιν, οὐδ᾽ ὑπενόουν), Τιβέριον μὲν Σεμπρώνιον Λόγγον ἐπὶ νεῶν ἑκατὸν ἑξήκοντα σὺν δύο στρατοῦ τέλεσιν ἐς Λιβύην ἐξέπεμπον (καὶ ὅσα Λόγγος τε καὶ οἱ λοιποὶ Ῥωμαίων στρατηγοὶ περὶ Λιβύην ἔπραξαν, ἐν τῇ Καρχηδονιακῇ βύβλῳ συγγέγραπται), (54) Πούπλιον δὲ Κορνήλιον Σκιπίωνα ἔστελλον ἐς Ἰβηρίαν ἐπὶ νεῶν ἑξήκοντα μετὰ πεζῶν μυρίων καὶ ἱππέων ἑπτακοσίων καὶ πρεσβευτὴν αὐτῷ συνέπεμπον Γναῖον Κορνήλιον Σκιπίωνα τὸν ἀδελφόν. (55) τούτοιν ὁ μὲν Πούπλιος παρὰ Μασσαλιωτῶν ἐμπόρων πυθόμενος Ἀννίβαν διὰ τῶν Ἀλπείων ὀρῶν ἐς τὴν Ἰταλίαν ὑπερβάντα, δείσας, μὴ ἀδοκήτως τοῖς Ἰταλιώταις ἐπιπέσοι, παραδοὺς Γναίῳ τῷ ἀδελφῷ τὴν ἐν Ἰβηρίᾳ στρατιὰν διέπλευσεν ἐπὶ πεντήρους ἐς Τυρρηνίαν. (56) καὶ ὅσα ἔπραξεν ἐν τῇ Ἰταλίᾳ οὗτός τε καὶ ὅσοι μετ᾽ αὐτὸν ἄλλοι στρατηγοὶ τοῦδε τοῦ πολέμου ἐγένοντο, ἕως Ἀννίβαν ἑκκαιδεκάτῳ μόλις ἔτει τῆς Ἰταλίας ἐξήλασαν, ἡ ἑξῆς βίβλος ὑποδείκνυσιν, ἣ τὰ ἔργα Ἀννίβου τὰ ἐν Ἰταλίᾳ πάντα περιλαμβάνει καὶ παρ᾽ αὐτὸ λέγεται Ῥωμαϊκῶν Ἀννιβαϊκή.

15 (57) Γναῖος δὲ οὐδέν, ὅ τι καὶ εἰπεῖν, ἔπραξεν «ἐν» τοῖς Ἴβηρσι, πρὶν αὐτῷ Πούπλιον τὸν ἀδελφὸν ἐπανελθεῖν· Ῥωμαῖοι γάρ, ληγούσης τῆς ἀρχῆς τῷ Πουπλίῳ, πρὸς μὲν Ἀννίβαν ἐς τὴν Ἰταλίαν τοὺς μετὰ τὸν

---

48 προαγορεύειν Exc.: προσαγορεύειν VM　**52** Ἀλπείων Steph.: Ἀλπίων VM　<τὴν Πυρήνην> διῆλθεν Gouk.　**52-3** lacunam ind. M. <καταλιπών. οἱ δὲ Ῥωμαῖοι προορῶντες πρὸς Καρχηδονίους καὶ ἐν Ἰβηρίᾳ> addidi, ex Sec. et Ald.　**53** βίβλῳ V, corr. ex βύβλῳ, et M　**56** βίβλος VM　Ἀννιβιακή VM: Ἀννιβαϊκή Steph.　**57** <ἐν> add. Steph.

13 (48) The Romans sent ambassadors to Carthage, to demand of the Carthaginians that they hand over Hannibal as a violator of the treaty, unless they considered that his action was on behalf of the state; and if they did not surrender him, to declare war against them immediately. (49) This is what the ambassadors did, and, as the Carthaginians did not surrender Hannibal, they declared war against them. This is said to be the way it happened. When the ambassador realised they were mocking him, he pointed to the fold of his clothing and said, "Here, Carthaginians, I bring you peace and war. Take whichever you choose." (50) They replied, "You give us whichever you wish." When he offered them war, they all cried out together, "We accept it." They immediately sent a message to Hannibal to overrun the whole of Iberia without fear, as the treaty was dissolved. (51) He marched against all the tribes in his vicinity and subdued them, persuading some, terrifying others and overthrowing others by force; and he brought together a large army, concealing the reason for it, because he was planning to invade Italy. (52) He sent ambassadors to the Gauls and investigated the passes through the Alps, and crossed them, leaving his brother, Hasdrubal, in Iberia.

14 (53) The Romans, reckoning that the war against the Carthaginians would be in Iberia and Libya (for they did not even imagine that the Libyans would ever invade Italy), sent Tiberius Sempronius Longus with one hundred and sixty ships and two legions to Libya (what Longus and the other Roman commanders did in Libya has been recorded in my book on the wars with Carthage). (54) They also sent Publius Cornelius Scipio to Iberia in sixty ships with ten thousand infantry and seven hundred cavalry, and with him his brother Gnaeus Cornelius Scipio as his legate. (55) Of these two, Publius, learning from Massiliote merchants that Hannibal had crossed the Alps into Italy, and fearing that he would attack the Italians before they were prepared for him, handed over to his brother Gnaeus the army in Iberia and sailed in a quinquereme to Etruria. (56) What he and the other commanders in this war who followed him did in Italy, until at last after fifteen years they drove Hannibal out of Italy, are set down in the next book, which deals with all the deeds of Hannibal in Italy and is therefore called the Hannibalic book of the Roman History.

15 (57) Gnaeus on the other hand did nothing worth recording among the Iberians before his brother Publius rejoined him. At the end of Publius' period of office, the Romans sent the consuls elected after Publius against Hannibal in Italy and

Πούπλιον ὑπάτους ἐξέπεμψαν, αὐτὸν δ' ἀνθύπατον ἀποφήναντες ἐς Ἰβηρίαν αὖθις ἔστειλαν. (58) καὶ ἀπὸ τοῦδε οἱ δύο Σκιπίωνες τὸν ἐν Ἰβηρίᾳ πόλεμον διέφερον, Ἀσρούβου σφίσιν ἀντιστρατηγοῦντος, μέχρι Καρχηδόνιοι μὲν ὑπὸ Σύφακος, τοῦ τῶν Νομάδων δυνάστου, πολεμούμενοι τὸν Ἀσρούβαν καὶ μέρος τῆς ὑπ' αὐτῷ στρατιᾶς μετεπέμψαντο, τῶν δ' ὑπολοίπων οἱ Σκιπίωνες εὐμαρῶς ἐκράτουν. (59) καὶ πολλαὶ τῶν πόλεων ἐς αὐτοὺς ἑκοῦσαι μετετίθεντο· καὶ γὰρ ἤστην πιθανωτάτω στρατηγῆσαί τε καὶ προσαγαγέσθαι.

16 (60) θέμενοι δ' οἱ Καρχηδόνιοι πρὸς Σύφακα εἰρήνην αὖθις ἐξέπεμπον εἰς Ἰβηρίαν Ἀσρούβαν μετὰ πλέονος στρατοῦ καὶ ἐλεφάντων τριάκοντα καὶ σὺν αὐτῷ ἄλλους δύο στρατηγούς, Μάγωνά τε καὶ Ἀσρούβαν ἕτερον, ὃς Γίσκωνος ἦν υἱός. καὶ χαλεπώτερος ἦν τοῖς Σκιπίωσιν ὁ πόλεμος ἀπὸ τοῦδε, ἐκράτουν δὲ καὶ ὧς. (61) καὶ πολλοὶ μὲν τῶν Λιβύων, πολλοὶ δὲ τῶν ἐλεφάντων ἐφθάρησαν, μέχρι χειμῶνος ἐπιλαβόντος οἱ μὲν Λίβυες ἐχείμαζον ἐν Τυρδιτανίᾳ, τῶν δὲ Σκιπιώνων ὁ μὲν Γναῖος ἐν Ὀρσῶνι, ὁ δὲ Πούπλιος ἐν Καστολῶνι. (62) ἔνθα αὐτῷ προσιὼν ὁ Ἀσρούβας ἀπηγγέλθη· καὶ προελθὼν τῆς πόλεως μετ' ὀλίγων ἐς κατασκοπὴν στρατοπέδου ἔλαθε πλησιάσας τῷ Ἀσρούβᾳ, καὶ αὐτὸν ἐκεῖνος καὶ τοὺς σὺν αὐτῷ πάντας ἱππεῦσι περιδραμὼν ἀπέκτεινεν. (63) ὁ δὲ Γναῖος οὐδέν τι προμαθὼν ἐς τὸν ἀδελφὸν ἐπὶ σῖτον ἔπεμπε στρατιώτας, οἷς ἕτεροι Λιβύων συντυχόντες ἐμάχοντο. καὶ πυθόμενος ὁ Γναῖος ἐξέδραμεν, ὡς εἶχεν, μετὰ τῶν εὐζώνων ἐπ' αὐτούς. οἳ δὲ τούς τε προτέρους ἀνῃρήκεσαν ἤδη καὶ τὸν Γναῖον ἐδίωκον, ἕως ἐσέδραμεν ἔς τινα πύργον. καὶ τὸν πύργον ἐνέπρησαν οἱ Λίβυες, καὶ ὁ Σκιπίων κατεκαύθη μετὰ τῶν συνόντων.

17 (64) οὕτω μὲν οἱ Σκιπίωνες ἀπέθανον ἄμφω, ἄνδρες ἐς πάντα ἀγαθοὶ γενόμενοι· καὶ αὐτοὺς ἐπεπόθησαν Ἴβηρες, ὅσοι δι' αὐτοὺς ἐς Ῥωμαίους μετέθεντο. (65) πυθόμενοι δ' οἱ ἐν ἄστει βαρέως τε ἤνεγκαν καὶ Μάρκελλον ἐκ Σικελίας ἄρτι ἀφιγμένον καὶ σὺν αὐτῷ Κλαύδιον ἐπὶ νεῶν ἐξέπεμπον ἐς Ἰβηρίαν μετὰ χιλίων ἱππέων καὶ πεζῶν μυρίων καὶ χορηγίας ἱκανῆς. (66) οὐδενὸς δὲ λαμπροῦ παρὰ τῶνδε γιγνομένου τὰ Λιβύων ὑπερηύξητο, καὶ πᾶσαν σχεδὸν Ἰβηρίαν εἶχον, ἐς βραχὺ Ῥωμαίων ἐν τοῖς ὄρεσι τοῖς Πυρηναίοις κατακεκλεισμένων. (67) πάλιν οὖν οἱ ἐν ἄστει πυνθανόμενοι μᾶλλον ἐταράσσοντο· καὶ φόβος ἦν, μὴ Ἀννίβου πορθοῦντος τὰ πρόσω τῆς Ἰταλίας καὶ οἵδε οἱ Λίβυες ἐς τὰ ἕτερα αὐτῆς

---

60 Γίσκωνος V (m.2) M: Τίσκωνος V (m.1) Γέσκωνος Mend. (ex *Lib.* 9.34, 10.37).   **65** Μάρκελλον Steph.: Μάκελον VM   post νεῶν lacunam ind. Steph.   **66** κατακεκλεισμένων Leidl: κατἄκεκλημένων VM

appointed him as proconsul and sent him back to Iberia. (58) From this time on the two Scipios carried on the war in Iberia, with Hasdrubal being the general opposed to them, until the Carthaginians, under attack from Syphax, ruler of the Numidians, sent for Hasdrubal and part of his army, at which point the Scipios easily overcame the remainder. (59) Many cities also came over to them voluntarily, for both as generals and as diplomats they were extremely persuasive.

16 (60) The Carthaginians made peace with Syphax and sent Hasdrubal back to Iberia with a larger army and thirty elephants, and along with him two other generals, Mago and another Hasdrubal, the son of Gisgo. From this time on, the war was more difficult for the Scipios, but even so they were successful. (61) Many of the Libyans and many elephants were destroyed, until, with the onset of winter, the Libyans went into winter quarters in Turdetania and of the Scipios, Gnaeus wintered at Orso and Publius at Castulo. (62) News was brought to him that Hasdrubal was advancing against him there, and, setting out from the city with a small number of soldiers to reconnoitre the enemy camp, he came upon Hasdrubal unexpectedly, who surrounded him with his cavalry and killed him along with all those with him. (63) Gnaeus, who knew nothing of this, sent soldiers to his brother to collect corn, who were met by another Libyan force who engaged with them. When Gnaeus learned of this, he set out rapidly with his light-armed forces against them. The Libyans had already disposed of the first group, and pursued Gnaeus until he took refuge in a tower. The Libyans burned down the tower, and Scipio and those with him were burnt to death.

17 (64) So died both the Scipios, excellent men in all respects; and those Iberians who had joined with the Romans grieved over them. (65) When those in Rome learned of this, they were dismayed by the news, and sent to Iberia Marcellus, who had recently returned from Sicily, and with him Claudius, with ships and one thousand cavalry and ten thousand infantry and adequate supplies. (66) These men achieved nothing remarkable and the Libyan cause flourished and they held almost the whole of Iberia, with the Romans closed into a small space in the Pyrenean mountains. (67) Once again when this was learned by those in Rome, they were even more greatly disturbed, and there was a panic lest, while Hannibal was laying waste the further parts of Italy, these Libyans might invade the rest of it. As a result,

ἐσβάλοιεν. ὅθεν οὐδ' ἀποσχέσθαι τῆς Ἰβηρίας βουλομένοις αὐτοῖς δυνατὸν ἦν, δέει τοῦ μὴ καὶ τόνδε τὸν πόλεμον ἐς τὴν Ἰταλίαν ἐπαγαγέσθαι.

18 (68) προύγραφον οὖν ἡμέραν, ἐν ᾗ χειροτονήσουσιν στρατηγὸν εἰς Ἰβηρίαν. καὶ οὐδενὸς παραγγέλλοντος ἔτι πλείων ἐγίγνετο φόβος, καὶ σιωπὴ σκυθρωπὸς ἐπεῖχε τὴν ἐκκλησίαν, ἐς οὗ Κορνήλιος Σκιπίων, ὁ Ποπλίου Κορνηλίου τοῦ ἀναιρεθέντος ἐν Ἴβηρσιν υἱός, νέος μὲν ὢν κομιδῇ (τεσσάρων γὰρ καὶ εἴκοσιν ἐτῶν ἦν), σώφρων δὲ καὶ γενναῖος εἶναι νομιζόμενος, ἐς τὸ μέσον ἐλθὼν ἐσεμνολόγησεν ἀμφί τε τοῦ πατρὸς καὶ ἀμφὶ τοῦ θείου καὶ τὸ πάθος αὐτῶν ὀδυράμενος ἐπεῖπεν οἰκεῖος εἶναι τιμωρὸς ἐκ πάντων πατρὶ καὶ θείῳ καὶ πατρίδι. (69) ἄλλα τε πολλὰ ἀθρόως καὶ λάβρως ὥσπερ ἔνθους ἐπαγγειλάμενος, οὐκ Ἰβηρίαν λήψεσθαι μόνην, ἀλλ' ἐπ' αὐτῇ καὶ Λιβύην καὶ Καρχηδόνα, τοῖς μὲν ἔδοξε κουφολογῆσαι νεανικῶς, τὸν δὲ δῆμον ἀνέλαβε κατεπτηχότα (χαίρουσι γὰρ ἐπαγγελίαις οἱ δεδιότες) καὶ ᾑρέθη στρατηγὸς ἐς Ἰβηρίαν ὡς πράξων τι τῆς εὐτολμίας ἄξιον. (70) οἱ πρεσβύτεροι δ' αὐτὴν οὐκ εὐτολμίαν, ἀλλὰ προπέτειαν ἐκάλουν. καὶ ὁ Σκιπίων αἰσθόμενος ἐς ἐκκλησίαν αὖθις αὐτοὺς συνεκάλει τε καὶ ἐσεμνύνετο ὅμοια· (71) καὶ τὴν ἡλικίαν εἰπὼν οὐδὲν ἐμποδὼν οἱ γενήσεσθαι προυκαλεῖτο ὅμως, εἴ τις ἐθέλοι τῶν πρεσβυτέρων τὴν ἀρχὴν παραλαβεῖν ἑκόντος αὐ τοῦ παραδιδόντος. (72) οὐδενὸς δ' ἑλομένου μᾶλλον ἐπαινούμενός τε καὶ θαυμαζόμενος ἐξῄει μετὰ μυρίων πεζῶν καὶ ἱππέων πεντακοσίων· οὐ γὰρ ἐνεχώρει πλέονα στρατὸν ἐξάγειν, Ἀννίβου δῃοῦντος τὴν Ἰταλίαν. ἔλαβεν δὲ καὶ χρήματα καὶ παρασκευὴν ἄλλην καὶ ναῦς μακρὰς ὀκτὼ καὶ εἴκοσι, μεθ' ὧν ἐς Ἰβηρίαν διέπλευσε.

19 (73) παραλαβών τε τὴν ἐκεῖ στρατιὰν καὶ οὓς ἦγεν ἐς ἓν συναγαγὼν ἐκάθηρε καὶ διελέχθη καὶ τοῖσδε μεγαληγόρως. δόξα τε διέδραμεν ἐς ὅλην αὐτίκα τὴν Ἰβηρίαν, βαρυνομένην τε τοὺς Λίβυας καὶ τῶν Σκιπιώνων τὴν ἀρετὴν ἐπιποθοῦσαν, ὅτι στρατηγὸς αὐτοῖς ἥκοι Σκιπίων ὁ Σκιπίωνος κατὰ θεόν. οὗ δὴ καὶ αὐτὸς αἰσθανόμενος ὑπεκρίνετο πάντα ποιεῖν πειθόμενος θεῷ. (74) πυνθανόμενος δ', ὅτι οἱ ἐχθροὶ σταθμεύουσι μὲν ἐν τέσσαρσι στρατοπέδοις, μακρὰν διεστηκότες ἀπ' ἀλλήλων, ἀνὰ δισμυρίους καὶ πεντακισχιλίους πεζοὺς καὶ ἱππέας πεντακοσίους ἐπὶ δισχιλίοις, τὴν δὲ παρασκευὴν τῶν τε χρημάτων καὶ σίτου καὶ ὅπλων καὶ βελῶν καὶ νεῶν καὶ αἰχμαλώτων καὶ ὁμήρων τῶν ἐξ ὅλης Ἰβηρίας ἔχουσιν ἐν τῇ πρότερον μὲν Ζακάνθῃ, τότε δὲ ἤδη Καρχηδόνι, καὶ φρουρὸς αὐτῶν ἐστι Μάγων μετὰ μυρίων Καρχηδονίων, (75) ἔκρινε πρῶτον ἐς τούτους ἐπιδραμεῖν διά τε τὴν ὀλιγότητα τοῦ στρατοῦ τοῦ μετὰ Μάγωνος καὶ τὸ μέγεθος τῆς παρασκευῆς καὶ ὡς ὁρμητήριον ἀσφαλὲς ἐκ γῆς καὶ θαλάσσης ἕξων ἐπὶ

although they wanted to withdraw from Iberia, they were unable to do so, for fear that the war there might also be transferred to Italy.

18 (68) They therefore specified a day on which they would elect a commander for Iberia. When no one came forward there was still more terror and a sullen silence gripped the assembly, until Cornelius Scipio, the son of that Publius Cornelius who had perished among the Iberians, came forward into the middle of the meeting. He was only a young man (for he was twenty-four years old), but had a reputation for good judgement and a noble spirit. He spoke in solemn terms about his father and his uncle, and lamented their fate, adding that he of all people was the proper person to avenge his father, his uncle and his country. (69) He spoke fluently and forcefully, as though inspired, saying that he would not only take Iberia but also Libya and Carthage. Some thought this was the thoughtless language of a young man, but he stirred up the people, who were cowering with fear (for those who are terrified rejoice at promises made to them) and he was chosen as commander for Iberia, as someone who would achieve something worthy of his bravery. (70) The older people however said that this was not bravery but foolhardiness. When Scipio heard this, he again summoned them into the assembly and again addressed them in solemn words. (71) He said that his youth would be no obstacle to him, but that, if any of the older men wished to take on the command, he would willingly yield it. (72) When no one offered to do so, he was praised and admired all the more, and set out with ten thousand infantry and five hundred horse. He could not take a larger army, for Hannibal was plundering Italy. He took money and other armaments and twenty-eight war-ships, with which he sailed for Iberia.

19 (73) Taking over the army that was already there and joining them into one body with those he brought with him, he performed a ritual cleansing, and addressed them also in grandiloquent style. The story immediately ran through the whole of Iberia, tired as it was of the Libyans and longing for the courage of the Scipios, that through the intervention of a god Scipio the son of Scipio had come to them as a general. When he discovered this, he represented himself as doing everything under the influence of a god. (74) He learned that the enemy were stationed in four camps, separated from one another by a great distance, consisting of twenty five thousand infantry and two thousand five hundred cavalry, but that they kept their store of money, corn, armour, weapons, ships, prisoners and hostages from the whole of Iberia in what had previously been Saguntum but was at that time called Carthage, and that it was guarded by Mago with ten thousand Carthaginians. (75) He decided first of all to attack these soldiers, both because of the small size of Mago's army and the great quantity of the supplies, and because he believed that it was a secure

ὅλην τὴν Ἰβηρίαν πόλιν ἀργυρεῖα καὶ χώραν εὐδαίμονα καὶ πλοῦτον πολὺν ἔχουσαν καὶ τὸν διάπλουν ἐς Λιβύην βραχύτατον.

20 (76) ὃ μὲν δὴ τοσοῖσδε λογισμοῖς ἐπαιρόμενος, οὐδενὶ προειπών, ὅπῃ χωρήσειν ἔμελλεν, ἡλίου δύναντος ἦγε τὴν στρατιὰν δι' ὅλης τῆς νυκτὸς ἐπὶ τὴν Καρχηδόνα. καὶ αὐτὴν ἅμα ἕῳ τῶν Λιβύων καταπλαγέντων περιταφρεύσας ἐς τὴν ἐπιοῦσαν ἡμέραν ἡτοιμάζετο, κλίμακάς τε καὶ μηχανὰς πάντῃ περιτιθεὶς χωρὶς ἑνὸς μέρους, ᾗ τὸ μὲν τεῖχος ἦν βραχύτατον, ἕλος δ' αὐτῷ καὶ θάλασσα προσέκλυζε καὶ δι' αὐτὸ καὶ οἱ φύλακες ἀμελῶς εἶχον. (77) νυκτὸς δὲ πάντα πληρώσας βελῶν καὶ λίθων καὶ τοῖς λιμέσι τῆς πόλεως ναῦς ἐπιστήσας, ἵνα μὴ αἱ νῆες αὐτὸν αἱ τῶν πολεμίων διαφύγοιεν (ὑπὸ γὰρ δὴ μεγαλοψυχίας ἤλπιζε πάντως αἱρήσειν τὴν πόλιν), πρὸ ἕω τὴν στρατιὰν ἀνεβίβαζεν ἐπὶ τὰς μηχανάς, τοὺς μὲν ἄνωθεν ἐγχειρεῖν κελεύων τοῖς πολεμίοις, τοὺς δὲ κάτω τὰς μηχανὰς ὠθεῖν ἐς τὸ πρόσω. (78) Μάγων δὲ τοὺς μὲν μυρίους ἐπέστησεν ταῖς πύλαις ὡς ἐκπηδήσοντας, ὅτε καιρὸς εἴη, μετὰ μόνων ξιφῶν (οὐ γὰρ εἶναι δόρασιν ἐν στενῷ χρῆσθαι), τοὺς δ' ἄλλους ἐς τὰς ἐπάλξεις ἀνῆγε. καὶ πολλὰ καὶ ὅδε μηχανήματα καὶ λίθους καὶ βέλη καὶ καταπέλτας ἐπιστήσας εἴχετο τοῦ ἔργου προθύμως. (79) γενομένης δὲ βοῆς καὶ παρακελεύσεως ἑκατέρωθεν, οὐδέτεροι μὲν ὁρμῆς καὶ προθυμίας ἐνέλειπον, καὶ λίθους τε καὶ βέλη καὶ ἀκόντια ἀφιέντες, οἱ μὲν ἀπὸ χειρῶν, οἱ δ' ἀπὸ μηχανῶν, οἱ δ' ἀπὸ σφενδόνης, εἴ τέ τις ἦν ἄλλη παρασκευὴ καὶ δύναμις, ἐχρῶντο προθύμως ἅπασιν.

21 (80) ἐκακοπάθει δὲ τὰ τοῦ Σκιπίωνος, καὶ οἱ μύριοι Καρχηδονίων, οἳ περὶ τὰς πύλας ἦσαν, ἐκδραμόντες σὺν τοῖς ξίφεσι γυμνοῖς ἐνέπιπτον ἐς τοὺς τὰ μηχανήματα ὠθοῦντας καὶ πολλὰ μὲν ἔδρων, οὐχ ἥσσω δ' ἀντέπασχον, μέχρι τῷ φιλοπόνῳ καὶ ταλαιπώρῳ τὰ Ῥωμαίων ὑπανίστατο. (81) καὶ μεταβολῆς γενομένης οἵ τε ἐπὶ τῶν τειχῶν ἔκαμνον ἤδη, καὶ αἱ κλίμακες αὐτοῖς προσεπέλαζον. οἱ δὲ ξιφήρεις τῶν Καρχηδονίων ἐς τὰς πύλας ἐσέτρεχον καὶ ἀποκλείσαντες αὐτὰς ἀνεπήδων ἐπὶ τὰ τείχη. (82) καὶ τοῖς Ῥωμαίοις αὖθις ἦν ὁ πόνος πολύς τε καὶ χαλεπός, ἐς οὗ Σκιπίων ὁ στρατηγὸς πάντῃ περιθέων τε καὶ βοῶν καὶ παρακαλῶν εἶδε περὶ μεσημβρίαν, ᾗ τὸ βραχὺ τεῖχος ἦν καὶ τὸ ἕλος προσέκλυζε, τὴν θάλασσαν ὑποχωροῦσαν· ἄμπωτις γὰρ ἐφήμερός ἐστιν. καὶ ὁ κλύδων ἐπῄει μὲν ἐς μαστούς, ὑπεχώρει δ'. ἐς μέσας κνήμας. (83) ὅπερ ὁ Σκιπίων τότε ἰδὼν καὶ περὶ τῆς φύσεως αὐτοῦ πυθόμενος, ὡς ἔχοι τὸ λοιπὸν τῆς

---

75 ἀργυρεῖα Steph.: ἀργυρία V   χώραν καὶ πλοῦτον εὐδαίμονα καὶ πολὺν VM, corr, Schweig. 76 αὐτῷ Mend.: αὐτὸ VM 79 καὶ ante λίθους del. Viereck-Roos. 80 ἔδρων Steph.: ἔδρον VM 81 ἀποκλείσαντες Leidl: ἀποκλη≡αντες (littera post η erasa) V 82 ἕλος Steph.; ἔλεος VM

base for operations by land and sea against the whole of Iberia, possessing silver mines, fertile land and great wealth, and the shortest possible sea-crossing to Libya.

20 (76) Excited by these plans, he told no one of where he intended to go, and starting at sunset he led his army through the night against Carthage. Catching the Libyans by surprise, he dug ditches around the city at day-break and prepared the siege through the following day, placing ladders and siege-engines everywhere, except for one place where the wall was very low, but the lagoon and the sea washed up against it, and for that reason the guards were careless. (77) Having filled all his engines with missiles and stones and stationed his ships in front of the city's harbours, to prevent the enemy ships escaping him (for in his mood of confidence he expected to capture the city for certain), he sent his soldiers to the siege-engines before dawn, ordering those in the upper part to engage with the enemy and those below to push the engines forward. (78) Mago placed his ten thousand men by the gates so as to be able to sally out at the appropriate moment with swords alone (for it was not possible to use spears in the confined space), and sent others up to battlements. He also put many engines, stones, missiles and catapults in place, and set about the work with enthusiasm. (79) A shout of encouragement went up on both sides, and neither was lacking in panache or enthusiasm, throwing stones, missiles and javelins, some by hand, others from the engines and others from slings, and whatever other means were available, they used them all enthusiastically.

21 (80) Scipio's side suffered badly, and the ten thousand Carthaginians who were by the gates, running out with swords drawn, attacked those who were pushing forward the engines. They achieved a great deal, but also suffered as much damage, until the Roman side began to prevail through their hard labour and endurance. (81) As the change of fortune began, those on the walls were already becoming exhausted and ladders were brought up against them. The Carthaginian swordsmen retreated through the gates, bolted them shut and climbed up onto the walls. (82) This again caused much hardship and labour to the Romans, until their general, Scipio, who was moving amongst them, calling out to them and encouraging them, saw at about mid-day that the sea was going out, where the wall was low and the lagoon washed against it; for there is an ebb-tide each day. When the tide was in, the water reached breast-height, but when it was out it reached only to the mid-calf. (83) Scipio saw this and was told about the natural cause of the phenomenon, and that it would take the rest of the day before the sea came in again. He ran about

ἡμέρας, πρὶν ἐπανελθεῖν τὸ πέλαγος, ἔθει πάντῃ βοῶν· "νῦν ὁ καιρός, ὦ ἄνδρες, νῦν ὁ σύμμαχός μοι θεὸς ἀφῖκται. πρόσιτε τῷ μέρει τῷδε τοῦ τείχους. ἡ θάλασσα ἡμῖν ὑποκεχώρηκε. φέρετε τὰς κλίμακας, ἐγὼ δ' ἡγήσομαι."

22 (84) καὶ πρῶτος ἁρπάσας τινὰ τῶν κλιμάκων μετέφερέν τε καὶ ἀνέβαινεν, οὔπω τινὸς ἀναβάντος ἄλλου, μέχρι περισχόντες αὐτὸν οἵ τε ὑπασπισταὶ καὶ ἡ ἄλλη στρατιὰ τόνδε μὲν ἐπέσχον, αὐτοὶ δὲ πολλὰς ὁμοῦ κλίμακας προσετίθεσάν τε καὶ ἀνεπήδων. (85) βοῆς δὲ καὶ ὁρμῆς ἑκατέρωθεν γενομένης καὶ ποικίλων ἔργων καὶ παθῶν, ἐκράτησαν ὅμως οἱ Ῥωμαῖοι καὶ πύργων τινῶν ἐπέβησαν ὀλίγων, οἷς ὁ Σκιπίων σαλπικτὰς καὶ βυκανιστὰς ἐπιστήσας ἐξοτρύνειν ἐκέλευσε καὶ θορυβεῖν ὡς τῆς πόλεως εἰλημμένης ἤδη. (86) ἕτεροί τε περιθέοντες ὁμοίως διετάρασσον, καὶ καθαλόμενοί τινες ἀνέῳξαν τῷ Σκιπίωνι τὰς πύλας· ὁ δ' εἰσεπήδησε μετὰ τῆς στρατιᾶς δρόμῳ. καὶ τῶν ἔνδον οἱ μὲν ἐς τὰς οἰκίας ἀπεδίδρασκον, ὁ δὲ Μάγων τοὺς μυρίους ἐς τὴν ἀγορὰν συνεκάλει. (87) ταχὺ δὲ καὶ τούτων κατακοπέντων ἐς τὴν ἄκραν σὺν ὀλίγοις ἀνεχώρει. τοῦ δὲ Σκιπίωνος καὶ ἐπὶ τὴν ἄκραν εὐθὺς ἐπιόντος, οὐδὲν ἔτι δρᾶν σὺν ἡττημένοις τε καὶ κατεπτηχόσιν ἔχων ἐνεχείρισεν ἑαυτὸν τῷ Σκιπίωνι.

23 (88) ὃ δὲ τόλμῃ καὶ τύχῃ πόλιν εὐδαίμονα καὶ δυνατὴν ἑλὼν ἡμέρᾳ μιᾷ, τετάρτῃ τῆς ἐπ' αὐτὴν ἀφίξεως, ἐπήρτο μεγάλως καὶ μᾶλλον ἐδόκει κατὰ θεὸν ἕκαστα δρᾶν· αὐτός τε οὕτως ἐφρόνει καὶ οὕτως ἐλογοποίει καὶ τότε καὶ ἐς τὸν ἔπειτα βίον, ἀρξάμενος ἐξ ἐκείνου. (89) πολλάκις γοῦν ἐς τὸ Καπιτώλιον ἐσῄει μόνος καὶ τὰς θύρας ἐπέκλειεν ὥσπερ τι παρὰ τοῦ θεοῦ μανθάνων. καὶ νῦν ἔτι τὴν εἰκόνα τὴν Σκιπίωνος ἐν ταῖς πομπαῖς μόνου προφέρουσιν ἐκ τοῦ Καπιτωλίου, τῶν δ' ἄλλων ἐξ ἀγορᾶς φέρονται. (90) τότε δ' εἰρηνικὸν ὁμοῦ καὶ πολεμικὸν ταμιεῖον παραλαβὼν ὅπλα τε πολλὰ ἐν αὐτῷ καὶ βέλη καὶ μηχανήματα καὶ νεωσοίκους καὶ ναῦς μακρὰς τρεῖς καὶ τριάκοντα καὶ σῖτον καὶ ἀγορὰν ποικίλην καὶ ἐλέφαντα καὶ χρυσὸν καὶ ἄργυρον, τὸν μὲν ἐν σκεύεσι πεποιημένον, τὸν δὲ ἐπίσημον, τὸν δὲ ἀσήμαντον, ὅμηρά τε Ἰβήρων καὶ αἰχμάλωτα καὶ ὅσα Ῥωμαίων αὐτῶν προείληπτο, ἔθυε τῆς ἐπιούσης καὶ ἐθριάμβευε καὶ τὴν στρατιὰν ἐπῄνει καὶ τῇ πόλει μετὰ τὴν στρατιὰν ἐδημηγόρει τῶν τε Σκιπιώνων αὐτοὺς ἀναμνήσας ἀπέλυε τοὺς αἰχμαλώτους εἰς τὰ ἴδια, θεραπεύων τὰς πόλεις. (91) ἀριστεῖα δ' ἐδίδου τῷ μὲν ἐς τὸ τεῖχος ἀναβάντι πρώτῳ μέγιστα, τῷ δ' ἑξῆς τὰ ἡμίσεα τούτων, τῷ δὲ τρίτῳ τὰ τρίτα καὶ τοῖς ἄλλοις κατὰ λόγον. τὰ δὲ λοιπὰ ἐς Ῥώμην ἔπεμψεν ἐπὶ τῶν εἰλημμένων νεῶν, ὅσα χρυσὸς ἢ ἄργυρος ἦν ἢ ἐλέφας. (92) ἡ μὲν δὴ

---

89 πολλάκις Steph.: πολλάκι VM   **91** ἀριστεῖα Musgrave et Schweig.: ἀριστεῖ VM   τῷ Steph.: τό VM   τὰ δὲ λοιπὰ δ' ἐς Ῥώμην V, corr. Leidl et Gouk.

shouting everywhere, "Now is the moment, men! Now the god has come to my aid! Attack this part of the wall. The sea has retreated for us. Bring up the ladders. I will lead you."

22 (84) He was the first to seize one of the ladders, carry it across and was climbing up. No one else was climbing up, until those round him, both his body-guard and the rest of the army, restrained him, and themsleves set up many ladders together and mounted them. (85) On both sides there was a shouting and a rushing forward, with various things done and suffered, but the Romans prevailed and captured a few of the towers. Scipio sent trumpeters and buglers up these towers and ordered them to make a rousing noise, as though the city had already been taken. (86) Others then came running up and spread the confusion in a similar way, and some jumped down from the walls and opened the gates to Scipio. He ran in with the army. Of those within the town, some ran away into their houses, but Mago summoned his ten thousand soldiers into the market-place. (87) When these were quickly cut to pieces, Mago retreated with a few men into the citadel. When Scipio immediately attacked the citadel, Mago, as there was nothing that he and his defeated and shattered forces could do, surrendered himself to Scipio.

23 (88) Having taken a rich and powerful city by daring and good fortune in one day, the fourth from his arrival, he was greatly elated and it appeared even more that he was achieving everything through the influence of a god. He himself thought this, and said so both then and throughout the rest of his life, beginning from this moment. (89) Often he went into the Capitoline temple by himself and shut the doors, as though he was discovering something from the god. Even now they bring the statue of Scipio alone out of the Capitoline temple during processions, while those of others they bring from the Forum. (90) On this occasion he took possession there of a store of material for both military and peaceful uses, much armour and many missiles, siege-engines, dock-yards and thirty-three war ships, and corn and various kinds of provisions as well as ivory, gold and silver, some in the form of dishes, some coined and some uncoined; and also Iberian hostages and prisoners, some taken previously from the Romans themselves. On the following day he sacrificed to the gods, conducted a triumph, and praised the army. After speaking to the army, he addressed the people in the city. Reminding them of the Scipios, he freed the captives to their own homes, thus seeking to appease their cities. (91) He gave rewards.to his soldiers, the greatest to the man who first scaled the wall, half as much to the next, one third to the third, and to the others in a similar ratio. The rest of the gold, silver and ivory he sent to Rome aboard the ships he had captured.

πόλις ἔθυεν ἐπὶ τρεῖς ἡμέρας, ὡς τῆς πατρῴας εὐπραξίας ἐκ πόνων πολλῶν αὖθις ἀνακυπτούσης, ἡ δὲ Ἰβηρία καὶ οἱ ἐν αὐτῇ Φοίνικες κατεπεπλήγεσαν τῷ μεγέθει καὶ τάχει τοῦ τολμήματος.

24 (93) ὁ δὲ φρουρὰν μὲν Καρχηδόνι ἐπέστησε καὶ τὸ τεῖχος ἐκέλευσε τὸ παρὰ τὴν ἄμπωτιν ἐς ὕψος ἐγεῖραι· τὴν δ' ἄλλην Ἰβηρίαν αὐτός τε ἐπιὼν καὶ τοὺς φίλους ἐς ἕκαστα περιπέμπων ὑπήγετο καὶ τἆλλα τὰ ἀντέχοντα ἐβιάζετο. (94) Καρχηδονίων δ' οἱ στρατηγοί, δύο ὄντε λοιπὼ καὶ δύο Ἀσρούβα, ὁ μὲν τοῦ Ἀμίλχαρος πορρωτάτω παρὰ Κελτίβηρσιν ἐξενολόγει, ὁ δὲ τοῦ Γίσκωνος ἐς μὲν τὰς πόλεις τὰς ἔτι βεβαίους περιέπεμπεν, ἀξιῶν Καρχηδονίοις ἐμμένειν ὡς στρατιᾶς ἐλευσομένης αὐτίκα ἀπείρου τὸ πλῆθος, Μάγωνα δ' ἕτερον ἐς τὰ πλησίον περιέπεμπεν ξενολογεῖν, ὁπόθεν δυνηθείη, καὶ αὐτὸς ἐς τὴν Λέρσα γῆν τῶν ἀφισταμένων ἐνέβαλεν καί τινα αὐτῶν πόλιν ἔμελλεν πολιορκήσειν. (95) ἐπιφανέντος δ' αὐτῷ τοῦ Σκιπίωνος ἐς Βαιτύκην ὑπεχώρει καὶ πρὸ τῆς πόλεως ἐστρατοπέδευεν· ἔνθα τῆς ἐπιούσης εὐθὺς ἡσσᾶτο, καὶ τὸν χάρακα αὐτοῦ καὶ τὴν Βαιτύκην ἔλαβεν ὁ Σκιπίων.

25 (96) ὁ δὲ τὴν στρατιὰν τὴν Καρχηδονίων τὴν ἔτι οὖσαν ἐν Ἰβηρίᾳ συνέλεγεν ἐς Καρμώνην πόλιν, ὡς ὁμοῦ πᾶσιν ἀμυνούμενος τὸν Σκιπίωνα. καὶ αὐτῷ συνῆλθον πολλοὶ μὲν Ἰβήρων, οὓς Μάγων ἦγεν, πολλοὶ δὲ Νομάδων, ὧν ἦρχε Μασανάσσης. (97) καὶ τούτων ὁ μὲν Ἀσρούβας μετὰ τῶν πεζῶν ὑπὸ χάρακι ἐστρατοπέδευεν, ὁ δὲ Μασανάσσης καὶ ὁ Μάγων ἱππαρχοῦντες αὐτῷ προηυλίζοντο τοῦ στρατοπέδου. (98) ὧδε δὲ ἔχουσιν αὐτοῖς ὁ Σκιπίων τοὺς ἰδίους ἱππέας ἐπιδιῄρει καὶ Λαίλιον μὲν ἐπὶ Μάγωνα ἔπεμπεν, αὐτὸς δ' ἐπὶ Μασανάσσην ἐτράπετο. (99) μέχρι μὲν οὖν τινος ἦν ἐν ἀγῶνι καὶ πόνῳ δυσχερεῖ, τῶν Νομάδων αὐτὸν ἀκοντιζόντων τε καὶ ὑποχωρούντων, εἶτ' αὖθις ἐπελαυνόντων· ὡς δὲ παρήγγειλεν ὁ Σκιπίων ἀμεταστρεπτὶ διώκειν αὐτούς, τὰ δόρατα προβαλόντας, οὐκ ἔχοντες ἀναστροφὴν οἱ Νομάδες κατέφυγον ἐς τὸ στρατόπεδον. καὶ ὁ Σκιπίων ἀποσχὼν δέκα σταδίους ἐστρατοπέδευσεν εὐσταθῶς, ᾗπερ ἐβούλετο. (100) ἦν δὲ ἡ μὲν τῶν ἐχθρῶν σύμπασα δύναμις ἑπτακισμύριοι πεζοὶ καὶ ἱππεῖς πεντακισχίλιοι καὶ ἐλέφαντες ἓξ καὶ τριάκοντα· Σκιπίωνι δὲ τούτων οὐδὲ τριτημόριον ἦν. διὸ καὶ μέχρι τινὸς ἐνεδοίαζε καὶ μάχης οὐ κατῆρχε, ἀλλ' ἀκροβολισμοῖς ἐχρῆτο μόνοις.

---

94 Λέρσα γῆν τῶν V: Τυρδιτανῶν vel Λυσιτανῶν Schweig. Καρπητανῶν Nipperdey Ἰλεργητῶν Schulten et Gouk. **95** Βαιτύκην VM; Βαικύλη Wesseling **96** Καρμώνην Wesseling: Καρεώνην VM **99** ἀμεταστρεπτὶ Bekker: ἀμεταστρεπτεῖ VM **100** τριτη- μόριον Steph: τριτημόριος VM

(92) At Rome there was a three-day festival, because their ancestral good-fortune was emerging once again after many troubles. Iberia and the Phoenicians there were astounded by the extent and speed of this daring achievement.

24 (93) Scipio established a garrison at Carthage, and ordered that the wall should be raised in height where the tide washed against it. He then set out against the rest of Iberia, and, sending friends to each place, won them over and subdued forcibly the remainder which still opposed him. (94) Of the generals of the Carthaginians, there were two remaining, both called Hasdrubal. Hasdrubal, son of Hamilcar, was enlisting mercenaries far away among the Celtiberians; Hasdrubal, son of Gisgo, sent messengers to those cities which were still on their side, encouraging them to remain with the Carthaginians, because an army of immense size was just about to come, and he sent another man called Mago to those that were close by, to enlist mercenaries wherever he could, while he himself invaded the territory of Lersa, where they had gone into revolt, and intended to besiege one of their towns. (95) When Scipio approached him, he retreated into Baetyca, and encamped in front of the town. There he was defeated on the following day, and Scipio captured his camp and also Baetyca.

25 (96) Hasdrubal gathered together such of the army of the Carthaginians as remained in Iberia at the town of Carmona, so as to resist Scipio with all their forces at once. Many Iberians, led by Mago, came to join him, and many Numidians, led by Massinissa. (97) Of these, Hasdrubal garrisoned the camp with the infantry, and Massinissa and Mago, in command of the cavalry, bivouacked in front of the camp. (98) With the enemy arranged in this fashion, Scipio disposed his own cavalry against them, and sent Laelius against Mago while he himself turned towards Massinissa. (99) For some time he was in a critical, difficult and laborious situation, with the Numidians discharging their javelins at him and retreating, and then driving forward again; but when Scipio ordered his troops to pursue them without deviating, with their spears levelled, the Numidians, who had no room to turn, fled back to the camp. Scipio moved ten *stadia* away and set up his camp in a good position, which he had chosen. (100) The entire enemy force was seventy thousand infantry, five thousand cavalry and thirty-six elephants, while Scipio did not have even a third as many. For this reason, he was for some time uncertain what to do and did not engage in battle, but skirmished with missiles.

26 (101) ἐπεὶ δ' ἐπέλειπεν αὐτὸν ἡ ἀγορὰ καὶ λιμὸς ἥπτετο τοῦ στρατοῦ, ἀναζεῦξαι μὲν οὐκ εὐπρεπὲς ἡγεῖτο εἶναι Σκιπίων· θυσάμενος δὲ καὶ εὐθὺς ἐπὶ ταῖς θυσίαις τὴν στρατιὰν ἐς ἐπήκοον ἐλάσας καὶ τὸ βλέμμα καὶ τὸ σχῆμα διαθεὶς πάλιν ὥσπερ ἔνθους, ἔφη τὸ δαιμόνιον ἥκειν τὸ σύνηθες αὐτῷ καὶ καλεῖν ἐπὶ τοὺς πολεμίους· χρῆναι δὲ θαρρεῖν θεῷ μᾶλλον ἢ πλήθει στρατοῦ· καὶ γὰρ τῶν πρότερον ἔργων κατὰ θεόν, οὐ κατὰ πλῆθος κρατῆσαι. (102) ἔς τε πίστιν τῶν λεγομένων τὰ ἱερὰ παραφέρειν ἐς τὸ μέσον ἐκέλευε τοὺς μάντεις. καὶ λέγων ὁρᾷ τινας οἰωνοὺς πετομένους, οὓς μεθ' ὁρμῆς καὶ βοῆς αὐτόθεν ἐπιστραφεὶς ἐδείκνυέν τε καὶ ἔλεγεν, ὅτι οἱ σύμβολα νίκης οἱ θεοὶ καὶ τάδε ἔπεμψαν. (103) συνεκινεῖτο δὲ πρὸς αὐτὰ ἐνθέως ὁρῶν καὶ βοῶν· καὶ ἡ στρατιὰ πᾶσα ἐς τὰς ἐκείνου φαντασίας, περιφερομένου δεῦρο κἀκεῖσε, συνεπεστρέφετο, καὶ πάντες ὡς ἐπὶ νίκην ἕτοιμον ἠρεθίζοντο. (104) ὁ δ' ἐπεὶ πᾶν εἶχεν, ὅσον τι καὶ ἐβούλετο, οὐκ ἀνέθετο οὐδ' εἴασε τὴν ὁρμὴν ἐκλυθῆναι, ἀλλ' ὡς ἔτι ὢν θεόληπτος ἔφη δεῖν ἐπὶ τοῖσδε τοῖς σημείοις εὐθὺς ἀγωνίσασθαι. καὶ φαγόντας ἐκέλευεν ὁπλίσασθαι καὶ ἐπῆγεν ἀδοκήτως τοῖς πολεμίοις, τοὺς μὲν ἱππέας Σιλανῷ, τοὺς δὲ πεζοὺς Λαιλίῳ καὶ Μαρκίῳ παραδούς.

27 (105) Ἀσρούβας δὲ καὶ Μάγων καὶ Μασανάσσης, ἐπιόντος αὐτοῖς τοῦ Σκιπίωνος ἄφνω, σταδίων ὄντων ἐν μέσῳ δέκα μόνων, ἄσιτον οὖσαν ἔτι τὴν στρατιὰν ὥπλιζον μετὰ σπουδῆς καὶ θορύβου καὶ βοῆς. (106) γενομένης δὲ ὁμοῦ πεζομαχίας τε καὶ ἱππομαχίας οἱ μὲν ἱππῆς οἱ τῶν Ῥωμαίων ἐκράτουν ὑπὸ τῆς αὐτῆς μηχανῆς, ἀμεταστρεπτὶ τοὺς Νομάδας διώκοντες, ὑποχωρεῖν εἰθισμένους καὶ ἐπελαύνειν· οἷς τὰ ἀκόντια διὰ τὴν ἐγγύτητα οὐδὲν ἦν ἔτι χρήσιμα· οἱ πεζοὶ δ' ἐπονοῦντο ὑπὸ τοῦ πλήθους τῶν Λιβύων καὶ ἡττῶντο δι' ὅλης ἡμέρας. (107) οὐδὲ τοῦ Σκιπίωνος αὐτοὺς ἐπιθέοντός τε καὶ παρακαλοῦντος μετετίθεντο, μέχρι τὸν ἵππον Σκιπίων τῷ παιδὶ παραδοὺς καὶ παρά τινος ἀσπίδα λαβὼν ἐξέδραμεν, ὡς εἶχε, μόνος ἐς τὸ μεταίχμιον, κεκραγώς· "ἐπικουρεῖτε, ὦ Ῥωμαῖοι, κινδυνεύοντι ὑμῶν τῷ Σκιπίωνι". (108) τότε γὰρ οἱ μὲν ἐγγὺς ὁρῶντες, οἷ κινδύνου φέρεται, οἱ δὲ πόρρω πυνθανόμενοι καὶ πάντες ὁμοίως αἰδούμενοί τε καὶ περὶ τῷ στρατηγῷ δεδιότες ἐσέδραμον ἐς τοὺς πολεμίους μετ' ἀλαλαγμοῦ καὶ βίας, ἣν οὐκ ἐνεγκόντες οἱ Λίβυες ἐνέδωκαν, ἐπιλειπούσης αὐτοὺς ἅμα τῆς δυνάμεως ὑπὸ τῆς ἀσιτίας περὶ ἑσπέραν· καὶ πολὺς αὐτῶν δι' ὀλίγου τότε φόνος ἐγίγνετο. (109) τοῦτο μὲν δὴ τέλος ἦν Σκιπίωνι τῆς περὶ Καρμώνην μάχης, ἐπισφαλοῦς ἐς πολὺ γενομένης. ἀπέθανον δ' ἐν αὐτῇ Ῥωμαίων μὲν ὀκτακόσιοι, τῶν δὲ πολεμίων μύριοι καὶ πεντακισχίλιοι.

---

102 πετομένους Steph.: πετωμένους VM   106 ἀμεταστρεπτὶ Bekker: ἀμεταστρεπτεὶ VM ἀπελαύνειν VM: ἐπελαύνειν Steph.   109 Καρμώνην Schweig.; Καρβώνην V (m.1) M; Ναρβωνην V (m.2)

26 (101) When his supplies began to fail and hunger was afflicting the army, Scipio thought it unacceptable to withdraw, and so he performed a sacrifice and immediately after the sacrifice, brought the army to hear him. Adopting the appearance and the attitude of someone inspired by the gods, he said to them that the god had come to him as usual, and had ordered him to attack the enemy; that they ought to trust the god rather than the numbers of the army, especially because in their previous exploits, they had been victorious through the god's help, not because of numbers. (102) In order that they should believe what he said, he ordered the priests to bring the victims which had been sacrificed into the assembly. While he was speaking, he sees some birds flying overhead, and, turning towards them immediately with a vigorous movement and a shout, he pointed them out, saying that the gods had sent him this sign of victory. (103) He followed their movement, looking towards them and calling out like one inspired; and the whole army, seeing him turning this way and that, turned with him, and all were fired with the notion that the victory was theirs already. (104) When he had everything as he wanted, he did not hesitate nor let the impetus dissipate, but said, as though still possessed by the god, that they must, after such signs as these, immediately go to fight. He ordered them, once they had eaten, to arm themselves, and, assigning the cavalry to Silanus and the infantry to Laelius and Marcius, he led them against the enemy, who had no expectation of their coming.

27 (105) Hasdrubal, Mago and Massinissa, as Scipio was coming on them suddenly (there were only ten *stadia* between them), armed their forces in a hurry, amidst confusion and shouting, even though the soldiers had not been fed. (106) An infantry battle and a cavalry battle took place simultaneously: the Roman cavalry were successful, using the same tactic they had employed before, pursuing without any deviating the Numidians, whose normal practice was to retreat and then attack again, and who were not able to use their javelins because of the lack of space; but the infantry were in trouble because of the number of the Libyans and had the worst of it throughout the whole day. (107) Even though Scipio went among them and cheered them on, they were unable to improve their position, until, handing his horse to a slave and seizing a shield from someone, he ran out alone just as he was into the space between the armies, shouting out, "Romans, rescue your Scipio in his danger!" (108) Then those who were near saw what danger he was in, and those who were far away heard it, and all of them, out of shame and out of fear for their general, charged against the enemy violently and with a great cry. The Libyans were unable to withstand the charge and gave way, for they were also losing strength as it was towards evening and they had had no food. Then in a short time a great slaughter of them took place. (109) Such was the outcome for Scipio of the battle of Carmona, which was in doubt for a long time. Eight hundred Romans died there, and fifteen thousand of the enemy.

28 (110) μετὰ δὲ τοῦθ᾽ οἱ μὲν Λίβυες ὑπεχώρουν ἀεὶ μετὰ σπουδῆς, ὁ δὲ Σκιπίων αὐτοῖς εἵπετο, βλάπτων τι καὶ λυπῶν, ὁσάκις καταλάβοι. (111) ὡς δ᾽ οἱ μὲν ὀχυρόν τι χωρίον προύλαβον, ἔνθα καὶ ὕδωρ ἦν ἄφθονον καὶ ἀγορὰ καὶ οὐδὲν ἄλλο ἢ πολιορκεῖν αὐτοὺς ἔδει, Σκιπίωνα δ᾽ ἤπειγον ἔτεραι χρεῖαι, Σιλανὸν μὲν ἀπέλιπε τούσδε πολιορκεῖν, αὐτὸς δ᾽ ἐπῄει τὴν ἄλλην Ἰβηρίαν καὶ ὑπήγετο. (112) Λιβύων δὲ τῶν ὑπὸ Σιλανοῦ πολιορκουμένων αὖθις ὑποχωρούντων, ἕως ἐπὶ τὸν πορθμὸν ἀφικόμενοι ἐς Γάδειρα ἐπέρασαν, ὁ Σιλανός, ὅσα δυνατὸν ἦν, βλάψας ἀνεζεύγνυεν ἐς Καρχηδόνα πρὸς Σκιπίωνα. (113) Ἀσρούβαν δὲ τὸν Ἀμίλχαρος περὶ τὸν βόρειον ὠκεανὸν στρατιὰν ἔτι συλλέγοντα ὁ ἀδελφὸς Ἀννίβας ἐκάλει κατὰ σπουδὴν ἐς τὴν Ἰταλίαν ἐσβαλεῖν. ὁ δέ, ἵνα λάθοι τὸν Σκιπίωνα, παρὰ τὸν βόρειον ὠκεανὸν τὴν Πυρήνην ἐς Γαλάτας ὑπερέβαινεν, μεθ᾽ ὧν ἐξενολογήκει Κελτιβήρων.

29 (114) καὶ ὁ μὲν Ἀσρούβας ὧδε ἐς τὴν Ἰταλίαν τῶν Ἰταλῶν ἀγνοούντων ἠπείγετο· Λεύκιος δ᾽ ἀπὸ Ῥώμης ἐπανιὼν ἔφραζε τῷ Σκιπίωνι, ὅτι αὐτὸν οἱ ἐν ἄστει Ῥωμαῖοι διανοοῦνται στρατηγὸν ἐς Λιβύην ἀποστέλλειν. (115) ὁ δὲ τοῦδε αὐτοῦ μάλιστα ἐπιθυμῶν ἐκ πολλοῦ καὶ ἐλπίζων ὧδε ἔσεσθαι Λαίλιον ἐπὶ νεῶν πέντε προύπεμπεν ἐς Λιβύην πρὸς τὸν δυνάστην Σύφακα, δωρεάς τε φέροντα καὶ τῶν Σκιπιώνων ὑπόμνησιν τῆς ἐς αὐτὸν Σύφακα φιλίας καὶ δέησιν Ῥωμαίοις, ἂν ἐπίωσι, συλλαμβάνειν. ὁ δὲ ὑπέσχετό τε ποιήσειν καὶ τὰ δῶρα ἔλαβεν καὶ ἀντέπεμψεν ἕτερα. (116) αἰσθανόμενοι δὲ τούτων οἱ Καρχηδόνιοι καὶ αὐτοὶ περὶ συμμαχίας ἐπρεσβεύοντο παρὰ τὸν Σύφακα. καὶ ὁ Σκιπίων, πυνθανόμενός τε καὶ μέγα ποιούμενος ἐπὶ Καρχηδονίοις προλαβεῖν καὶ βεβαιώσασθαι Σύφακα, ᾔει πρὸς αὐτὸν ἐπὶ νεῶν δύο σὺν τῷ Λαιλίῳ.

30 (117) καὶ αὐτῷ καταγομένῳ οἱ πρέσβεις τῶν Καρχηδονίων, ἔτι ὄντες παρὰ τῷ Σύφακι, ναυσὶν αἷς εἶχον μακραῖς ἐπανήγοντο, λαθόντες τὸν Σύφακα. (118) ἀλλ᾽ ὁ μὲν ἱστίῳ χρώμενος παρέπλευσεν αὐτοὺς ἀδεῶς καὶ κατήχθη, ὁ δὲ Σύφαξ ἐξένιζεν ἀμφοτέρους καὶ τῷ Σκιπίωνι συνθέμενος ἰδίᾳ καὶ πίστεις παρασχὼν ἀπέπεμπε καὶ τοὺς Καρχηδονίους ἐφεδρεύοντας αὖθις αὐτῷ κατεῖχεν, ἕως ἐν βεβαίῳ τῆς θαλάσσης γένοιτο ὁ Σκιπίων. (119) παρὰ μὲν δὴ τοσοῦτον ἦλθε κινδύνου Σκιπίων, καταγόμενός τε καὶ πλέων· λέγεται δ᾽ ἐν Σύφακος ἑστιώμενος συγκατακλιθῆναι τῷ Ἀσρούβᾳ καὶ αὐτὸν ὁ Ἀσρούβας περὶ πολλῶν ἐρόμενος καταπλαγῆναι τῆς σεμνότητος καὶ πρὸς τοὺς φίλους εἰπεῖν, ὅτι μὴ μόνον πολεμῶν οὗτος ὁ ἀνήρ, ἀλλὰ καὶ ἑστιώμενος φοβερὸς εἴη.

---

110 εἵπετο Steph.: ἥπετο VM   **111** Σκιπίωνα δ᾽ Steph.: Σκιπίων δ᾽ VM   **116** μέγα ποιούμενος Steph.: μεταποιούμενος VM   **119** πλέων VM Exc.: ἀναπλέων Viereck-Roos ἀποπλεων Schweig.

28 (110) After this the Libyans retreated hurriedly, and Scipio pursued them, damaging and harassing them whenever he caught up with them. (111) But when some of them captured a strong place, where there was a plentiful supply of water and provisions and there was no alternative but to lay siege to them, Scipio was called away by other important matters, and he left Silanus to undertake the siege, while he himself went into the rest of Iberia and subdued it. (112) The Libyans, whom Silanus was besieging, retreated again until they came to the straits and reached Gades. Silanus, having done them as much damage as he could, marched back to Scipio at Carthage. (113) Hasdrubal, the son of Hamilcar, who was still gathering an army near the northern ocean, was summoned by his brother Hannibal to invade Italy with all speed. In order to avoid Scipio, he moved along the northern shore and across the Pyrenees into Gaul, with the Celtiberians he had recruited.

29 (114) In this way Hasdrubal was forcing his way into Italy without the knowledge of the Italians. Lucius, however, on his return from Rome, informed Scipio that the Romans in the city were considering sending him to Libya as general. (115) This had been what Scipio was longing for for a long time and now hoped that matters would turn out as he wished. So he sent Laelius with five ships to Libya to king Syphax, taking gifts and reminding Syphax of the friendship of the Scipios towards him, and asking him from the Romans to take their side if they invaded. He promised that he would do so, and took the gifts and sent others in return. (116) When the Carthaginians discovered this, they themselves sent an embassy to Syphax about making an alliance. Scipio heard of it, and, thinking it a matter of importance to take Syphax as a partner against the Carthaginians and secure his help, went to meet him with two ships, accompanied by Laelius.

30 (117) As he approached the shore, the Carthaginian ambassadors, who were still with Syphax, came out against him with the war-ships which they had with them, without Syphax noticing what they were doing. (118) He however hoisted his sails and sailed passed them boldly and reached the shore; and Syphax treated both parties as his guests. Having agreed secretly with Scipio and given him pledges of loyalty, Syphax sent him away and kept the Carthaginians in discussion with him until Scipio was safe out at sea. (119) Such was the extent of the danger that Scipio risked, both in landing and in sailing away. It is said that Scipio, at a banquet in Syphax' residence, lay on a couch next to Hasdrubal, and that Hasdrubal, having questioned him on many topics, was impressed with his dignity of bearing and said to his friends that this was a man who was to be feared not only in battle but also at the dinner-table.

31 (120) τῷ δ' αὐτῷ χρόνῳ Μάγωνί τινες Κελτιβήρων καὶ Ἰβήρων ἔτι ἐμισθοφόρουν, ὧν αἱ πόλεις ἐς Ῥωμαίους μετετέθειντο· καὶ ὁ Μάρκιος αὐτοῖς ἐπιθέμενος χιλίους μὲν καὶ πεντακοσίους διέφθειρεν, οἱ δὲ λοιποὶ διέφυγον αὐτὸν ἐς τὰς πόλεις. (121) ἑτέρους δὲ ἑπτακοσίους ἱππέας καὶ πεζοὺς ἑξακισχιλίους, Ἄννωνος αὐτῶν ἡγουμένου, συνήλασεν ἐς λόφον, ὅθεν ἀποροῦντες ἁπάντων ἐπρεσβεύοντο πρὸς τὸν Μάρκιον περὶ σπονδῶν. (122) ὁ δ' ἐκέλευεν αὐτοὺς Ἄννωνα καὶ τοὺς αὐτομόλους ἐκδόντας αὐτῷ τότε πρεσβεύειν. οἱ μὲν δὴ καὶ τὸν Ἄννωνα στρατηγὸν ὄντα σφῶν συναρπάσαντες, ἔτι τῶν λεγομένων ἀκροώμενον, καὶ τοὺς αὐτομόλους παρέδοσαν· ὁ δὲ Μάρκιος ᾔτει καὶ τὰ αἰχμάλωτα. (123) λαβὼν δὲ καὶ ταῦτ' ἐκέλευεν αὐτοὺς τακτὸν ἀργύριον κατενεγκεῖν ἅπαντας ἔς τι τοῦ πεδίου χωρίον· οὐ γὰρ ἁρμόζειν τὰ ὑψηλότερα τοῖς παρακαλοῦσιν. καταβάντων δ' ἐς τὸ πεδίον ἔφη· (124) "ἄξια μὲν θανάτου δεδράκατε, οἳ τὰς πατρίδας ἔχοντες ὑφ' ἡμῖν εἵλεσθε μετὰ τῶν ἐχθρῶν ἐπ' αὐτὰς στρατεύειν· δίδωμι δ' ὑμῖν, τὰ ὅπλα καταθεῖσιν, ἀπαθέσιν ἀπιέναι." (125) ἀγανακτησάντων δ' εὐθὺς ὁμοῦ πάντων καὶ ἀνακραγόντων οὐκ ἀποθήσεσθαι τὰ ὅπλα μάχη γίγνεται καρτερά. καὶ τὸ μὲν ἥμισυ τῶν Κελτιβήρων πολλὰ δρασάντων κατεκόπη, τὸ δ' ἥμισυ πρὸς Μάγωνα διεσώθη. (126) ὁ δ' ἄρτι μὲν ἐς τὸ στρατόπεδον τὸ Ἄννωνος κατεπεπλεύκει ναυσὶν ἑξήκοντα μακραῖς, μαθὼν δὲ τὴν Ἄννωνος συμφορὰν ἐς Γάδειρα διέπλει καὶ λιμῷ κακοπαθῶν περιεσκόπει τὸ μέλλον.

32 (127) καὶ Μάγων μὲν ἐπὶ ἀργίας ἦν, Σιλανὸς δ' ἀπέσταλτο μὲν ὑπὸ τοῦ Σκιπίωνος Κάστακα πόλιν προσαγαγέσθαι, πολεμικῶς δ' αὐτῷ τῶν Καστακαίων ἐχόντων παρεστρατοπέδευε· καὶ τοῦτο ἐμήνυε τῷ Σκιπίωνι. (128) ὃ δὲ προπέμψας τινὰ παρασκευὴν πολιορκίας εἵπετο· καὶ παροδεύων ἐνέβαλλεν ἐς Ἰλυργίαν πόλιν, ἣ Ῥωμαίων μὲν ἦν φίλη κατὰ τὸν πρότερον Σκιπίωνα, ἀναιρεθέντος δ' ἐκείνου κρύφα μετετέθειτο καὶ στρατιὰν ὑποδεξαμένη Ῥωμαίων ὡς ἔτι φίλη Καρχηδονίοις ἐκδεδώκει. (129) ὧν χάριν ὁ Σκιπίων σὺν ὀργῇ τέσσαρσιν ὥραις ἐξεῖλεν αὐτήν, τρωθεὶς μὲν τὸν αὐχένα, τῆς δὲ μάχης οὐκ ἀνασχών, ἕως ἐκράτησεν. καὶ ἡ στρατιὰ δι' αὐτόν, οὐδενὸς ἐπικελεύσαντος, ὑπεριδοῦσα τῆς ἁρπαγῆς ἔκτεινον ὁμαλῶς καὶ παιδία καὶ γυναῖκας, μέχρι καὶ τὴν πόλιν αὐτοῖς ἐπικατέσκαψαν. (130) ἀφικόμενος δ' ἐς τὴν Κάστακα ὁ Σκιπίων τὸν μὲν στρατὸν ἐς τρία διεῖλε καὶ τὴν πόλιν ἐφρούρει, μάχης δ' οὐκ ἦρχε, διδοὺς ἔτι τοῖς Καστακαίοις μεταγνῶναι· καὶ γὰρ ἤκουεν αὐτοὺς οὕτω φρονεῖν. οἱ δὲ τοῖς φρουροῦσι σφᾶς ἐμποδὼν οὖσιν ἐπιθέμενοι καὶ κρατήσαντες ἐνεχείρισαν τὴν πόλιν τῷ Σκιπίωνι. (131) καὶ τοῖσδε μὲν φρουρὰν ὁ Σκιπίων ἐπέστησε καὶ τὴν πόλιν ἐπέτρεψεν ἑνὶ τῶν Καστακαίων ἐπὶ δόξης ὄντι ἀγαθῆς· αὐτὸς δ' ἐς

---

127 ἀργίας Steph.: ἀργείας VM

31 (120) At this time, some of the Celtiberians and Iberians, whose cities had gone over to the Romans, were still serving as mercenaries with Mago. Marcius attacked them and killed one thousand five hundred of them, and the rest fled from him to their cities. (121) Another seven hundred cavalry and six thousand infantry, under the command of Hanno, he forced together onto a hill, where, because they were running short of all provisions, they sent an embassy to Marcius to ask for a truce. (122) He told them that he would negotiate with them once they had surrendered Hanno and the deserters. They seized Hanno, even though he was their commander and was listening to the discussion, and handed over the deserters; but Marcius demanded the prisoners as well. (123) Having received these too, he ordered them all to come down to the plain, bringing a specified sum of money, because the raised ground was not an appropriate place for those who were asking for favours. (124) When they came down to the plain, he said to them, "What you have done is worthy of death, for when your countries are under our control, you have chosen to fight with the enemy against them; but if you lay down your arms, I will allow you to go away unpunished." (125) They all immediately became very angry and shouted out that they would not lay down their arms; and a fierce battle began. Half the Celtiberians were cut down, after much fighting, and the other half escaped to join Mago. (126) He had just sailed into Hanno's camp with sixty war-ships, but, learning Hanno's disaster, sailed to Gades and, though suffering from lack of supplies, watched to see what would happen next.

32 (127) While Mago was inactive, Silanus was sent by Scipio to bring over the town of Castax; but as the Castacians were showed themselves hostile, he set up camp against them, and informed Scipio he had done this. (128) Scipio sent on ahead the equipment needed for a siege, and began to follow himself. He left his route and attacked the town of Ilyrgia, which had been friendly to the Romans in the time of the elder Scipio, but, when he was killed, welcomed a Roman army, as though still friendly, but handed it over to the Carthaginians. (129) For this reason Scipio captured it in four hours in a furious attack, and, although he was wounded in the neck, would not give up the fight until he had taken it. The army, for his sake and without being ordered to do so, neglected the opportunity for plunder and slaughtered everyone, even the women and children, until they pulled down the town on top of them. (130) When he arrived at Castax, Scipio divided his army into three sections and set a watch on the town; but he did not begin the battle, giving the Castacians time to change their minds, since he had heard that they intended to do so. They set upon those who were guarding the town and were opposed to this intention and overcame them, and then handed over the town to Scipio. (131) Scipio put in a garrison over them and entrusted the town to one of the Castacians who had

Καρχηδόνα ἀνεζεύγνυε, Σιλανὸν καὶ Μάρκιον περιπέμψας ἐπὶ τὸν πορθμὸν δῃοῦν, ὅσα δύναιντο.

33 (132) Ἀσταπὰ δ᾽ ἦν πόλις Καρχηδονίοις αἰεὶ διαμείνασα ὁμαλῶς· οἱ τότε τοῦ Μαρκίου σφᾶς περικαθημένου συγγιγνώσκοντες, ὅτι Ῥωμαῖοι λαβόντες αὐτοὺς ἀνδραποδιοῦνται, τὴν περιουσίαν σφῶν ἐς τὴν ἀγορὰν συνήνεγκαν καὶ ξύλα περιθέντες αὐτῇ τὰ τέκνα καὶ τὰ γύναια ἐπέβησαν ἐπὶ τὴν ὕλην. (133) πεντήκοντα δὲ σφῶν ὥρκωσαν τοὺς ἀρίστους, ὅταν ἡ πόλις ἁλίσκηται, τὰ γύναια καὶ τοὺς παῖδας ἀνελεῖν καὶ τὸ πῦρ ἅψαι καὶ ἑαυτοὺς ἐπικατασφάξαι. (134) οἱ μὲν δὴ μάρτυρας τῶνδε ποιησάμενοι τοὺς θεοὺς ἐξέδραμον ἐπὶ τὸν Μάρκιον οὐχ ὑφορώμενον οὐδέν, ὅθεν αὐτοῦ τοὺς ψιλοὺς καὶ τοὺς ἱππέας ἐτρέψαντο. (135) ὁπλισαμένης δὲ τῆς φάλαγγος τὰ μὲν τῶν Ἀσταπαίων ἦν ἄριστα, ἐξ ἀπογνώσεως μαχομένων, Ῥωμαῖοι δ᾽ ὅμως ἐκράτουν αὐτῶν διὰ τὸ πλῆθος· οὐ γὰρ δὴ τῇ γε ἀρετῇ χείρους ἦσαν οἱ Ἀσταπαῖοι. (136) πεσόντων δ᾽ ἁπάντων οἱ πεντήκοντα τὰς γυναῖκας καὶ τὰ παιδία κατέσφαξαν καὶ τὸ πῦρ ἐγείραντες ἑαυτοὺς ἐπέρριψαν, ἀκερδῆ τοῖς πολεμίοις τὴν νίκην ἐργασάμενοι. ὁ δὲ Μάρκιος τὴν ἀρετὴν τῶν Ἀσταπαίων καταπλαγεὶς οὐκ ἐνύβρισεν ἐς τὰ οἰκόπεδα αὐτῶν.

34 (137) μετὰ δὲ τοῦθ᾽ ὁ μὲν Σκιπίων ἐς ἀρρωστίαν ἐνέπεσεν, καὶ ὁ Μάρκιος αὐτῷ διῴκει τὸ στρατόπεδον· ὅσοι δὲ τῶν στρατιωτῶν ὑπ᾽ ἀσωτίας ἀναλώκεσαν τὰ πεπορισμένα, ἡγούμενοι τῶν μὲν πόνων οὐδὲν ἄξιον εὑρῆσθαι παρὰ τὸ μηδὲν ἔχειν, σφετερίζεσθαι δ᾽ αὐτῶν τὰ ἔργα καὶ τὴν δόξαν Σκιπίωνα, ἀφίσταντο ἀπὸ τοῦ Μαρκίου καὶ ἐφ᾽ ἑαυτῶν ἐστρατοπέδευον. (138) ἔκ τε τῶν φρουρίων αὐτοῖς πολλοὶ συνέτρεχον, καὶ παρὰ Μάγωνός τινες ἀργύριον φέροντες ἔπειθον αὐτοὺς ἐς τὸν Μάγωνα μεταθέσθαι. οἱ δὲ τὸ μὲν ἀργύριον ἔλαβον, στρατηγοὺς δ᾽ ἀπὸ σφῶν ἑλόμενοι καὶ ταξιάρχους καὶ τἆλλα διακοσμηθέντες ἐφ᾽ ἑαυτῶν ἐτάσσοντο καὶ συνώμνυον ἀλλήλοις. (139) πυθόμενος δ᾽ ὁ Σκιπίων ἐπέστελλεν ἐν μέρει μὲν τοῖς ἀφεστηκόσιν, ὅτι διὰ τὴν νόσον αὐτοὺς οὐκ ἀμείψατό πω, ἐν μέρει δὲ τοῖς ἄλλοις, ἵνα μεταπείθωσιν αὐτοὺς πλανωμένους, κοινῇ δ᾽ ἅπασιν ἐπιστολὴν ἄλλην ὡς ἤδη συνηλλαγμένοις, ὅτι αὐτοὺς αὐτίκα ἀμείψεται. καὶ ἐκέλευεν εὐθὺς ἥκειν ἐπὶ σῖτον ἐς Καρχηδόνα.

35 (140) ἀναγινωσκομένων δὲ τούτων οἱ μὲν ὑπώπτευον, οἱ δὲ πιστεύειν ἠξίουν καὶ συνετίθεντο, καὶ πάντες ᾤδευον ἐς τὴν Καρχηδόνα ὁμοῦ. (141) προσιόντων δ᾽ αὐτῶν ὁ Σκιπίων προσέταξε τοῖς συνοῦσίν οἱ βουλευταῖς ἕκαστον τῶν ἐξάρχων τινὰ τῆς στάσεως προσεταιρίσασθαι προσιόντα καὶ

---

137 εὑρῆσθαι Viereck-Roos: εὑρῖσθαι VM ηὑρῆσθαιMend.   **138** συνέτρεχον Steph.: συντρεχον VM

a good reputation. He marched to Carthage, and sent Silanus and Marcius to the straits to do as much damage as they could by plundering.

33 (132) There was a town called Astapa, which had always remained completely on the side of the Carthaginians. When at this time Marcius besieged it, since they knew that when the Romans captured it, they would sell them into slavery, they brought their wealth into the market-place and, piling wood around it, they placed their children and women on the pile of wood. (133) They made fifty of their chief citizens swear that, if the city was taken, they would kill the women and children, set fire to the pyre and kill themselves on it. (134) Then, calling the gods as witnesses to these promises, they charged out against Marcius, who was not expecting anything, and so they routed his light-armed troops and cavalry. (135) Even when the Romans were equipped with their full armour, the Astapians had the best of it, for they fought out of despair; but the Romans eventually overcame them through weight of numbers, for the Astapians were not inferior to them in courage. (136) When all of them had fallen, the fifty killed the women and children, and, having set light to the fire, threw themselves onto it, ensuring that their enemies got no profit from their victory. Marcius was struck by the courage of the Astapians, and did not do any damage to their houses.

34 (137) After this Scipio fell ill and Marcius took the command of the camp in his place. Some of the soldiers had spent their money wastefully, and thinking that they had not had adequate recompense for all their labours, to the extent of having nothing at all, and that Scipio was taking to himself what they had done and the glory of it, rebelled against Marcius and set up camp by themselves. (138) Many joined them from the garrisons, and some came to them from Mago bringing money, and urged them to desert to Mago. They took the money, but chose generals and centurions from their own number and set up the rest of their organisation, and placed themselves under their own officers and swore oaths to one another. (139) When Scipio heard of this, he wrote to the rebellious soldiers that because of his illness he had not yet been able to reward them properly, and separately to the others that they should persuade those who had gone astray to change their minds; and he wrote another letter to all of them together, as though they were already conciliated, saying that he would give them their reward immediately; and he ordered them to come to Carthage to collect their provisions.

35 (140) When these letters were read, some were suspicious, but the rest thought they were to be trusted and they came to an agreement, and all together travelled immediately to Carthage. (141) While they were on their way, Scipio ordered those senators who were with him each to associate with one of the leaders of the mutiny

ὡς ἀπ' εὐνοίας διορθοῦντα ὑποδέξασθαί τε καὶ δῆσαι λαθόντα. (142) προσέταξεν δὲ καὶ τοῖς χιλιάρχοις τοὺς πιστοτάτους ἕκαστον ἀφανῶς ἅμα ἕῳ ξιφήρεις ἔχειν καὶ τὰ εὔκαιρα τῆς ἐκκλησίας ἐκ διαστημάτων καταλαβόντας, ἤν τις ἐπανιστῆται, κατακεντεῖν καὶ κατακαίνειν αὐτίκα ἄνευ παραγγέλματος. (143) αὐτὸς δ' ἄρτι φαινομένης ἡμέρας ἐπὶ τὸ βῆμα ἐκομίζετο καὶ τοὺς κήρυκας ἐς ἐκκλησίαν ἐποτρύνειν περιέπεμπεν. οἱ δέ, αἰφνιδίου μὲν αὐτοῖς τοῦ κηρύγματος γενομένου, αἰδούμενοι δ' ἔτι νοσοῦντα τὸν στρατηγὸν σφῶν παρακρατεῖν καὶ νομίζοντες ἐπὶ τὰς ἀμοιβὰς καλεῖσθαι, συνέθεον ὁμοῦ πάντοθεν, οἱ μὲν ἄζωστοι τὰ ξίφη, οἱ δὲ καὶ ἐν χιτῶσι μόνοις, οὐ φθάσαντες οὐδὲ τὴν ἐσθῆτα πᾶσαν ἐπιθέσθαι.

36 (144) Σκιπίων δέ, φρουρὰν ἔχων ἀμφ' αὑτὸν ἀφανῆ, πρῶτα μὲν αὐτοῖς ἐπεμέμφετο τῶν γεγονότων, εἶτ' ἔφη τὴν αἰτίαν ἀναθήσειν μόνοις τοῖς ἄρξασιν, "οὓς ἐγὼ κολάσω δι' ὑμῶν". καὶ λέγων ἔτι προσέταξε τοῖς ὑπηρέταις διαστῆσαι τὸ πλῆθος. (145) οἱ μὲν δὴ διίστανον, οἱ δὲ βουλευταὶ τοὺς αἰτίους παρῆγον ἐς τὸ μέσον. ἀναβοησάντων δ' αὐτῶν καὶ τοὺς συστρατιώτας βοηθῆσαι σφίσι παρακαλούντων τοὺς ἐπιφθεγγομένους εὐθὺς ἔκτεινον οἱ χιλίαρχοι. (146) καὶ τὸ μὲν πλῆθος, ἐπειδὴ τὴν ἐκκλησίαν φρουρουμένην εἶδεν, ἐφ' ἡσυχίας ἦν σκυθρωποῦ· ὁ δὲ Σκιπίων, τοὺς εἰς τὸ μέσον παραχθέντας αἰκισάμενος, καὶ μᾶλλον αὐτῶν τοὺς ἐκβοήσαντας, ἐκέλευσε τοὺς αὐχένας ἁπάντων ἐς τοὔδαφος παττάλοις προσδεθέντας ἀποτμηθῆναι καὶ τοῖς ἄλλοις ἀμνηστίαν ἐκήρυξεν διδόναι.

37 (147) ὧδε μὲν τὸ στρατόπεδον καθίστατο τῷ Σκιπίωνι· Ἰνδίβιλις δέ, τῶν συνθεμένων τις αὐτῷ δυναστῶν, στασιαζούσης ἔτι τῆς Ῥωμαϊκῆς στρατιᾶς κατέδραμέν τι τῆς ὑπὸ τῷ Σκιπίωνι γῆς. (148) καὶ αὐτῷ τοῦ Σκιπίωνος ἐπελάσαντος ὑπέστη μὲν τὸν ἀγῶνα γενναίως καὶ χιλίους καὶ διακοσίους Ῥωμαίων διέφθειρεν, ἀπολομένων δ' αὐτῷ δισμυρίων ἐδεῖτο προσπέμψας. καὶ ὁ Σκιπίων αὐτὸν χρήμασι ζημιώσας συνηλλάσσετο. (149) λαθὼν δὲ καὶ Μασανάσσης Ἀσρούβαν ἐπέρασε τὸν πορθμὸν καὶ φιλίαν τῷ Σκιπίωνι συνθέμενος ὤμοσε συμμαχήσειν, ἂν ἐς Λιβύην στρατεύῃ. ἔπραξεν δὲ τοῦτο ἀνὴρ ἐς πάντα βέβαιος διὰ τοιάνδε αἰτίαν. (150) Ἀσρούβου τοῦ τότε οἱ συνόντος στρατηγοῦ θυγάτηρ ἐς γάμον ἐγγε γύητο Μασανάσσῃ· Σύφακα δ' ἄρα τὸν δυνάστην ἔρως ἔκνιζε τῆς παιδός, καὶ οἱ Καρχηδόνιοι, μέγα ποιούμενοι Σύφακα ἐπὶ Ῥωμαίους προσλαβεῖν, ἔδωκαν αὐτῷ τὴν παῖδα, οὐδὲν τοῦ Ἀσρούβου πυθόμενοι. καὶ τῶνδε πραχθέντων ὁ μὲν Ἀσρούβας αὐτὰ ἐπέκρυπτε, τὸν Μασανάσσην αἰδούμενος, ὁ δὲ αἰσθόμενος συνέθετο τῷ Σκιπίωνι. (151) Μάγων δ' ὁ ναύαρχος, ἀπογνοὺς ἀπὸ τῶν

---

143 γενομένου Steph.: γενομέοι VM **146** διδόναι Steph.: διδομέναι VM **148** ἐπελάσαντος Steph.: ἐπελάσιτος VM (ιτος in ras. a m.2, V)

who was coming and to welcome him as though setting matters to rights in a friendly fashion, and to put them in chains before it was noticed. (142) He instructed the military tribunes that each should, without being observed, have his most reliable men equipped with swords at dawn and positioned at strategic points at intervals in the assembly, if anyone caused a disturbance, to stab him and cut him down without further order. (143) As soon as the sun arose, he himself was carried to the speaker's platform and sent the heralds to summon everyone to an assembly. Although the summons was unexpected, they were ashamed to keep their general waiting when he was still sick, and, believing that they were being called to receive their rewards, ran together from all sides, some without belting on their swords and some only wearing their tunics, not even having had time to put on all their clothing.

36 (144) Scipio, with a guard around him but out of sight, first blamed them for what had happened, and then said that he would attach blame only to the leaders, "And these I shall punish with your help." While he was still speaking, he ordered the lictors to divide the crowd into two sections. (145) While they were dividing them, the senators dragged those responsible into the space in the middle. These cried out and called upon their fellow soldiers to help them, but any who responded the tribunes immediately cut down. (146) When the crowd saw that the assembly was surrounded with armed men, they fell into a sullen silence. Scipio had those who had been dragged into the middle tortured, those who shouted out being treated worst; and he ordered the necks of all of them to be fixed to the ground with pegs and their heads cut off. To the rest he announced an amnesty.

37 (147) Thus did Scipio restore order to his army. But Indibilis, one of the kings who had joined him, invaded part of the territory under Scipio's control while the Roman army was still in a state of mutiny. (148) When Scipio marched against him, he fought bravely and killed one thousand two hundred Romans, but, having lost twenty thousand men, he sent to ask for peace. Scipio demanded money from him in recompense and came to terms with him. (149) Massinissa crossed the straits without Hasdrubal's knowledge, and having established friendship with Scipio, swore to fight in alliance with him if the war was fought in Libya. Although he was a man who remained constant under all circumstances, he acted in this way for the following reason. (150) The daughter of Hasdrubal, under whom he was now serving, had been engaged in marriage to Massinissa. However king Syphax fell in love with the girl, and the Carthaginians, thinking it important to secure Syphax' alliance against the Romans, gave him the girl without knowing what Hasdrubal had done. After this had happened, Hasdrubal kept it secret, out of regard for Massinissa; but once Massinissa found out about it, he came to an agreement with Scipio. (151) The admiral Mago, despairing of the situation in Iberia, sailed to the

παρόντων τὰ ἐν Ἰβηρίᾳ, πλεύσας ἐς Λίγυας καὶ Κελτοὺς ἐξενολόγει.

38 (152) καὶ ὃ μὲν περὶ ταῦτ' ἦν, καὶ τὰ Γάδειρα ἐκλειφθέντα ὑπὸ τοῦ Μάγωνος οἱ Ῥωμαῖοι παρέλαβον· στρατηγοὺς δὲ Ἰβηρίας ἐτησίους ἐς τὰ ἔθνη τὰ εἰλημμένα ἔπεμπον ἀπὸ τοῦδε ἀρξάμενοι, μικρὸν πρὸ τῆς τετάρτης καὶ τεσσαρακοστῆς καὶ ἑκατοστῆς ὀλυμπιάδος, ἁρμοστὰς ἢ ἐπιστάτας αὐτοῖς τῆς εἰρήνης ἐσομένους. (153) καὶ αὐτοῖς ὁ Σκιπίων ὀλίγην στρατιὰν ὡς ἐπὶ εἰρήνῃ καταλιπὼν συνῴκισε τοὺς τραυματίας ἐς πόλιν, ἣν ἀπὸ τῆς Ἰταλίας Ἰταλικὴν ἐκάλεσε· καὶ πατρίς ἐστι Τραϊανοῦ τε καὶ Ἀδριανοῦ, τῶν ὕστερον Ῥωμαίοις ἀρξάντων τὴν αὐτοκράτορα ἀρχήν. (154) αὐτὸς δ' ἐς Ῥώμην ἐπὶ στόλου πολλοῦ διέπλει, λαμπρῶς τε κεκοσμημένου καὶ καταγέμοντος αἰχμαλώτων ὁμοῦ καὶ χρημάτων καὶ ὅπλων καὶ λαφύρων ποικίλων. (155) καὶ ἡ πόλις αὐτὸν ἐπιφανῶς ἐξεδέχετο μετὰ δόξης ἀοιδίμου τε καὶ παραλόγου διά τε νεότητα καὶ ταχυεργίαν καὶ μέγεθος εὐπραξίας. οἵ τε φθονοῦντες αὐτῷ τὴν πάλαι κουφολογίαν ὡμολόγουν ἐς ἔργον ἀποβῆναι. (156) καὶ Σκιπίων μὲν θαυμαζόμενος ἐθριάμβευεν, Ἰνδίβιλις δ' οἰχομένου τοῦ Σκιπίωνος αὖθις ἀφίστατο. καὶ αὐτὸν οἱ στρατηγοὶ τῆς Ἰβηρίας τὸν στρατὸν ἀγείραντες, ὅσος αὐτοῖς ἦν περὶ τὰ φρούρια, καὶ δύναμιν ἄλλην ἀπὸ τῶν ὑπηκόων συναγαγόντες ἔκτειναν. (157) τοὺς δ' αἰτίους τῆς ἀποστάσεως ἐς κρίσιν παραγαγόντες θανάτῳ μετῆλθον καὶ τὰ ὄντα αὐτοῖς ἐδήμευσαν. τά τε ἔθνη τὰ συναράμενα αὐτῷ χρήμασιν ἐζημίωσαν καὶ τὰ ὅπλα αὐτῶν παρείλοντο καὶ ὅμηρα ᾔτησαν καὶ φρουρὰς δυνατωτέρας αὐτοῖς ἐπέστησαν.

39 (158) καὶ τάδε μὲν ἦν εὐθὺς μετὰ Σκιπίωνα, καὶ ἡ πρώτη Ῥωμαίων ἐς Ἰβηρίαν πεῖρα ἐς τοῦτο ἔληγε· χρόνῳ δ' ὕστερον, ὅτε Ῥωμαῖοι Κελτοῖς τε τοῖς περὶ Πάδον ἐπολέμουν καὶ Φιλίππῳ τῷ Μακεδόνι, ἐνεωτέρισαν αὖθις ἐς τὴν ἀσχολίαν αὐτῶν οἱ Ἴβηρες. (159) καὶ αὐτοῖς ἐπεπέμφθησαν ἐκ Ῥώμης στρατηγοὶ τοῦδε τοῦ πολέμου Σεμπρώνιός τε Τουδιτανὸς καὶ Μᾶρκος Ἕλουιος, μετὰ δ' ἐκείνους Μινούκιος. (160) καὶ ἐπὶ τούτῳ μείζονος ἔτι τῆς κινήσεως γιγνομένης μετὰ πλέονος δυνάμεως ἐπέμφθη Κάτων, νέος μὲν ὢν ἔτι πάμπαν, αὐστηρὸς δὲ καὶ φιλόπονος συνέσει τε γνώμης καὶ δεινότητι λόγων ἀριπρεπής, ὥστε αὐτὸν ἐπὶ τοῖς λόγοις ἐκάλουν οἱ Ῥωμαῖοι Δημοσθένη, πυνθανόμενοι τὸν ἄριστον ἐν τοῖς Ἕλλησι ῥήτορα γεγενῆσθαι Δημοσθένη.

40 (161) ὡς δὲ κατέπλευσε τῆς Ἰβηρίας ἐς τὸ καλούμενον Ἐμπόριον ὁ Κάτων, οἱ μὲν πολέμιοι πάντοθεν ἐπ' αὐτὸν ἐς τετρακισμυρίους ἀγηγέρατο, (162) ὁ δ' ἐπὶ μέν τι τὴν στρατιὰν ἐγύμναζεν, ὡς δ' ἔμελλε

---

159 ἐπέπμφθησαν Mend.: ἐπέμφθησαν VM   Τουδιτανὸς Schweig.: Τουδερτῖνος VM
Ἕλουιος Schweig.: Ἑλουίδιος VM

Ligurians and the Celts and recruited mercenaries.

38 (152) While Mago was occupied with this business, the Romans took Gades, which he had left. The Romans from this time, shortly before the one hundred and forty-fourth Olympiad, began to send praetors of Iberia annually to those peoples they had captured, to act as governors and to ensure the peace there. (153) Scipio left them a small army suitable for peaceful conditions, and established a town for his wounded men, which he named Italica, taking the name from Italy. This is the place of origin of Trajan and Hadrian, who later ruled the Romans as emperors. (154) He himself sailed to Rome with a large fleet, brilliantly adorned and packed with prisoners, money, arms and spoils of different kinds. (155) The city welcomed him magnificently and honoured him to a famous and unprecedented extent, both because of his youth and the speed and extent of his success. Even those who were jealous of him admitted that what had previously seemed empty boasting had in fact been achieved. (156) While Scipio celebrated a triumph amidst all this admiration, Indibilis, once Scipio had gone, again went into revolt. The praetors in Iberia gathered together the army, which had been left them for a garrison, and added to it further troops from those who were subject to them, and killed him. (157) They brought to trial those who were responsible for the uprising and punished them with death and confiscated their property. They imposed fines on those tribes which had supported him, took away their weapons, demanded hostages and installed stronger garrisons to watch them.

39 (158) These things happened immediately after Scipio left, and at this point the first enterprise of the Romans against Iberia came to an end. Afterwards, when the Romans were fighting with the Celts of the Po valley and with Philip the Macedonian, the Iberians, taking advantage of the Romans' preoccupations, rebelled again. (159) The generals sent against them from Rome for this war were Sempronius Tuditanus and Marcus Helvius, and after them Minucius. (160) As the revolt grew still greater, Cato was sent with larger forces, since, even though he was still very young, he was austere, hard-working and outstanding in the intelligence of his thought and the power of his speech, so that because of his speeches the Romans called him Demosthenes, since they knew that Demosthenes had been the greatest orator amongst the Greeks.

40 (161) When Cato sailed to Spain, arriving at the place called Emporion, the enemy gathered together against him from all parts to the number of forty thousand. (162) He trained up his army in a short time and, when he was about to engage in

συνενεχθήσεσθαι μάχῃ, τὰς ναῦς, ἃς εἶχεν, ἐς Μασσαλίαν ἀπέπεμψεν καὶ τὸν στρατὸν ἐδίδασκεν οὐ τοῦτ' εἶναι φοβερόν, ὅτι πλήθει προύχουσιν οἱ πολέμιοι (τὴν γὰρ εὐψυχίαν αἰεὶ τοῦ πλέονος ἐπικρατεῖν), ἀλλ' ὅτι νεῶν ἀποροῦμεν, ὡς οὐκ ἔχειν, εἰ μὴ κρατοῖμεν, οὐδὲ σωτηρίαν. (163) ταῦτα εἰπὼν αὐτίκα συνέβαλλεν, οὐκ ἐπελπίσας ὥσπερ ἕτεροι τὸν στρατόν, ἀλλὰ φοβήσας. γενομένης δ' ἐν χερσὶν τῆς μάχης ἐς πάντα μετεπήδα παρακαλῶν καὶ παροξύνων. (164) ἀκρίτου δ' αὐτῆς ἐς δείλην ἑσπέραν ἔτι οὔσης καὶ πολλῶν πιπτόντων ἑκατέρωθεν ἔς τινα λόφον ὑψηλὸν μετὰ τριῶν τάξεων ἐφέδρων ἀνέδραμεν, τὸ ἔργον ὁμοῦ πᾶν ἐποψόμενος. (165) ὡς δὲ εἶδε τοὺς μέσους τῶν ἰδίων μάλιστα ἐνοχλουμένους, ὥρμησεν ἐς αὐτοὺς προκινδυνεύων ἔργῳ τε καὶ βοῇ συνετάραξε τοὺς ἐχθροὺς καὶ πρῶτος κατῆρξε τῆς νίκης. (166) διώξας τε νυκτὸς ὅλης ἐκράτησεν αὐτῶν τοῦ στρατοπέδου καὶ πολλοὺς ἀπέκτεινεν. ἐπανιόντι δ' ὡς ἡγεμόνι τῆς νίκης συνήδοντο συμπλεκόμενοι. καὶ μετὰ τοῦτο ἀνέπαυε τὴν στρατιὰν καὶ τὰ λάφυρα ἐπίπρασκεν.

41 (167) πρεσβευόντων δ' ἐς αὐτὸν ἁπάντων ὅμηρά τε ᾔτησεν ἄλλα καὶ βιβλία ἐσφραγισμένα ἐς ἑκάστους περιέπεμπε καὶ τοὺς φέροντας ἐκέλευεν ἡμέρᾳ μιᾷ πάντας ἀποδοῦναι· καὶ ὥριζε τὴν ἡμέραν τεκμηράμενος, ὅτε μάλιστα ἐς τὴν πορρωτάτω πόλιν ἀφίξονται. (168) ἐκέλευεν δ' ἡ γραφὴ ταῖς ἀρχαῖς τῶν πόλεων ἁπάσαις καθαιρεῖν τὰ τείχη σφῶν αὐτῆς ἡμέρας, ᾗ τὰ γράμματα λάβοιεν· εἰ δὲ ἀνάθοιντο τὴν ἡμέραν, ἀνδραποδισμὸν ἠπείλει. (169) οἱ δ' ἄρτι μὲν ἡττημένοι μεγάλῃ μάχῃ, ὑπὸ δ' ἀγνοίας, εἴτε μόνοις, εἴθ' ἅπασι ταῦτα προσετάχθη, φοβούμενοι μόνοι μὲν ὡς εὐκαταφρόνητοι, μετὰ ⟨δὲ⟩ τῶν ἄλλων, μὴ μόνοι βραδύνωσι, καιρόν τε οὐκ ἔχοντες περιπέμψαι πρὸς ἀλλήλους καὶ τοὺς στρατιώτας τοὺς ἐληλυθότας μετὰ τῶν γραμμάτων ἐφεστῶτας σφίσιν εὐλαβούμενοι, τὸ σφέτερον ἀσφαλὲς ἕκαστοι προύργου τιθέμενοι, τὰ τείχη καθῄρουν μετὰ σπουδῆς. ἐν ᾧ γὰρ ἅπαξ ὑπακούειν ἐδόκει, καὶ τὸ ταχέως εἰργάσθαι προσλαβεῖν ἐφιλοτιμοῦντο. (170) οὕτω μὲν αἱ πόλεις αἱ περὶ Ἴβηρα ποταμὸν μιᾶς ἡμέρας ὑφ' ἑνὸς στρατηγήματος αὐταὶ τὰ τείχη τὰ ἑαυτῶν καθῄρουν καὶ Ῥωμαίοις ἐς τὸ μέλλον εὐέφοδοι γενόμεναι διέμειναν ἐς πλεῖστον ἐπὶ εἰρήνης.

42 (171) ὀλυμπιάσι δ' ὕστερον τέσσαρσιν, ἀμφὶ τὰς πεντήκοντα καὶ ἑκατόν, πολλοὶ τῶν Ἰβήρων γῆς ἀποροῦντες ἀπέστησαν ἀπὸ Ῥωμαίων, ἄλλοι τε καὶ Λούσονες, οἳ περὶ τὸν Ἴβηρα ᾤκηνται. (172) στρατεύσας οὖν ἐπ' αὐτοὺς ὕπατος Φούλβιος Φλάκκος ἐνίκα μάχῃ. καὶ πολλοὶ μὲν αὐτῶν

---

162 ἀπέπεμψεν Schweig.: π≡∈πεμψ≡ν V πέπεμψεν M   163 ταῦτα Steph.: ταῦτα δ' VM ἐπελπίσας Steph.: ἐλπίσας VM   169 ⟨δὲ⟩ add. Steph.

battle, sent the ships which he had away to Massilia and told the army 'not to be afraid that the enemy would overwhelm with their numbers (for a good courage was always stronger than superior numbers), but, because we have no ships, unless we are victorious, we have nothing, not even our safety.' (163) Having said this, he immediately began the battle, having filled his army not with hope, as other generals did, but with fear. When the fighting was hand to hand, he leapt from one place to another in all parts of the conflict, encouraging and urging on his men. (164) When the issue still remained in doubt into the late afternoon, and many had fallen on both sides, he climbed a high hill with three cohorts of the reserves, in order to see the whole battle at once. (165) When he saw that the centre of his own forces was struggling the most, he rushed in amongst them, exposing himself to danger, and by his actions and by his loud shouting he threw the enemy into confusion and was the first to begin the victory. (166) He pursued them through the whole night and captured their camp and killed many. On his return, the soldiers rejoiced with him as the leader of the victory and embraced him. After this, he rested the army and sold the booty.

41 (167) They all came as ambassadors to him, and he demanded further hostages, and sent sealed letters to each and ordered all those who were carrying them to hand them over on one day. He fixed the day by calculating when they would reach the farthest town. (168) The text of the letters ordered the authorities in all the towns to take down their wall on the very day that they received the letters; and if they put off the day, he threatened them with enslavement. (169) As they had recently been defeated in a great battle and were in ignorance whether they alone or whether all the towns had been given these orders, they were afraid that, if they were alone, they would count for nothing, and, if they were with others, that they alone would be delaying. As they had no time to send messages to one another and were anxious about the soldiers who had come with the letters and were standing in front of them, they each reckoned their own safety to be of the greatest importance and took down their walls with haste. Once they had decided to obey the order, they competed with one another to carry it into effect rapidly. (170) In this way the towns along the river Ebro themselves destroyed their walls on one day as a result of one single stratagem, and, because for the future they were open of access to the Romans, they remained at peace for the most part.

42 (171) Four Olympiads later, about the 150th, many of the Iberians who had too little land, and in particular the Lusones, who lived beside the Ebro, revolted against the Romans. (172) The consul, Fulvius Flaccus, was put in command against them and defeated them in battle. Many of them dispersed to their towns, but those who

κατὰ πόλεις διελύθησαν· ὅσοι δὲ μάλιστα γῆς ἠπόρουν καὶ ἐξ ἄλης ἐβιότευον, ἐς Κομπλέγαν πόλιν συνέφυγον, ἣ νεόκτιστός τε ἦν καὶ ὀχυρὰ καὶ ηὔξετο ταχέως. (173) ὅθεν ὁρμώμενοι τὸν Φλάκκον ἐκέλευον, καταθέντα σφίσιν ὑπὲρ τῶν ἀνῃρημένων ἑκάστου σάγον τε καὶ ἵππον καὶ ξίφος, ἀποτρέχειν ἐξ Ἰβηρίας, πρίν τι κακὸν παθεῖν. ὁ δὲ πολλοὺς αὐτοῖς ἔφη σάγους οἴσειν καὶ τοῖς πρέσβεσιν αὐτῶν ἑπόμενος τῇ πόλει παρεστρατοπέδευσεν. (174) οἱ δὲ ἀνομοίως ταῖς ἀπειλαῖς σφῶν αὐτίκα ἀπεδίδρασκον καὶ τὰ τῶν ἐγγὺς βαρβάρων ἐλήζοντο. χρῶνται δὲ διπλοῖς ἱματίοις παχέσιν, ἀντὶ χλαμύδων αὐτὰ περιπορπώμενοι, καὶ τοῦτο σάγον ἡγοῦνται.

43 (175) Φλάκκῳ μὲν οὖν διάδοχος ἦλθεν ἐπὶ τὴν στρατηγίαν Τιβέριος Σεμπρώνιος Γράκχος. Κάραυιν δὲ πόλιν, ἣ Ῥωμαίων ἦν φίλη, δισμύριοι Κελτιβήρων ἐπολιόρκουν· καὶ ἐπίδοξος ἦν ἁλώσεσθαι, Γράκχου σφόδρα μὲν ἐπειγομένου βοηθῆσαι τῇ πόλει, περιόντος δ᾽ ἐν κύκλῳ τοὺς πολεμίους καὶ οὐκ ἔχοντος οὐδὲ μηνῦσαι τῇ πόλει περὶ ἑαυτοῦ. (176) τῶν οὖν τις ἰλάρχων, Κομίνιος, ἐνθυμηθεὶς πρὸς ἑαυτὸν καὶ Γράκχῳ τὸ τόλμημα ἀνενεγκών, ἐνεπορπήσατο σάγον Ἰβηρικῶς καὶ λαθὼν ἀνεμίχθη τοῖς χορτολογοῦσιν τῶν πολεμίων συνεισῆλθέ τε αὐτοῖς ὡς Ἴβηρ ἐς τὸ στρατόπεδον καὶ εἰς τὴν Κάραουιν διαδραμὼν ἐμήνυσεν, ὅτι Γράκχος ἐπίοι. (177) οἱ μὲν δὴ διεσώθησαν, ἐγκαρτερήσαντες τῇ πολιορκίᾳ, μέχρι Γράκχος αὐτοῖς ἐπῆλθε μετὰ τρίτην ἡμέραν καὶ οἱ πολιορκοῦντες ἀπανέστησαν· (178) δισμύριοι δ᾽ ἐκ τῆς Κομπλέγας διέτρεχον ἐς τὸ Γράκχου στρατόπεδον σὺν ἱκετηρίαις καὶ πλησιάσαντες ἀδοκήτως ἐπέθεντο αὐτῷ καὶ συνετάραξαν. ὁ δ᾽ εὐμηχάνως ἐξέλιπεν αὐτοῖς τὸ στρατόπεδον καὶ ὑπεκρίνατο φεύγειν· εἶτα διαρπάζουσιν ἐπιστραφεὶς ἐπέπεσέν τε καὶ πλείστους ἔκτεινεν καὶ τῆς Κομπλέγας κατέσχε καὶ τῶν περιοίκων. (179) τοὺς δὲ ἀπόρους συνῴκιζε καὶ γῆν αὐτοῖς διεμέτρει καὶ πᾶσιν ἔθετο τοῖς τῇδε συνθήκας ἀκριβεῖς, καθ᾽ ἃς Ῥωμαίων ἔσονται φίλοι· ὅρκους τε ὤμοσεν αὐτοῖς καὶ ἔλαβεν, ἐπιποθήτους ἐν τοῖς ὕστερον πολέμοις πολλάκις γενομένους. δι᾽ ἃ καὶ ἐν Ἰβηρίᾳ καὶ ἐν Ῥώμῃ διώνυμος ἐγένετο ὁ Γράκχος καὶ ἐθριάμβευσε λαμπρῶς.

44 (180) ἔτεσιν δὲ οὐ πολλοῖς ὕστερον πόλεμος ἄλλος ἠγέρθη περὶ Ἰβηρίαν χαλεπὸς ἐκ τοιᾶσδε προφάσεως. Σεγήδη πόλις ἐστὶ Κελτιβήρων τῶν Βελλῶν λεγομένων μεγάλη τε καὶ δυνατὴ καὶ ἐς τὰς Σεμπρωνίου Γράκχου συνθήκας ἐνεγέγραπτο. (181) αὕτη τὰς βραχυτέρας πόλεις ἀνῴκιζεν ἐς αὑτὴν καὶ τεῖχος ἐς τεσσαράκοντα σταδίους κύκλῳ περιεβάλετο Τίτθους τε ὅμορον γένος ἄλλο συνηνάγκαζεν ἐς ταῦτα. (182)

---

172 Κομπλέγαν Steph.: Κομπλεγὸν VM   **178** Κομπλέγας Steph.: Κονπλέγας VM   **179** καθ" ἃς Steph.: καθα VM καθ᾽ ἃ Bekker

were particularly lacking in land and lived a nomadic existence fled together to the town of Complega, which had recently been founded and made secure, and which grew rapidly. (173) Basing themselves there, they demanded that Flaccus give them a plaid, a horse and a sword in recompense for each of those that had been killed, and that he should leave Iberia before something bad happened to him. He said that he would bring them many plaids, and, following their ambassadors, encamped in front of the town. (174) Despite their threats, they immediately ran away, plundering the property of the barbarians who lived near. They wear a heavy outer garment of double thickness, fastening them round themselves in place of a military cloak, and this they call a *sagos* (plaid).

43 (175) The man who came to succeed Flaccus in the command was Tiberius Sempronius Gracchus. Twenty thousand Celtiberians were laying siege to Caravis, a town which was friendly to the Romans. It was likely that the town would be captured and Gracchus pressed on to bring it help, but, though he marched right round the enemy, he could not even let the city know that he was there. (176) Then Cominius, a commander of a cavalry squadron, having thought the matter through himself and taken his daring plan to Gracchus, wrapped himself round with a plaid in the Iberian fashion and secretly mixed with those of the enemy who were gathering fodder and went with them into their camp as though he were an Iberian, and, passing through into Caravis, told them that Gracchus was coming. (177) They were saved in this way, resisting the siege until Gracchus reached them on the third day and the besiegers withdrew. (178) But twenty thousand others came to Gracchus' camp from Complega with olive branches in their hands, and, when they came near, attacked him unexpectedly and caused much confusion. He however cleverly left the camp to them and pretended to fly. Then he turned and fell on them while they were engaged in plundering, killed most of them and seized Complega and the people round about it. (179) Those who were poor he settled and distributed land to them, and imposed precise treaties on all, according to which they were to be the friends of the Romans. He swore oaths to them and received oaths in return, which were often longed for in the wars which followed. As a result Gracchus became renowned both in Iberia and in Rome and celebrated a magnificent triumph.

44 (180) Not many years after, another problematic war broke out in Iberia, and this was the explanation of it. Segeda is a large and powerful city, belonging to those Celtiberians called the Belli, and it was included in Sempronius Gracchus' treaties. (181) This city caused smaller towns to move to its site, and built a wall of some forty *stadia* in circumference around itself, and forced the Titthi, another neighbouring tribe, to join with it. (182) The senate learned of this and forbade them

ἡ δὲ σύγκλητος πυθομένη τό τε τεῖχος ἀπηγόρευε τειχίζειν καὶ φόρους ἤτει τοὺς ὁρισθέντας ἐπὶ Γράκχου στρατεύεσθαί τε Ῥωμαίοις προσέτασσε· καὶ γὰρ τοῦθ' αἱ Γράκχου συνθῆκαι ἐκέλευον. (183) οἱ δὲ περὶ μὲν τοῦ τείχους ἔλεγον ἀπηγορεῦσθαι Κελτίβηρσιν ὑπὸ Γράκχου μὴ κτίζειν πόλεις, οὐ τειχίζειν τὰς ὑπαρχούσας· τῶν δὲ φόρων καὶ τῆς ξεναγίας ὑπ' αὐτῶν ἔφασαν Ῥωμαίων ἀφεῖσθαι μετὰ Γράκχον. καὶ τῷ ὄντι ἦσαν ἀφειμένοι, δίδωσι δ' ἡ βουλὴ τὰς τοιάσδε δωρεὰς ἀεὶ προστιθεῖσα κυρίας ἔσεσθαι, μέχρι ἂν αὐτῇ καὶ τῷ δήμῳ δοκῇ.

45 (184) στρατηγὸς οὖν ἐπ' αὐτοὺς Νωβελίων ἐπέμπετο μετὰ στρατιᾶς οὐ πολὺ τρισμυρίων ἀνδρῶν ἀποδεούσης· ὃν ἐπειδὴ σφίσιν οἱ Σεγηδαῖοι προσιόντα ἔγνωσαν, οὔπω τὸ τεῖχος ἐκτελέσαντες ἔφευγον ἐς Ἀρουακοὺς μετὰ παίδων καὶ γυναικῶν καὶ σφᾶς ὑποδέχεσθαι τοὺς Ἀρουακοὺς παρεκάλουν. (185) οἱ δ' ὑποδέχονταί τε καὶ Κάρον αὐτῶν Σεγηδαίων, πολεμικὸν εἶναι νομιζόμενον, αἱροῦνται στρατηγόν. ὁ δὲ τρίτῃ μετὰ τὴν χειροτονίαν ἡμέρᾳ δισμυρίους πεζοὺς καὶ ἱππέας πεντακισχιλίους ἔς τινα λόχμην ἐνεδρεύσας παροδεύουσι τοῖς Ῥωμαίοις ἐπέθετο καὶ τῆς μάχης ἐπὶ πολὺ ἀγχωμάλου γενομένης ἐκράτει τε λαμπρῶς καὶ Ῥωμαίων τῶν ἐξ ἄστεως ἔκτεινεν ἐς ἑξακισχιλίους, ὡς μέγα τῇ πόλει γενέσθαι τὸ ἀτύχημα. (186) ἀτάκτου δ' αὐτῷ τῆς διώξεως ἐπὶ τῇ νίκῃ γενομένης οἱ τὰ σκευοφόρα Ῥωμαίων φυλάσσοντες ἱππῆς ἐπέδραμον καὶ Κάρον τε αὐτὸν ἀριστεύοντα ἔκτειναν καὶ ἑτέρους ἀμφ' αὐτόν, οὐκ ἐλάσσους καὶ οἵδε τῶν ἑξακισχιλίων, μέχρι νὺξ ἐπελθοῦσα διέλυσεν. (187) ἐγίγνετο δὲ ταῦθ', ὅτε Ῥωμαῖοι τῷ Ἡφαίστῳ τὴν ἑορτὴν ἄγουσιν· ὅθεν οὐδεὶς ἂν ἑκὼν ἄρξειεν ἐξ ἐκείνου μάχης παρὰ τήνδε τὴν ἡμέραν.

46 (188) Ἀρουακοὶ μὲν οὖν εὐθὺς αὐτῆς νυκτὸς ἐς Νομαντίαν, ἣ δυνατωτάτη πόλις ἦν, συνελέγοντο καὶ στρατηγοὺς Ἄμβωνα καὶ Λεύκωνα ᾑροῦντο· Νωβελίων δ' αὐτοῖς τρισὶν ἡμέραις ὕστερον ἐπελθὼν παρεστρατοπέδευσεν ἀπὸ σταδίων τεσσάρων καὶ εἴκοσιν. (189) παραγενομένων δέ οἱ Νομάδων ἱππέων τριακοσίων, οὓς Μασανάσσης ἐπεπόμφει, καὶ ἐλεφάντων δέκα τὴν στρατιὰν ἐπῆγε τοῖς πολεμίοις, ἄγων ὀπίσω τὰ θηρία λανθάνοντα. (190) καὶ γενομένης ἐν χερσὶ τῆς μάχης οἱ μὲν ἄνδρες διέστησαν, τὰ δὲ θηρία ἐξεφαίνετο· καὶ οἱ Κελτίβηρες αὐτοί τε καὶ οἱ ἵπποι σφῶν, οὐ πρὶν ἑωρακότες ἐλέφαντας ἐν πολέμοις, ἐθορυβοῦντο καὶ κατέφευγον ἐς τὴν πόλιν. (191) ὁ δὲ καὶ τοῖς τείχεσιν αὐτοὺς ἐπῆγε καὶ ἐμάχετο γενναίως, μέχρι τῶν ἐλεφάντων τις ἐς τὴν κεφαλὴν λίθῳ μεγάλῳ καταπίπτοντι πληγεὶς ἠγριώθη τε καὶ ἐκβοήσας

---

183 προστιθεῖσα Steph.: προτιθεῖσα VM   **184** Ἀρουακοὺς Schweig.: Ἀρουασκοὺς VM
188 δυνατωτάτη Steph.: δυνωτωτάτη VM   **190** ἐξεφαίνετο Steph.: ἐξαιφαίνετο

to build the wall and demanded from them the taxes laid down by Gracchus and ordered them to provide troops to fight with the Romans, since this was required by Gracchus' treaties. (183) They replied that, so far as the wall was concerned, the Celtiberians were forbidden by Gracchus to found cities, not to wall existing ones; and as to the taxes and the recruitment, they said that they had been released from these by the Romans themselves after the time of Gracchus. And in fact they had been released from these obligations, but the senate, in giving such concessions, always adds that they shall be in force for so long as seems good to the senate and the people.

45 (184) Therefore Nobilior was sent as general against them with an army of not far short of thirty thousand men. When the Segedans heard that he was coming, since they had not yet completed the wall, they fled to the Arevaci with their women and children and begged the Arevaci to take them in. (185) They did take them in and chose Carus, one of these very Segedans and a man renowned for his skill at warfare, as their general. On the third day after his election, he set twenty thousand foot and five thousand horse in ambush in a wood and attacked the Romans, who were in column of march. Though the battle was for a long time evenly balanced, he won decisively and killed six thousand Roman citizens, so that on that day the city of Rome was afflicted with a great disaster. (186) But his pursuit after the battle was disorderly and the Roman cavalry that was guarding the baggage counterattacked, and they killed Carus, who defended himself bravely, and those with him, no less than six thousand also, until the onset of night put an end to the battle. (187) These things happened on the day on which the Romans keep the feast of Vulcan, and as a result no one since that time willingly starts a battle on that day.

46 (188) The Arevaci immediately, on that very night, gathered at Numantia, which was a very strong city, and chose Ambo and Leuco as their generals. Nobilior moved against them three days later and encamped twenty four *stadia* away. (189) Having with him three hundred Numidian cavalry, which Massinissa had sent, and three elephants, he led his army against the enemy, keeping the animals out of sight at the rear. (190) When the battle was engaged, the men stood aside and revealed the animals. The Celtiberians and their horses, never before having seen elephants on the field of battle, were thrown into confusion and fled for the city. (191) Nobilior led them up to the walls and fought bravely, until one of the elephants, struck on the head by a falling stone, became enraged and, letting out a huge bellow, turned on its

μέγιστον ἐς τοὺς φίλους ἐπεστρέφετο καὶ ἀνῄρει τὸν ἐν ποσίν, οὐ διακρίνων ἔτι φίλιον ἢ πολέμιον. (192) οἵ τε ἄλλοι ἐλέφαντες πρὸς τὴν ἐκείνου βοὴν διαταραχθέντες ὅμοια πάντες ἔδρων καὶ τοὺς Ῥωμαίους συνεπάτουν τε καὶ ἀνέτεμνον καὶ ἀνερρίπτουν· ὅπερ ἀεὶ θορυβηθέντες οἱ ἐλέφαντες εἰώθασι πάσχειν καὶ πάντας ἡγεῖσθαι πολεμίους· καί τινες διὰ τήνδε τὴν ἀπιστίαν αὐτοὺς καλοῦσι κοινοὺς πολεμίους. (193) φυγὴ οὖν τῶν Ῥωμαίων ἐγίγνετο ἄτακτος· ἣν οἱ Νομαντῖνοι κατιδόντες ἀπὸ τῶν τειχῶν ἐξέθορον καὶ διώκοντες ἔκτειναν ἄνδρας μὲν ἐς τετρακισχιλίους, ἐλέφαντας δὲ τρεῖς ὅπλα τε πολλὰ καὶ σημεῖα ἔλαβον. Κελτιβήρων δ' ἀπέθανον ἐς δισχιλίους.

47 (194) καὶ ὁ Νωβελίων μικρὸν ἐκ τοῦ πταίσματος ἀναλαβὼν ἀγορᾷ μέν τινι τῶν πολεμίων ἐπεχείρει περὶ Ἀξείνιον πόλιν σεσωρευμένῃ, οὐδὲν δὲ ἀνύσας, ἀλλὰ κἀνταῦθα πολλοὺς ἀποβαλὼν ἐπανῆλθε νυκτὸς ἐς τὸ στρατόπεδον. (195) ὅθεν Βιήσιον ἵππαρχον ἐπὶ συμμαχίαν ἔς τι γειτονεῦον ἔθνος ἔπεμπεν, ἱππέων δεόμενος. οἳ δὲ συνέπεμψαν αὐτῷ τινας ἱππέας, οὓς ἐρχομένους ἐλόχων οἱ Κελτίβηρες· καὶ τῆς ἐνέδρας ἐκφανείσης οἱ μὲν σύμμαχοι διεδίδρασκον, ὁ δὲ Βιήσιος μαχόμενος αὐτός τε καὶ σὺν αὐτῷ πολλοὶ Ῥωμαίων ἀπέθανον. (196) συνεχῶν δὲ τοιῶνδε πταισμάτων αὐτοῖς ἐπιγιγνομένων πόλις Ὄκιλις, ἔνθα ἡ ἀγορὰ καὶ τὰ χρήματα ἦν τὰ Ῥωμαίων, μετέθετο ἐς τοὺς Κελτίβηρας. (197) καὶ ὁ Νωβελίων ἀπιστῶν ἅπασιν ἐν τῷ στρατοπέδῳ διεχείμαζε, στεγάσας, ὡς ἐδύνατο, καὶ τὴν ἀγορὰν ἔχων ἔνδον καὶ κακοπαθῶν αὐτῆς τε τῆς ἀγορᾶς τῇ ὀλιγότητι καὶ νιφετοῦ πυκνότητι καὶ κρύους χαλεπότητι, ὥστε πολλοὶ τῶν στρατιωτῶν οἱ μὲν ἐν τοῖς φρυγανισμοῖς, οἱ δὲ καὶ ἔνδον ὑπὸ στενοχωρίας καὶ κρύους ἀπώλλυντο.

48 (198) τοῦ δ' ἐπιόντος ἔτους Νωβελίωνι μὲν ἐπὶ τὴν στρατηγίαν ἀφικνεῖται διάδοχος Κλαύδιος Μάρκελλος, ἄγων πεζοὺς ὀκτακισχιλίους καὶ ἱππέας πεντακοσίους· λοχώντων δὲ καὶ τόνδε τῶν πολεμίων διῆλθε πεφυλαγμένως καὶ σύμπαντι τῷ στρατῷ παρὰ τὴν Ὄκιλιν ἐστρατοπέδευσεν. (199) ἐπιτυχὴς δὲ τὰ πολέμια ὢν τὴν πόλιν αὐτίκα παρεστήσατο καὶ συγγνώμην ἔδωκεν, ὅμηρά τινα καὶ ἀργυρίου τάλαντα τριάκοντα λαβών. (200) Νεργόβριγες δ', αὐτοῦ περὶ τῆσδε τῆς μετριοπαθείας πυθόμενοι, πέμψαντες ἠρώτων, τί ἂν πράξαντες εἰρήνης ἐπιτύχοιεν. (201) ὡς δὲ αὐτοὺς ἐκέλευεν ἑκατὸν ἱππέας δοῦναι συστρατεύσοντας, οἱ μὲν ὑπισχνοῦντο δώσειν, κατὰ δ' ἄλλο μέρος τοῖς οὐραγοῦσιν ἐπετίθεντο καὶ τῶν σκευοφόρων τι περιέσπων. (202) εἶτ' ἀφίκοντο τοὺς ἑκατὸν ἱππέας ἄγοντες ὡς δὴ κατὰ τὸ συγκείμενον περί τε τῶν ἐπὶ τῆς οὐραγίας γενομένων ἔλεγόν τινας ἀγνοοῦντας τὰ

---

192 ἀνερρίπτουν Stph.: ἀνερίπτουν VM 197 ἀπώλλυντο Steph.: ἀπώλυντο VM

own troops and destroyed whoever was at its feet, making no distinction between friend and foe. (192) The other elephants, disturbed by the cry of the first, all began to behave in the same way, and trampled the Romans, wounding them and tossing them about. Elephants are always likely to act like this when they are aroused and to regard everyone as an enemy, and some, because of their untrustworthy nature, call them the common enemy of all. (193) The Romans broke into disorderly fight, and, when the Numantines saw it, they sallied out from their walls and pursued them, killing about four thousand men and three elephants and seizing many weapons and military standards. Of the Celtiberians about two thousand were killed.

47 (194) Nobilior, recovering a little from this misfortune, attacked a supply-base collected together by the enemy at the town of Axeinion, but having achieved nothing but rather having lost many men there, he returned to his encampment by night. (195) From there he sent Biesius, a cavalry commander, to a neighbouring tribe to arrange an alliance, asking for cavalry. They sent some cavalrymen back with him, whom the Celtiberians ambushed as they travelled; and when it became clear that it was an ambush, the allies ran away, but Biesius fought on and he and many Romans who were with him were killed. (196) While these misfortunes afflicted them one after another, the town of Ocilis, where the supply-base and money of the Romans were, went over to the Celtiberians. (197) Nobilior, having lost all confidence, took up winter quarters in his encampment, roofing it over so far as he could, and kept his provisions inside. He suffered much from the scarcity of these supplies and the heavy falls of snow and the harshness of the frost, with the result that many of the soldiers died, some while gathering firewood and others inside the camp from the shortage of space and from the cold.

48 (198) The following year Claudius Marcellus arrived as successor to Nobilior in the command, bringing eight thousand infantry and five hundred cavalry. The enemy set an ambush for him too, but he made his way through them circumspectly and camped outside Ocilis with all his army. (199) As he was successful in military matters, he brought the town over to his side immediately, taking some hostages and thirty talents of silver. (200) The Nergobriges, hearing about his moderation, sent to ask what they would have to do to obtain peace. (201) When he instructed them to provide one hundred cavalrymen to fight along with him, they promised they would do so, but in another part they attacked the rear-guard and carried off some of the baggage train. (202) They then arrived with the one hundred cavalrymen according to the terms laid down, and said, with regard to what had happened to the rear-guard that some of them had made a mistake, because they did not know about the

ὡμολογημένα ἁμαρτεῖν. (203) ὁ δὲ τοὺς μὲν ἑκατὸν ἱππέας ἔδησε, τοὺς δ' ἵππους αὐτῶν ἀποδόμενος καὶ τὸ πεδίον καταδραμὼν τὴν λείαν διεῖλεν τῷ στρατῷ καὶ τῇ πόλει παρεστρατοπέδευσε. (204) Νεργόβριγες δέ, προσαγομένων αὐτοῖς μηχανημάτων ἅμα καὶ χωμάτων, κήρυκα πέμψαντες λυκῆν ἀντὶ κηρυκείου περικείμενον ᾔτουν συγγνώμην. ὁ δὲ οὐκ ἔφη δώσειν, εἰ μὴ πάντες Ἀρουακοὶ καὶ Βελλοὶ καὶ Τίτθοι δεηθεῖεν ὁμοῦ. (205) ὧν τὰ μὲν ἔθνη πυθόμενα προθύμως ἐπρεσβεύετο καὶ τὸν Μάρκελλον ἠξίουν, ποινὴν αὐτοῖς ἐπιθέντα μετρίαν, ἐς τὰς Γράκχου συνθήκας ἀναγαγεῖν· ἀντέλεγον δ' αὐτοῖς ἐπιχώριοί τινες ὑπ' ἐκείνων πεπολεμημένοι.

49 (206) καὶ ὁ Μάρκελλος ἐξ ἑκατέρων πρέσβεις ἐς Ῥώμην ἔπεμπεν ἀντιλέξοντας ἀλλήλοις, ἰδίᾳ δ' ἐπέστελλε τῇ βουλῇ προτρέπων ἐς τὰς διαλύσεις· ἐβούλετο γὰρ ἐφ' ἑαυτοῦ τὸν πόλεμον ἐκλυθῆναι, δόξαν οἱ χρηστὴν καὶ ἀπὸ τοῦδε νομίζων ἔσεσθαι. (207) τῶν δὲ πρέσβεων οἱ μὲν ἐκ τῆς φιλίας ἐς τὴν πόλιν ἐσελθόντες ἐξενίζοντο, οἱ δὲ ἐκ τῶν πολεμίων, ὡς ἔθος ἐστίν, ἔξω τειχῶν ἐστάθμευον. (208) ἀποδοκιμάζουσα δ' ἡ βουλὴ τὴν εἰρήνην καὶ χαλεπῶς φέρουσα, ὅτι μή, καθάπερ αὐτοὺς ἠξίου Νωβελίων, ὁ πρὸ Μαρκέλλου, Ῥωμαίοις αὐτοὺς ἐπετετρόφεσαν, Μάρκελλον αὐτοῖς ἐξοίσειν ἔφη τὰ δόξαντα. (209) καὶ στρατιὰν εὐθὺς ἐκλήρουν ἐς Ἰβηρίαν τότε πρῶτον ἀντὶ καταλέξεως· πολλῶν γὰρ αἰτιωμένων τοὺς ὑπάτους ἀδίκως ποιεῖσθαι τὰς καταγραφὰς καί τινας ἐς τὰς κουφοτέρας στρατείας καταλέγειν ἔδοξεν ἀπὸ κλήρου τότε συναγαγεῖν. (210) ὧν ἐστρατήγει Λικίνιος Λούκουλλος ὕπατος, πρεσβευτῇ χρώμενος Κορνηλίῳ Σκιπίωνι, τῷ Καρχηδόνα μετ' οὐ πολὺ ἑλόντι καὶ Νομαντίαν ὕστερον.

50 (211) ὁ μὲν δὴ Λούκουλλος ὥδευεν, ὁ δὲ Μάρκελλος τόν τε πόλεμον προεῖπε τοῖς Κελτίβηρσι καὶ τὰ ὅμηρα αἰτοῦσιν ἀπέδωκε. τὸν δ' ἐν Ῥώμῃ τοὺς λόγους διαθέμενον ὑπὲρ τῶν Κελτιβήρων ἰδίᾳ πρὸς αὐτὸν ἀνακαλέσας ἐπὶ πολὺ διέτριβεν· (212) ὑπὲρ ὅτου δὴ καὶ ὑπωπτεύετο μὲν καὶ τότε, μᾶλλον δ' ἐπιστώθη τοῖς ὕστερον γενομένοις, ὅτι αὐτοὺς ἀνέπειθεν ἑαυτῷ τὰ κατὰ σφᾶς ἐπιτρέψαι, ἐπειγόμενος ἄρα πρὸ τοῦ Λουκούλλου τὸν πόλεμον καταλυθῆναι. (213) μετὰ γὰρ τὴν συνουσίαν Νεργόβριγα μὲν Ἀρουακῶν πεντακισχίλιοι κατέλαβον, Μάρκελλος δ' ἐπὶ Νομαντίαν ἐχώρει καὶ πέντε σταδίους ἀποσχὼν παρεστρατοπέδευεν αὐτοῖς καὶ συνεδίωκεν ἐς τὴν πόλιν, (214) ἕως ὁ τῶν Νομαντίνων στρατηγὸς Λιτέννων ὑποστὰς ἐβόα βούλεσθαι Μαρκέλλῳ συνελθεῖν ἐς λόγους καὶ

203-4 παρεστρατοπέδευσεν. Ἐργόβριγες VM, corr. Steph.   κηρυκείου Steph.: κηρυκίου VM Exc.   **205** Μάρκελλον VM: Κλαύδιον Μάρκελλον Exc. Κλαύδιον Gouk.   **206** ἐπέστελλε Exc.: ἐπέστελλον VM   **208** Νωβελίων, ὁ πρὸ add.V (m.1) in marg.   καὶ ante Μάρκελλον add. V   **209** ἀδίκως Mend.: ἀδίκους VM Exc.   **211** διέτριβεν Exc.: διέτριβον V (sed o eras.) M

agreement. (203) He imprisoned the hundred cavalrymen, and, having sold their horses and ravaged the fields, distributed the booty to the army and besieged their town. (204) The Nergobriges, once the engines and siege-mounds were brought up against them, sent a herald, wearing a wolf-skin instead of carrying a herald's staff, and asked for pardon. Marcellus said that he would not grant this, unless all the Arevaci, Belli and Titthi asked for it at the same time. (205) When these tribes heard of this, they sent urgent embassies and asked Marcellus to give them a light penalty and to go back to the treaties of Gracchus; but some of the peoples living there, against whom they had made war, spoke against them.

49 (206) Marcellus sent the ambassadors from both sides to Rome to speak against one another, but privately he sent messages to the senate, urging a cessation of hostilities. He wanted the war to be concluded by himself, thinking that he would gain a valuable reputation from this also. (207) Those of the ambassadors who were friends of the Romans entered the city and were treated as guests, but those from the enemy side took up lodgings, as usual, outside the walls. (208) The senate rejected the peace and was offended that they had not surrendered themselves to the Romans, as Nobilior, Marcellus' predecessor, had demanded of them; and said that Marcellus would declare its decree to them. (209) For the first time they chose an army by lot to serve in Spain, instead of by conscription. Because many people were complaining that the consuls were conducting the levy unfairly and that some were being enrolled for easier campaigns, they decided on this occasion to recruit by use of the lot. (210) Licinius Lucullus, the consul, was appointed general, with Cornelius Scipio, who soon after captured Carthage and later Numantia, as his legate.

50 (211) While Lucullus was on the way, Marcellus told the Celtiberians of the war, and returned their hostages to them at their request. He summoned privately the man who had presented the argument on behalf of the Celtiberians in Rome and spent a long time with him. (212) Because of this it was suspected at the time, and confirmed still more by what followed, that he had persuaded them to entrust their affairs to him, being anxious to end the war before Lucullus arrived. (213) For after the meeting, five thousand of the Arevaci captured Nergobriga, and Marcellus moved against Numantia and encamped five *stadia* from them and pursued them into the city. (214) Then the general of the Numantines, Litenno, stopped and called out that he wanted to meet Marcellus to talk. When they met, he said that the Belli,

συνελθὼν ἔφη Βελλοὺς καὶ Τίτθους καὶ Ἀρουακοὺς ἑαυτοὺς ἐπιτρέπειν Μαρκέλλῳ. ὁ δ' ἄσμενος ἀκούσας ὅμηρά τε καὶ χρήματα πάντας ᾔτησε καὶ λαβὼν ἀφῆκεν ἐλευθέρους.

51 (215) ὁ μὲν δὴ πόλεμος ὁ Βελλῶν τε καὶ Τίτθων καὶ Ἀρουακῶν ἔληγεν οὕτω πρὸ Λουκούλλου· ὁ δὲ Λούκουλλος, δόξης τε ἐπιθυμῶν καὶ ἐκ πενίας χρῄζων χρηματισμοῦ, ἐς Οὐακκαίους, ἕτερον γένος Κελτιβήρων, ἐνέβαλεν, οἳ γείτονες τῶν Ἀρουακῶν εἰσιν, οὔτε τινὸς αὐτῷ ψηφίσματος γεγονότος οὔτε Οὐακκαίων Ῥωμαίοις πεπολεμηκότων οὐδ' ἐς αὐτόν τι Λούκουλλον ἁμαρτόντων. (216) περάσας δὲ τὸν ποταμὸν τὸν καλούμενον Τάγον ἀφίκετο πρὸς Καύκαν πόλιν καὶ παρεστρατοπέδευσεν. οἱ δ' ἐπύθοντο μὲν αὐτοῦ, τίνος ἥκοι δεόμενος ἢ τί πολέμου χρῄζων, φήσαντος δέ, ὅτι Καρπητανοῖς ὑπὸ Οὐακκαίων ἀδικουμένοις βοηθοίη, τότε μὲν ἀνεχώρουν ἐς τὴν πόλιν, ξυλευομένῳ δ' αὐτῷ καὶ· χορτολογοῦντι ἐπέκειντο καὶ κτείνουσι πολλοὺς καὶ τοὺς λοιποὺς διώκουσιν ἐς τὸ στρατόπεδον. (217) γενομένης δὲ καὶ παρατάξεως οἱ Καυκαῖοι ψιλοῖς ἐοικότες ἐκράτουν ἐπὶ πολὺ τοῦ Λουκούλλου, μέχρι σφῶν τὰ ἀκόντια πάντα ἐξαναλώθη· καὶ τότε ἔφευγον, οὐκ ὄντες μενέμαχοι, περί τε τὰς πύλας αὐτῶν ὠθουμένων ἀνῃρέθησαν ἀμφὶ τοὺς τρισχιλίους.

52 (218) τῆς δ' ἐπιούσης οἱ πρεσβύτατοι στεφανωσάμενοί τε καὶ φέροντες ἱκετηρίας τὸν Λούκουλλον αὖθις ἠρώτων, τί ποιοῦντες ἂν εἶεν φίλοι. ὁ δὲ αὐτοὺς ὅμηρά τε ᾔτει καὶ ἀργυρίου τάλαντα ἑκατὸν καὶ τοὺς ἱππέας αὐτῶν ἐκέλευέν οἱ συστρατεύειν. (219) ὡς δὲ πάντα ἔλαβεν, ἠξίου φρουρὰν ἐς τὴν πόλιν ἐσαγαγεῖν. δεξαμένων δὲ καὶ τοῦτο τῶν Καυκαίων ἐσήγαγε δισχιλίους ἀριστίνδην ἐξειλεγμένους, οἷς ἐσελθοῦσιν εἴρητο γίγνεσθαι περὶ τὰ τείχη. καταλαβόντων δ' αὐτὰ τῶν δισχιλίων ἐσήγαγε τὴν ἄλλην στρατιὰν ὁ Λούκουλλος καὶ τῇ σάλπιγγι ὑπεσήμαινε κτείνειν Καυκαίους ἅπαντας ἡβηδόν. (220) οἱ μὲν δὴ πίστεις τε καὶ θεοὺς ὁρκίους ἐπικαλούμενοι καὶ Ῥωμαίους ἐς ἀπιστίαν λοιδοροῦντες διεφθείροντο ὠμῶς, ἐκ δισμυρίων ἀνδρῶν κατὰ πύλας ἀποκρήμνους διαφυγόντων ὀλίγων· ὁ δὲ Λούκουλλος τὴν πόλιν διήρπαζε καὶ δόξης Ῥωμαίους ἐνεπίμπλη κακῆς. (221) οἱ δ' ἄλλοι βάρβαροι συνέθεον ἐκ τῶν πεδίων, οἱ μὲν ἐς τὰ ἀπόκρημνα, οἱ δὲ ἐς τὰς ὀχυρωτέρας πόλεις, συμφέροντες ἃ δύναιντο, καὶ ἐμπιμπράντες ὅσα λείποιεν, τοῦ μηδὲν ἔτι Λούκουλλον εὑρεῖν.

53 (222) ὁ δὲ πολλὴν γῆν ἔρημον ὁδεύσας ἔς τινα πόλιν Ἰντερκατίαν ἀφίκετο, ἔνθα πεζοὶ μὲν ὑπὲρ δισμυρίους συνεπεφεύγεσαν, ἱππεῖς δὲ

---

215 Οὐακκαίων V (οὐ suprasr.m.2): ἀκκαίων M τούτων Exc. 216 ὑπὸ Οὐακκαίων Schweig.: ὑποκαίων V (sed in marg. γρ. καυκαίων ἢ οὐακκαίων) M ὑπο Καυκαίων Gouk. 222 Ἰντερκατίαν Steph.: Ἐντερκατίαν VM ἱππεῖς Steph.: ἱππῆς VM

the Titthi and the Arevaci surrendered themselves to Marcellus. He was delighted to hear this, and demanded hostages and money from all of them and then let them go free.

51 (215) In this way the war with the Belli, the Titthi and the Arevaci came to an end before Lucullus arrived. Lucullus, however, who was keen for glory and needed money because of his lack of it, attacked the Vaccaei, another Celtiberian tribe who were neighbours of the Arevaci, even though there had been no vote to support him in this and the Vaccaei had not fought against the Romans nor done Lucullus himself any wrong. (216) Crossing the river called the Tagus, he arrived at the town of Cauca, and encamped against it. They sent to ask him what he wanted in coming to them or why he was seeking to fight them. He answered that he was coming to the assistance of the Carpetani who had been wronged by the Vaccaei. They then retreated into their town, but attacked him as he was gathering wood and fodder and killed many men and chased the rest to their camp. (217) There was then a pitched battle and the Caucaei, whose armour was like that of light-armed troops, were for the most part successful against Lucullus, until they had used up all their javelins. Then they fled, since they were not able to hold a position in battle, and, as they pushed against one another at the gates, about three thousand of them were destroyed.

52 (218) On the following day the elders, wearing crowns and carrying olive branches, asked Lucullus again what they should do to be friends. He demanded from them hostages and one hundred talents of silver and ordered that their cavalry should fight on his side. (219) When he had taken all this, he required that a garrison be installed in the town. The Caucaei accepted this also, and he led in two thousand men, chosen for their bravery, whom he told to take positions on the walls after they had entered. When the two thousand had seized the walls, Lucullus led in the rest of the army, and signalled with a trumpet blast to kill the Caucaei who were of age. (220) The Caucaei, calling to witness the gods in whose name good faith was promised and oaths were sworn and reviling the Romans for their lack of faith, were destroyed cruelly, with only a few of the twenty thousand men escaping through precipitous passages. Lucullus sacked the town and brought infamy upon the Romans. (221) The other barbarians together escaped from the plains, some into inaccessible rocky places, and others into more defensible towns, carrying with them what they could, and burning whatever they left, so that Lucullus should find nothing.

53 (222) He travelled through a great tract of desert land and arrived at a town called Intercatia, to which about twenty thousand foot soldiers had fled and two thousand

δισχίλιοι. καὶ αὐτοὺς ὁ Λούκουλλος ἐς συνθήκας ὑπὸ ἀνοίας προυκαλεῖτο· οἱ δ' ἐπ' ὀνείδει τὰ Καυκαίων αὐτῷ προύφερον καὶ ἐπυνθάνοντο, εἰ ἐπὶ τὰς ἐκείνων πίστεις αὐτοὺς καλοίη. (223) ὁ δ', οἷον ἅπαντες οἱ ἁμαρτόντες, ἀνθ' ἑαυτοῦ τοῖς ὀνειδίζουσιν χαλεπαίνων ἔκειρεν αὐτῶν τὰ πεδία καὶ περικαθίσας κύκλῳ τὴν πόλιν χώματα ἤγειρε πολλὰ καὶ συνεχῶς ἐξέτασσε προκαλούμενος ἐς μάχην. (224) οἱ δ' οὔπω μὲν ἀντεξέτασσον, ἀλλ' ἦσαν ἀκροβολισμοὶ μόνοι· θαμινὰ δέ τις τῶν βαρβάρων ἐξίππευεν ἐς τὸ μεταίχμιον, κεκοσμημένος ὅπλοις περιφανῶς, καὶ προυκαλεῖτο Ῥωμαίων ἐς μονομαχίαν τὸν ἐθέλοντα, οὐδενὸς δ' ὑπακούοντος ἐπιτωθάσας καὶ τῷ σχήματι κατορχησάμενος ἀπεχώρει. (225) γιγνομένου δὲ τούτου πολλάκις ὁ Σκιπίων, ἔτι νέος ὤν, ὑπερήγησέν τε καὶ προπηδήσας ὑπέστη τὸ μονομάχιον, εὐτυχῶς δ' ἐκράτησεν ἀνδρὸς μεγάλου σμικρὸς ὤν.

54 (226) καὶ τόδε μὲν ἐπῆρε Ῥωμαίους, νυκτὸς δὲ φόβοι πολλοὶ κατεῖχον· οἱ γὰρ ἱππῆς, ὅσοι τῶν βαρβάρων, πρὶν ἀφικέσθαι Λούκουλλον, ἐπὶ χορτολογίαν προεληλύθεσαν, οὐκ ἔχοντες ἐσελθεῖν ἐς τὴν πόλιν Λουκούλλου περικαθημένου, περιθέοντες ἐβόων καὶ συνετάρασσον· καὶ συνεπήχουν οἱ ἔνδον αὐτοῖς. (227) ὅθεν ὁ φόβος ἦν τοῖς Ῥωμαίοις ποικίλος. ἔκαμνον δὲ καὶ τῇ φυλακῇ δι' ἀγρυπνίαν καὶ ἀήθειαν τροφῶν ἐπιχωρίων· οἴνου γὰρ οὐκ ὄντος οὐδ' ἁλῶν οὐδ' ὄξους οὐδ' ἐλαίου πυροὺς καὶ κριθὰς καὶ ἐλάφων κρέα πολλὰ καὶ λαγωῶν χωρὶς ἁλῶν ἑψόμενα σιτούμενοι κατερρήγνυντο τὰς γαστέρας, καὶ πολλοὶ καὶ ἀπώλλυντο, μέχρι ποτὲ τὸ χῶμα ἠγέρθη καὶ τὰ τείχη τῶν πολεμίων τύπτοντες μηχαναῖς μέρος μέν τι κατέβαλον καὶ ἐσέδραμον ἐς τὴν πόλιν· (228) μετὰ δ' οὐ πολὺ βιασθέντες τε καὶ ἀναχωροῦντες ἐσπίπτουσιν ἔς τινα δεξαμενὴν ὕδατος ὑπὸ ἀγνωσίας, ἔνθα οἱ πλείους ἀπώλοντο. καὶ νυκτὸς οἱ βάρβαροι τὰ πεσόντα ἀνῳκοδόμουν. (229) πάνυ δ' ἑκατέρων κακοπαθούντων (ὁ γὰρ λιμὸς ἀμφοῖν ἥπτετο) Σκιπίων ἀνεδέχετο τοῖς βαρβάροις οὐδὲν ἔσεσθαι παράσπονδον καὶ πιστευθεὶς κατὰ κλέος ἀρετῆς διέλυσε τὸν πόλεμον ἐπὶ τοῖσδε, Λουκούλλῳ δοθῆναι παρὰ τῶν Ἰντερκατίων σάγους μυρίους καὶ θρεμμάτων τι πλῆθος ὡρισμένον καὶ πεντήκοντα ἄνδρας ἐς ὅμηρα. (230) χρυσὸν δὲ καὶ ἄργυρον Λούκουλλος αἰτῶν, οὗ δὴ χάριν ἡγούμενος ὅλην Ἰβηρίαν πολύχρυσον εἶναι καὶ πολυάργυρον ἐπολέμει, οὐκ ἔλαβεν· οὐ γὰρ εἶχον, οὐδ' ἐν δόξῃ ταῦτ' ἐκεῖνοι Κελτιβήρων τίθενται.

55 (231) ἐπὶ δὲ Παλλαντίαν ᾔει πόλιν, ἣ δόξαν τε ἀρετῆς εἶχε μείζω καὶ πολλοὶ συνεπεφεύγεσαν ἐς αὐτήν· ὅθεν αὐτῷ συνεβούλευόν τινες ἀποχωρεῖν πρὸ πείρας. ὁ δὲ πολυχρήματον εἶναι πυνθανόμενος οὐκ ἀνεχώρει, μέχρι σιτολογοῦντα αὐτὸν οἱ Παλλάντιοι συνεχῶς ἱππεῦσιν

---

231 Παλλαντίαν Steph.: Παλαντίαν VM ᾔει Steph.: ἤιει V (sed ι eras.) ᾔει M

horsemen. Lucullus stupidly proposed that they enter an alliance. They upbraided him with the case of the Caucaei, and asked if he were offering them the same good faith that he had to them. (223) He, as happens with all who commit evil, was angry with those who upbraided him rather than with himself, ravaged their fields, and having encircled the city, set many siege mounds against it, and continually drew up his troops in line of battle to challenge them to fight. (224) They did not draw up their line in response, but used projectiles only. Often one of the barbarians rode out into the space between the lines, splendidly arrayed in armour, and challenged any of the Romans who wished to single combat; and when none answered him, he jeered at them, performed a dance and went back to his lines. (225) When this had happened many times, Scipio, still a young man, was aggrieved beyond bearing and, jumping up, accepted the challenge, and was fortunate to kill him, though he was small and his opponent large.

54 (226) This lifted the Romans' spirits, but at nightfall many fears gripped them. For some horsemen from among the barbarians, who had gone out foraging before Lucullus arrived, not being able to enter the city because Lucullus was surrounding it, ran round it shouting out and causing confusion, and those inside echoed their shouts. (227) As a result, the Romans suffered various terrors. They were weary of the watching through lack of sleep and the strangeness of the local food. As there was no wine, no salt, no vinegar and no oil, they lived on wheat and barley and large quantities of the flesh of deer and hares, boiled without salt and suffered from diarrhoea, and many of them died. Eventually the mound was set up, and by striking against the walls of the enemy with their siege engines, they threw down a part of it and ran into the town. (228) After a little they were overcome and in retreat, because they did not know the place, they fell into a water cistern, where most of them died. In the night, the barbarians built up again the walls that had fallen down. (229) When both sides were suffering badly (for famine was affecting both) Scipio undertook to the barbarians that nothing would be done to break a treaty and, since he was believed because of his high reputation for virtue, he brought the war to an end on the following terms: Lucullus was to be given by the Intercatians ten thousand plaids, a fixed number of animals and fifty men as hostages. (230) Lucullus asked for gold and silver, for the sake of which he undertook the war, believing that the whole of Iberia was full of gold and silver, but he got none, since they did not have any, and these Celtiberians do not hold it to be of value.

55 (231) He then went to Pallantia, a city which was still more renowned for its bravery and to which many had fled for refuge. For this reason some advised him to go away without attempting it. But he, learning that it was very rich, did not retreat from it, until the Pallantians continually harassed him with their cavalry while

ἠνώχλουν τε καὶ σιτολογεῖν ἐκώλυον. (232) ἀπορῶν δὲ τροφῶν ὁ Λούκουλλος ἀνεζεύγνυ, τετράγωνον ἐν πλινθίῳ τὸν στρατὸν ἄγων, ἑπομένων αὐτῷ καὶ τότε τῶν Παλλαντίων μέχρι Δορίου ποταμοῦ, ὅθεν οἱ μὲν Παλλάντιοι νυκτὸς ἀνεχώρουν, ὁ δ' ἐς τὴν Τυρδιτανῶν χώραν διελθὼν ἐχείμαζε. (233) καὶ τοῦτο τέλος ἦν τοῦ Οὐακκαίων πολέμου, παρὰ ψήφισμα Ῥωμαίων ὑπὸ Λουκούλλου γενομένου. καὶ ὁ Λούκουλλος ἐπὶ τῷδε οὐδὲ ἐκρίθη.

56 (234) τοῦ δ' αὐτοῦ χρόνου μέρος ἄλλο Ἰβήρων αὐτονόμων, οἳ Λυσιτανοὶ καλοῦνται, Πουνίκου σφῶν ἡγουμένου, τὰ Ῥωμαίων ὑπήκοα ἐλήζοντο καὶ τοὺς στρατηγοῦντας αὐτῶν, Μανίλιόν τε καὶ Καλπούρνιον Πείσωνα, τρεψάμενοι κτείνουσιν ἑξακισχιλίους καὶ ἐπ' αὐτοῖς Τερέντιον Οὐάρρωνα ταμίαν. (235) οἷς ἐπαρθεὶς ὁ Πούνικος τὰ μέχρι ὠκεανοῦ κατέδραμεν καὶ Οὐέττωνας ἐς τὴν στρατείαν προσλαβὼν ἐπολιόρκει Ῥωμαίων ὑπηκόους τοὺς λεγομένους Βλαστοφοίνικας, οἷς φασιν Ἀννίβαν τὸν Καρχηδόνιον ἐποικίσαι τινὰς ἐκ Λιβύης καὶ παρὰ τοῦτο κληθῆναι Βλαστοφοίνικας. (236) Πούνικος μὲν οὖν λίθῳ πληγεὶς ἐς τὴν κεφαλὴν ἀπέθανεν, διαδέχεται δ' αὐτὸν ἀνήρ, ᾧ ὄνομα ἦν Καίσαρος. οὗτος ὁ Καίσαρος Μουμμίῳ, μετὰ στρατιᾶς ἄλλης ἐπελθόντι ἀπὸ Ῥώμης, ἐς μάχην συνηνέχθη καὶ ἡττώμενος ἔφυγε. (237) Μουμμίου δ' αὐτὸν ἀτάκτως διώκοντος ἐπιστραφεὶς ἔκτεινεν ἐς ἐνακισχιλίους καὶ τήν τε λείαν τὴν ἡρπασμένην καὶ τὸ οἰκεῖον στρατόπεδον ἀνεσώσατο καὶ τὸ Ῥωμαίων προσέλαβέ τε καὶ διήρπασεν ὅπλα καὶ σημεῖα πολλά, ἅπερ οἱ βάρβαροι κατὰ τὴν Κελτιβηρίαν ὅλην περιφέροντες ἐπετώθαζον.

57 (238) Μούμμιος δ' ὑπολοίπους ἔχων πεντακισχιλίους ἐγύμναζεν ἔνδον ἐν τῷ στρατοπέδῳ, δεδιὼς ἄρα προελθεῖν ἐς τὸ πεδίον, πρὶν τοὺς ἄνδρας ἀναθαρρῆσαι. φυλάξας δέ, εἴ τι μέρος οἱ βάρβαροι τῆς ἀφηρημένης λείας παρέφερον, ἀδοκήτως αὐτοῖς ἐπέθετο καὶ πολλοὺς διαφθείρας ἔλαβε τὴν λείαν καὶ τὰ σημεῖα. (239) Λυσιτανῶν δ' οἱ ἐπὶ θάτερα τοῦ Τάγου ποταμοῦ, κἀκεῖνοι Ῥωμαίοις πεπολεμωμένοι, Καυκαίνου σφῶν ἡγουμένου, Κουνέους ἐπόρθουν, οἳ Ῥωμαίοις ἦσαν ὑπήκοοι, καὶ πόλιν αὐτῶν μεγάλην εἷλον Κονίστοργιν. (240) παρά τε τὰς στήλας τὰς Ἡρακλείους τὸν ὠκεανὸν ἐπέρων, καὶ οἱ μὲν τὴν ἄλλην Λιβύην κατέτρεχον, οἱ δ' Ὀκίλην πόλιν ἐπολιόρκουν. (241) Μούμμιος δ', ἑπόμενος ἐνακισχιλίοις πεζοῖς καὶ ἱππεῦσι πεντακοσίοις, ἔκτεινε τῶν μὲν δῃούντων ἐς μυρίους καὶ πεντακισχιλίους, τῶν δ' ἑτέρων τινάς, καὶ τὴν πολιορκίαν διέλυσε τὴν

---

232 ἐν πλινθίῳ Steph.: ἐμπλινθίῳ VM   Τυρδιτανῶν Steph.: Τυριδιτανῶν VM   **234** Οὐάρρωνα Steph.: οὐ ἄρωνα VM   **235** στρατείαν Schweig.: στρατιὰν VM   Βλαστοφοίνικας VM: Βαστουλοφοίνικας Schweig.   **241** ἱππεῦσι Steph.; ἱππεας V (sed α eras.) ἱππευς M

foraging and prevented him collecting forage. (232) As he was running short of food, Lucullus withdrew, leading his army in a square formation, with the Pallantians still following him as far as the river Durius, where the Pallantians withdrew by night, and he went away into the country of the Turdetani to winter. (233) And this was the end of the war against the Vaccaei, undertaken by Lucullus without the authority of any vote from the Romans; and Lucullus was not even put on trial because of it.

56 (234) At the same time another group of independent Iberians, called the Lusitanians, under the leadership of Punicus, were plundering the possessions of those subject to the Romans and, routing their commanders, Manilius and Calpurnius Piso, killed six thousand men, including the quaestor, Terentius Varro. (235) Excited by this, Punicus overran the territory as far as the Ocean and, after adding the Vettones to his army, besieged some subjects of the Romans called the Blastophoenicians. Hannibal the Carthaginian is said to have settled some people from Libya among them, and consequently they are called Blastophoenicians. (236) Punicus was struck on the head by a stone and died, and a man named Caesaros was chosen in his place. This Caesaros joined battle with Mummius, who came from Rome with another army, and was defeated and fled. (237) When Mummius pursued him in a disorderly fashion, he turned and killed about six thousand, recaptured the booty that had been taken and his own camp, and took the Roman camp and seized many weapons and standards, which the barbarians carried throughout Celtiberia in mockery of the Romans.

57 (238) Mummius took his remaining five thousand troops and trained them within his camp, being afraid to go out into the plain before his men had recovered their courage. He kept watch to see if the barbarians might come carrying any part of the booty they had captured, and attacked them unawares, killed many of them and took the booty and the standards. (239) Those Lusitanians who lived on the other side of the Tagus, who were themselves at war with the Romans, under the leadership of Caucaenus, besieged the Cunei, who were subjects of the Romans, and took Conistorgis, a large city of theirs. (240) They crossed the Ocean near the Pillars of Herakles, and some of them ravaged the rest of Libya while some laid siege to the city of Ocile. (241) Mummius however pursued them with nine thousand infantry and five hundred cavalry and killed about fifteen thousand of the plunderers and

Όκίλης. (242) ἐντυχὼν δὲ καὶ τοῖς φέρουσιν, ἃ σεσυλήκεσαν, ἔκτεινε καὶ τούσδε πάντας, ὡς μηδ' ἄγγελον ἀπὸ τοῦ κακοῦ διαφυγεῖν. τὴν δὲ λείαν διαδοὺς τῷ στρατῷ τὴν δυνατὴν φέρεσθαι τὰ λοιπὰ τοῖς θεοῖς τοῖς ἐνυαλίοις ἔκαυσε.

58 (243) καὶ Μούμμιος μὲν τάδε πράξας ἐπανῆλθεν ἐς Ῥώμην καὶ ἐθριάμβευσεν, ἐνδέχεται δ' αὐτὸν Μᾶρκος Ἀτίλιος, ὃς Λυσιτανῶν μὲν ἐς ἑπτακοσίους ἐπιδραμὼν ἀπέκτεινε καὶ τὴν μεγίστην πόλιν ἐξεῖλεν, ἧ ὄνομα Ὀξθράκαι, τὰ δ' ἐγγὺς καταπληξάμενος ἅπαντα ἐπὶ συνθήκαις παρέλαβε. καὶ τούτων ἦν ἔνια τοῦ Οὐεττώνων ἔθνους, ὁμόρου τοῖς Λυσιτανοῖς. (244) ὡς δ' ἀνεζεύγνυε χειμάσων ὁ Ἀτίλιος, αὐτίκα πάντες μετετίθεντο καί τινας Ῥωμαίοις ὑπηκόους ἐπολιόρκουν· οὓς ἐπειγόμενος ἐξελεῖν τῆς πολιορκίας Σέρουιος Γάλβας, ὁ Ἀτιλίου διάδοχος, ἡμέρᾳ μιᾷ καὶ νυκτὶ πεντακοσίους σταδίους διελθὼν ἐπιφαίνεται τοῖς Λυσιτανοῖς καὶ εὐθὺς ἐς μάχην ἐξέτασσε, κατάκοπον τὸν στρατὸν ἔχων. (245) τρεψάμενος δ' εὐτυχῶς τοὺς πολεμίους ἐπέκειτο φεύγουσιν ἀπειροπολέμως. ὅθεν ἀσθενοῦς αὐτῷ καὶ ἀσυντάκτου τῆς διώξεως οὔσης διὰ κόπον οἱ βάρβαροι κατιδόντες αὐτοὺς διεσπασμένους τε καὶ ἀναπαυομένους κατὰ μέρη συνελθόντες ἐπέθεντο καὶ κτείνουσιν ἐς ἑπτακισχιλίους. (246) ὁ δὲ Γάλβας μετὰ τῶν ἀμφ' αὐτὸν ἱππέων κατέφυγεν ἐς Καρμώνην πόλιν, ἔνθα τοὺς διαφυγόντας ἀνελάμβανε, καὶ συμμάχους ἀθροίσας ἐς δισμυρίους διῆλθεν ἐς Κουνέους καὶ παρεχείμαζεν ἐν Κονιστόργει.

59 (247) Λούκουλλος δέ, ὁ τοῖς Οὐακκαίοις ἄνευ ψηφίσματος πολεμήσας, ἐν Τυρδιτανίᾳ τότε χειμάζων ᾔσθετο Λυσιτανῶν ἐς τὰ πλησίον ἐμβαλόντων καὶ περιπέμψας τοὺς ἀρίστους τῶν ἡγεμόνων ἔκτεινε τῶν Λυσιτανῶν ἐς τετρακισχιλίους. (248) περί τε Γάδειρα τὸν πορθμὸν ἑτέρων περώντων ἔκτεινεν ἐς χιλίους καὶ πεντακοσίους καὶ τοὺς λοιποὺς συμφυγόντας εἴς τινα λόφον ἀπετάφρευσε πλῆθός τε ἔλαβεν ἀνδρῶν ἄπειρον. καὶ τὴν Λυσιτανίαν ἐπιὼν κατὰ μέρος ἐπόρθει. (249) ἐπόρθει δὲ καὶ Γάλβας ἐπὶ θάτερα. καί τινων πρεσβευομένων ἐς αὐτὸν καὶ θελόντων βεβαιοῦν καὶ ὅσα Ἀτιλίῳ τῷ πρὸ αὐτοῦ στρατηγῷ συνθέμενοι παρεβεβήκεσαν, ἐδέχετο καὶ ἐσπένδετο καὶ ὑπεκρίνετο αὐτοῖς καὶ συνάχθεσθαι ὡς δι' ἀπορίαν λῃστεύουσί τε καὶ πολεμοῦσι καὶ παρεσπονδηκόσιν. (250) "τὸ γὰρ λυπρόγεων," ἔφη, "καὶ πενιχρὸν ὑμᾶς ἐς ταῦτα ἀναγκάζει· δώσω δ' ἐγὼ πενομένοις φίλοις γῆν ἀγαθὴν καὶ ἐν ἀφθόνοις συνοικιῶ, διελὼν ἐς τρία."

242 ἃ σεσυλήκεσαν Schweig.: ἃς ἐσυλήκεσαν VM   243 Οὐεττώνων Steph.: Οὐεττόνων VM   244 Ῥωμαίοις Steph.: Ῥωμαίους VM   Σέρουιος Schweig.: Σερουίλιος VM   246 Καρμώνην Schweig.: Καρμένην VM   Κουνέους Steph.: Κονέους VM   249 παρεσπονδηκόσιν Steph.: παρεσπονδηκασι VM

some of the others, and raised the siege of Ocile. (242) Coming across some carrying away their booty, he killed all of them too, so that none was left to escape with news of the disaster. He distributed to the army as much of the loot as they could carry and burnt the remainder in honour of the gods of war.

58 (243) Mummius, having done these things, returned to Rome and celebrated a triumph. Marcus Atilius succeeded him. He invaded the Lusitanians and killed some seven hundred, and captured their largest town, which was called Oxthracae, and having terrified all those in the vicinity, he made a truce with them. Some of these were of the tribe of the Vettones, who were neighbours of the Lusitanians. (244) When Atilius went away into winter quarters, they changed their minds and laid siege to some of the subjects of the Romans. Servius Galba, who was Atilius' successor, hastened to lift the siege, and, having covered five hundred *stadia* in a day and a night, appeared among the Lusitanians and immediately drew up his forces for battle, though his army was exhausted. (245) He was fortunate in routing the enemy, but pursued them as they fled in a way which revealed his lack of experience in warfare. As the pursuit was weak and disorderly as a result of tiredness, the barbarians, seeing that they were scattered and pausing in groups for a rest, regrouped and attacked, killing some seven thousand. (246) Galba, with the cavalry which accompanied him, fled to the town of Carmona and there gathered together those that had fled. He assembled about twenty thousand allied troops and advanced into the territory of the Cunei and wintered at Conistorgis.

59 (247) Lucullus, who had waged war against the Vaccaei without a vote having been taken, was then wintering in Turdetania. He learned that the Lusitanians were invading the territory close to him and, sending the best of his commanders against them, he killed about four thousand of the Lusitanians. (248) He killed another one thousand five hundred of them as they were crossing the strait at Gades. The rest of them fled onto a hill, which he surrounded with a trench, and captured an immense number of men. He invaded Lusitania and ravaged it area by area. (249) Galba ravaged it also from the other side. When some envoys came to him, requesting that they re-establish the agreement that they had made with Atilius, his predecessor as general, and then broken, he received them and made a truce and pretended to sympathise with them, on the grounds that it was because of their poverty that they indulged in banditry, went to war and broke agreements. (250) "For it is the poor quality of the soil," he said, "and your lack of resources that compels you to do these things. I will give my poor friends good land and settle them in rich country, dividing them into three sections."

60 (251) οἱ μὲν δὴ τάδε προσδοκῶντες ἀπὸ τῶν ἰδίων ἀνίσταντο καὶ συνῆεσαν, οἷ προσέτασσεν ὁ Γάλβας· ὁ δὲ αὐτοὺς ἐς τρία διῄρει καὶ πεδίον ἑκάστοις τι ὑποδείξας ἐκέλευεν ἐν τῷ πεδίῳ περιμένειν, μέχρι πολίσειεν αὐτοὺς ἐπελθών. (252) ὡς δ᾽ ἧκεν ἐπὶ τοὺς πρώτους, ἐκέλευεν ὡς φίλους θέσθαι τὰ ὅπλα, θεμένους δ᾽ ἀπετάφρευέν τε καὶ μετὰ ξιφῶν τινας ἐσπέμψας ἀνεῖλεν ἅπαντας, ὀδυρομένους τε καὶ θεῶν ὀνόματα καὶ πίστεις ἀνακαλοῦντας. (253) τῷ δ᾽ αὐτῷ τρόπῳ καὶ τοὺς δευτέρους καὶ τρίτους ἐπειχθεὶς ἀνεῖλεν, ἀγνοοῦντας ἔτι τὰ πάθη τὰ τῶν προτέρων, ἀπιστίᾳ μὲν ἄρα ἀπιστίαν μετιών, οὐκ ἀξίως δὲ Ῥωμαίων μιμούμενος βαρβάρους. (254) ὀλίγοι δ᾽ αὐτῶν διέφυγον, ὧν ἦν Οὐρίατθος, ὃς μετ᾽ οὐ πολὺ ἡγήσατο Λυσιτανῶν καὶ ἔκτεινε πολλοὺς Ῥωμαίων καὶ ἔργα μέγιστα ἐπεδείξατο. ἀλλὰ τάδε μὲν ὕστερον γενόμενα ὕστερον λέξω· (255) τότε δ᾽ ὁ Γάλβας, Λουκούλλου φιλοχρηματώτερος ὤν, ὀλίγα μέν τινα τῆς λείας τῇ στρατιᾷ διεδίδου καὶ ὀλίγα τοῖς φίλοις, τὰ λοιπὰ δ᾽ ἐσφετερίζετο, καίτοι πλουσιώτατος ὢν ὁμοῦ τι Ῥωμαίων· ἀλλ᾽ οὐδὲ ἐν τῇ εἰρήνῃ φασὶν αὐτὸν διαλιπεῖν ψευδόμενόν τε καὶ ἐπιορκοῦντα διὰ κέρδη. μισούμενος δὲ καὶ κατηγορούμενος διέφευγε διὰ τὸν πλοῦτον.

61 (256) οὐ πολὺ δὲ ὕστερον, ὅσοι διέφευγον ἐκ τῆς Λουκούλλου καὶ Γάλβα παρανομήσεως, ἁλισθέντες ἐς μυρίους τὴν Τυρδιτανίαν κατέτρεχον. (257) καὶ αὐτοῖς ἀπὸ Ῥώμης ἐπελθὼν Γάϊος Οὐετίλιος, ἄγων τέ τινα στρατὸν ἄλλον καὶ τοὺς ἐν Ἰβηρίᾳ προσλαβών, ἅπαντας ἔχων ἐς μυρίους, ἐπέπεσε προνομεύουσι καὶ πολλοὺς ἀνελὼν συνέωσε τοὺς λοιποὺς ἔς τι χωρίον, οἷ κινδυνεύειν τε μένοντας ἐχρῆν ὑπὸ λιμοῦ καὶ ἀπιόντας ὑπὸ Ῥωμαίων· ὧδε γὰρ εἶχε δυσχωρίας. (258) καὶ διὰ τοῦτο πρέσβεις ἐς τὸν Οὐετίλιον ἔπεμπον σὺν ἱκετηρίαις, γῆν ἐς συνοικισμὸν αἰτοῦντες ὡς ἀπὸ τοῦδε ἐσόμενοι Ῥωμαίων ἐς πάντα κατήκοοι. ὁ δ᾽ ὑπισχνεῖτο δώσειν καὶ συνετίθετο ἤδη. (259) Οὐρίατθος δ᾽, ὁ ἐκ τῆς Γάλβα παρανομίας ἐκφυγών, τότε συνὼν αὐτοῖς ὑπεμίμνησκε τῆς Ῥωμαίων ἀπιστίας, ὁσάκις τε αὐτοῖς ὀμόσαντες ἐπιθοῖντο καὶ ὡς ὅδε πᾶς ὁ στρατὸς ἐκ τοιῶνδε ἐπιορκιῶν Γάλβα καὶ Λουκούλλου διαφύγοιεν. οὐδ᾽ ἀπορεῖν ἔφη σωτηρίας ἀπὸ τοῦδε τοῦ χωρίου, ἂν ἐθέλωσι πείθεσθαι.

62 (260) ἐρεθισθέντων δ᾽ αὐτῶν καὶ ἐν ἐλπίσι γενομένων ᾑρέθη τε στρατηγὸς καὶ πάντας ἐκτάξας ἐς μέτωπον ὡς ἐπὶ μάχῃ τοὺς μὲν ἄλλους ἐκέλευσεν, ὅταν αὐτὸς ἐπιβῇ τοῦ ἵππου, διαιρεθέντας ἐς μέρη πολλὰ φεύγειν, ὡς δύνανται, κατ᾽ ἄλλας καὶ ἄλλας ὁδοὺς ἐς Τριβόλαν πόλιν, ἔνθα αὐτὸν περιμένειν, χιλίους δὲ μόνους ἐπιλεξάμενος ἐκέλευσεν αὐτῷ συνίστασθαι. (261) καὶ γιγνομένων τούτων οἳ μὲν εὐθὺς ἔφυγον,

---

254 Οὐρίατθος Steph.: Οὐρίαθος VM   256 Τυρδιτανίαν Steph.: Τορδιτανίαν VM

60 (251) With these expectations they left their own territory and gathered at the place which Galba had arranged. He divided them into three sections and showed each a stretch of open land, ordering them to stay in this open country until he could come to provide them with a town. (252) When he came to the first group, he ordered them, as friends, to lay down their arms. When they had done so, he surrounded them with a trench and sent in men with swords and killed them all, lamenting and calling on the names of the gods and the promises that they had received. (253) He hurried on and killed the second and third groups in the same way while they were still in ignorance of what had happened to the others. Thus he paid back treachery with treachery, imitating barbarians in a way that was unworthy of the Romans. (254) However a few of the escaped, one of whom was Viriathus, who not long after led the Lusitanians and killed many of the Romans and performed great exploits. But these happened afterwards, and I shall tell of them afterwards. (255) At this time Galba, who was greedier for money than Lucullus, gave a little of the booty to the army and a little to his friends and appropriated the rest for himself, even though he was already the richest of all the Romans; but not even in time of peace, so they say, did he abstain from lying and perjury for the sake of profit. Although he was hated and the subject of accusations, he was acquitted because of his wealth.

61 (256) Not long after, those who escaped from Lucullus' and Galba's treachery assembled together, about ten thousand in number, and invaded Turdetania. (257) Gaius Vetilius came out against them from Rome, bringing with him another army and taking over the soldiers in Iberia, having in all about ten thousand men. He fell on them while they were foraging, killed many of them and forced the rest into a place where, if they stayed, they would be in danger from famine, and if they left, from the Romans, such was the difficulty of the terrain. (258) Therefore they sent envoys to Vetilius with olive branches, asking for land on which to settle, and thereafter they would obey the Romans in all matters. He agreed to give them this and an agreement was reached. (259) Viriathus, however, who had escaped from Galba's treachery, was with them at that time, and reminded them of the unreliability of the Romans, and how often they had sworn oaths and then attacked them, and how everyone in the army had escaped the perjured oaths of Galba and Lucullus. They would manage to escape from the place, he said, if they would follow his orders.

62 (260) They were stirred up by this and began to become hopeful; and he was chosen as their general and, having drawn them all up in line of battle as though for a fight, he ordered some of them to divide in many groups and to flee, as soon as he mounted his horse, as best they could by different routes to the town of Tribola and there to wait for him; and he chose just one thousand of them and ordered them to remain with him. (261) When all this was in place, they fled when Viriathus

ἐπειδὴ ὁ Οὐρίατθος τὸν ἵππον ἀνέβη, ὁ δὲ Οὐετίλιος αὐτοὺς δείσας διώκειν ἐς πολλὰ διῃρημένους, ἐπὶ τὸν Οὐρίατθον ἑστῶτα καὶ ἐφεδρεύοντα τῷ γενησομένῳ τραπεὶς ἐμάχετο. (262) ὁ δ' ὠκυτάτοις ἵπποις αὐτὸν ἐνοχλῶν καὶ ὑποφεύγων καὶ πάλιν ἱστάμενος καὶ ἐπιὼν ἐκείνην τε τὴν ἡμέραν ἐν τῷ αὐτῷ πεδίῳ καὶ τὴν ἐπιοῦσαν ὅλην διέτριψε περιθέων. (263) ὡς δ' εἴκασεν ἀσφαλῶς ἔχειν τῆς φυγῆς τοὺς ἑτέρους, τότε νυκτὸς ὁρμήσας δι' ὁδῶν ἀτριβῶν κουφοτάτοις ἵπποις ἀπέδραμεν ἐς Τριβόλαν, Ῥωμαίων αὐτὸν διώκειν ὁμοίως οὐ δυναμένων διά τε βάρος ὅπλων καὶ ἀπειρίαν ὁδῶν καὶ ἵππων ἀνομοιότητα. (264) ὧδε μὲν ἐξ ἀέλπτου στρατὸν ἀπογιγνώσκοντα αὑτοῦ περιέσωσε, καὶ τὸ στρατήγημα τόδε περιφερόμενον ἐς τοὺς τῇδε βαρβάρους ἐξῆρεν αὐτόν, καὶ πολλοὶ πανταχόθεν αὐτῷ προσε χώρουν.

63 (265) ὁ δ' ἐς ὀκτὼ ἔτη Ῥωμαίοις ἐπολέμει· καί μοι δοκεῖ τὸν Οὐριάτθου πόλεμον σφόδρα τε ἐνοχλήσαντα Ῥωμαίοις καὶ δυσεργότατον αὐτοῖς γενόμενον συναγαγεῖν, ἀναθέμενον, εἴ τι τοῦ αὐτοῦ χρόνου περὶ Ἰβηρίαν ἄλλο ἐγίγνετο. (266) Οὐετίλιος μὲν δὴ αὐτὸν διώκων ἦλθεν ἐπὶ τὴν Τριβόλαν, ὁ δ' Οὐρίατθος ἐν λόχμαις ἐνέδραν ἐπικρύψας ἔφυγε, μέχρι τὰς λόχμας ὑπερελθόντος τοῦ Οὐετιλίου αὐτός τε ἐπεστρέφετο καὶ οἱ ἐκ τῆς ἐνέδρας ἀνεπήδων καὶ Ῥωμαίους ἑκατέρωθεν ἔκτεινόν τε καὶ ἐζώγρουν καὶ ἐς τὰς φάραγγας ἐώθουν. ἐζωγρήθη δὲ καὶ ὁ Οὐετίλιος· καὶ αὐτὸν ὁ λαβὼν ἀγνοῶν, γέροντα ὑπέρπαχυν ὁρῶν, ἔκτεινεν ὡς οὐδενὸς ἄξιον. (267) Ῥωμαίων δὲ μόλις ἐκ μυρίων ἑξακισχίλιοι διέδρασαν ἐς Καρπησσόν, ἐπὶ θαλάσσῃ πόλιν, ἣν ἐγὼ νομίζω πρὸς Ἑλλήνων πάλαι Ταρτησσὸν ὀνομάζεσθαι καὶ Ἀργανθώνιον αὐτῆς βασιλεῦσαι, ὃν ἐς πεντήκοντα καὶ ἑκατὸν ἔτη ἀφικέσθαι φασί. (268) τοὺς μὲν οὖν ἐς τὴν Καρπησσὸν διαφυγόντας ὁ ταμίας, ὃς εἵπετο τῷ Οὐετιλίῳ, συνέτασσεν ἐπὶ τειχῶν δεδιότας· παρὰ δὲ Βελλῶν καὶ Τίτθων αἰτήσας πεντακισχιλίους συμμάχους καὶ λαβὼν προύπεμψεν ἐπὶ τὸν Οὐρίατθον. ὁ δὲ πάντας ἔκτεινεν, ὡς μηδ' ἄγγελον διαφυγεῖν. καὶ ὁ ταμίας ἡσύχαζεν ἐν τῇ πόλει, περιμένων τινὰ βοήθειαν ἀπὸ Ῥώμης.

64 (269) Οὐρίατθος δὲ τὴν Καρπητανίαν, εὐδαίμονα χώραν, ἐπιὼν ἀδεῶς ἐλεηλάτει, ἕως ἧκεν ἐκ Ῥώμης Γάιος Πλαύτιος, ἄγων πεζοὺς μυρίους καὶ ἱππέας χιλίους ἐπὶ τριακοσίοις. (270) τότε δ' αὖθις ὑπεκρίνατο φεύγειν ὁ Οὐρίατθος, καὶ ὁ Πλαύτιος αὐτὸν ἔπεμψε διώ κειν ἐς τετρακισχιλίους, οὓς ἐπιστραφεὶς ὁ Οὐρίατθος ἔκτεινε χωρὶς ὀλίγων. (271) καὶ τὸν Τάγον

---

261 Οὐετίλιος Steph.: Οὐετίνος VM   265 ὀκτὼ Schweig.: τρία VM   266 Οὐετιλίου Steph.: ἐτιλίου VM   ἐπεστρέφετο Steph.: ἐπιστρέφετο VM   267 Καρπησσόν Steph.: Καρπισσόν VM (sed Καρπησσ- §§7 et 268)

mounted his horse; but Vetilius, afraid of pursuing those who were divided into many groups, turned against Viriathus, who stood there, awaiting what would happen next, and fought against him. (262) He, surrounding himself with the fastest horses, ran away and then stopped and attacked, and so used up that day and the whole of the next running around the same battlefield. (263) When he reckoned that the rest had safely made their escape, he set out by night and reached Tribola along unmarked paths on very agile horses, while the Romans were unable to pursue him in the same way because of the weight of their armour, their ignorance of the routes and the inferiority of their horses. (264) In this way he saved his despairing army against the odds, and the story of his stratagem reached the barbarians in the area and increased his reputation, and many came to join him from many different places.

63 (265) He waged war against the Romans for eight years. I intend to deal with the war with Viriathus, which was very troublesome and difficult for the Romans, postponing any other events in Iberia which took place at the same time. (266) Vetilius, then, pursued him to Tribola; and Viriathus, having concealed an ambush in some thickets, fled, until Vetilius reached the thickets, and then turned on him and those in the ambush launched their attack; and they killed and captured the Romans on both sides and forced them over the cliffs. Vetilius himself was captured, and the man who took him did not recognise him, seeing only a fat old man, and killed him as someone of no importance. (267) Of the ten thousand Romans, six thousand with difficulty reached Carpessus, a town by the sea which I believe was in ancient times called Tartessus by the Greeks and Arganthonius was its king, who, they say, lived to the age of one hundred and fifty years. (268) The quaestor who was assigned to Vetilius marshalled those who fled to Carpessus on the walls, though they were in a state of dread. He requisitioned five thousand allied soldiers from the Belli and the Titthi, and when he received them, he sent them against Viriathus. He killed them all, and so no one escaped to bring the news of the disaster. The quaestor remained in peace within the town, waiting for assistance from Rome.

64 (269) Viriathus invaded Carpetania, a prosperous region, and plundered it freely, until Gaius Plautius came from Rome, bringing ten thousand infantry and one thousand three hundred cavalry. (270) On this occasion again Viriathus pretended to flee, and Plautius sent four thousand men in pursuit, against whom Viriathus turned and killed all but a few. (271) He crossed the river Tagus and camped on a

ποταμὸν διαβὰς ἐστρατοπέδευεν ἐν ὄρει περιφύτῳ μὲν ἐλάαις, Ἀφροδίτης δ' ἐπωνύμῳ, ἔνθα ὁ Πλαύτιος καταλαβὼν καὶ τὸ πταῖσμα ἀναλαβεῖν ἐπειγόμενος συνέβαλεν. ἡττηθεὶς δὲ φόνου πολλοῦ γενομένου διέφυγεν ἀκόσμως ἐς τὰς πόλεις καὶ ἐκ μέσου θέρους ἐχείμαζεν, οὐ θαρρῶν οὐδαμοῖ προϊέναι. (272) ὁ δ' Οὐρίατθος τὴν χώραν ἀδεῶς περιιὼν ᾔτει τοὺς κεκτημένους τιμὴν τοῦ ἐπικειμένου καρποῦ καὶ παρ' ὧν μὴ λάβοι, διέφθειρεν.

65 (273) ὧν οἱ ἐν ἄστει Ῥωμαῖοι πυνθανόμενοι Φάβιον Μάξιμον Αἰμιλιανόν, Αἰμιλίου Παύλου τοῦ Περσέα τὸν Μακεδόνων βασιλέα ἀνελόντος υἱόν, ἔπεμπον ἐς Ἰβηρίαν καὶ στρατιὰν ἑαυτῷ καταγράφειν ἐπέτρεπον. (274) ὁ δέ, Ῥωμαίων ἄρτι Καρχηδόνα καὶ τὴν Ἑλλάδα ἑλόντων καὶ τὸν τρίτον ἐν Μακεδονίᾳ πόλεμον κατωρθωκότων, φειδοῖ τῶν ἀνδρῶν τῶν ἐκεῖθεν ἐληλυθότων κατέλεγεν πρωθήβας, οὐ πρὶν πολέμου πεπειραμένους, ἐς δύο τέλη. καὶ παρὰ τῶν συμμάχων στρατὸν ἄλλον αἰτήσας ἧκεν ἐς Ὄρσωνα τῆς Ἰβηρίας, σύμπαντας ἔχων πεζοὺς μυρίους καὶ πεντακισχιλίους καὶ ἱππέας ἐς δισχιλίους. (275) ὅθεν οὔπω μάχης ἄρχων, μέχρι τὴν στρατιὰν γυμνάσειεν, ἐς Γάδειρα διέπλευσε τὸν πορθμόν, Ἡρακλεῖ θύσων. ὁ δὲ Οὐρίατθος αὐτοῦ τῶν ξυλευομένων τισὶν ἐπιπεσὼν ἔκτεινε πολλοὺς καὶ ἐφόβησε τοὺς λοιπούς. (276) τοῦ δ' ὑποστρατήγου συντάξαντος αὐτοὺς αὖθις ὁ Οὐρίατθος ἐκράτει καὶ πολλὴν λείαν περιεσύρατο. ἀφικομένου τε τοῦ Μαξίμου συνεχῶς ἐξέτασσε προκαλού μενος. (277) ὁ δὲ ὅλῳ μὲν οὐ συνεμίσγετο τῷ στρατῷ, γυμνάζων αὐτοὺς ἔτι, κατὰ δὲ μέρη πολλάκις ἠκροβολίζετο, πεῖράν τε ποιούμενος τῶν πολεμίων καὶ τοῖς ἰδίοις ἐντιθεὶς θάρσος. χορτολογῶν τε ἐνόπλους ἀεὶ τοῖς γυμνοῖς περιίστη καὶ περιέτρεχε μεθ' ἱππέων αὐτός, οἷα Παύλῳ τῷ πατρὶ συστρατευόμενος ἐν Μακεδόσιν ἑώρα. (278) μετὰ δὲ χειμῶνα γεγυμνασμένῳ τῷ στρατῷ τρέπεται δεύτερος ὅδε τὸν Οὐρίατθον καλῶς ἀγωνισάμενον καὶ πόλεις αὐτοῦ δύο τὴν μὲν διήρπασεν, τὴν δ' ἐνέπρησεν, αὐτόν τε φεύγοντα ἐς χωρίον, ᾧ ὄνομα ἦν Βαικόρ, διώκων ἔκτεινε πολλούς. καὶ ἐχείμαζεν ἐν Κορδύβῃ.

66 (279) ἐφ' οἷς ὁ Οὐρίατθος, οὐχ ὁμοίως ἔτι καταφρονῶν, Ἀρουακοὺς καὶ Τίτθους καὶ Βελλούς, ἔθνη μαχιμώτατα, ἀπέστησεν ἀπὸ Ῥωμαίων. (280) καὶ πόλεμον ἄλλον οἵδε ἐφ' ἑαυτῶν ἐπολέμουν, ὃν ἐκ πόλεως αὐτῶν μιᾶς Νομαντῖνον ἡγοῦνται, μακρόν τε καὶ ἐπίπονον Ῥωμαίοις γενόμενον, καὶ συνάξω καὶ τόνδε ἐς ἓν μετὰ Οὐρίατθον. (281) Οὐρίατθος μὲν ἐπὶ θάτερα

---

271 προϊέναι Schweig.: προσιέναι VM   274 πρωθήβας Schweig. ex Suda: πρὸ Θήβης VM   277 αὐτός Schweig.: αὐτοὺς VM   278 ἐν Κορδύβῃ deletum in V punctis singulis letteris suppositis: habet M   281 Κοϊνίτῳ VM: Κοίντῳ Gouk.

mountain, covered with olive trees, called the mountain of Aphrodite. Plautius caught up with him there and, being keen to redeem his disaster, attacked him. He was defeated with much slaughter and fled in a disorderly fashion to the towns and went into winter quarters in the middle of summer, not daring to venture out again. (272) Viriathus went around the area freely, demanding from the owners the price of the crop that was growing there and destroying the crops of those from whom he did not receive it.

65 (273) When the Romans in the city of Rome learned of these events, they sent Fabius Maximus Aemilianus, the son of Aemilius Paullus who had defeated Perseus, king of the Macedonians, to Iberia, and ordered him to enrol an army for himself. (274) Since the Romans had recently taken Carthage and Greece and had successfully completed the third war in Macedonia, he enlisted two legions of young men, who had had no previous experience of war, in order to spare those who had returned from these places. Having requisitioned another force from the allies, he arrived at Orso in Iberia, having altogether fifteen thousand infantry and about two thousand cavalry. (275) As he did not intend to start the campaign until he had trained his army, he sailed from there through the straits to Gades, to sacrifice to Herakles. Viriathus fell upon some of his men while they were cutting wood and killed many of them and terrified the rest. (276) When the legate drew them up in order of battle, Viriathus again defeated them and seized much booty. When Maximus arrived, he continuously led out his forces, challenging Maximus. (277) He, however, did not engage with his whole force, for he was still training it, but frequently skirmished using part of them, testing the enemy and encouraging his own troops. When foraging he always surrounded his light-armed with fully armed soldiers and himself roamed the country with his cavalry, as he had seen done when serving with his father against the Macedonians. (278) After the winter, with his army now trained up, he routs Viriathus, though he fought well, being the second to do so, and took two of his towns, of which he plundered one and burnt the other, and pursued Viriathus, who fled to a place, of which the name was Baecor, and killed many men. Then he went into winter quarters in Corduba.

66 (279) After this Viriathus, who no longer despised the enemy in the same way, won over the Arevaci, the Titthi and the Belli, extremely warlike peoples, from the Romans. (280) They waged another war on their own behalf, which is called the Numantine war from one of their towns, and which was a lengthy and troublesome war for the Romans. I shall deal with it as a sequel after Viriathus. (281) Viriathus

τῆς Ἰβηρίας ἑτέρῳ στρατηγῷ Ῥωμαίων Κοϊντίῳ συνεπλέκετο καὶ
ἡσσώμενος ἐς τὸ Ἀφροδίσιον ὄρος ἀνέστρεφεν. (282) ὅθεν ἐπιστραφεὶς
ἔκτεινε τῶν Κοϊντείων χιλίους καὶ σημεῖά τινα ἥρπασε· τοὺς δὲ λοιποὺς
ἐς τὸ στρατόπεδον αὐτῶν συνεδίωξε καὶ τὴν ἐν Ἰτύκκῃ φρουρὰν ἐξέβαλε
καὶ τὴν Βαστιτανῶν χώραν ἐλῄζετο, Κοϊντίου διὰ δειλίαν καὶ ἀπειρίαν
οὐκ ἐπιβοηθοῦντος, ἀλλ' ἐν Κορδύβῃ χειμάζοντος ἐκ μέσου μετοπώρου καὶ
Γάιον Μάρκιον θαμινὰ ἐπιπέμποντος αὐτῷ, ἄνδρα Ἴβηρα ἐκ πόλεως
Ἰταλικῆς.

67 (283) τοῦ δ' ἐπιόντος ἔτους Κοϊντίῳ μὲν ὁ ἀδελφὸς Αἰμιλιανοῦ, Φάβιος
Μάξιμος Σερουιλιανός, ἦλθεν ἐπὶ τὴν στρατηγίαν διάδοχος, δύο ἄλλα τέλη
Ῥωμαίων ἄγων καὶ συμμάχους τινάς, ἅπαντας ἐς μυρίους καὶ
ὀκτακισχιλίους πεζοὺς καὶ ἱππέας ἑξακοσίους ἐπὶ χιλίοις. (284)
ἐπιστείλας δὲ καὶ Μικίψῃ, τῷ Νομάδων βασιλεῖ, πέμψαι οἱ τάχιστα
ἐλέφαντας ἐς Ἰτύκκην ἠπείγετο, τὴν στρατιὰν ἄγων κατὰ μέρος· καὶ τὸν
Οὐρίαθον ἑξακισχιλίοις ἀνδράσιν ἐπιόντα οἱ μετά τε κραυγῆς καὶ
θορύβου βαρβαρικοῦ καὶ κόμης μακρᾶς, ἣν ἐν τοῖς πολέμοις ἐπισείουσι
τοῖς ἐχθροῖς, οὐδὲν ὑποπτήξας ὑπέστη τε γενναίως καὶ ἀπεώσατο
ἄπρακτον. (285) ὡς δέ οἱ καὶ τὸ ἄλλο πλῆθος ἀφῖκτο καὶ ἐκ Λιβύης
ἐλέφαντες δέκα σὺν ἱππεῦσι τριακοσίοις, στρατόπεδον ὠχύρου μέγα καὶ
προεπεχείρει τῷ Οὐρίαθῳ καὶ τρεψάμενος αὐτὸν ἐδίωκεν. (286) ἀτάκτου
δὲ τῆς διώξεως γενομένης, ἰδὼν ἐν τῇ φυγῇ τοῦτο ὁ Οὐρίαθος ἐπανῆλθε
καὶ κτείνας ἐς τρισχιλίους τοὺς λοιποὺς συνήλασεν ἐς τὸ στρατόπεδον
καὶ προσέβαλε καὶ τῷδε, ὀλίγων μόλις αὐτὸν ὑφισταμένων περὶ τὰς
πύλας, τῶν δὲ πλεόνων ἐς τὰς σκηνὰς καταδύντων ὑπὸ δέους καὶ μόλις
ὑπὸ τοῦ στρατηγοῦ καὶ τῶν χιλιάρχων ἐξαγομένων. (287) τότε μὲν οὖν
Φάνιός τε, ὁ Λαιλίου κηδεστής, λαμπρῶς ἠρίστευε, καὶ νὺξ ἐπελθοῦσα
Ῥωμαίους περιέσωσεν· ὁ δὲ Οὐρίαθος, ἢ νυκτὸς ἢ καύματος ὥρᾳ θαμινὰ
ἐπιὼν καὶ οὔ τινα καιρὸν ἀδόκητον ἐκλείπων, ψιλοῖς ἀνδράσι καὶ ἵπποις
ταχυτάτοις ἠνώχλει τοῖς πολεμίοις, μέχρι τὸν Σερουιλιανὸν ἐς Ἰτύκκην
ἀναστῆσαι.

68 (288) τότε δ' ἤδη τροφῶν τε ἀπορῶν ὁ Οὐρίαθος καὶ τὸν στρατὸν
ἔχων ἐλάττω, νυκτὸς ἐμπρήσας τὸ στρατόπεδον, ἐς Λυσιτανίαν ἀνεχώρει.
καὶ αὐτὸν ὁ Σερουιλιανὸς οὐ καταλαβὼν ἐς Βαιτουρίαν ἐνέβαλε καὶ πέντε
πόλεις διήρπαζεν, αἳ τῷ Οὐρίαθῳ συνεπεπράχεσαν. (289) μετὰ δὲ τοῦτο
ἐστράτευεν ἐς Κουνέους, ὅθεν ἐς Λυσιτανοὺς ἐπὶ τὸν Οὐρίαθον αὖθις
ἠπείγετο. καὶ αὐτῷ παροδεύοντι δύο λήσταρχοι μετὰ μυρίων ἀνδρῶν

282 τῶν Κοϊντείων Schweig.: τοὺς Κοϊντείους VM τῶν Κοίντου Gouk.   Ἰτύκκῃ Steph.:
Ἰτύκῃ VM Βαστιτανῶν Steph.: Βασσιτανῶν VM Κοϊντίου Steph.: Κιντίου VM Κοίντου
Gouk.   **283** Κοϊντίῳ Steph.: Κοίντῳ V Σερουιλιανός Pighius: Αἰμιλιανός VM   **284**
Ἰτύκκην V (priore κ in ras.)   **286** προσέβαλε Steph.: προσέβαλλε VM αὐτὸν Musgrave:
αὐτῶν VM   **287** ἐκλείπων Steph.: ἐκλιπὼν VM

in the other part of Iberia became entangled with Quinctius, another praetor of the Romans, and, being defeated by him, returned to the mountain of Aphrodite. (282) From there he turned again and killed a thousand of Quinctius' men and captured some of their standards. The rest he pursued into their encampment and attacked the garrison at Itucca and ravaged the territory of the Bastitani, while Quinctius, out of cowardice and inexperience, rendered no assistance but went into winter quarters at Corduba from the middle of autumn and frequently sent Gaius Marcius, an Iberian from the town of Italica, against him.

67 (283) The following year Fabius Maximus Servilianus, the brother of Aemilianus, came as Quinctius' successor in the command, bringing two further legions of Romans and some allies, in all about eighteen thousand infantry and one thousand six hundred cavalry. (284) He sent a message to Micipsa, the king of the Numidians, to send him elephants as quickly as possible, and he hurried to Itucca, with his army in separate sections. When Viriathus attacked him with six thousand men, and with the shouting and clangour of the barbarians and their long hair, which they shake at their enemies in warfare, he was not frightened but stood bravely and repelled him without his having achieved anything. (285) When the rest of his force arrived and also ten elephants and three hundred horsemen from Libya, he constructed a large camp and moved out against Viriathus and routed and pursued him. (286) The pursuit became disorderly, and Viriathus, noticing this in the course of his flight, rallied, killed about three thousand and drove the rest into the camp and attacked even this, with a few resisting him with difficulty at the gates, while the majority were slinking away into their tents out of fear and were only driven out of them with difficulty by their commander and the tribunes. (287) At this point Fannius, the son-in-law of Laelius, behaved bravely, and the onset of night saved the Romans; but Viriathus, attacking frequently at night or in the heat of the day and making use of any moment at which he might not be expected, harassed the enemy with light armed men and rapid horses, until he forced Servilianus back to Itucca.

68 (288) Since by that time Viriathus was running short of food-supplies and had a smaller army, he burnt his camp and retreated into Lusitania. Servilianus failed to catch up with him and invaded Baeturia and plundered five towns that had collaborated with Viriathus. (289) After this he marched against the Cunei, and from there again invaded the Lusitanians in pursuit of Viriathus. As he was on the way, two bandit chieftains, Curius and Apuleius, attacked him with ten thousand men,

ἐπιθέμενοι, Κούριός τε καὶ Ἀπουλήιος, ἐθορύβησαν καὶ τὴν λείαν ἀφείλοντο. (290) καὶ Κούριος μὲν ἐν τῷ ἀγῶνι ἔπεσεν, ὁ δὲ Σερουιλιανὸς τήν τε λείαν μετ' οὐ πολὺ ἀνέλαβε καὶ πόλεις εἷλεν Εἰσκαδίαν τε καὶ Γέμελλαν καὶ Ὀβόλκολαν, φρουρουμένας ὑπὸ τῶν Οὐριάθου, καὶ διήρπαζεν ἑτέρας καὶ συνεγίγνωσκεν ἄλλαις. (291) αἰχμάλωτα δ' ἔχων ἀμφὶ τὰ μύρια πεντακοσίων μὲν ἀπέτεμεν τὰς κεφαλάς, τοὺς δὲ λοιποὺς ἀπέδοτο. καὶ [ἐχείμαζε, δεύτερον ἔτος ἤδη στρατηγῶν τοῦδε τοῦ πολέμου. καὶ τάδε μὲν ὁ Σερουιλιανὸς ἐργασάμενος ἐς Ῥώμην ἀπῆρε διαδεξαμένου τὴν ἀρχὴν Κοΐντου Πομπηίου Αὔλου. ὁ δὲ ἀδελφὸς αὐτοῦ Μάξιμος Αἰμιλιανὸς] Κοννόβαν μέν τινα λήσταρχον ἑαυτὸν ἐγχειρίσαντα λαβὼν καὶ φεισάμενος αὐτοῦ μόνου τοὺς σὺν αὐτῷ πάντας ἐχειροκόπησεν.

69 (292) Οὐρίαθον δὲ διώκων Ἐρισάνην αὐτοῦ πόλιν ἀπετάφρευεν, ἐς ἣν ὁ Οὐρίαθος ἐσδραμὼν νυκτὸς ἅμα ἕῳ τοῖς ἐργαζομένοις ἐπέκειτο, μέχρι τὰ σκαφεῖα ῥίψαντες ἔφευγον. (293) τήν τε ἄλλην στρατιάν, ἐκταχθεῖσαν ὑπὸ τοῦ Σερουιλιανοῦ, τρεψάμενος ὁμοίως Οὐρίαθος ἐδίωκε καὶ συνήλασεν ἐς κρημνούς, ὅθεν οὐκ ἦν τοῖς Ῥωμαίοις διαφυγεῖν. (294) Οὐρίαθος δὲ ἐς τὴν εὐτυχίαν οὐχ ὕβρισεν, ἀλλὰ νομίσας ἐν καλῷ θήσεσθαι τὸν πόλεμον ἐπὶ χάριτι λαμπρᾷ συνετίθετο Ῥωμαίοις, καὶ τὰς συνθήκας ὁ δῆμος ἐπεκύρωσεν, Οὐρίαθον εἶναι Ῥωμαίων φίλον καὶ τοὺς ὑπ' αὐτῷ πάντας ἧς ἔχουσι γῆς ἄρχειν. (295) ὧδε μὲν ὁ Οὐριάθου πόλεμος ἐδόκει πεπαῦσθαι, χαλεπώτατός τε Ῥωμαίοις γενόμενος καὶ ἐπὶ εὐεργεσίᾳ καταλυθείς, οὐ μὴν ἐπέμεινεν οὐδ' ἐς βραχὺ τὰ συγκείμενα.

70 (296) ὁ γὰρ ἀδελφὸς Σερουιλιανοῦ, τοῦ ταῦτα συνθεμένου, Καιπίων, διάδοχος αὐτῷ τῆς στρατηγίας γενόμενος, διέβαλλε τὰς συνθήκας καὶ ἐπέστελλε Ῥωμαίοις ἀπρεπεστάτας εἶναι. (297) καὶ ἡ βουλὴ τὸ μὲν πρῶτον αὐτῷ συνεχώρει κρύφα λυπεῖν τὸν Οὐρίαθον, ὅ τι δοκιμάσειεν· ὡς δὲ αὖθις ἠνώχλει καὶ συνεχῶς ἐπέστελλεν, ἔκρινε λῦσαί τε τὰς σπονδὰς καὶ φανερῶς πολεμεῖν αὖθις Οὐριάθῳ. (298) ἐψηφισμένου δὴ σαφῶς ὁ Καιπίων Ἄρσαν τε πόλιν ἐκλιπόντος Οὐριάθου παρέλαβε καὶ αὐτὸν Οὐρίαθον φεύγοντά τε καὶ τὰ ἐν παρόδῳ φθείροντα περὶ Καρπητανίαν κατέλαβεν, πολὺ πλείονας ἔχων. (299) ὅθεν ὁ Οὐρίαθος, οὐ δοκιμάζων αὐτῷ συμπλέκεσθαι διὰ τὴν ὀλιγότητα, κατὰ μέν τινα φάραγγα ἀφανῆ τὸ πλέον τοῦ στρατοῦ περιέπεμψεν ἀπιέναι, τὸ δὲ λοιπὸν αὐτὸς ἐκτάξας ἐπὶ λόφου δόξαν παρεῖχε πολεμήσοντος. (300) ὡς δ' ᾔσθετο τῶν

---

291 verba uncis inclusa non Appiani esse susp. Viereck-Roos. ad §278 haec verba transf. Schweig. Κοΐντου Πομπηίου Αὔλου del. Gouk, ut gloss., et add. <τοῦ ἀδελφοῦ> **293** Σερουιλιανοῦ Schweig.: Αἰμιλιανοῦ VM **296** Σερουιλιανοῦ Schweig.: Αἰμιλιανοῦ VM Καιπίων Schweig.: Κεπίων VM (hic et deinceps) Σκιπίων Exc. **298** ἐκλιπόντος Mend.: ἐλειπόντος VM

threw his forces into confusion and carried off booty. (290) Curius fell in the struggle, and Servilianus shortly afterwards recovered the booty and captured the towns of Eiskadia, Gemella and Obulcula, which had been garrisoned by Viriathus, plundered some others and pardoned others again. (291) He took about ten thousand prisoners, of whom he beheaded five hundred and sold the rest. [And he went into winter quarters, being a commander in this war for the second year. And Servilianus did these things and then returned to Rome, being succeeded in the command by Quintus Pompeius, son of Aulus. His brother, Maximus Aemilianus,] He captured Connobas, a bandit chieftain, who surrendered to him, and pardoned him alone but cut off the hands of all those who were with him.

69 (292) Pursuing Viriathus, he encircled his town of Erisane with a trench, but Viriathus entered it by night and at dawn attacked those who were working on the trench, so that they fled, throwing away their spades. (293) Once Servilianus had marshalled the rest of the army, Viriathus routed that too and forced them into a precipitous place, from which the Romans could not escape. (294) Viriathus was not arrogantly self-confident about his good fortune but, thinking this a good opportunity to stop the war made an agreement with the Romans on notably generous terms, and the people ratified the agreement, that Viriathus was to be a friend of the Romans and that those under his control should all rule over the land which they held. (295) In this way the war with Viriathus, which had been very problematic for the Romans, appeared to have come to an end, resolved by an act of generosity. The agreement did not, however, last long.

70 (296) Caepio, the brother of Servilianus, who had made this agreement, was his successor in the command, and he spoke against the agreement and wrote home, representing it as highly dishonourable to the Romans. (297) The senate at first gave him permission to annoy Viriathus in whatever way he saw fit; and when he again kept fussing over the matter and continually sent letters, it decided to break the treaty and openly go to war with Viriathus again. (298) Once this had been voted on clearly, Caepio took the town of Arsa, which Viriathus left, and, having far more forces, caught up with Viriathus himself, as he fled, destroying property throughout Carpetania along his way. (299) Viriathus therefore. reckoning that he should not engage because of the small number of his forces, instructed the greater part of his army to slip away through a hidden ravine, and himself drew up the remainder on a hill and gave the impression that he was about to fight. (300) When he concluded

προαπεσταλμένων ἐν ἀσφαλεῖ γεγονότων, ἐξίππευσεν ἐς αὐτοὺς μετὰ καταφρονήσεως, ὀξέως οὕτως, ὡς μηδ' αἰσθέσθαι τοὺς διώκοντας, ὅποι διέδραμεν. ὁ δὲ Καιπίων, ἐς Οὐέττωνας καὶ Καλλαίκους τραπείς, τὰ ἐκείνων ἐδήου.

71 (301) καὶ ζήλῳ τῶν ἔργων Οὐριάτθου τὴν Λυσιτανίαν ληστήρια πολλὰ ἄλλα ˙ἐπιτρέχοντα ἐπόρθει. Σέξτος δὲ Ἰούνιος Βροῦτος, ἐπὶ ταῦτα πεμφθείς, ἀπέγνω μὲν αὐτὰ διώκειν διὰ χώρας μακρᾶς, ὅσην ὁ Τάγος τε καὶ Λήθης καὶ Δόριος καὶ Βαίνις ποταμοὶ ναυσίποροι περιέχουσιν, ὀξέως, οἷα δὴ ληστήρια, μεθιπταμένους δυσεργὲς ἡγούμενος εἶναι καταλαβεῖν καὶ αἰσχρὸν οὐ καταλαβόντι καὶ νικήσαντι τὸ ἔργον οὐ λαμπρόν· (302) ἐς δὲ τὰς πόλεις αὐτῶν ἐτράπετο, δίκην τε λήψεσθαι προσδοκῶν καὶ τῇ στρατιᾷ πολὺ κέρδος περιέσεσθαι · καὶ τοὺς λῃστὰς ἐς ἑκάστην ὡς πατρίδα κινδυνεύουσαν διαλυθήσεσθαι. (303) ὁ μὲν δὴ ταῦτ' ἐνθυμού μενος ἐδήου τὰ ἐν ποσὶν ἅπαντα, συμμαχομένων τοῖς ἀνδράσι τῶν γυναικῶν καὶ συναναιρουμένων καὶ οὔ τινα φωνὴν οὐδ' ἐν ταῖς σφαγαῖς ἀφιεισῶν. εἰσὶ δ' οἳ καὶ εἰς τὰ ὄρη, μεθ' ὧν ἐδύναντο, ἀνεπήδων· καὶ αὐτοῖς δεομένοις συνεγίγνωσκεν ὁ Βροῦτος καὶ τὰ ὄντα ἐμερίζετο.

72 (304) καὶ τὸν Δόριον περάσας πολλὰ μὲν πολέμῳ κατέδραμεν, πολλὰ δὲ παρὰ τῶν αὐτοὺς ἐνδιδόντων ὅμηρα αἰτήσας ἐπὶ Λήθην μετήει, πρῶτος ὅδε Ῥωμαίων ἐπινοῶν τὸν ποταμὸν τόνδε διαβῆναι. (305) περάσας δὲ καὶ τόνδε καὶ μέχρι Νίμιος, ἑτέρου ποταμοῦ, προελθών, Βρακάρων αὐτῷ φερομένην ἀγορὰν ἁρπασάντων, ἐστράτευεν ἐπὶ τοὺς Βρακάρους, οἵ εἰσιν ἔθνος ⟨μαχιμώτατον⟩ καὶ ἅμα ταῖς γυναιξὶν ὡπλισμέναις καὶ οἵδε ἐμάχοντο καὶ προθύμως ἔθνησκον, οὐκ ἐπιστρεφόμενος αὐτῶν οὐδεὶς οὐδὲ τὰ νῶτα δεικνὺς οὐδὲ φωνὴν ἀφιέντες. (306) ὅσαι δὲ κατήγοντο τῶν γυναικῶν, αἱ μὲν αὐτὰς διεχρῶντο, αἱ δὲ καὶ τῶν τέκνων αὐτόχειρες ἐγίγνοντο, χαίρουσαι τῷ θανάτῳ μᾶλλον τῆς αἰχμαλωσίας. (307) εἰσὶ δέ τινες τῶν πόλεων, αἳ τότε μὲν τῷ Βρούτῳ προσετίθεντο, οὐ πολὺ δ' ὕστερον ἀφίσταντο, καὶ αὐτὰς ὁ Βροῦτος κατεστρέφετο αὖθις.

73 (308) ἐπὶ δὲ Ταλάβριγα πόλιν ἐλθών, ἣ πολλάκις μὲν αὐτῷ συνετέθειτο, πολλάκις δ' ἀποστᾶσα ἠνώχλει, παρακαλούντων αὐτὸν καὶ τότε τῶν Ταλαβρίγων καὶ διδόντων αὐτούς, ἐς ὅ τι χρήζοι, πρῶτα μὲν τοὺς αὐτομόλους Ῥωμαίων ᾔτει καὶ τὰ αἰχμάλωτα καὶ ὅπλα, ὅσα εἶχον, καὶ ὅμηρα ἐπὶ τούτοις, εἶτ' αὐτοὺς ἐκέ λευσε σὺν παισὶ καὶ γυναιξὶν

---

301 Βαίνις Viereck-Roos: Βαίτης VM   **305** Νίμιος VM: Μινίου ci. Casaubon lacunam ind. Schweig., qui ⟨μαχιμώτατον⟩ sugg., exempli gratia   **308** Ταλάβριγα Steph.: τὰ Λάβρίγα VM   τῶν Ταλαβρίγων Steph.: τῶν τε Λαβρίγων VM

that those he had sent away were safe, he rode after them with total disregard for the enemy and with such speed that those who pursued him could not tell which way he had gone. Caepio then turned against the Vettones and the Callaeci and ravaged their property.

71 (301) Spurred on by the deeds of Viriathus, many other groups of bandits invaded and ravaged Lusitania. Sextus Iunius Brutus, who was sent out to deal with them, gave up the idea of chasing them through the long stretches of territory bordered by the Tagus, the Lethes, the Durius and the Baenis (all navigable rivers), thinking it difficult to catch up with men who moved rapidly from place to place, as bandits do, disgraceful to fail to catch them and to conquer them a matter of no great glory. (302) He turned against their towns, in the expectation that he would be able to inflict punishment on them, that there would be much profit in it for the army and that the bandits would scatter each to his own homeland when it was in danger. (303) With these notions in mind, he plundered everything he came across, the women fighting and dying alongside the men and not uttering a cry, even in the midst of the slaughter. Some fled to the mountains, laden with all they could carry; and Brutus granted pardon to these when they asked for it, dividing up their property.

72 (304) Having crossed the Durius, he overran a great area in the course of the fighting and, having demanded many hostages from those who surrendered to him, reached the Lethes, being the first Roman to contemplate going across this river. (305) Having crossed this and advanced to the Nimis, another river, he marched against the Bracari, who had plundered supplies as they were being brought to him. They are a most warlike people, and fight with their women alongside them in full armour and died willingly, not one of them turning or showing his back or uttering a cry. (306) Of the women who were taken, some killed themselves and some murdered their children with their own hands, preferring death to slavery. (307) Some of the towns which surrendered to Brutus at this time, revolted not long afterwards, and Brutus subdued them a second time.

73 (308) On his advancing against the town of Talabriga, which had often submitted to him and as often revolted and caused him problems, they appealed to him on this occasion also and surrendered themselves to him, to do as he wished. He first demanded from them the Roman deserters and such prisoners and weapons as they had, and in addition hostages, and then ordered then, with their women and children,

ἐκλιπεῖν τὴν πόλιν. (309) ὡς δὲ καὶ τοῦθ' ὑπέστησαν, τὴν στρατιὰν
αὐτοῖς περιστήσας ἐδημηγόρει, καταλέγων, ὁσάκις ἀποσταῖεν καὶ ὅσους
πολέμους πολεμήσειαν αὐτῷ. φόβον δὲ καὶ δόξαν ἐμφήνας ἐργασομένου τι
δεινὸν ἐπὶ τῶν ὀνειδῶν ἔληξε καὶ τοὺς μὲν ἵππους αὐτῶν καὶ τὸν σῖτον
καὶ χρήματα, ὅσα κοινὰ ἦν, ἢ εἴ τις ἄλλη δημοσία παρασκευή, πάντα
περιεῖλε, τὴν δὲ πόλιν αὖθις οἰκεῖν ἔδωκεν ἐξ ἀέλπτου. (310) τοσάδε μὲν
δὴ Βροῦτος ἐργασάμενος ἐς Ῥώμην ἀπῄει. καὶ αὐτὰ ἐς τὴν Οὐριάτθου
γραφὴν συνήγαγον, ἐν τῷ αὐτῷ χρόνῳ διὰ τὸν ἐκείνου ζῆλον ὑπὸ
λῃστηρίων ἄλλων ἀρξάμενα γίγνεσθαι.

74 (311) Οὐρίατθος δὲ Καιπίωνι περὶ συμβάσεων τοὺς πιστοτάτους αὐτῷ
φίλους ἐπέπεμπεν, Αὔδακα καὶ Διτάλκωνα καὶ Μίνουρον, οἳ διαφθαρέντες
ὑπὸ τοῦ Καιπίωνος δώροις τε μεγάλοις καὶ ὑποσχέσεσι πολλαῖς
ὑπέστησαν αὐτῷ κτενεῖν τὸν Οὐρίατθον. (312) καὶ ἔκτειναν ὧδε·
ὀλιγοϋπνότατος ἦν διὰ φροντίδα καὶ πόνους ὁ Οὐρίατθος καὶ τὰ πολλὰ
ἔνοπλος ἀνεπαύετο, ἵνα ἐξεγρόμενος εὐθὺς ἐς πάντα ἕτοιμος εἴη. τοῖς
οὖν φίλοις ἐξῆν καὶ νυκτερεύοντι ἐντυγχάνειν. (313) ᾧ δὴ καὶ τότε ἔθει
οἱ περὶ τὸν Αὔδακα φυλάξαντες αὐτὸν ἀρχομένου ὕπνου παρῆλθον ἐς τὴν
σκηνήν, ὡς δή τινος ἐπείγοντος, καὶ κεντοῦσιν ὡπλισμένον ἐς τὴν
σφαγήν· οὐ γὰρ ἦν ἄλλοθι. (314) οὐδεμιᾶς δ' αἰσθήσεως γενομένης διὰ
τὴν τῆς πληγῆς εὐκαιρίαν διέδρασαν ἐς Καιπίωνα καὶ τὰς δωρεὰς ἤτουν.
ὁ δὲ αὐτίκα μὲν αὐτοῖς ἔδωκεν ἀδεῶς ἔχειν, ὅσα ἔχουσι, περὶ δὲ ὧν
ἤτουν, ἐς Ῥώμην αὐτοὺς ἔπεμπεν. (315) οἱ δὲ θεραπευτῆρες Οὐριάτθου καὶ
ἡ ἄλλη στρατιά, γενομένης ἡμέρας, ἀναπαύεσθαι νομίζοντες αὐτόν,
ἐθαύμαζον διὰ τὴν ἀήθειαν, μέχρι τινὲς ἔμαθον, ὅτι νεκρὸς κέοιτο
ἔνοπλος. (316) καὶ εὐθὺς ἦν οἰμωγή τε καὶ πένθος ἀνὰ τὸ στρατόπεδον,
ἀλγούντων τε ἐπ' ἐκείνῳ καὶ περὶ σφῶν δεδιότων καὶ ἐνθυμουμένων, ἐν
οἵοις εἰσὶ κινδύνοις καὶ οἵου στρατηγοῦ στέρονται. μάλιστα δὲ αὐτούς,
ὅτι τοὺς δράσαντας οὐχ εὕρισκον, ὑπερήλγυνεν.

75 (317) Οὐρίατθον μὲν δὴ λαμπρότατα κοσμήσαντες ἐπὶ ὑψηλοτάτης
πυρᾶς ἔκαιον ἱερεῖά τε πολλὰ ἐπέσφαττον αὐτῷ, καὶ κατὰ ἴλας οἵ τε
πεζοὶ καὶ οἱ ἱππῆς ἐν κύκλῳ περιθέοντες αὐτὸν ἔνοπλοι βαρβαρικῶς
ἐπῄνουν μέχρι τε σβεσθῆναι τὸ πῦρ παρεκάθηντο πάντες ἀμφ' αὐτό. καὶ
τῆς ταφῆς ἐκτελεσθείσης ἀγῶνα μονομάχων ἀνδρῶν ἤγαγον ἐπὶ τοῦ
τάφου. (318) τοσοῦτον αὐτοῦ πόθον κατέλιπεν Οὐρίατθος, ἀρχικώτατος μὲν
ὡς ἐν βαρβάροις γενόμενος, φιλοκινδυνότατος δ' ἐς ἅπαντα πρὸ ἁπάντων
καὶ ἰσομοιρότατος ἐν τοῖς κέρδεσιν. οὐ γάρ ποτε πλέον ὑπέστη λαβεῖν,

to leave the town. (309) When they obeyed even this command, he surrounded them with his army and made a speech to them, recounting how many times they had revolted and all the wars they had waged against him. Having set before them the fear and belief that he was about to inflict something terrible, he went no further than to upbraid them, and took away from them their horses, their grain and such of their money as was held in common or any other public property, and gave them back their town to live in, quite contrary to what they expected. (310) When he had done these things, Brutus left for Rome. I have brought together these events with the history of Viriathus because they began to be undertaken at the same time by bandits in emulation of him.

74 (311) Viriathus sent to Caepio his most trusted friends, Audax, Ditalco and Minurus, to enter into negotiations. These men were corrupted by Caepio with large gifts and many promises and undertook to kill Viriathus. (312) And this is how they killed him: Viriathus slept very little because of his anxieties and hard work and generally rested in full armour, so that on waking he would immediately be ready for anything. For this reason his friends were able to come to meet him during the night. (313) Relying on this habit, those involved with Audax watched him and, just as sleep was coming upon him, entered the tent as though there were some pressing business, and stabbed him in the throat, armoured as he was, for there was no other place at which they could do it. (314) Because they were fortunate with their thrust, nothing was noticed, and they escaped to Caepio and demanded their bribes. He immediately granted them to have what they had in safety and sent them to Rome with regard to their demands. (315) At day-break Viriathus' attendants and the rest of the army, thinking that he was asleep, were surprised at this change of routine, until some of them discovered that he lay dead, in full armour. (316) Immediately there was lamentation and grief throughout the army, mourning him, and fearing for themselves, as they considered the dangers they were in and the qualities of the general they had lost. They were especially grieved that they could not find the men who had done the deed.

75 (317) They dressed Viriathus in splendid garments and burned him on a high pyre, and made many sacrifices on his behalf. The infantry and the cavalry in their squadrons ran around him in full armour in the barbarian fashion and recited praises of him, and they all sat around him until the pyre burnt down. When the funeral rites were over, they conducted gladiatorial games by the tomb. (318) So great was the longing that Viriathus left, who was among the barbarians a leader of outstanding abilities, the most eager for danger on behalf of all his followers in all

αἰεὶ παρακαλούντων· ὁ δὲ καὶ λάβοι, τοῖς ἀριστεύσασιν ἐδίδου. (319) ὅθεν αὐτῷ, δυσχερέστατον ἔργον καὶ οὐδενί πω στρατηγῶν εὐμαρῶς ἐγγενόμενον, ἔτεσιν ὀκτὼ τοῦδε τοῦ πολέμου παμμιγὴς στρατὸς ἀστασίαστος ἦν καὶ κατήκοος ἀεὶ καὶ ἐς τοὺς κινδύνους ὀξύτατος. (320) τότε δὲ σφῶν Ταύταλον ἑλόμενοι στρατηγεῖν ἐπὶ Ζάκανθαν ἐφέροντο, ἣν Ἀννίβας καθελὼν ἔκτισεν καὶ ἀπὸ τῆς αὐτοῦ πατρίδος Καρχηδόνα προσεῖπεν. (321) ἀποκρουσθεῖσι δ' αὐτοῖς ἐκεῖθεν καὶ τὸν Βαῖτιν ποταμὸν περῶσιν ὁ Καιπίων ἐπέκειτο, μέχρι κάμνων ὁ Ταύταλος αὐτόν τε καὶ τὴν στρατιὰν τῷ Καιπίωνι παρέδωκεν ὡς ὑπηκόοις χρῆσθαι. ὁ δὲ ὅπλα τε αὐτοὺς ἀφείλετο ἅπαντα καὶ γῆν ἔδωκεν ἱκανήν, ἵνα μὴ λῃστεύοιεν ἐξ ἀπορίας.

76 (322) ὁ μὲν δὴ Οὐριάθου πόλεμος ἐς τοῦτο ἐτελεύτα, ἐπάνεισι δ' ἐς τὸν Οὐακκαίων καὶ Νομαντίνων πόλεμον ἡ γραφή, οὓς Οὐρίατθος μὲν ἠρέθισεν ἐς ἀπόστασιν, Καικίλιος δ' αὐτοῖς Μέτελλος ἀπὸ Ῥώμης ἐπιπεμφθεὶς μετὰ πλέονος στρατοῦ Οὐακκαίους μὲν ἐχειρώσατο, σὺν ἐκπλήξει καὶ τάχει θερίζουσιν ἐμπίπτων, Τερμεντία δ' αὐτῷ καὶ Νομαντία ἔτι ἔλειπον. (323) ἦν δ' ἡ Νομαντία ποταμοῖς δύο καὶ φάραγξιν ἀπόκρημνος, ὑλαί τε αὐτῇ πυκναὶ περιέκειντο, καὶ μία κάθοδος ἦν ἐς τὸ πεδίον, ἣ τάφρων ἐπεπλήρωτο καὶ στηλῶν. (324) αὐτοὶ δ' ἦσαν ἄριστοι μὲν ἱππῆς τε καὶ πεζοί, πάντες δ' ἀμφὶ τοὺς ὀκτακισχιλίους· καὶ τοσοίδε ὄντες ὅμως ὑπ' ἀρετῆς ἐς μέγα ἠνώχλησαν τὰ Ῥωμαίων. (325) Μέτελλος μὲν δὴ μετὰ χειμῶνα τὴν στρατιὰν Κοΐντῳ Πομπηίῳ Αὔλου ‹υἱῷ›, διαδόχῳ τῆς στρατηγίας οἱ γενομένῳ, παρέδωκεν, τρισμυρίους πεζοὺς καὶ δισχιλίους ἱππέας ἄριστα γεγυμνασμένους, ὁ δὲ Πομπήιος τῇ Νομαντίᾳ παραστρατοπεδεύων ᾤχετό ποι, καὶ ἱππέας αὐτοῦ μεταθέοντας αὐτὸν οἱ Νομαντῖνοι καταβάντες ἔκτειναν. (326) ἐπανελθὼν οὖν παρέ τασσεν ἐς ‹τὸ› πεδίον, καὶ οἱ Νομαντῖνοι καταβάντες ὑπεχώρουν κατ' ὀλίγον οἷα φεύγοντες, μέχρι ταῖς στήλαις καὶ φάραγξιν ὁ Πομπήιος ‹ἐνέπεσεν ...›

77 (327) καὶ καθ' ἡμέραν ἐν ταῖς ἀκροβολίαις ἐλασσούμενος ὑπ' ἀνδρῶν πολὺ ἐλασσόνων μετέβαινεν ἐπὶ Τερμεντίαν ὡς εὐχερέστερον ἔργον. (328) ὡς δὲ καὶ τῇδε συμβαλὼν ἑπτακοσίους τε ἀπώλεσε καὶ τὸν τὴν ἀγορὰν αὐτῷ φέροντα χιλίαρχον οἱ Τερμεντεῖς ἐτρέψαντο καὶ τρίτῃ πείρᾳ κατὰ τὴν αὐτὴν ἡμέραν ἐς ἀπόκρημνα τοὺς Ῥωμαίους συνελάσαντες πολλοὺς αὐτῶν πεζούς τε καὶ ἱππέας αὐτοῖς ἵπποις κατέωσαν ἐς τὰ ἀπόκρημνα, περιφόβως ἔχοντες οἱ λοιποὶ διενυκτέρευον ἔνοπλοι. καὶ ἅμα ἕῳ

---

319 post εὐμαρῶς add. εὐμαροῦς VM **320** Ζάκανθαν Steph.: Ζάκανθον VM **322** Οὐακκαίων VM: Ἀρουακῶν Schweig. Καικίλιος Steph.: Κεκίλιος VM (ut semper) Οὐακκαίους VM: Ἀρουακους Schweig. **325** Αὔλου ‹υἱῷ› Viereck-Roos: Αὔλῳ VM ‹τῷ› Αὔλου ci. Schweig. ἑκατὸν ci. Schweig.: αὐτὸν VM καταβάντες del. Gouk. **326** ‹τὸ› add. Mend. lacunam stat. Musgrave et Schweig; ‹ἐνέπεσεν› suppl. Schulten

circumstances and the fairest in the sharing out of the spoils. He never took the largest share, though his followers always urged him to do so, and what he did take he gave to those who had showed themselves bravest. (319) So it was that through the eight years of this war his army, though made up of different elements, never broke up into factions but always obeyed orders and was keen to face dangers — by no means an easy achievement for any commander. (320) After this, they chose Tautalus as their commander and launched an expedition against Saguntum, which Hannibal founded after his capture of it and called it Carthage after his homeland. (321) They were driven away from there, and, as they crossed the river Baetis, Caepio attacked them, until Tautalus, in a state of exhaustion, surrendered his army to Caepio, to become subjects. He removed all their weapons from them and gave them enough land that they should not revert to banditry as a result of their poverty.

76 (322) So the war with Viriathus came to an end. Our account reverts to the war with the Vaccaei and the Numantines, whom Viriathus had stirred up to revolt. Caecilius Metellus was sent out from Rome against them, with a larger army and subdued the Vaccaei, attacking them with terrifying speed as they were gathering their harvest. Termantia and Numantia remained to be dealt with. (323) Numantia was difficult to reach because of two rivers and ravines, and thick woods surrounded it. There was only one route down to the plain, and it had been closed off with ditches and blocks of stone. (324) They were excellent cavalry and infantry soldiers, about eight thousand in all; and this was the number who through their courage caused such great problems for the Romans. (325) After the winter, Metellus handed over to Quintus Pompeius, son of Aulus, who was his successor in the command, an army consisting of thirty thousand infantry and two thousand cavalry, excellently trained. Pompeius, who was encamped over against Numantia, set off for some other place, and the Numantines came down upon and killed one hundred of the cavalry who were trying to catch up with him. (326) Having returned, he marshalled his troops onto the plain, and the Numantines, having come forward, moved back a little, as though they were in flight, until Pompeius [found himself] among the blocks of stone and the ravines ...

77 (327) Having been defeated day after day in skirmishes by a much smaller number of men, he moved to Termantia, as being an easier piece of work. (328) When he attacked it, he lost seven hundred men, and the Termantines routed the tribune who was bringing him supplies; and on the same day in a third encounter they drove the Romans into a rocky area and forced many of them, both infantry and cavalry with their horses, onto the rocks (the rest were terrified and spent the night

προσιόντων τῶν πολεμίων ἐκταξάμενοι τὴν ἡμέραν ὅλην ἠγωνίζοντο ἀγχωμάλως καὶ διεκρίθησαν ὑπὸ νυκτός. (329) ὅθεν ὁ Πομπήιος ἐπὶ πολίχνης Μαλίας ἤλασεν, ἣν ἐφρούρουν οἱ Νομαντῖνοι. καὶ οἱ Μαλιεῖς, τοὺς φρουροὺς ἀνελόντες ἐξ ἐνέδρας, παρέδοσαν τὸ πολίχνιον τῷ Πομπηίῳ. (330) ὁ δὲ τά τε ὅπλα αὐτοὺς καὶ ὅμηρα αἰτήσας μετῆλθεν ἐπὶ Σηδητανίαν, ἣν ἐδῄου λήσταρχος ὄνομα Ταγγῖνος· καὶ αὐτὸν ὁ Πομπήιος ἐνίκα καὶ πολλοὺς ἔλαβεν αἰχμαλώτους. (331) τοσοῦτον δ' ἦν φρονήματος ἐν τοῖς λῃσταῖς, ὥστε τῶν αἰχμαλώτων οὐδεὶς ὑπέμεινε δουλεύειν, ἀλλ' οἱ μὲν αὐτούς, οἱ δὲ τοὺς πριαμένους ἀνῄρουν, οἱ δὲ τὰς ναῦς ἐν τῷ διάπλῳ διετίτρων.

78 (332) ὁ δὲ Πομπήιος αὖθις ἐλάσας ἐπὶ Νομαντίαν ποταμόν τινα μετωχέτευεν ἐς τὸ πεδίον ὡς λιμῷ πιέσων τὴν πόλιν. οἱ δὲ ἐργαζομένῳ τε ἐπέκειντο καὶ σαλπικτῶν χωρὶς ἐκτρέχοντες ἀθρόοι τοὺς ὀχετεύοντας ἠνώχλουν. ἔβαλλον δὲ καὶ τοὺς ἀπὸ τοῦ χάρακος ἐπιβοηθοῦντας, ἕως κατέκλεισαν ἐς τὸ στρατόπεδον. (333) καὶ σιτολογοῦσιν ἑτέροις ἐπιδραμόντες καὶ τῶνδε πολλοὺς διέφθειραν Ὀππιόν τε χιλίαρχον ἐπ' αὐτοῖς ἀνεῖλον. καὶ κατ' ἄλλο μέρος τάφρον ὀρύσσουσι Ῥωμαίοις ἐπιδραμόντες ἔκτειναν ἐς τετρακοσίους καὶ τὸν ἡγούμενον αὐτῶν. (334) ἐφ' οἷς τῷ τε Πομπηίῳ σύμβουλοι παρῆσαν ἐκ Ῥώμης καὶ τοῖς στρατιώταις (ἓξ γὰρ ἔτη διεληλύθει στρατευομένοις) διάδοχοι νεοκατάγραφοί τε καὶ ἔτι ἀγύμναστοι καὶ ἀπειροπόλεμοι. (335) μεθ' ὧν ὁ Πομπήιος, αἰδούμενός τε τὰ ἐπταισμένα καὶ ἐπειγόμενος τὴν αἰσχύνην ἀναλαβεῖν, ἐπέμενε χειμῶνος ἐν τῷ στρατοπέδῳ. (336) καὶ οἱ στρατιῶται, κρύους τε ὄντος ἐν ἀστέγῳ σταθμεύοντες καὶ πρῶτον ἄρτι πειρώμενοι τοῦ περὶ τὴν χώραν ὕδατός τε καὶ ἀέρος, κατὰ γαστέρα ἔκαμνον, καὶ διεφθείροντο ἔνιοι. (337) μέρους δ' ἐπὶ σῖτον οἰχομένου κρύψαντες ἐνέδραν οἱ Νομαντῖνοι παρ' αὐτὸ τὸ Ῥωμαίων στρατόπεδον ἠκροβολίζοντο ἐρεθίζοντες, ἕως οἱ μὲν οὐ φέροντες ἐπεξῄεσαν, οἱ δ' ἐκ τῆς ἐνέδρας ἀνίσταντο· καὶ Ῥωμαῖοι πολλοὶ μὲν ἐκ τοῦ πλήθους, πολλοὶ δὲ τῶν ἐπιφανῶν ἀπέθανον. οἱ δὲ Νομαντῖνοι, καὶ τοῖς τὸν σῖτον φέρουσιν ἀπαντήσαντες, ἔκτειναν καὶ τῶνδε πολλούς.

79 (338) καὶ ὁ Πομπήιος, τοσοῖσδε συνενεχθεὶς κακοῖς, ἐς τὰς πόλεις μετὰ τῶν συμβούλων ἀνεζεύγνυε, χειμάσων τὸ ἐπίλοιπον, τοῦ ἔαρος προσδοκῶν ἥξειν οἱ διάδοχον. καὶ δεδιὼς κατηγορίαν ἔπρασσεν ἐς τοὺς Νομαντίνους κρύφα τοῦ πολέμου διαλύσεις. (339) οἱ δὲ καὶ αὐτοὶ κάμνοντες ἤδη φόνῳ τε πολλῷ ἀρίστων καὶ γῆς ἀργίᾳ καὶ τροφῶν ἀπορίᾳ καὶ μήκει τοῦ πολέμου, μακροῦ παρὰ προσδοκίαν γεγονότος, ἐπρέσβευον

---

334 τῷ τε Schweig.: τότε VM   338 τοσοῖσδε Exc.: τοσοῖς VM   κακοῖς Exc.: om. VM

in full armour). At dawn when the enemy came out, they took up position and fought the whole day with neither side prevailing, until night separated them. (329) From there, Pompeius attacked the little town of Malia, which the Numantines had garrisoned. The inhabitants of Malia killed the garrison in an ambush and handed over the village to Pompeius. (330) He demanded that they hand over their arms and provide hostages, and left for Sedetania, which was being ravaged by a bandit-chieftain called Tanginus. Pompeius defeated him and captured many prisoners. (331) The courage of the bandits was so great that none of those who were captured endured slavery, but some killed themselves, others those who had purchased them, and others sank the ships in which they were being transported away.

78 (332) Pompeius again attacked Numantia, and he diverted a certain river into the plain, in order to press hard on the city by means of starving it. The Numantines attacked him while he was engaged in this work and, without signals from trumpets, rushed out as a body and disrupted those who were digging the channels. They hurled missiles at those who came to help them from the palisade, until they shut them up in the camp. (333) They also attacked some other men who were collecting forage and killed many of them too, amongst others the tribune, Oppius. In another place, they attacked some Romans who were digging a ditch and killed about four hundred, including their leader. (334) At this point, there came to Pompeius from Rome senatorial commissioners and replacements for his soldiers, who had served six years, who had been newly recruited and were still untrained and inexperienced in war. (335) Pompeius, who was ashamed at the blunders he had made and was keen to remove the shame, remained with these recruits in camp during the winter. (336) The soldiers, who were camping without shelter, though it was cold, and were experiencing the water and air of the country for the first time, suffered sickness in the stomach, and some of them died. (337) When a section of the soldiers went out to collect forage, the Numantines hid in ambush near the Roman camp and provoked them by hurling missiles at them, until the Romans, unable to endure this, made a sortie, and the Numantines emerged from the ambush. Many Romans were killed, both ordinary soldiers and people of distinction. The Numantines also met up with those who were bringing in the forage and killed many of those also.

79 (338) Pompeius, having met with such disasters, retired with the senatorial commissioners to the cities, staying there for the remainder of the winter and expecting that his successor would come in the spring. Because he was afraid that he would be prosecuted, he secretly undertook negotiations with the Numantines about bringing the war to an end. (339) They for their part were now tired of the slaughter of many of their best men, their inability to work the land, their shortage of food and the length of the war, which had gone on far longer than they had expected,

ἐς Πομπήιον. (340) ὁ δ' ἐς μὲν τὸ φανερὸν ἐκέλευεν αὐτοὺς Ῥωμαίοις ἐπιτρέπειν (οὐ γὰρ εἰδέναι συνθήκας ἑτέρας Ῥωμαίων ἀξίας), λάθρᾳ δ' ὑπισχνεῖτο, ἃ ἔμελλεν ποιήσειν. (341) καὶ συνθεμένων ἐκείνων καὶ ἐπιτρεψάντων ἑαυτοὺς ὅμηρά τε καὶ αἰχμάλωτα ᾔτησε καὶ τοὺς αὐτομόλους καὶ πάντα ἔλαβεν. ᾔτησε δὲ καὶ ἀργυρίου τάλαντα τριάκοντα· ὧν μέρος αὐτίκα ἔδοσαν οἱ Νομαντῖνοι, καὶ τὰ λοιπὰ ὁ Πομπήιος ἀνέμενεν. (342) παραγενομένου δ' αὐτῷ διαδόχου Μάρκου Ποπιλίου Λαίνα, οἱ μὲν ἔφερον τὰ λοιπὰ τῶν χρημάτων, ὁ δ', ἀπηλλαγμένος μὲν τοῦ περὶ τοῦ πολέμου δέους τῷ παρεῖναι τὸν διάδοχον, τὰς δὲ συνθήκας εἰδὼς αἰσχράς τε καὶ ἄνευ Ῥωμαίων γενομένας, ἠρνεῖτο μὴ συνθέσθαι τοῖς Νομαντίνοις. (343) καὶ οἱ μὲν αὐτὸν ἤλεγχον ἐπὶ μάρτυσι τοῖς τότε παρατυχοῦσιν ἀπό τε βουλῆς καὶ ἱππάρχοις καὶ χιλιάρχοις αὐτοῦ Πομπηίου, ὁ δὲ Ποπίλιος αὐτοὺς ἐς Ῥώμην ἔπεμπε δικασομένους τῷ Πομπηίῳ. (344) κρίσεως δ' ἐν τῇ βουλῇ γενομένης Νομαντῖνοι μὲν καὶ Πομπήιος ἐς ἀντιλογίαν ἦλθον, τῇ βουλῇ δ' ἔδοξε πολεμεῖν Νομαντίνοις. (345) καὶ ὁ Ποπίλιος ἐνέβαλεν ἐς τοὺς γείτονας αὐτῶν Λούσονας, οὐδὲν δ' ἐργασάμενος (ἧκε γὰρ αὐτῷ διάδοχος ἐπὶ τὴν στρατηγίαν Ὁστίλιος Μαγκῖνος) ἀνέζευξεν ἐς Ῥώμην.

80 (346) ὁ δὲ Μαγκῖνος τοῖς Νομαντίνοις συμβαλὼν ἡττᾶτό τε πολλάκις καὶ τέλος ἀναιρουμένων πολλῶν ἐς τὸ στρατόπεδον ἔφυγεν. λόγου δὲ ψευδοῦς ἐμπεσόντος, ὅτι Νομαντίνοις ἔρχονται βοηθοῦντες Κάνταβροί τε καὶ Οὐακκαῖοι, δείσας ἄπυρον τὴν νύκτα διήγαγεν ὅλην ἐν σκότῳ, φεύγων ἐς ἔρημον τὸ Νωβελίωνός ποτε χαράκωμα. (347) καὶ μεθ' ἡμέραν ἐς αὐτὸ συγκλεισθείς, οὔτε κατεσκευασμένον οὔτε ὠχυρωμένον, περιεχόντων αὐτὸν τῶν Νομαντίνων καὶ πάντας ἀποκτενεῖν ἀπειλούντων, εἰ μὴ συνθοῖτο εἰρήνην, συνέθετο ἐπὶ ἴσῃ καὶ ὁμοίᾳ Ῥωμαίοις καὶ Νομαντίνοις. (348) καὶ ὁ μὲν ἐπὶ τούτοις ὤμνυε τοῖς Νομαντίνοις, οἱ δ' ἐν ἄστει πυθόμενοι χαλεπῶς ἔφερον ὡς ἐπὶ αἰσχίσταις πάνυ σπονδαῖς καὶ τὸν ἕτερον τῶν ὑπάτων Αἰμίλιον Λέπιδον ἐς Ἰβηρίαν ἐξέπεμπον, Μαγκῖνον δ' ἀνεκάλουν ἐς κρίσιν. (349) καὶ τῷδε μὲν ἔσποντο πρέσβεις Νομαντίνων· ὁ δ' Αἰμίλιος, ἀναμένων καὶ ὅδε τὰς ἐκ Ῥώμης ἀποκρίσεις καὶ τὴν ἀργίαν οὐ φέρων (ὡς γὰρ ἐπὶ δόξαν ἢ κέρδος ἢ θριάμβου φιλοτιμίαν ἐξῆεσάν τινες ἐς τὰς στρατηγίας, οὐκ ἐπὶ τὸ τῇ πόλει συμφέρον), Οὐακκαίων κατεψεύδετο ὡς ἀγορὰν ἐν τῷδε τῷ πολέμῳ Νομαντίνοις παρασχόντων· (350) καὶ τὴν γῆν αὐτῶν κατέτρεχεν Παλλαντίαν τε πόλιν, ἣ μεγίστη Οὐακκαίων ἐστίν, οὐδὲν ἐξαμαρτοῦσαν ἐς τὰ συγκείμενα, ἐπολιόρκει καὶ

---

345 Ὁστίλιος Schweig.: Ἀτείλιος V Ἀτίλιος M **346** πολλάκις Exc.: πολλάκι VM **347** περιεχόντων Exc.: περισχόντων VM τῶν Exc.: om. VM ἀποκτενεῖν Steph.: ἀποκτείνειν VM Exc. **350** τε Exc.: om. VM

and sent ambassadors to Pompeius. (340) Publicly he ordered them to surrender to the Romans, saying that he knew that no other terms would be regarded as acceptable by the Romans; but secretly he promised them what he would do. (341) The Numantines reached an agreement with him and surrendered themselves, and he demanded hostages and their prisoners of war and deserters and received all these. He also demanded thirty talents of silver, of which the Numantines gave him part and Pompeius awaited the arrival of the rest. (342) When his successor, Marcus Popilius Laenas, arrived they brought him the remainder of the money, but he, no longer being afraid of the war now his successor was present and knowing that the agreement was disgraceful and made without the assent of the Romans, denied that he had come to terms with the Numantines. (343) When they called as witnesses those from the senate who happened to be there and also Pompeius' own cavalry commanders and tribunes, Popilius sent them to Rome to lodge an accusation against Pompeius. (344) The trial took place in the senate, and the Numantines and Pompeius contradicted each other; but the senate decreed that the war against the Numantines should continue. (345) Popilius attacked their neighbours, the Lusones, but when his successor in the command, Hostilius Mancinus, arrived, he had achieved nothing and returned to Rome.

80 (346) Mancinus attacked the Numantines and was defeated many times, and finally, having lost many men, fled to his camp. When a false rumour arose that the Cantabrians and the Vaccaei were coming to help the Numantines, out of fear he spent the whole night in the dark without lighting a fire, and fled away in the darkness to a remote place where once Nobilior had built a camp. (347) When day came he shut himself up there, even though he neither had equipment nor had fortified his position; and when the Numantines encircled him and threatened to kill everyone if he did not agree to peace, he made an agreement on equal terms between the Romans and the Numantines. (348) He swore on oath to the Numantines on these terms; but when those in the capital learnt of it, they were outraged at this most disgraceful treaty and sent the other consul, Aemilius Lepidus, to Iberia and summoned Mancinus to trial. (349) Ambassadors from the Numantines followed him there; but Aemilius, who was also waiting for the decision from Rome and could not bear being idle (for some sought the command for glory or gain or the honour of a triumph, not for the benefit of the city), falsely alleged that the Vaccaei had provided the Numantines with supplies during the war. (350) He ravaged their land and laid siege to the city of Pallantia, which is the largest city of the Vaccaei,

Βροῦτον, ἐφ' ἕτερα τῆς Ἰβηρίας ἀπεσταλμένον, ὥς μοι προείρηται, κηδεστὴν ὄντα οἱ, τοῦδε τοῦ ἔργου μετασχεῖν ἔπεισεν.

81 (351) κατέλαβον δ' αὐτοὺς ἀπὸ Ῥώμης πρέσβεις Κίννας τε καὶ Καικίλιος, οἳ τὴν βουλὴν ἔφασαν ἀπορεῖν, εἰ τοσῶνδε πταισμάτων σφίσιν ἐν Ἰβηρίᾳ γενομένων ὁ Αἰμίλιος πόλεμον ἕτερον ἀρεῖται, καὶ ψήφισμα ἐπέδοσαν αὐτῷ προαγορεῦον Αἰμίλιον Οὐακκαίοις μὴ πολεμεῖν. (352) ὁ δὲ ἀρξάμενός τε ἤδη τοῦ πολέμου καὶ τὴν βουλὴν τοῦτ' ἀγνοεῖν ἡγούμενος, ἀγνοεῖν δ', ὅτι καὶ Βροῦτος αὐτῷ συνεπιλαμβάνει καὶ σῖτον καὶ χρήματα καὶ στρατιὰν Οὐακκαῖοι τοῖς Νομαντίνοις παρέσχον, ἔσεσθαι δὲ καὶ τὴν ἀνάζευξιν τοῦ πολέμου φοβερὰν ὑπολαβὼν καὶ σχεδὸν Ἰβηρίας ὅλης διάλυσιν, εἰ καταφρονήσειαν ὡς δεδιότων, τοὺς μὲν ἀμφὶ τὸν Κίνναν ἀπράκτους ἀπέλυσεν καὶ τάδε αὐτὰ ἐπέστειλε τῇ βουλῇ, αὐτὸς δ' ὀχυρωσάμενος φρούριον μηχανὰς ἐν αὐτῷ συνεπήγνυτο καὶ σῖτον συνέφερε. (353) Φλάκκος δ' αὐτῷ σιτολογῶν, ἐνέδρας ἐκφανείσης, εὐμηχάνως διέδωκεν, ὅτι Παλλαντίαν ἐξεῖλεν Αἰμίλιος· καὶ τοῦ στρατοῦ συναλαλάξαντος ὡς ἐπὶ νίκῃ, πυθόμενοι τούτων οἱ βάρβαροι καὶ ἀληθῆ νομίσαντες ἀπεχώρουν.

82 (354) Φλάκκος μὲν δὴ τὴν ἀγορὰν κινδυνεύουσαν ὧδε περιέσωζε, μακρᾶς δὲ τῆς ἐπὶ τῇ Παλλαντίᾳ πολιορκίας οὔσης αἱ τροφαὶ Ῥωμαίους ἐπέλειπον, καὶ λιμὸς ἥπτετο αὐτῶν, καὶ τὰ ὑποζύγια πάντα ἔφθαρτο, καὶ πολλοὶ τῶν ἀνθρώπων ἐξ ἀπορίας ἀπέθνησκον. (355) οἱ στρατηγοὶ δέ, Αἰμίλιός τε καὶ [ὁ] Βροῦτος, ἐς μὲν πολὺ διεκαρτέρουν, ἡσσώμενοι δ' ὑπὸ τοῦ κακοῦ νυκτὸς ἄφνω περὶ ἐσχάτην φυλακὴν ἐκέλευον ἀναζευγνύναι· χιλίαρχοί τε καὶ λοχαγοὶ περιθέοντες ἐπέσπευδον ἅπαντας ἐς τοῦτο πρὸ ἔω. (356) οἱ δὲ σὺν θορύβῳ τά τε ἄλλα πάντα καὶ τοὺς τραυματίας καὶ τοὺς νοσοῦντας ἀπέλιπον, συμπλεκομένους τε σφίσι καὶ δεομένους. καὶ αὐτοῖς ἀτάκτου καὶ θορυβώδους τῆς ἀναχωρήσεως γιγνομένης καὶ φυγῇ μάλιστα ὁμοίας οἱ Παλλάντιοι πανταχόθεν ἐπικείμενοι πολλὰ ἔβλαπτον ἐξ ἠοῦς ἐπὶ ἑσπέραν. (357) νυκτὸς δ' ἐπιλαβούσης Ῥωμαῖοι μὲν ἐς τὰ πεδία ἑαυτοὺς ἐρρίπτουν ἀνὰ μέρος, ὡς τύχοιεν, ἄσιτοί τε καὶ κατάκοποι, οἱ δὲ Παλλάντιοι θεοῦ σφᾶς ἀποτρέποντος ἀνεχώρουν.

83 (358) καὶ τάδε μὲν ἦν περὶ τὸν Αἰμίλιον, Ῥωμαῖοι δ' αὐτὰ πυθόμενοι τὸν μὲν Αἰμίλιον παρέλυσαν τῆς στρατηγίας τε καὶ ὑπατείας, καὶ ἰδιώτης ἐς Ῥώμην ὑπέστρεφεν καὶ χρήμασιν ἐπεζημιοῦτο· Μαγκίνῳ δ' ἐδίκαζον καὶ τοῖς πρέσβεσι τοῖς Νομαντίνων. (359) οἱ μὲν δὴ τὰς

---

351 ἀρεῖται Musgrave: αἱρεῖται VM αἱρεῖτε Exc.   **354** ἥπτετο αὐτῶν Schweig.: εἵπτετο αὐτοῖς VM   **355** ὁ del. Steph.   **358** ὑπατείας Steph.: ὑπατίας VM

even though it had done nothing contrary to the treaty; and persuaded Brutus, his kinsman by marriage, who had been sent (as I have stated already) to the other part of Iberia, to join him in this enterprise.

81 (351) Ambassadors from Rome, Cinna and Caecilius, caught up with them. They said that the senate was at a loss that, with so many disasters having befallen them in Iberia, Aemilius was undertaking another war, and they handed over to him a decree, forbidding Aemilius from fighting the Vaccaei. (352) He, however, had already begun the war and thought that the senate did not know this and also did not know that Brutus had joined him and that the Vaccaei had supplied food, money and troops to the Numantines; and also that a withdrawal from the war was something to be feared and would virtually mean the loss of Iberia, if the Iberians despised them as cowards. He sent away Cinna's party, which had failed to achieve any of their intentions, and sent a message stating these things to the senate. He himself fortified his encampment, constructed siege machinery inside it and brought in corn. (353) Flaccus was gathering corn for him when an ambush was discovered. Flaccus cleverly gave it out that Aemilius had captured Pallantia. The soldiers shouted out as at a victory, and the barbarians, hearing of this and believing it to be true, withdrew.

82 (354) In this way Flaccus saved the supplies which were in danger; but, as the siege of Pallantia went on for a long time, the Romans' food supplies ran out and they suffered from hunger. All their beasts of burden perished and many of the men died of starvation. (355) Their generals, Aemilius and Brutus, endured this for a long time, but, overcome by difficulties, they suddenly ordered a withdrawal one night at about the last watch. The tribunes and centurions ran about, urging all the men to their task before dawn broke. (356) In the confusion they left everything behind, including the wounded and the sick, who clung to them, begging not to be left. The withdrawal was disorderly and confused and much more like a rout. The Pallantians harried them on every side and inflicted much damage from dawn to dusk. (357) As night fell, the Romans threw themselves down onto the plains, section by section as they happened to be, without food and in a state of exhaustion; but the Pallantians, turned back by a god, withdrew.

83 (358) This is what happened to Aemilius. When the Romans heard of it, they relieved Aemilius of his command and his consulship and he returned to Rome as a private citizen and was punished with a monetary fine; and they were also deciding the case between Mancinus and the ambassadors of the Numantines. (359) They

συνθήκας, ἃς ἐπεποίηντο πρὸς Μαγκῖνον, ἐπεδείκνυον· ὁ δὲ τὴν αἰτίαν
αὐτῶν ἐς Πομπήιον ἀνέφερεν, τὸν πρὸ αὐτοῦ γενόμενον στρατηγόν, ὡς
ἀργὸν καὶ ἄπορον τὸν στρατὸν ἐγχειρίσαντά οἱ καὶ δι' αὐτὸ κἀκεῖνον
ἡσσημένον τε πολλάκις καὶ συνθήκας ὁμοίας αὐτῷ θέμενον πρὸς τοὺς
Νομαντίνους· ὅθεν ἔφη καὶ τὸν πόλεμον τόνδε, παρὰ τὰς συνθήκας
ἐκείνας ὑπὸ Ῥωμαίων ἐψηφισμένον, ἀπαίσιον αὐτοῖς γεγονέναι. (360) οἱ δ'
ἐχαλέπαινον μὲν ἀμφοτέροις ὁμοίως, ἀπέφυγε δ' ὅμως Πομπήιος ὡς περὶ
τῶνδε κριθεὶς καὶ πάλαι. Μαγκῖνον δ' ἔγνωσαν ἐκδοῦναι τοῖς Νομαντίνοις,
ἄνευ σφῶν αἰσχρὰς συνθήκας πεποιημένον, ᾧ λόγῳ καὶ Σαυνίταις οἱ
πατέρες, ὅμοια χωρὶς αὐτῶν συνθεμένους, ἡγεμόνας εἴκοσιν ἐξεδεδώκεσαν.
(361) Μαγκῖνον μὲν δὴ Φούριος ἀγαγὼν εἰς Ἰβηρίαν γυμνὸν παρεδίδου
τοῖς Νομαντίνοις· (362) οἱ δ' οὐκ ἐδέξαντο. στρατηγὸς δ' ἐπ' αὐτοὺς
αἱρεθεὶς Καλπούρνιος Πείσων οὐδ' ἤλασεν ἐπὶ Νομαντίαν, ἀλλ' ἐς τὴν
Παλλαντίων γῆν ἐσβαλὼν καὶ μικρὰ δῃώσας ἐχείμαζεν ἐν Καρπητανίᾳ τὸ
ἐπίλοιπον τῆς ἀρχῆς.

84 (363) ἐν δὲ Ῥώμῃ κάμνων ὁ δῆμος ἐπὶ τοῖς Νομαντίνοις, μακροῦ καὶ
δυσχεροῦς τοῦ πολέμου σφίσι παρὰ προσδοκίαν γεγονότος, ἡροῦντο
Κορνήλιον Σκιπίωνα, τὸν Καρχηδόνα ἑλόντα, αὖθις ὑπατεύειν, ὡς μόνον
ἐπικρατῆσαι τῶν Νομαντίνων δυνάμενον. (364) ὁ δὲ καὶ τότε ἦν ἔτι
νεώτερος τῆς νενομισμένης τοῖς ὑπατεύουσιν ἡλικίας· ἡ οὖν βουλὴ πάλιν,
ὥσπερ ἐπὶ Καρχηδονίοις αὐτοῦ χειροτονουμένου [Σκιπίωνος], ἐψηφίσατο
τοὺς δημάρχους λῦσαι τὸν περὶ τῆς ἡλικίας νόμον καὶ τοῦ ἐπιόντος
ἔτους ‹αὖθις› θέσθαι. (365) οὕτω μὲν ὁ Σκιπίων αὖθις ὑπατεύων ἐς
Νομαντίαν ἠπείγετο, στρατιὰν δ' ἐκ καταλόγου μὲν οὐκ ἔλαβεν, πολλῶν
τε πολέμων ὄντων καὶ πολλῶν ἀνδρῶν ἐν Ἰβηρίᾳ, ἐθελοντὰς δέ τινας, ἔκ
τε πόλεων καὶ βασιλέων ἐς χάριν ἰδίαν πεμφθέντας αὐτῷ, συγχωρούσης
τῆς βουλῆς, ἐπηγάγετο καὶ πελάτας ἐκ Ῥώμης καὶ φίλους πεντακοσίους,
οὓς ἐς ἴλην καταλέξας ἐκάλει φίλων ἴλην. (366) πάντας δὲ ἐς
τετρακισχιλίους γενομένους παραδοὺς ἄγειν ἀδελφιδῷ Βουτεῶνι σὺν
ὀλίγοις αὐτὸς προεξώρμησεν ἐς Ἰβηρίαν ἐπὶ τὸ στρατόπεδον,
πυνθανόμενος αὐτὸ γέμειν ἀργίας καὶ στάσεων καὶ τρυφῆς, εὖ εἰδώς, ὅτι
μὴ κρατήσει πολεμίων, πρὶν κατασχεῖν τῶν ἰδίων ἐγκρατῶς.

85 (367) ἐλθὼν δὲ ἐμπόρους τε πάντας ἐξήλαυνε καὶ ἑταίρας καὶ μάντεις
καὶ θύτας, οἷς διὰ τὰς δυσπραξίας οἱ στρατιῶται περιδεεῖς γεγονότες
ἐχρῶντο συνεχῶς· ἔς τε τὸ μέλλον ἀπεῖπε μηδὲν ἐσφέρεσθαι τῶν
περισσῶν, μηδὲ ἱερεῖον ἐς μαντείαν πεποιημένον. (368) ἐκέλευσεν δὲ καὶ

---

359 πολλάκις Exc.: πολλάκι VM   **360** ὅμως Steph.: ὁμοίως VM ὅμοίος V (m.2)   **361**
Φούριος Steph.: Φρούριος VM Exc.   **362** Καρπητανίᾳ Steph.: Καρπιτανίᾳ VM   **364**
Σκιπίωνος del. Nipperdey αὖθις add. Mend.   **365** φίλων Steph.: φιλον VM   **367** πεποι-
ημένον VM: πεπλασμένον Gouk.

produced the treaty which they had made with Mancinus; but he transferred the blame for the treaty onto Pompeius, who had been the general before him, as having passed on to him an army which was lazy and ill-equipped and because of which he too had been defeated on many occasions and had concluded a treaty with the Numantines, similar to that which he himself had made; as a result, he said, this war, which had been decreed by the Romans in violation of the treaty, had been ill-omened for them. (360) The Romans were angry with both to an equal extent, but Pompeius escaped condemnation, on the grounds that he had been tried on these matters already. They decreed that Mancinus should be surrendered to the Numantines for having made a disgraceful treaty without their permission, on the grounds that their ancestors had surrendered twenty officers to the Samnites, having made a similar treaty without their permission. (361) Furius took Mancinus to Iberia and handed him over naked to the Numantines, who refused to accept him. (362) Calpurnius Piso was chosen as general against them, but did not attack Numantia but invaded the territory of the Pallantians, and, having undertaken a small amount of plundering, wintered in Carpetania for the remainder of his command.

84 (363) In Rome the people, wearied by the Numantines because the war had been far longer and far more difficult for them than they had expected, chose Cornelius Scipio, who had captured Carthage, to be consul again, as the only man capable of defeating the Numantines. (364) Even at that date he was younger than the age fixed for those holding the consulship. Therefore the senate once again, just as when he was voted in to fight against the Carthaginians, decreed that the tribunes should repeal the age-law and introduce it again the following year. (365) Thus Scipio, consul once again, hurried to Numantia, but he did not recruit an army by a levy, since there were many wars going on and many men in Iberia, but took a number of volunteers, sent to him by cities and kings from personal goodwill, with the agreement of the senate; and five hundred clients and friends of his from Rome, whom he enrolled into a troop, which he called the troop of friends. (366) All these, some four thousand in total, he handed over to his nephew, Buteo, to lead, while he, with a few men pushed on ahead into Iberia to the army's camp, having heard that it was full of sloth, quarrels and luxury, and knowing well that he would not defeat the enemy before he had established a firm grip on his own soldiers.

85 (367) On his arrival, he expelled all the traders, prostitutes, clairvoyants and diviners, whom the soldiers consulted continually, having become extremely anxious because of their lack of success; and for the future he banned the bringing in to the camp of all unnecessary items, even a sacrificial victim, prepared for divination. (368) He also ordered the wagons and the superfluous items which were

τὰς ἁμάξας καὶ τὰ περισσὰ τῶν ἐς αὐτὰς τιθεμένων καὶ τὰ ὑποζύγια, χωρὶς ὧν αὐτὸς ὑπελείπετο, πραθῆναι. καὶ σκεῦος οὐκ ἐξῆν ἐς δίαιταν ἔχειν οὐδενὶ πλὴν ὀβελοῦ καὶ χύτρας χαλκῆς καὶ ἐκπώματος ἑνός. τά τε σιτία αὐτοῖς ὥριστο κρέα ζεστὰ καὶ ὀπτὰ εἶναι. (369) κλίνας τε ἀπεῖπεν ἔχειν καὶ πρῶτος ἐπὶ στιβάδων ἀνεπαύετο. ἀπεῖπεν δὲ καὶ ὁδεύοντας ἡμιόνοις ἐπικαθέζεσθαι· τί γὰρ ἐν πολέμῳ προσδοκᾶν ἔφη παρ' ἀνδρὸς οὐδὲ βαδίζειν δυναμένου; κἂν τοῖς ἀλείμμασι καὶ λουτροῖς ἑαυτοὺς ἤλειφον, ἐπισκώπτοντος τοῦ Σκιπίωνος, ὡς αἱ ἡμίονοι, χεῖρας οὐκ ἔχουσαι, χρήζουσι τριβόντων. (370) οὕτω μὲν αὐτοὺς ἐς σωφροσύνην μετέβαλλεν ἀθρόως, εἴθιζεν δὲ καὶ ἐς αἰδῶ καὶ φόβον, δυσπρόσιτος ὢν καὶ δυσχερὴς ἐς τὰς χάριτας, καὶ μάλιστα τὰς παρανόμους. (371) ἔλεγέν τε πολλάκις τοὺς μὲν αὐστηροὺς καὶ ἐννόμους τῶν στρατηγῶν τοῖς οἰκείοις, τοὺς δὲ εὐχερεῖς καὶ φιλοδώρους τοῖς πολεμίοις εἶναι χρησίμους· τὰ γὰρ στρατόπεδα τοῖς μὲν εἶναι κεχαρμένα τε καὶ καταφρονητικά, τοῖς δὲ σκυθρωπὰ μέν, εὐπειθῆ δὲ καὶ πᾶσιν ἕτοιμα.

86 (372) οὐ μὴν οὐδ' ὧς ἐτόλμα πολεμεῖν, πρὶν αὐτοὺς γυμνάσαι πόνοις πολλοῖς. τὰ οὖν ἀγχοτάτω πεδία πάντα περιιὼν ἑκάστης ἡμέρας ἄλλο μετ' ἄλλο στρατόπεδον ἤγειρέ τε καὶ καθήρει, καὶ τάφρους ὤρυσσε βαθυτάτας καὶ ἐνεπίμπλη, τείχη τε μεγάλα ᾠκοδόμει καὶ κατέφερεν, αὐτὸς ἐξ ἠοῦς ἐς ἑσπέραν ἅπαντα ἐφορῶν. (373) τὰς δὲ ὁδοιπορίας, ἵνα μή τις ὡς πάλαι διασκιδνῷτο, ἦγεν ἐν πλινθίοις ἀεί, καὶ τὴν δεδομένην ἑκάστῳ τάξιν οὐκ ἦν ἐναλλάξαι. περιιών τε τὴν ὁδοιπορίαν καὶ τὰ πολλὰ οὐραγῶν τοὺς μὲν ἀρρωστοῦντας ἐπὶ τοὺς ἵππους ἀνεβίβαζεν ἀντὶ τῶν ἱππέων, τὰ δὲ βαροῦντα τὰς ἡμιόνους ἐς τοὺς πεζοὺς διεμέριζεν. (374) εἰ δὲ σταθμεύοι, τοὺς μὲν προφύλακας τῆς ἡμέρας ἐκ τῆς ὁδοιπορίας ἔδει περὶ τὸν χάρακα ἵστασθαι καὶ ἱππέων ἑτέραν ἴλην περιτρέχειν· οἱ δ' ἄλλοι τὰ ἔργα διῄρηντο, καὶ τοῖς μὲν ταφρεύειν ἐτέτακτο, τοῖς δὲ τειχίζειν, τοῖς δὲ σκηνοποιεῖν, χρόνου τε μῆκος ὡρίζετο αὐτοῖς καὶ διεμετρεῖτο.

87 (375) ὅτε δ' εἴκασεν ὀξὺ καὶ εὐπειθὲς αὐτῷ καὶ φερέπονον γεγονέναι τὸ στράτευμα, μετέβαινεν ἀγχοῦ τῶν Νομαντίνων. προφυλακὰς δέ, ὥσπερ τινές, ἐπὶ φρουρίων οὐκ ἐποιεῖτο· οὐδὲ διήρει ποι τὸν στρατὸν ὅλως, τοῦ μή τινος ἐν ἀρχῇ γενομένου πταίσματος εὐκαταφρόνητον τοῖς πολεμίοις αὐτὸν γενέσθαι, καὶ τέως καταφρονοῦσιν. (376) οὐδ' ἐπεχείρει τοῖς ἐχθροῖς, ἔτι περισκοπῶν αὐτόν τε τὸν πόλεμον καὶ τὸν καιρὸν αὐτοῦ καὶ τὴν τῶν Νομαντίνων ὁρμήν, ἐς ὅ τι τρέψοιντο. τὰ δ' ὀπίσω τοῦ στρατοπέδου πάντα ἐχορτολόγει καὶ τὸν σῖτον ἔκειρεν ἔτι χλωρόν. (377) ὡς δὲ αὐτῷ ταῦτα ἐξετεθέριστο καὶ ἐς τὸ πρόσθεν ἔδει βαδίζειν, ὁδὸς

---

371 κεχαρμένα Steph.: κεχαρισμένα VM   375 ἐποιεῖτο Steph.: ἐποιήτο VM   376 ἔτι χλωρόν Steph.: ἐπίχλωρον VM

loaded onto them to be sold, and also the draught animals, except for those which he himself ordered to be kept. No one was permitted to possess any equipment for cooking except a spit, a bronze cooking-pot and one drinking-cup. Their food was limited to boiled and roasted meat. (369) He forbade them to have beds and was himself the first to take his rest on a straw mattress. He also prohibited them from riding on mules while on the march. "For what is to be expected in war," he said, "of a man incapable of marching on foot?" When they were rubbing themselves down with oil and when in the baths, they applied the oil themselves, since Scipio made a joke that it was those who, like mules, had no hands, that needed others to rub them down. (370) In this way he converted them all to self-control, and accustomed them to respect and fear him, since he was not easy of access and grudging in giving favours, especially those which were forbidden by regulations. (371) He often said that those generals who were austere and observed the rules were beneficial to their own, those who were easy-going and fond of giving presents were beneficial to the enemy; for the armies of the latter were happy but insubordinate, those of the former had a scowling face, but took orders and were ready for anything.

86 (372) Even so he did not dare to begin the war until he had trained them with many hard tasks. Going round all the plains that were nearest to hand, he erected each day another camp and then demolished it, dug deep ditches and then filled them in, built large walls and took them down again, he himself overseeing everything from dawn to dusk. (373) During the marches, to avoid men being scattered as had happened in the past, he led them in square formations, and no one was allowed to change the position assigned to him. Going along the line of march, and spending much time at the rear, he mounted the sick on horses in place of the cavalrymen, and distributed among the infantry loads that were weighing down the mules. (374) When he set up camp, those who had formed the advanced guard on the march during the day had to stand around the encampment while another troop of cavalry rode round the outskirts. The remainder divided up the various tasks: some he set to dig the ditches, some to build walls, some to set up the tents, and he defined and measured the time given to them for this.

87 (375) When he judged that the army had become eager, obedient to himself and capable of sustaining hard labour, he moved closer to the Numantines. He did not, as some do, place forward guards in fortified posts. He never in any way divided the army to avoid some disaster occurring at the outset and his being despised by the enemy, who were already contemptuous of the Romans. (376) He did not even attack the enemy, as he was still studying the war itself and the opportunities it offered and the intentions of the Numantines, should they take any particular turn. He gathered forage from all the land behind the camp and cut the corn while it was still green. (377) When all these had been harvested and he needed to move forward, there was a short way past Numantia to the plains and many advised him to go that

μὲν ἦν παρὰ τὴν Νομαντίαν ἐπὶ τὰ πεδία σύντομος, καὶ πολλοὶ συνεβούλευον ἐς αὐτὴν τραπέσθαι. ὃ δ᾽ ἔφη τὴν ἐπάνοδον δεδιέναι, κούφων μὲν τότε τῶν πολεμίων ὄντων, καὶ ἐκ πόλεως ὁρμωμένων καὶ ἐς πόλιν ἀφορμώντων· (378) "οἱ δ᾽ ἡμέτεροι βαρεῖς ἐπανίασιν ὡς ἀπὸ σιτολογίας καὶ κατάκοποι καὶ κτήνη καὶ ἀμάξας καὶ φορτία ἄγουσιν. δυσχερής τε ὅλως καὶ ἀνόμοιος ὁ ἀγών· ἡσσωμένοις μὲν γὰρ πολὺς ὁ κίνδυνος, νικῶσι δὲ οὐ μέγα τὸ ἔργον οὐδὲ ἐπικερδές." (379) εἶναι δ᾽ ἄλογον κινδυνεύειν ἐπὶ ὀλίγοις καὶ στρατηγὸν ἀμελῆ τὸν ἀγωνιζόμενον πρὸ τῆς χρείας, ἀγαθὸν δὲ τὸν ἐν μόναις παρακινδυνεύοντα ταῖς ἀνάγκαις. συγκρίνων δ᾽ ἔφη καὶ τοὺς ἰατροὺς μὴ χρῆσθαι τομαῖς μηδὲ καύσεσι πρὸ φαρμάκων. (380) ταῦτ᾽ εἰπὼν ἐκέλευσεν τοῖς ἡγεμόσιν τὴν μακροτέραν περιάγειν. καὶ συνεξῄει τότε μὲν ἐς τὸ πέραν τοῦ στρατοπέδου, ὕστερον δ᾽ ἐς τὰ Οὐακκαίων, ὅθεν οἱ Νομαντῖνοι τὰς τροφὰς ἐωνοῦντο, κείρων ἅπαντα καὶ τὰ χρήσιμα ἐς τὰς ἑαυτοῦ τροφὰς συλλέγων, τὰ δὲ περιττὰ σωρεύων τε καὶ κατακαίων.

88 (381) ἐν δέ τινι πεδίῳ τῆς Παλλαντίας, ὄνομα Κοπλανίῳ, πολλοὺς ἐπὶ τῶν ὀρῶν ὑπὸ λόφοις ἔκρυψαν οἱ Παλλάντιοι καὶ ἑτέροις ἐς τὸ φανερὸν τοὺς σιτολογοῦντας ἠνώχλουν. (382) ὁ δὲ Ῥουτίλιον Ῥοῦφον, συγγραφέα τῶνδε τῶν ἔργων, τότε χιλιαρχοῦντα, ἐκέλευσε τέσσαρας ἱππέων ἴλας λαβόντα ἀναστεῖλαι τοὺς ἐνοχλοῦντας. Ῥοῦφος μὲν οὖν ὑποχωροῦσιν αὐτοῖς ἀμέτρως εἵπετο καὶ φεύγουσιν ἐς τὸν λόφον συνανεπήδα, ἔνθα τῆς ἐνέδρας ἐκφανείσης ἐκέλευε τοὺς ἱππέας μήτε διώκειν μήτε ἐπιχειρεῖν ἔτι, ἀλλ᾽ ἐν προβολῇ τὰ δόρατα θεμένους ἑστάναι καὶ ἐπιόντας ἀμύνεσθαι μόνον. (383) ὁ δὲ Σκιπίων εὐθὺ ἀνατρέχοντος αὐτοῦ παρὰ τὸ πρόσταγμα δείσας εἵπετο κατὰ σπουδὴν καί, ὡς εὗρε τὴν ἐνέδραν, ἐς δύο διεῖλε τοὺς ἱππέας καὶ προσέταξεν αὐτῶν ἑκατέροις παρὰ μέρος ἐμπηδᾶν τοῖς πολεμίοις καὶ ἀκοντίσαντας ὁμοῦ πάντας εὐθὺς ἀναχωρεῖν, οὐκ ἐς τὸν αὐτὸν τόπον, ἀλλ᾽ αἰεὶ κατ᾽ ὀλίγον προστιθέντας ὀπίσω καὶ ὑποχωροῦντας. (384) οὕτω μὲν τοὺς ἱππέας ἐς τὸ πεδίον περιέσωσεν· ἀναζευγνύοντι δ᾽ αὐτῷ καὶ ἀναχωροῦντι ποταμὸς ἦν ἐν μέσῳ δύσπορός τε καὶ ἰλυώδης, καὶ παρ᾽ αὐτὸν ἐνήδρευον οἱ πολέμιοι. (385) ὁ δὲ μαθὼν ἐξέκλινε τῆς ὁδοῦ καὶ μακροτέραν ἦγε καὶ δυσενέδρευτον, νυκτός τε ὁδεύων διὰ τὸ δίψος καὶ φρέατα ὀρύσσων, ὧν τὰ πλέονα πικρὰ εὑρίσκετο. τοὺς μὲν οὖν ἄνδρας ἐπιμόχθως περιέσωσεν, ἵπποι δέ τινες αὐτοῦ καὶ ὑποζύγια ὑπὸ τῆς δίψης ἀπώλοντο.

89 (386) καὶ Καυκαίους δὲ παροδεύων, ἐς οὓς παρεσπόνδησε Λούκουλλος, ἐκήρυξε Καυκαίους ἐπὶ τὰ ἑαυτῶν ἀκινδύνως κατέρχεσθαι. (387) καὶ

---

377 σύντομος Steph.: συντόμως VM   383 αὐτῶν Steph.: αὐτῷ VM   385 δυσενέδρευτον Steph.: δυσέδρευτον VM

way. He said that he was worried about the return journey, when the enemy would be without burdens and had the city to sally forth from and to retire to. (378) "But our men will be heavy-laden as they return from gathering the grain and tired, and they will be driving loaded animals and wagons. The fight will be very difficult and uneven. There will be much danger if we are defeated, and we will have achieved little of value if we win. (379) It makes no sense to run a risk for a small gain, and it is a careless general who fights before it is necessary, while a good one only takes chances when compelled to do so." He drew as a parallel that doctors do not use surgery or cauterise before they have tried drugs. (380) So saying, he ordered the guides to take the longer route. On that occasion he led them to an area beyond the camp, but later into the territory of the Vaccaei, where the Numantines purchased their food-stuffs, cutting everything down, taking what could be used for their own consumption, and piling up the rest and burning it.

88 (381) On a plain in the territory of Pallantia called Coplanion, the Pallantians hid many men in the mountains below the crest, and with the rest openly attacked those who were gathering food. (382) He ordered Rutilius Rufus, who wrote a history of these exploits and was then a tribune, to take four troops of horse and to push back the attackers. Rufus followed them as they retreated in a disorderly fashion and chased along after them as they fled towards the crest of the hill. When he discovered the ambush, he ordered his cavalrymen neither to pursue nor to engage, but to stand with their spears at the ready and only to fend off those who attacked them. (383) As soon as he rushed up the hill contrary to his orders, Scipio became anxious and followed him hurriedly. When he saw the ambush, he divided the cavalry into two sections and instructed them to charge the enemy in turn, and, when they had hurled their javelins at the same time, to retreat immediately all together, not to the same point, but always adding a little distance as they withdrew. (384) In this way, he brought the cavalrymen safely onto the plain; but when he had struck camp and was retiring, there was a river in his way which was hard to cross and muddy, and beside which the enemy was waiting in ambush. (385) When he learnt of this, he left his route and went by a longer one which was less susceptible to ambush, travelling by night because of the danger of drought, and digging wells, most of which were found to be bitter. Thus he rescued the men with difficulty, but some of his horses and draught animals died of thirst.

89 (386) While marching through the territory of the Caucaei, whose treaty Lucullus had violated, he announced by a herald that the Caucaei could return to their own

παρῆλθεν ἐς τὴν Νομαντίνην χειμάσων, ἔνθα αὐτῷ καὶ Ἰογόρθας ἐκ Λιβύης ἀφίκετο, ὁ Μασσανάσσου υἱωνός, ἄγων ἐλέφαντας δυοκαίδεκα καὶ τοὺς συντασσομένους αὐτοῖς τοξότας τε καὶ σφενδονήτας. (388) αἰεὶ δέ τι δῃῶν καὶ τὰ περικείμενα πορθῶν, ἔλαθε περὶ κώμην ἐνεδρευθείς, ἣν ἐκ τοῦ πλέονος τέλμα πηλοῦ περιεῖχεν, ἐπὶ δὲ θάτερα φάραγξ ἦν, καὶ ἀφανὴς ἐν ἐκείνῃ λόχος ὑπεκρύπτετο. (389) τῆς οὖν στρατιᾶς τῷ Σκιπίωνι διῃρημένης οἱ μὲν τὴν κώμην ἐπόρθουν ἐσελθόντες, τὰ σημεῖα ἔξω καταλιπόντες, οἱ δὲ περιίππευον οὐ πολλοί. (390) τούτοις οὖν ἐμπίπτουσιν οἱ λοχῶντες. καὶ οἳ μὲν αὐτοὺς ἀπεμάχοντο, ὁ δὲ Σκιπίων (ἔτυχεν γὰρ πρὸ τῆς κώμης παρὰ τὰ σημεῖα ἑστώς) ἀνεκάλει τῇ σάλπιγγι τοὺς ἔνδον καί, πρὶν αὐτῷ γενέσθαι χιλίους, τοῖς ἱππεῦσιν ἐνοχλουμένοις ἐπεβοήθει. (391) τοῦ δὲ στρατοῦ τοῦ πλέονος ἐκ τῆς κώμης ἐκδραμόντος ἐτρέψατο μὲν ἐς φυγὴν τοὺς πολεμίους, οὐ μὴν ἐδίωκε φεύγοντας, ἀλλ᾽ ἐς τὸν χάρακα ἀνεχώρει πεσόντων ἑκατέρωθεν ὀλίγων.

90 (392) μετ᾽ οὐ πολὺ δὲ ἀγχοτάτω τῆς Νομαντίας δύο στρατόπεδα θέμενος τῷ μὲν ἐπέστησεν τὸν ἀδελφὸν Μάξιμον, τοῦ δ᾽ αὐτὸς ἡγεῖτο. Νομαντίνων δὲ θαμινὰ ἐκτασσόντων καὶ προκαλουμένων αὐτὸν ἐς μάχην ὑπερεώρα, οὐ δοκιμάζων ἀνδράσιν ἐξ ἀπογνώσεως μαχομένοις συμπλέκεσθαι μᾶλλον ἢ συγκλήσας αὐτοὺς ἑλεῖν λιμῷ. (393) φρούρια δ᾽ ἑπτὰ περιθείς, πολιορκίαν ⟨παρεσκεύασεν, ἅμα δὲ πρὸς τοὺς συμμάχους ἔπεμψεν⟩ ἐπιγράψας ἑκάστοις, οὓς ἔδει πέμπειν. ὡς δὲ ἦλθον, ἐς μέρη πολλὰ διεῖλεν αὐτοὺς καὶ τὴν ἑαυτοῦ στρατιὰν ἐπιδιεῖλεν· εἶθ᾽ ἡγεμόνας ἐπιστήσας ἑκάστῳ μέρει προσέταξεν περιταφρεύειν καὶ περιχαρακοῦν τὴν πόλιν. (394) ἦν δὲ ἡ περίοδος ἡ μὲν αὐτῆς Νομαντίας τέσσαρες καὶ εἴκοσι στάδιοι, ἡ δὲ τοῦ χαρακώματος ὑπὲρ τὸ διπλάσιον. καὶ τοῦτο διῃρεῖτο πᾶν οἱ κατὰ μέρος ἕκαστον. (395) καὶ προείρητο, εἴ τι ἐνοχλοῖεν οἱ πολέμιοι, σημεῖον ἐξαίρειν, ἡμέρας μὲν φοινικίδα ἐπὶ δόρατος ὑψηλοῦ, νυκτὸς δὲ πῦρ, ἵνα τοῖς δεομένοις ἐπιθέοντες αὐτός τε καὶ Μάξιμος ἀμύνοιεν. (396) ὡς δὲ ἐξείργαστο πάντα αὐτῷ καὶ τοὺς κωλύοντας εἶχεν ἱκανῶς ἀπομάχεσθαι, ἑτέραν τάφρον ὤρυσσεν οὐ μακρὰν ὑπὲρ ἐκείνην καὶ σταυροὺς αὐτῇ περιεπήγνυ καὶ τεῖχος ᾠκοδόμει, οὗ τὸ μὲν πάχος ἦν πόδες ὀκτώ, τὸ δὲ ὕψος δέκα χωρὶς τῶν ἐπάλξεων· πύργοι τε πανταχόθεν αὐτῷ διὰ πλέθρου περιέκειντο. (397) καὶ λίμνην συνάπτουσαν οὐκ ἐνὸν περιτειχίσαι χῶμα αὐτῇ περιέθηκεν ἴσον τῷ τείχει καὶ τὸ βάθος καὶ τὸ ὕψος, ὡς ἂν εἴη καὶ τόδε ἀντὶ τείχους.

---

387 Ἰογόρθας Steph.: Ἰουγόρθας VM   390 οὖν ἐμπίπτουσιν Schweig.: συνεμπίπτουσιν VM   391 τοῦ δὲ ci. Schweig.: τοῦδε δὲ τοῦ VM   392 τῷ Steph.: τὸ VM   393 post φρούρια δ" indicat lacunam Steph. πολιορκίαν ⟨παρεσκεύασεν, ἅμα δὲ πρὸς τοὺς συμμάχους ἔπεμψεν⟩ suppl. Schulten   394 διῃρεῖτο M: διῃρεῖτο V

lands without fear of danger. (387) He reached Numantia and went into winter quarters, and there Jugurtha, the grandson of Massinissa, joined him from Libya, bringing twelve elephants and the archers and slingers who were marshalled with them in battle. (388) While he continued his ravaging and pillaging of the country around, he stumbled into an ambush near a village, which was mostly surrounded by a muddy swamp, with a ravine on the other side, in which a troop of men was hidden out of sight. (389) Scipio's force was divided, with some of the men entering the village to plunder it, leaving their standards outside, while the rest, not many, were riding round the edge. (390) The men lurking in the ambush fell on these, and they in turn fought back against them; but Scipio, who happened to be standing in front of the village beside the standards, summoned back those who were inside the village with a trumpet call, and, before he had gathered a thousand, went to help the cavalry who were being attacked. (391) When the majority of the army had run out from the village, he put the enemy to flight, not pursuing them as they fled but retiring to his fortified camp, small numbers having fallen on each side.

90 (392) Not long after, he set up two camps very close to Numantia, putting his brother Maximus in charge of one and commanding the other himself. When the Numantines frequently drew themselves up in order of battle and challenged him to fight, he took no notice, reckoning it preferable not to engage with men fighting out of despair, but rather to shut them in and to take the city by starvation. (393) Having set seven forts round it, he prepared the siege <and at the same time sent to his allies>, writing to tell each whom they should send. When they came, he divided them into many sections and also divided his own army. Then he assigned leaders to each section and instructed them to dig a ditch and construct a fortification round the city. (394) The perimeter of Numantia was twenty-four *stadia*, and that of the fortified wall more than twice that. All this he divided up, section by section. (395) He instructed them beforehand, if the enemy should attack, to raise a signal, by day a red flag on a long spear, by night a fire, so that he and Maximus could rush to those in need and bring aid. (396) When he had completed all this and had made adequate provision to repel those attempting to prevent the work, he dug a second ditch not far in front of the first, fixed stakes in it and built a wall, eight feet thick and ten feet high, without counting the parapets. Towers were placed round the circuit, one every *plethron*. (397) As it was not possible to build a wall alongside the marsh which lay next to it, he set up an earth embankment around it, of the same size as the wall in height and depth, to take the place of the wall.

91 (398) οὕτω μὲν ὁ Σκιπίων ὅδε πρῶτος, ὡς ἐμοὶ δοκεῖ, περιετείχισε πόλιν οὐ φυγομαχοῦσαν· τόν τε Δόριον ποταμόν, συμφερόμενον τῷ περιτειχίσματι καὶ πολλὰ τοῖς Νομαντίνοις χρήσιμον ἔς τε ἀγορᾶς κομιδὴν καὶ διαπομπὴν ἀνδρῶν, ὅσοι κατ' αὐτὸν κολυμβηταί τε καὶ σκάφεσι μικροῖς ἐλάνθανον ἢ ἱστίοις, ὅτε λάβρον εἴη τὸ πνεῦμα, ἐβιάζοντο ἢ κώπαις κατὰ τὸ ῥεῦμα, ζεῦξαι μὲν οὐκ ἐδύνατο, πλατὺν ὄντα καὶ πάνυ ῥοώδη, φρούρια δὲ ἀντὶ γεφύρας αὐτῷ δύο περιθεὶς ἀπήρτησε καλῳδίοις δοκοὺς μακρὰς ἐξ ἑκατέρου φρουρίου καὶ ἐς τὸ πλάτος τοῦ ποταμοῦ μεθῆκεν, ἐχούσας ἐμπεπηγότα πυκνὰ ξίφη τε καὶ ἀκόντια. (399) αἱ δ' ὑπὸ τοῦ ῥοῦ, τοῖς ξίφεσι καὶ· τοῖς ἀκοντίοις ἐμπίπτοντος, αἰεὶ περιστρεφόμεναι οὔτε διανηχομένους οὔτ' ἐπιπλέοντας οὔτε ὑποδύνοντας εἴων λαθεῖν. (400) τοῦτο δ' ἦν, οὗ μάλιστα ὁ Σκιπίων ἐπεθύμει, μηδενὸς αὐτοῖς ἐπιμιγνυμένου μηδ' εἰσιόντος ἀγνοεῖν αὐτούς, ὅ τι γίγνοιτο ἔξω· οὕτω γὰρ ἀπορήσειν ἀγορᾶς τε καὶ μηχανῆς πάσης.

92 (401) ὡς δὲ ἡτοίμαστο πάντα καὶ καταπέλται μὲν ἐπέκειντο τοῖς πύργοις ὀξυβελεῖς τε καὶ λιθοβόλοι, ταῖς δ' ἐπάλξεσιν παρέκειντο λίθοι καὶ βέλη καὶ ἀκόντια, τὰ δὲ φρούρια τοξόται καὶ σφενδονῆται κατεῖχον, ἀγγέλους μὲν ἐπέστησε πυκνοὺς κατὰ τὸ ἐπιτείχισμα πᾶν, οἳ νυκτός τε καὶ ἡμέρας ἔμελλον ἄλλοι παρ' ἄλλων τὸν λόγον ἐκδεχόμενοι μηνύσειν αὐτῷ τὰ γιγνόμενα, (402) κατὰ δὲ πύργον ἐκέλευσεν, εἴ τι γίγνοιτο, σημεῖον ἐκ πρώτου τοῦ πονοῦντος αἴρεσθαι καὶ τὸ αὐτὸ πάντας ἐπαίρειν, ὅταν τὸν ἀρξάμενον θεάσωνται, ἵνα τὸ μὲν κίνημα παρὰ τοῦ σημείου θᾶσσον ἐπιγιγνώσκοι, τὸ δὲ ἀκριβὲς παρὰ τῶν ἀγγέλων. (403) τῆς δὲ στρατιᾶς οὔσης σὺν τοῖς ἐπιχωρίοις ἐς ἑξακισμυρίους, τὸ μὲν ἥμισυ διετέτακτο αὐτῷ τειχοφυλακεῖν καὶ ἐς τὰ ἀναγκαῖα, εἴ πη δεήσειε, μεταχωρεῖν, δισμύριοι δὲ τειχομαχήσειν ἔμελλον, ὅτε χρεία γένοιτο, καὶ τούτοις ἐφεδρεύειν ἕτεροι μύριοι. (404) χωρίον δὲ καὶ τούτων ἑκάστοις διετέτακτο· καὶ μεταπηδᾶν, εἰ μὴ κελεύσειεν, οὐκ ἐξῆν. ἐς δὲ τὸ τεταγμένον εὐθὺς ἀνεπήδων, ὅτε τι σημεῖον ἐπιχειρήσεως ἐπαρθείη.

93 (405) οὕτω μὲν τῷ Σκιπίωνι πάντα ἀκριβῶς διετέτακτο· οἱ δὲ Νομαντῖνοι πολλάκις μὲν τοῖς φυλάσσουσιν ἐπεχείρουν, ἄλλοτε ἄλλη κατὰ μέρη, ταχεῖα δ' αὐτίκα καὶ καταπληκτικὴ τῶν ἀμυνομένων ἡ ὄψις ἦν, (406) σημείων τε ὑψηλῶν πανταχόθεν αἰρομένων καὶ ἀγγέλων διαθεόντων καὶ τῶν τειχομάχων ἀθρόως ἀναπηδώντων ἐς τὰ τείχη σαλπικτῶν τε κατὰ πάντα πύργον ἐξοτρυνόντων, ὥστε τὸν κύκλον ὅλον εὐθὺς ἅπασιν εἶναι φοβερώτατον, ἐς πεντήκοντα σταδίους ἐπέχοντα ἐν περιόδῳ, καὶ τόνδε τὸν κύκλον ὁ Σκιπίων ἑκάστης ἡμέρας τε καὶ νυκτὸς ἐπισκοπῶν περιῄει.

---

401 ἄλλων Steph.: ἄλλους VM   **406** ἀναπηδώντων Steph.: ἀναπηδόντων VM   ἐπέχοντα Steph.: ἀπέχοντα VM   περιῄει Steph.: περιηίη V (sed prius η eras.) περιίη M

91 (398) Thus Scipio was the first, so it seems to me, to wall in a city which was willing to fight a battle. The river Durius crossed the fortification and was very useful to the Numantines both for bringing in supplies and sending out men, who were able to slip through either as individual divers or in small boats, either driven by sails, when the wind was strong, or carried along by the stream using oars. This he was unable to bridge, since it was broad and had a strong current; but in place of a bridge, he set two forts alongside it and attached long beams to each of the forts by ropes, which he placed across the width of the river, with many swords and javelins fixed into them. (399) These rotated continuously as a result of the pressure of the stream on the swords and javelins, and prevented people swimming or sailing or diving past them. (400) What Scipio wanted above all was that no one should have contact with or enter the city, so that they would not know what was happening outside, for in this way they would be deprived of supplies and all means of survival.

92 (401) When everything had been prepared and catapults placed in the towers to hurl sharpened missiles and rocks, and rocks and missiles and javelins had been placed along the parapets, and archers and slingers were in position in the guard-posts, he stationed messengers at frequent intervals along the fortification, who would be able by night and by day, by passing the word from one to another, to inform him of what was going on; (402) and he gave orders to each tower that, if anything did happen, a signal should be raised first by the one that was in difficulty, and that all the others should raise the same signal, when they saw the one that had done so first, so that he would know of the disturbance more rapidly through the signals, and its precise details through the messengers. (403) The army, including the indigenous forces, numbered about sixty thousand, half of which was drawn up so as to protect the wall and to move to any point of difficulty as need arose; twenty thousand were to fight on the wall whenever it was needed; and the other ten thousand was to act as a reserve. (404) A position was assigned to each of these, and they were not to change their station unless ordered to do so. They moved to the place assigned whenever the signal of an attack was raised.

93 (405) In this way Scipio arranged everything precisely. The Numantines, however, often attacked those who were on guard in different places and at different times, but the appearance of those warding them off was rapid and striking, (406) and with the signals everywhere raised aloft and the messengers running backwards and forwards and those defending the walls rushing to their places in a body and the trumpets sounding from every tower, the whole circuit became extremely formidable to all along the fifty *stadia* of the perimeter; and Scipio made a tour of inspection of the circuit every night.

94 (407) ὁ μὲν δὴ τοὺς πολεμίους ὧδε συγκλήσας οὐκ ἐς πολὺ ἀρκέσειν ἐνόμιζεν, οὔτε τροφῆς ἔτι προσιούσης σφίσιν οὔτε ὅπλων οὔτ' ἐπικουρίας· Ῥητογένης δέ, ἀνὴρ Νομαντῖνος, ᾧ Καραύνιος ἐπίκλησις ἦν, ἄριστος ἐς ἀρετὴν Νομαντίνων, πέντε πείσας φίλους, σὺν παισὶν ἄλλοις τοσοῖσδε καὶ ἵπποις τοσοῖσδε ἐν νυκτὶ συννεφεῖ διῆλθε λαθὼν τὸ μεταίχμιον, κλίμακα φέρων πτυκτήν, (408) καὶ φθάσας ἐς τὸ περιτείχισμα ἀνεπήδησεν αὐτός τε καὶ οἱ φίλοι καὶ τοὺς ἑκατέρωθεν φύλακας ἀνελόντες τοὺς μὲν θεράποντας ἀπέπεμψαν ὀπίσω, τοὺς δ' ἵππους διὰ τῆς κλίμακος ἀναγαγόντες ἐξίππευσαν ἐς τὰς Ἀρουακῶν πόλεις σὺν ἱκετηρίαις, δεόμενοι Νομαντίνοις συγγενέσιν οὖσιν ἐπικουρεῖν. (409) τῶν δ' Ἀρουακῶν οἱ μὲν οὐδ' ὑπήκουον αὐτῶν, ἀλλ' εὐθὺς ἀπέπεμπον δεδιότες, Λουτία δὲ πόλις ἦν εὐδαίμων, τριακοσίους σταδίους ἀφεστῶσα ἀπὸ Νομαντίνων, ἧς οἱ μὲν νέοι περὶ τοὺς Νομαντίνους ἐσπουδάκεσαν καὶ τὴν πόλιν ἐς συμμαχίαν ἐνῆγον, οἱ πρεσβύτεροι δ' ἐμήνυσαν κρύφα τῷ Σκιπίωνι. (410) καὶ ὁ Σκιπίων ὀγδόης ὥρας πυθόμενος ἐξήλαυνεν αὐτίκα σὺν εὐζώνοις ὅτι πλείστοις καὶ ἅμα ἕω τὴν Λουτίαν φρουρᾷ περιλαβὼν ᾔτει τοὺς ἐξάρχους τῶν νέων. ἐπεὶ δ' ἐξωρμηκέναι τῆς πόλεως αὐτοὺς ἔλεγον, ἐκήρυξε διαρπάσειν τὴν πόλιν, εἰ μὴ τοὺς ἄνδρας παραλάβοι. (411) οἱ μὲν δὴ δείσαντες προσῆγον αὐτούς, ἐς τετρακοσίους γενομένους· ὁ δὲ τὰς χεῖρας αὐτῶν ἐκτεμὼν ἀνέστησε τὴν φρουρὰν καὶ διαδραμὼν αὖθις ἅμ' ἕω τῆς ἐπιούσης παρῆν ἐς τὸ στρατόπεδον.

95 (412) Νομαντῖνοι δὲ κάμνοντες ὑπὸ λιμοῦ πέντε ἄνδρας ἔπεμπον ἐς τὸν Σκιπίωνα, οἷς εἴρητο μαθεῖν, εἰ μετριοπαθῶς σφίσι χρήσεται παραδοῦσιν αὐτούς. Αὔαρος δὲ αὐτῶν ἡγούμενος πολλὰ μὲν περὶ τῆς προαιρέσεως καὶ ἀνδρείας τῶν Νομαντίνων ἐσεμνολόγησε καὶ ἐπεῖπεν, ὡς οὐδὲ νῦν ἁμάρτοιεν, ὑπὲρ παίδων καὶ γυναικῶν καὶ ἐλευθερίας πατρίου κακοπαθοῦντες ἐς τοσόνδε κακοῦ. (413) "διὸ καὶ μάλιστα", εἶπεν, "ὦ Σκιπίων, ἄξιόν ἐστι σέ, τοσῆσδε ἀρετῆς γέμοντα, φείσασθαι γένους εὐψύχου τε καὶ ἀνδρικοῦ καὶ προτεῖναι τὰ φιλανθρωπότερα τῶν κακῶν ἡμῖν, ἃ καὶ δυνησόμεθα ἐνεγκεῖν, ἄρτι πειρώμενοι μεταβολῆς. ὡς οὐκ ἐφ' ἡμῖν ἔτι ἐστίν, ἀλλ' ἐπὶ σοὶ τὴν πόλιν ἢ παραλαβεῖν, εἰ τὰ μέτρια κελεύοις, ἢ μαχομένην ὑπεριδεῖν ἀπολέσθαι." (414) ὁ μὲν Αὔαρος ὧδε εἶπεν, ὁ δὲ Σκιπίων (ᾔσθετο γὰρ παρὰ τῶν αἰχμαλώτων τὰ ἔνδον) ἔφη δεῖν αὐτοὺς ἐγχειρίσαι τὰ κατὰ σφᾶς καὶ σὺν ὅπλοις παραδοῦναι τὴν πόλιν. (415) ὧν ἀπαγγελθέντων οἱ Νομαντῖνοι, χαλεποὶ καὶ τέως ὄντες ὀργὴν ὑπ' ἐλευθερίας ἀκράτου καὶ ἀηθείας ἐπιταγμάτων, τότε καὶ μᾶλλον ὑπὸ τῶν συμφορῶν ἠγριωμένοι τε καὶ ἀλλόκοτοι γεγονότες, τὸν Αὔαρον

---

410 ᾔτει τοὺς ἐξάρχους τῶν νέων VM: ἐξῄτει τῶν ἐξάρχων τοὺς νέους Gouk. **414** ᾔσθετο Steph.: ἠσθετο VM

94 (407) Having thus shut in his enemies, Scipio thought they would be not able to hold out for long, with no food or arms or assistance coming in to them. However Rhetogenes, a Numantine, surnamed Caraunios, the most courageous of the Numantines, persuaded five friends, and with an equal number of slaves and horses on a cloudy night, slipped across the space between the city and the walls without being observed, carrying a folding scaling-bridge. (408) Arriving first at the fortification, he climbed it and he and his friends killed the guards on either side, sent the servants back and, having led the horses up the scaling-bridge, rode out to the cities of the Arevaci, bearing olive branches and begging them to help the Numantines, who were their kinsmen. (409) Some of the Arevaci refused to listen to them and sent them away immediately out of fear, but the city of Lutia was wealthy and situated three hundred *stadia* from Numantia, and there the young men were eager to support the Numantines and urged that the city make an alliance with them, but the older men secretly informed Scipio. (410) Scipio, hearing of this at the eighth hour, set out with as many light-armed soldiers as possible, surrounded Lutia with a guard at dawn and demanded the surrender of the leaders of the young men. When they said that they had left the city in a hurry, he announced through a herald that he would sack the city if it did not hand over the men. (411) Scared by this, they produced them, about four hundred in number. He cut off their hands, withdrew his guard and, making all speed, was back in his camp at dawn the following day.

95 (412) The Numantines were being worn out by hunger and sent five men to Scipio, who were instructed to discover whether he would treat them moderately if they surrendered. Their leader, Avarus, produced a long and verbose speech about the policy and bravery of the Numantines and added that even now they had done nothing wrong and were suffering to such an extent because they were defending their children and women and their ancestral freedom. (413) "For this reason, Scipio," he said, "it is particularly appropriate for you, a man full of so much virtue, to spare a people who are courageous and brave, and to offer us terms more humane than our present evils, which we shall be able to bear, tested as we are by change of fortune. It is now your choice, not ours, either to receive the surrender of the city, if your demands are moderate, or to watch its destruction as it resists you." (414) So spoke Avarus, but Scipio, who knew of the situation inside the city from the men he had captured, said that they must hand themselves and their property over to him and surrender their city and their weapons. (415) When these man reported back, the Numantines, who even before this had been terrible in their anger as a result of their unfettered freedom and unused to receiving orders, now were still further enraged by their disaster and became completely inhuman. They killed Avarus and the five

καὶ τοὺς σὺν αὐτῷ πέντε πρέσβεις ἀπέκτειναν ὡς κακῶν ἀγγέλους καὶ τὸ σφέτερον ἀσφαλὲς ἴσως διῳκημένους παρὰ τῷ Σκιπίωνι.

96 (416) μετὰ δ' οὐ πολὺ πάντων αὐτοὺς τῶν ἐδεστῶν ἐπιλιπόντων, οὐ καρπὸν ἔχοντες, οὐ πρόβατον, οὐ πόαν, πρῶτα μέν, ὥσπερ τινὲς ἐν πολέμων ἀνάγκαις, δέρματα ἕψοντες ἐλιχμῶντο, ἐπιλιπόντων δ' αὐτοὺς καὶ τῶν δερμάτων ἐσαρκοφάγουν ἕψοντες τὰ ἀνθρώπεια, πρῶτα μὲν τὰ τῶν ἀποθνησκόντων κοπτόμενα ἐν μαγειρείοις, ἐπὶ δ' ἐκείνοις τῶν νοσούντων κατεφρόνουν, καὶ τοὺς ἀσθενεστέρους ἐβιάζοντο οἱ δυνατώτεροι. (417) κακῶν τε οὐδὲν αὐτοῖς ἀπῆν, ἠγριωμένοις μὲν τὰς ψυχὰς ὑπὸ τῶν τροφῶν, τεθηριωμένοις δὲ τὰ σώματα ὑπὸ λιμοῦ καὶ λοιμοῦ καὶ κόμης καὶ χρόνου. οὕτω δ' ἔχοντες αὐτοὺς ἐπέτρεπον τῷ Σκιπίωνι. (418) ὁ δ' ἐκέλευεν αὐτοὺς τῆς μὲν ἡμέρας ἐκείνης συνενεγκεῖν τὰ ὅπλα, ἔνθα συνέταξε, τῆς δ' ἐπιούσης προσελθεῖν ἐς ἕτερον χωρίον. οἱ δ' ὑπερεβάλοντο τὴν ἡμέραν, ὁμολογήσαντες, ὅτι πολλοὶ τῆς ἐλευθερίας ἔτι ἔχονται καὶ ἐθέλουσιν αὐτοὺς ἐξαγαγεῖν τοῦ βίου. τὴν οὖν ἡμέραν ᾔτουν ἐς τοῦ θανάτου τὴν διάθεσιν.

97 (419) τοσόσδε ἔρως ἐλευθερίας καὶ ἀνδραγαθίας ἦν ἐν πόλει βαρβάρῳ τε καὶ σμικρᾷ. ἐς γὰρ ὀκτακισχιλίους ἐπ' εἰρήνης γενόμενοι οἷα μὲν καὶ ὅσα Ῥωμαίους ἔδρασαν, οἵας δὲ συνθήκας αὐτοῖς ἔθεντο ἐπὶ ἴσῃ καὶ ὁμοίᾳ, οὐδέσι τοιαῦτα συνθέσθαι Ῥωμαίων ὑποστάντων, οἷον δὲ ὄντα τὸν τελευταῖον στρατηγόν, ἐξ μυριάσιν αὐτοὺς περικαθήμενον, προυκαλέσαντο πολλάκις ἐς μάχην. (420) ὁ δὲ ἦν ἄρα στρατηγικώτερος αὐτῶν, ἐς χεῖρας οὐκ ἰὼν θηρίοις, ἀλλὰ τῷ λιμῷ σφᾶς κατεργαζόμενος, ἀμάχῳ κακῷ, ᾧ δὴ καὶ μόνῳ ληφθῆναί τε δυνατὸν ἦν ἄρα Νομαντίνους καὶ ἐλήφθησαν μόνῳ. (421) ἐμοὶ μὲν δὴ ταῦτα περὶ Νομαντίνων εἰπεῖν ἐπῆλθεν, ἐς τὴν ὀλιγότητα αὐτῶν καὶ φερεπονίαν ἀφορῶντι καὶ ἔργα πολλὰ καὶ χρόνον, ὅσον διεκαρτέρησαν· (422) οἱ δὲ πρῶτα μὲν αὐτούς, οἱ βουλόμενοι, διεχρῶντο, ἕτερος ἑτέρως· οἱ λοιποὶ δ' ἐξῄεσαν τρίτης ἡμέρας ἐς τὸ δεδομένον χωρίον, δυσόρατοί τε καὶ ἀλλόκοτοι πάμπαν ὀφθῆναι, οἷς τὰ μὲν σώματα ἦν ἀκάθαρτα καὶ τριχῶν καὶ ὀνύχων καὶ ῥύπου μεστά, ὀδώδεσαν δὲ χαλεπώτατον, καὶ ἐσθὴς αὐτοῖς ἐπέκειτο πιναρὰ καὶ ἥδε καὶ οὐχ ἧσσον δυσώδης. (423) ἐφαίνοντο δὲ τοῖς πολεμίοις ἐλεεινοὶ μὲν ἀπὸ τῶνδε, φοβεροὶ δ' ἀπὸ τῶν βλεμμάτων· ἔτι γὰρ αὐτοὺς ἐνεώρων ἔκ τε ὀργῆς καὶ λύπης καὶ πόνου καὶ συνειδότος ἀλληλοφαγίας.

---

416 τὰ τῶν Steph.: τὰ τατῶν VM   419 τοιαῦτα Nauk: ταῦτα VM τάυτα Gouk.   421 ἀφορῶντι Steph.: ἀφορῶν τε VM   422 πάμπαν Steph.: πανπαν VM καὶ ὀρύπων ante καὶ ῥύπου eras. in V

ambassadors who went with him as being the bearers of bad news and perhaps having negotiated their own safety with Scipio.

96 (416) Not long after this, when all their foodstuffs had run out and they had no produce, not a single sheep nor any grass, first, as some do under the necessities of war, they boiled hides and licked them. When no more hides were left, they boiled and ate human flesh, first that of those who had died, chopped up in the butchers' shops, and after that they began to lose all respect for the sick and the stronger began to seize hold of the weaker. (417) There was no limit to the evils they suffered, growing savage in their souls as a result of the food they ate, and becoming like animals in their bodies as a result of hunger, disease, their long hair and the duration of the siege. In this state, they handed themselves over to Scipio. (418) He ordered them to bring their weapons on that very day to a place he specified, and to come on the next day to another place. They put off the day, stating that many of them still clung to their liberty and wished to take their lives themselves. They asked therefore for a day to prepare for death.

97 (419) Such was the love of liberty and of bravery in a city that was both barbarian and tiny. Although they were only about eight thousand strong in time of peace, they inflicted so many and such great defeats on the Romans, concluded such treaties on terms of absolute equality, even though the Romans never consented to make such treaties with anyone, such was the quality of the last general sent against them, who surrounded them with sixty thousand men, while they frequently challenged him to fight. (420) He was, to be sure, a greater general than they were, a man who refused to engage with wild animals, but wore them down with hunger, an evil that requires no fighting, through which alone it was possible to capture the Numantines and through which alone they were captured. (421) This then is what I want to say about the Numantines, concerning their small numbers, their endurance, their many deeds and the length of time they held out. (422) First of all, all those who wished to killed themselves, each in his own way; the rest came out on the third day to the place that had been appointed, an appalling spectacle and looking altogether inhuman, with their bodies unwashed, full of hair and nails and filth; they smelt horribly and their clothing was unwashed and just as stinking. (423) To their enemies they seemed pitiable because of this; but their faces made them seem terrifying, for they looked at the Romans, in a way which expressed their pride and grief, what they had endured and the consciousness of their cannibalism.

98 (424) ἐπιλεξάμενος δ᾿ αὐτῶν πεντήκοντα ὁ Σκιπίων ἐς θρίαμβον, τοὺς λοιποὺς ἀπέδοτο καὶ ⟩ τὴν πόλιν κατέσκαψεν, δύο μὲν τάσδε πόλεις δυσμαχωτάτας ἑλὼν στρατηγὸς ὅδε Ῥωμαίων, (425) Καρχηδόνα μὲν αὐτῶν Ῥωμαίων ψηφισαμένων διὰ μέγεθος πόλεώς τε καὶ ἀρχῆς καὶ εὐκαιρίαν γῆς καὶ θαλάσσης, Νομαντίαν δὲ σμικράν τε καὶ ὀλιγάνθρωπον, οὔπω τι Ῥωμαίων περὶ αὐτῆς ἐγνωκότων, αὐτός, (426) εἴτε συμφέρειν Ῥωμαίοις ἡγούμενος, εἴτε ἄκρος ὢν ὀργὴν καὶ φιλόνεικος ἐς τὰ λαμβανόμενα, εἴθ᾿, ὡς ἔνιοι νομίζουσι, τὴν δόξαν ἡγούμενος διώνυμον ἐπὶ τοῖς μεγάλοις γίγνεσθαι κακοῖς. καλοῦσι γοῦν αὐτὸν οἱ Ῥωμαῖοι μέχρι νῦν, ἀπὸ τῶν συμφορῶν, ἃς ἐπέθηκεν ταῖς πόλεσιν, Ἀφρικανόν τε καὶ Νομαντῖνον. (427) τότε δὲ τὴν γῆν τὴν Νομαντίνων τοῖς ἐγγὺς οἰκοῦσι διελὼν καὶ ταῖς ἄλλαις πόλεσι χρηματίσας καί, εἴ τι ἦν ὕποπτον, ἐπιπλήξας τε καὶ ζημιώσας χρήμασιν ἀπέπλευσεν ἐπ᾿ οἴκου.

99 (428) Ῥωμαῖοι δέ, ὡς ἔθος, ἐς τὰ προσειλημμένα τῆς Ἰβηρίας ἔπεμψαν ἀπὸ τῆς βουλῆς ἄνδρας δέκα τοὺς καταστησομένους αὐτὰ εἰς εἰρήνην, ὅσα Σκιπίων τε ἔλαβε καὶ Βροῦτος πρὸ τοῦ Σκιπίωνος ὑπηγάγετο ἢ ἐχειρώσατο. (429) χρόνῳ δ᾿ ὕστερον ἀποστάσεων ἄλλων ἐν Ἰβηρίᾳ γενομένων Καλπούρνιος Πείσων στρατηγὸς ᾑρέθη. (430) καὶ αὐτὸν διεδέξατο μὲν Σέρουιος Γάλβας, Κίμβρων δ᾿ ἐπιστρατευόντων τῇ Ἰταλίᾳ καὶ Σικελίας πολεμουμένης τὸν δεύτερον δουλικὸν πόλεμον στρατιὰν μὲν ἐς Ἰβηρίαν οὐκ ἔπεμπον ὑπ᾿ ἀσχολίας, πρέσβεις δ᾿ ἀπέστελλον, οἳ τὸν πόλεμον ἔμελλον, ὅπῃ δύναιντο, καταθήσεσθαι. (431) Κίμβρων δ᾿ ἐξελαθέντων Τίτος Δείδιος ἐπελθὼν Ἀρουακῶν μὲν ἔκτεινεν ἐς δισμυρίους, Τερμησὸν δέ, μεγάλην πόλιν αἰεὶ δυσπειθῆ Ῥωμαίοις γενομένην, ἐξ ἐρυμνοῦ κατήγαγεν ἐς τὸ πεδίον καὶ ἐκέλευσεν οἰκεῖν ἀτειχίστους. (432) Κολένδαν δὲ προσκαθίσας ἐνάτῳ μηνὶ παρέλαβεν ἐγχειρίσασαν ἑαυτὴν καὶ τοὺς Κολενδέας ἅπαντας μετὰ παίδων καὶ γυναικῶν ἀπέδοτο.

100 (433) πόλιν δ᾿ ἑτέραν τῆς Κολένδης πλησίον ᾤκουν μιγάδες Κελτιβήρων, οὓς Μᾶρκος Μάριος συμμαχήσαντας αὐτῷ κατὰ Λυσιτανῶν, τῆς βουλῆς ἐπιτρεπούσης, ᾠκίκει πρὸ πέντε ἐνιαυτῶν. (434) ἐλήστευον δ᾿ ἐξ ἀπορίας οὗτοι· καὶ κρίνας αὐτοὺς ὁ Δείδιος ἀνελεῖν, συνθεμένων αὐτῷ τῶν δέκα πρέσβεων ἔτι παρόντων, ἔφη τοῖς ἐπιφανέσιν αὐτῶν ἐθέλειν τὴν Κολενδέων χώραν αὐτοῖς προσορίσαι πενομένοις. (435) ἀσπαζομένους δὲ ὁρῶν ἐκέλευεν, τῷ δήμῳ ταῦτα μετενεγκόντας, ἥκειν μετὰ γυναικῶν καὶ παίδων τὴν χώραν μεριουμένους. ἐπεὶ δ᾿ ἀφίκοντο, προσέταξε τοὺς

431 ἐξελαθέντων Steph.: ἐξελασθέντων VM ʹΑρουακῶν Schweig.: Οὐαρκαίων V (κ supra ρ α m.2) M Οὐακκαίων Steph. **432** προσκαθίσας Steph.: προσκαθήσας VM **434** πενομένοις Steph.: πενομένος VM

98 (424) Scipio chose fifty of them for his triumph, sold the remainder and destroyed the city, this one Roman general thus having captured the two cities that had given the most trouble in war. (425) Carthage he destroyed after the Romans themselves had decreed it, because of the greatness of the city and its power and its prosperity by land and sea, but Numantia, which was small and had a small population, he destroyed himself, without the Romans having made any decision about it, (426) either believing it to be of benefit to the Romans, or because he was hot tempered and passionate against the places he captured, or, as some think, believing that he would have the glory of two names from these great calamities. Certainly the Romans even now call him both Africanus and Numantinus, from the defeats he inflicted on these cities. (427) He then divided the territory of the Numantines between those who lived close to them, and, having negotiated with the other cities and, if there were any grounds for suspicion, punished and fined them, he sailed for home.

99 (428) The Romans, as usual, sent out ten men from the senate to those parts of Iberia which had been captured to arrange matters on the basis of peace, both those parts which Scipio had taken and those which Brutus before Scipio had made subject or defeated. (429) After this time there were other revolts in Iberia and Calpurnius Piso was chosen general. (430) Servius Galba succeeded him, but as the Cimbri were invading Italy, and Sicily was also embroiled in the second slave war, they did not send an army to Iberia, because they were so preoccupied with these matters, but sent ambassadors to put an end to the war by whatever means they could. (431) Once the Cimbri had been driven away, Titus Didius came and killed twenty thousand of the Arevaci, and moved Termessus, a large city which had always been disinclined to obey the Romans, from the strong position it occupied down to the plain, and ordered then to live there without building walls. (432) Having besieged Colenda, he took it in the ninth month, after it had surrendered itself, and sold all the inhabitants with their children and wives.

100 (433) There lived in another city near Colenda a mixed race of Celtiberians, whom Marcus Marius had settled five years earlier, with the agreement of the senate, after they had fought with him against the Lusitanians. (434) These had taken to brigandage because of their poverty. Didius decided to exterminate them, with the agreement of the ten commissioners, who were still present. He said to their leaders that he wanted to add the territory of the Colendans to theirs, because they were poor. (435) When they welcomed this, he ordered them, after they had informed the people of this matters, to come with their women and children to divide up the land. When they arrived, he ordered his soldiers to come out from

στρατιώτας ἐκ τοῦ χάρακος ἐξελθεῖν καὶ τοὺς ἐνεδρευομένους εἴσω παρελθεῖν ὡς ἀπογραψόμενος αὐτῶν ἔνδον τὸ πλῆθος, ἐν μέρει μὲν ἀνδρῶν, ἐν μέρει δὲ παίδων καὶ γυναικῶν, ἵν᾽ ἐπιγνοίη, πόσην χώραν αὐτοῖς δέοι διελεῖν. (436) ὡς δὲ παρῆλθον ἐς τὴν τάφρον καὶ τὸ χαράκωμα, περιστήσας αὐτοῖς τὸν στρατὸν ὁ Δείδιος ἔκτεινε πάντας. καὶ ἐπὶ τοῖσδε Δείδιος μὲν καὶ ἐθριάμβευσεν, πάλιν δὲ τῶν Κελτιβήρων ἀποστάντων Φλάκκος ἐπιπεμφθεὶς ἔκτεινε δισμυρίους. (437) ἐν δὲ Βελγήδῃ πόλει ὁ μὲν δῆμος ἐς ἀπόστασιν ὁρμῶν τὴν βουλὴν ὀκνοῦσαν ἐνέπρησεν αὐτῷ βουλευτηρίῳ, ὁ δὲ Φλάκκος ἐπελθὼν ἔκτεινε τοὺς αἰτίους.

101 (438) τοσάδε μὲν εὗρον ἄξια λόγου Ῥωμαίοις ἐς τότε πρὸς Ἴβηρας αὐτοὺς γενόμενα· χρόνῳ δ᾽ ὕστερον στασιαζόντων ἐν Ῥώμῃ Σύλλα τε καὶ Κίννα καὶ ἐς ἐμφυλίους πολέμους καὶ στρατόπεδα κατὰ τῆς πατρίδος διῃρημένων Κόιντος Σερτώριος, ἐκ τῆς Κίννα στάσεως αἱρεθεὶς τῆς Ἰβηρίας ἄρχειν, (439) Ἰβηρίαν τε αὐτὴν ἐπανέστησε Ῥωμαίοις καὶ πολὺν στρατὸν ἀγείρας καὶ βουλὴν τῶν ἰδίων φίλων ἐς μίμημα τῆς συγκλήτου καταλέξας ἤλαυνεν ἐς Ῥώμην ἐπὶ τόλμης καὶ φρονήματος λαμπροῦ, καὶ τἆλλα ὢν ἐς θρασύτητα περιώνυμος, (440) ὥστε τὴν βουλὴν δείσασαν ἑλέσθαι τοὺς παρὰ σφίσιν ἐπὶ μεγίστης τότε δόξης στρατηγούς, Καικίλιόν τε Μέτελλον μετὰ πολλοῦ στρατοῦ καὶ Γναῖον Πομπήιον ἐπ᾽ ἐκείνῳ μεθ᾽ ἑτέρου στρατοῦ, ἵνα τὸν πόλεμον, ὅπῃ δύναιντο, ἐξωθοῖεν ἐκ τῆς Ἰταλίας ἐν διχοστασίᾳ τότε μάλιστα οὔσης. (441) ἀλλὰ Σερτώριον μὲν τῶν στασιωτῶν τις αὐτοῦ Περπέρνας ἀνελὼν ἑαυτὸν ἐπὶ Σερτωρίῳ στρατηγὸν ἀπέφηνε τῆς ἀποστάσεως, Περπέρναν δ᾽ ἔκτεινε μάχῃ Πομπήιος, καὶ ὁ πόλεμος ὅδε, θορυβήσας δὴ τῷ φόβῳ μάλιστα Ῥωμαίους, διελύθη. τὸ δ᾽ ἀκριβὲς αὐτοῦ δηλώσει τὰ περὶ Σύλλαν ἐμφύλια.

102 (442) μετὰ δὲ τὸν Σύλλα θάνατον Γάιος Καῖσαρ αἱρεθεὶς Ἰβηρίας στρατηγεῖν, ὥστε καὶ πολεμεῖν, οἷς δεήσειεν, ὅσα τῶν Ἰβήρων ἐσαλεύετο ἢ Ῥωμαίοις ἔτι ἔλειπεν, πολέμῳ συνηνάγκασεν πάντα ὑπακούειν. (443) καί τινα αὖθις ἀφιστάμενα Ἰούλιος Καῖσαρ, ὁ τοῦ Γαίου παῖς, ὁ Σεβαστὸς ἐπίκλην, ἐχειρώσατο. (444) καὶ ἐξ ἐκείνου μοι δοκοῦσι Ῥωμαῖοι τὴν Ἰβηρίαν, ἣν δὴ νῦν Ἰσπανίαν καλοῦσιν, ἐς τρία διαιρεῖν καὶ στρατηγοὺς ἐπιπέμπειν, ἐτησίους μὲν ἐς τὰ δύο ἡ βουλή, τὸν δὲ τρίτον βασιλεύς, ἐφ᾽ ὅσον δοκιμάσειεν.

---

435 διελεῖν Reiske et Schweig.: διελθεῖν VM   442 ἔλειπεν Steph.: ἔλιπεν VM

their encampment, and those whom he intended to entrap to go into it, so that inside he could record the number of them, the men in one part and the children and women in another, so that he could reckon how much land he would need to distribute to them. (436) When they had come inside the ditch and the rampart, Didius surrounded them with his soldiers and killed them all. For this Didius even celebrated a triumph, but when the Celtiberians went into revolt again, Flaccus was sent out and killed twenty thousand. (437) In the city of Belgeda the people, who were determined to revolt, burnt the council, which was hesitating, in the very council-house, but Flaccus arrived and killed those who were responsible.

101 (438) These are the things worthy of record that I have discovered that the Romans did against the Iberians themselves. Afterwards, when Sulla and Cinna were struggling together in Rome and the Romans were divided through the civil wars and the forming of armies against the state, Quintus Sertorius, who had been chosen from among Cinna's party to command in Iberia, raised Iberia itself in rebellion against the Romans, and, having assembled a large army and enrolled a council of his friends in imitation of the senate, marched against Rome with boldness and outstanding brilliance, being already famed for his boldness in other matters. (440) As a result, the senate in terror chose to send against him those generals from amongst them who at that time had the greatest reputations, Caecilius Metellus with a large army, and after him Gnaeus Pompeius with another army, to keep, by whatever means they could, the war away from Italy, which was at that time particularly divided between the two parties. (441) But Perperna, a man of his own party, killed Sertorius and set himself up in Sertorius' place as the commander of the rebellion. Pompeius killed Perperna in battle, and this war, which had especially alarmed the Romans, was brought to an end. The details of this war will be seen in my book about the Civil Wars which deals with Sulla.

102 (442) After the death of Sulla, Gaius Caesar was chosen to command in Iberia, to fight wherever he needed, and he compelled by force of arms all those Iberians who were still uncertain or were not yet belonging to the Romans into total obedience. (443) Some, who again went into revolt, were defeated by Julius Caesar, the son of Gaius, surnamed Augustus. (444) It seems to me that since that time the Romans have divided Iberia, which they now call Hispania, into three and send generals, the senate sending two each year and the emperor sending the third, for as long a period as he decides.

Commentary

Chs. 1-3: Introduction

1

1 **The Pyrenean range of mountains:** Appian begins with a geographic and ethnographic note, with enough early history to set the scene for the arrival of the Romans. There is a similar introduction to his books on the wars in Illyria (*Illyr.* 1.1-3.7) and in Libya (*Lib.* 1.1-2.10). Probably there were similar introductions to some of the other books on wars in geographical areas, which do not survive, or are only fragmentary. He clearly considered the geographical setting of significance, if only to emphasise the immensity of the achievement of the Romans, and begins the Preface of his work with a survey of the territory and peoples included within the empire (*Proem.* 1.1-5.18).

the Celts, who are now generally called Galatians or Gauls: Appian's view on the location of the Iberian peninsula, as is common among ancient writers, places it further north and on a different axis from geographical reality (see below on 1.3); with the Pyrenees running north-south, so that the Gauls lived to the east of the mountains and the Iberians and Celtiberians to the west (P. Janni, *La mappa e il periplo* (Rome 1984), p. 100). Of the various names of these people, he himself normally calls them Celts (Κελτοί; thus at 2.5; and, referring to those outside the peninsula 4.15; 37.151 and 39.158). Galatians (Γαλάται) is the normal Greek name for those in Gaul and north Italy, and Gauls (Γάλλοι) the Roman name.

Before the arrival of the Carthaginians and Romans, the inhabitants of the peninsula can be distinguished into two groups: those who lived in the high central plateau of the *meseta* and the northern and western coasts, who were semi-nomadic, with a basically pastoral economy, and seem to be for the most part of Celtic origin (those in the north-eastern corner of the *meseta* being known as Celtiberians, who were more settled than those further west); and a second group, living along the Mediterranean coast and in the valley of the Guadalquivir, who were known by the ancients by the general name, Iberians. These last seem to have been more urbanised. It is by no means certain whether 'Iberian' represented a true ethnic or cultural unity, and, as Strabo observed (3.4.19), the name 'Iberia' was used by the ancients to cover different areas. In addition, there were Phoenician and Greek colonies, mostly round the coastline from Catalunya to Cadiz (see below on 2.5).

the Pyrenees, the largest of the European mountains: Appian is wrong here, of course, as the Alps are both higher and more extensive. The highest mountain of the Pyrenees is Possets at 3367 m, while the highest of the Alpine mountains, the Matterhorn, is 4474 m. Diodorus Siculus (5.35.2), writing in the first century BC, also believed the Pyrenees to be the highest and largest range.

2 **the Tyrrhenian sea:** Appian uses this term to refer to the northern part of the western Mediterranean in general, as do most authors (see E. C. Semple, *The Geography of the Mediterranean region: its Relation to Ancient History* (London 1932), p. 60).
the Pillars of Herakles: The Straits of Gibraltar (see 2.8 below).

the western or the northern ocean: The Atlantic and the Bay of Biscay.

3   This crossing takes half a day: Appian believed, as did other writers such as Caesar (*Bell. Gall.* 5.13.2), Strabo (3.1.3), Pliny the elder (*NH* 4.102) and Tacitus (*Agricola* 10), that the Iberian peninsula lay further north than it really does, and with the north-south axis lying roughly from Cape Finisterre to Cartagena. For this reason he thought that north-western Spain was close to the southern coast of Britain. However, he places Iberia far closer to Britain than other authors (P. Janni, *La mappa*, p. 114).

4   The size of Iberia: Strabo (2.4.4 and 3.1.3) describes the peninsula as like an ox-hide, 6,000 *stadia* long and 5,000 *stadia* wide, almost half the size suggested by Appian. At this period the *stadion* is usually equivalent to one eighth of a Roman mile (and thus approximately 187 m.), in which case Strabo's figures are approximately correct, since the distance in a straight line from Cape Finisterre to Cartagena is c.920 km. and from Cape St Vincent to the Mediterranean end of the Pyrenees c.1170 km. Obviously both authors are only giving approximations. Strabo also emphasises throughout his account the excellence of the large rivers of Iberia for transport.

Hispania as some now call it rather than Iberia: *Hispania* is the Latin name for the whole peninsula, and is found already as early as the beginning of the second century BC (Plautus, *Menaech.* 235 (*Hispanos*); Ennius, *Ann.* 471 (Skutsch)). Appian himself uses the Greek name, Iberia, throughout this work, noting again at the very end (102.444) that the Romans now call it Hispania. Strabo (3.4.19) mentions the two usages, and also explains that *Iberia* meant different areas at different times. Polybius (3.37.10) states that in his time (probably the later half of the second century BC) *Iberia* was the name of the land from the Pyrenees to the Pillars of Herakles (Gibraltar) (see F. W. Walbank, *Historical Commentary* 1.378-9).

2

5   the Celts crossed the Pyrenees at some time in the past: There is much debate among archaeologists about the arrival of Celtic civilisation in Iberia. For a recent account, see Maria Cruz Fernández Castro, *Iberia in prehistory* (Oxford 1995). The Phoenicians had been colonising the southern coast of Spain and the mining areas of the Guadalquivir valley since the eighth century BC, when they also established their major western settlement at Carthage in north Africa. The Greek colonies in Spain are mostly on the more northerly part of the Mediterranean coastline, the most notable being Emporion (modern Empúries), and all seem to originate from Massilia (modern Marseilles) to which the inhabitants of Phocaea in Asia Minor had fled, after the destruction of their city by the Persians in about 546 BC. On Phoenician and Greek colonisation, see R. J. Harrison, *Spain at the dawn of history: Iberians, Phoenicians and Greeks* (London 1988), chs. 3-5.

6   Arganthonius, king of Tartessus: This king is mentioned in a story in Herodotus (1.163-5) as ruling over the kingdom of Tartessus for eighty years, and dying at the age of 120. He is said to have welcomed merchants from the Greek city of Phocaea in the seventh or sixth century BC. Another story in Herodotus (4.152) describes a Samian merchant, named Colaeus, who was allegedly blown off-course and found Tartessus, where he also traded profitably. The second story describes Tartessus as being beyond the Pillars of Herakles, and it has been identified with a civilisation based on the Atlantic coast, between Seville and Huelva, which produced remarkable goods in

bronze and gold, under the influence of Phoenician colonies in southern Spain. For a short account, see Harrison, *Spain*, ch. 4.

7 **Carpessus:** This place is unknown apart from this mention, and a similar note at 63.267, which makes the identification with Tartessus seem to be a conjecture of Appian's. Other writers identify Tartessus with Carteia, which is on the coast just inside the Straits of Gibraltar (Strabo 3.2.14; Pliny, *NH* 3.1.3; Pausanias 6.19.3; Pomp. Mel. 2.6.96).

8 **the temple of Herakles:** This temple was actually at Gades (modern Cadiz), and was famous in the ancient world (see Strabo 3.5.3). The divinity worshipped there was originally the Phoenician god Melkart, already identified by Herodotus with Herakles (Herodotus 2.43), in whose temple at Tyre Alexander the Great wanted to sacrifice, but was refused. Arrian, describing this event, discusses the relationship between the cult of Herakles at Thebes, that at Tyre and the cult at Tartessus (Arrian, *Anab.* 2.16). On the temple in Gades, see R. J. Harrison, *Spain*, pp. 123-6.

3

10 **They have divided it into three parts and send three praetors out to them:** Appian is describing the position in the peninsula after the creation of the three provinces of Baetica, Lusitania and Hispania citerior (Tarraconensis) in the reign of Augustus. The word translated as *praetors* (στρατηγοί) is ambiguous, as it is used both in an non-specific sense as meaning 'commanders' or 'generals', and, in a Roman context, as describing holders of the praetorship. Appian's usage elsewhere indicates that here he means the latter, but if so, he is in error (see below, on 38.152 and 102.444; and on the governors in Augustus' period, Richardson, *The Romans in Spain* (Oxford 1996), pp. 164-5).

12 **my history of Sicily:** Appian's *Sikelike*, the fifth book of his *Roman History*, survives only fragments preserved in the Byzantine *Excerpta* (see Introduction, pp. 3 and 5).

Chs. 4-38: The Hannibalic war

In 261 BC, the Romans responded to an appeal by a group of mercenaries, holding the Sicilian city of Messana (modern Messene), and invaded Sicily in order to ensure that the Carthaginians, who had been a major presence in the island since the fifth century, did not gain control of the Straits of Messene. After a long and difficult war, in which the Romans had for the first time to develop a competent navy, with which, after many defeats, they were at last able to defeat the Carthaginians at the battle of the Aegetes Islands in 241 BC. The undefeated Carthaginian general on Sicily, Hamilcar Barca, was forced to withdraw, and the Carthaginians were compelled to pay a large indemnity. Shortly after the end of this, the first Punic war, Carthage was faced with a revolt of her mercenary armies (which Appian, 4.15, calls the 'Libyan' war), in the course of which Rome seized Sardinia in 238 BC. In response to this, Hamilcar Barca began to develop Carthaginian power in Spain The Barca family seem to have been the main proponents of Carthaginian expansion in the area, since at Hamilcar's death his place was taken by his son-in-law, Hasdrubal, who was in turn succeeded by Hamilcar's own son, Hannibal. When Hannibal left Spain in 218 BC to march through southern France and across the Alps into Italy, he left his brother, also called Hasdrubal, in charge, supported by another brother, Mago, who was the last Carthaginian commander to leave the peninsula in 206 BC (see below, 37.151). The family link with Spain was further strengthened by Hannibal's marriage to a Spanish princess from Castulo in the upper Guadalquivir valley (Livy 24.41.7; Silius Italicus, 3.97-103, calls her Imilce). On the influence of the Barca family in Spain, see Richardson, *Hispaniae*, pp. 18-20 and 59-60.

The war in Spain last from the attack by Hannibal on Saguntum in 219 BC to the final departure of Mago. It formed an essential part of the overall Roman strategy in defeating Hannibal, who left the peninsula in 218 BC on his famous journey across the Alps, but who must have hoped to use his bases in Spain (particularly New Carthage) as a source of supply for his relatively small army. The main success of the brothers, P. and Cn. Scipio, in the years 218 to 211 BC, was in keeping the route to Italy closed, so that, despite Hannibal's spectacular series of victories in Italy (at the river Ticinus and the river Trebia in 218, Lake Trasimene in 217 and Cannae in 216) he was never able to restore his losses of men or draw fresh supplies from Spain. This made his reliance on winning over Rome's allies in Italy even more important to him than would otherwise have been the case, and this in turn restricted what he could do. Also important was Hannibal's inability to gain access to the siege machinery that he had accumulated in New Carthage, and which was captured there by the younger Scipio in 209 BC (see below on 23.90). This hampered his activity in Italy, and in particular made a siege of Rome itself out of the question. Only after losing the battle of Baecula in 208 BC, did Hannibal's brother, Hasdrubal, succeed in escaping from the peninsula to bring aid to the forces in Italy, and he was defeated at the battle of the river Metaurus in 207. (Appian confuses Hasdrubal with another Hasdrubal, the son of Gisgo, and so misdates this event: see below on 28.113). The campaigns in Spain were therefore crucial in the war of attrition which eventually led to Hannibal's withdrawal from Italy in 203 BC.

4

13   **The first external war:** Appian is here distinguishing between those wars fought outside Italy (which he calls *external*) from those within Italy, though of course these too were external to the city of Rome, and would have been seen as such in the early and middle republic. Even so, in describing the Hannibalic war as the second external war, he is forgetting the war fought against the Illyrians in 229 BC, which Polybius calls the first to be fought in Greece by the Romans (Polybius 2.11-12). The reason for putting together the first Punic war and the war in Iberia appears to be his wish to present both as wars between the two great powers over territory in the western Mediterranean. This is misleading, since, as the accounts in both Polybius and Livy show, the original intention of the Romans in sending an army to Iberia was to prevent Hannibal from invading Italy. The Hannibalic war was not essentially a war for the possession of the Iberian peninsula, as Appian appears to represent it here.

14   **They began to fight in about the one hundred and fortieth Olympiad:** The Olympiad was a four-year period, reckoned from the first celebration of the Olympic games in 776 BC (see E. J. Bickerman, *The chronology of the ancient world* (London 1968), pp. 75-76). The 140th Olympiad was the period from 220 to 216 BC, and was used by Polybius as the starting point of his history (Polybius 1.3.1; 2.37.2; 4.1.3). Appian also concludes his account of the Hannibalic war in Spain with an Olympiad date (see below 38.152). For Appian's use of the Olympiad system, see Leidl, pp. 100-101.

The reason given for the breaking of the treaty was as follows: The account which follows blames the outbreak of the Hannibalic war entirely on the Carthaginians, and more specifically on the Barca family. Polybius, who examines the causes of the war in great detail (Polybius 3.6-30), considers that Hamilcar Barca was a major cause, but because of his exasperation at the Roman defeat of the Carthaginians in the first war, and the subsequent seizure by the Romans of the island of Sardinia (Polybius 3.9.6-10.13). However Polybius rejects the account of the Roman historian Fabius Pictor, who put the blame on Hasdrubal, Hamilcar's son-in-law, because (according to Fabius) he had established a separate and powerful rule in Iberia, and wanted to dominate Carthage also; in this account, Hannibal was following Hasdrubal's policy in attacking Saguntum, contrary to the wishes of the Carthaginians (Polybius 3.8; the account in Diodorus 25.12 also sounds as though it has come from Fabius). It is likely that Appian's version has its origins in Fabius' history, though what he gives is more elaborate and even more anti-Barca than the other accounts of Fabius. For a discussion of these sources, see Walbank, *Historical Commentary*, 1.310-11; and for a brief account of the Carthaginians in Iberia, H. H. Scullard, 'The Carthaginians in Spain', *CAH* VIII², pp. 17-43.

15 **the Libyan war against the Carthaginians:** This war, the 'Mercenary War', was notorious for the cruelty displayed on both sides, and seems to have lasted from just after the end of the first Punic war in 241 to late in 238. Polybius gives a full account (Polybius 1.65-88; see Walbank, *Historical Commentary*, 1.130-49). Polybius also mentions Iberians and Celts among the mercenaries, together with 'Libyans' (*i.e.* native north Africans). Appian uses the term 'Libya' to refer to north Africa, and especially that part dominated by Carthage, so that his eighth book, which he calls *Karchedoniake* ('Carthaginian') in the preface to his *Roman History* (*praef,* 57) is called *Libyke* in the manuscripts.

and surrendered Sardinia to the Romans: This was seen by Polybius as one of the two major explanations of the cause of the Hannibalic war (Polybius 3.30). He states that the Romans had no reason for taking the island, specifically rebutting the account which Appian produces here, and which probably also originates in Fabius Pictor's version (Polybius 3.28; see Walbank, *Historical Commentary*, 1.149-50).

16 **Hanno, who was called 'the Great':** Hanno was the leader of the anti-Barca faction in Carthage. In Polybius' account of the Mercenary War, he is represented as being a very ineffective commander, and the war as being only brought into control by the Carthaginians as a result of Hamilcar's appointment in his place, and by Hamilcar's decision to unite the forces which Hanno was still commanding with his own. At the end of the war, according to Polybius, they made a public reconciliation, and together besieged towns in Numidia (Polybius 1.87-8). He is only called 'the Great' by Appian and the Byzantine historian Zonaras (8.22.6). We know little about the nature of politics in Carthage, but it appears to be similar to that of Rome in the same period, based on families and within an oligarchic framework (see Lazenby, *Hannibal's War*, pp. 4-5).

the Numidians: Numidia was an independent kingdom, west of Carthage in north Africa, which was often in conflict with Carthage (see also on the kings of Numidia: Syphax, below 15.58 and 29.115; and Massinissa 25.96, 30.118 and 37.149-50).

5

17   **plundered the possessions of the Iberians, who were doing him no wrong:** As might be expected, Polybius gives a much more positive account of Hamilcar's period in Iberia, saying that he won over the Iberians by war and diplomacy, and after nine years was killed in a battle against the most war-like of the Iberians (Polybius 2.1.5-9). On the Iberians, here used in a very general sense, see above on 1.1.

  his son-in-law, Hasdrubal: On the Barca family, see note before ch. 4 above.

20   **the Iberians set fire to the wagons:** This stratagem is first attributed to the opponents of Hamilcar by Frontinus, *Strat.* 2.4.17, writing on military tactics at the end of the first century AD.

6

23   **Hannibal, ... who was Barca's son and the brother of Hasdrubal's wife:** See note on Barca family, at ch. 4.

  This young man: Hannibal was 25 or 26 when he succeeded Hasdrubal in 221 BC (Nepos, *Hann.* 3.2) and nine when he accompanied his father, Hamilcar, to Spain in 238 BC (Polybius 2.1.6). As Hamilcar died in 229 BC (Polybius 3.10.7), Hannibal will have been about eighteen years old when Hasdrubal took over the Spanish command. For the parallel with Scipio Africanus, see below at 18.68

24   **the river Ebro, which cuts Iberia approximately in half and flows into the northern sea:** As often, Appian's geography is poor. The Ebro flows into the Mediterranean, not the Atlantic, and reaches the sea at Tortosa, some 150 km. down the coast from Barcelona. It is true that the Ebro flows most of the way across the peninsula, rising about 40 km. south of Santander, on the Atlantic coast. It cannot be said, however, that it cuts the peninsula in half, even approximately.

7

25   **The Saguntines, colonists from the Zakynthians:** Several ancient authors refer to the Greek origin of Saguntum (so Livy 21.7.2; Strabo 3.4.6; Pliny, *NH* 16.79.216), probably because of the similarity of its name in Greek (Ζάκυνθα) to that of the Ionian island of Zacynthus. The archaeology of the site, on a high ridge on the edge of the mountains some 20 km. north of Valencia, and still dominating the coastal plain, shows it to have been an Iberian town with no observable Greek settlement, and its coinage gives the name *Arse* (see Michael H. Crawford, *Coinage and Money under the Roman Republic* (London 1985), p. 88 and Appendix J). It is possible that this is the reason for Livy's assertion that there were also Italian colonists from Ardea among the inhabitants (Livy 21.7.2). The origin of both the Greek and the Roman names is uncertain, but it suits the argument of both Appian and Livy to suggest that the Saguntines were from the beginning aligned with the Greeks and Italians rather than with the Carthaginians or even with the Iberians. This also explains Appian's mention of 'the other Greeks' as being anxious about Carthaginian expansion, along with the Saguntines.

  situated half way between the Pyrenees and the river Ebro: Once again, Appian's geography is at fault, since Saguntum is some 150 km. south of the Ebro. In three other places in this work, he identifies Saguntum with New Carthage, which is approximately 250 km. south of Saguntum (12.47; 19.74; 75.320). The reason for his error in this place, however, is his confusion over the treaty between the Romans and Hasdrubal (see below on 7.27 and 10.39), which is also the context in which he places Saguntum north of the Ebro at *Iber.* 10.79 and *Hann.* 3.12.

27 **The two sides agreed:** The treaty agreed between the Romans and Hasdrubal in 226 is described in Polybius (2.13) and Livy (21.2.7). Appian's account is the most confused and the most intricate. He combines the negotiations with Hasdrubal with the appeal to the Romans from the Saguntines, which the other two keep separate, and represents the agreement as resulting in an addition to a pre-existing treaty between Rome and Carthage. Polybius describes a compact between the Romans and Hasdrubal (as opposed to the authorities in Carthage); and Livy describes it as a renewal by the Roman people and Hasdrubal of an earlier treaty about the boundaries of the two 'empires' (*imperia*) of the Romans and the Carthaginians, with an explicit clause preserving the freedom of the Saguntines. The version given by Polybius, that the agreement simply required the Carthaginians not to cross the Ebro under arms, with no mention of any other part of the peninsula, is probably the closest to the truth, and the agreement would then be intended (as Polybius indicates) to keep the Carthaginians away from the Gauls, who were about to invade Italy. This was then altered by later pro-Roman writers, who wanted to blame Hannibal and the Carthaginians for the outbreak of the Hannibalic war. This tradition may have originated in the writings of Fabius Pictor, but was clearly progressively elaborated by Livy and Appian. For an analysis of the sources and of the significance of the Ebro treaty, see Richardson, *Hispaniae*, pp. 20-30 and H. H. Scullard, 'The Carthaginians in Spain', *CAH* VIII², pp. 28-31 (both with further bibliography); J. W Rich, 'The origins of the second Punic war', in T. J. Cornell et al. edd., *The Second Punic War: a reappraisal* (*BICS suppl.* 67, 1996), pp. 1-37.

8

28 **a slave ... surprised him while hunting and killed him:** The version Appian gives of the death of Hasdrubal (and also at *Hann.* 2.8) is that, given with slightly different details, by a number of other authors (Diodorus Siculus 25.12; Livy 21.2.6; Val. Max. 3.3, ext.7; Justin 44.5.5), all of whom present a picture of a cruel and blood-thirsty man, whose murder was avenged by the tortures inflicted on the slave concerned. Polybius gives a slightly different account (2.36.1-2), in which he emphasises the virtues of Hasdrubal as a general and a diplomat. See Walbank, *Historical Commentary* 1.214.

29 **The army then declared Hannibal to be their commander:** Although all the sources which describe Hannibal's appointment agree that he was the choice of the army, the majority of the others (and even Appian himself at *Hann.* 3.8) state explicitly or imply that this was ratified by the assembly of the people at Carthage, while Appian states that it was the council which confirmed it (cf. Polybius 3.13.4; Livy 21.3.1; Nepos, *Hann.* 3.1). ·Only the twelfth-century historian, Zonaras (8.21), in an imprecise phrase, suggests that it was another authority in the city. It is possible but unlikely that Appian was following a different source here, which has left no other trace. More probably he wanted to present the accusations which the enemies of the Barcids bought against Hannibal and his supporters as having popular support (see below 8.31), which would have seemed very odd if the same people had just voted Hannibal the command with

great enthusiasm. Livy, who reports the accusations, states that the group bringing them was led by Hanno, the opponent of the Barcids, but he was not supported by the majority (Livy 21.3.2-4.1; on Hanno, see note on 5.16 above). It is possible also that Appian is making a contrast between the election of Scipio in 210, chosen by the people despite the reservations of the older people, and the appointment of Hannibal, chosen by the army and the oligarchy (see below 18.68-72).

The Carthaginian council: There were properly speaking two councils in Carthage, a smaller one (called the *gerusia* by Greek authors, probably of about thirty; and a larger (the *synkletos* or senate), which seems to have had little impact on events in practice. Appian here uses the term *boule*, which could refer to either, but it is probable that the smaller council took decisions of this type (cf. Polybius 1.21.6 and 10.18.1; and Walbank's comments on theses passages in *Historical Commentary*, 1.76 and 2.218). Elsewhere, in his book on the Hannibalic war, Appian says Hannibal was appointed by the people in Carthage, rather than the council (*Hann.* 3.8-10).

30 **despised Hannibal because of his youth:** The difficulties Hannibal experienced because of his age are a parallel to those of Scipio. See below on 18.68, and on Hannibal's age, above on 6.23.

31 **The people sided with the prosecutors:** This is probably another example of Appian's anti-Barcid bias (see last note).

9

33 **He decided that he would not endure being in perpetual fear:** The notion that generals started wars in order to distract attention from their personal difficulties is found elsewhere in Hellenistic historians. See, for example, the stories that Pericles began the Peloponnesian war to avoid being prosecuted for financial and other misdemeanours (Plutarch, *Pericles* 31-2; Aristodemus 16.1). The story that Hannibal acted in this way does not occur elsewhere, except in Appian, *Hann.* 3.9; and Hannibal's fear at the outcome of various uncertainties is also found at *Hann.* 40.173 (contemplating the attack on Rome) and 58.243 (fearing that he might be blamed for having started the war by his attack on the Romans in Spain).

34 **while he was still a boy his father had him swear an oath:** This story appears in almost all the sources, and, according to Polybius, goes back to Hannibal himself, who told it to king Antiochus III of Syria in 195 to explain his undying hatred of the Romans (Polybius 3.11.1-12.6). Polybius attaches importance to the story, since he argues that the first cause of the Hannibalic war was the hatred that Hamilcar felt for the Romans, which was passed on to his son (Polybius 3.9.6-8). For the later Roman tradition, this story fitted so well with the idea that it was the Carthaginians, and especially Hannibal himself, who were responsible for the war, that it became a standard part of their account of it. Thus Livy, 21.1.4, includes it in the first chapter of his first book on the war, and it recurs regularly in both historians and poets (Nepos, *Hann.* 2.4; Val. Max. 9.3. ext.3; Florus 1.22.2; Appian, *Hann.* 3.10; Orosius 4.14.3; *de vir. ill.* 42. Martial 9.43.9; Sil. It. 1.81ff.)

35 **and that he, if he were successful, would gain immortal fame:** According to the satirist Juvenal (*sat.* 10.147-67) this topic was a common exercise for declamations by school-boys.

37 **Libya and those parts of Iberia which were subject to Carthage:** Libya is the area of north Africa subject to Carthage (see above on 4.13); and Iberia, as usual, simply means the whole peninsula (see above on 1.4).

10

36 **it would make an outstanding start if he crossed the Ebro:** Once again Appian's geography is faulty (see note on 7.25 above). Polybius states that the first campaign that Hannibal undertook was against the Vaccaei and other tribes in the northern part of the central *meseta*, as a result of which everyone south of the river Ebro, with the exception of the Saguntines was afraid of him (Polybius 3.14).

the Torboletae, who are neighbours of the Saguntines: These people are otherwise unknown. Schulten, *FHA* 3.27-8, identifies their territory with that of Tartessus, which he believes had its frontier at the river Júcar down to the period of Carthaginian control (see above on 2.6). They are called the Turdetani by Livy, 21.6.1 and 12.5, which is the name of a large group of people, living far away in the valley of the Guadalquivir (the Roman Baetis); and in later passage are called the Turduli (Livy 28.39.8), a name which is also used for the Turdetani of Baetica (Livy 34.17.4 and 34.20.2). Polybius' account, in which a Roman embassy, which warned Hannibal not to interfere in Saguntum, was answered by Hannibal with the charge that the Romans had themselves interfered in an internal dispute there, seems quite different, though Polybius does say that Hannibal then wrote to Carthage, accusing the Saguntines of having injured some Carthaginian allies, relying on their alliance with the Romans (Polybius 3.15.1-8). This is coherent with Appian's account here.

39 **on the following night crossed the Ebro with his entire army:** Appian's phraseology here seems designed to show that, in the very act of attacking Saguntum, Hannibal had clearly broken the Ebro treaty (see above, on 7.27). He is wrong, of course, in stating that Hannibal had to cross the Ebro to reach Saguntum, an error which results from his placing Saguntum north of the river (see above on 7.25).

11

40 **the Saguntines sent an embassy to Rome:** Appian's account here of the diplomatic exchanges before the outbreak of the war involves the Saguntines to a greater extent than either Polybius' or Livy's version, and seems to present the whole matter as being conducted in the more complex style of diplomacy which he also ascribed to the process leading to the Ebro treaty (see above 7.27, and note). This is no doubt to emphasise the importance of this event, and of the Saguntines within it.

43 **When this was reported at Rome:** The decision of the senate not to intervene seems odd here, and Polybius certainly implies that the senate had decided, when Saguntum was threatened, to go to war if it was attacked (Polybius 3.20.2). In each case, the account of the senate's decision seems to be determined by the desire of the author to put the Romans in a good light: Polybius showing that they did care about the Saguntines (he mentions the earlier vote to show that there was no need for the senate to decide whether or not to fight Hannibal when the war was declared in 218, because they had already come to the necessary decision); and Appian providing an excuse for the long delay between the news that Saguntum had fallen and the eventual outbreak of the

war. Leidl, pp.151-2, points out that Appian echoes the words of the Ebro treaty (as he has presented it: see above 7.27) to demonstrate the rightness of the Roman case.

12

44-7 The account of the siege of Saguntum is similar to that in Livy (21.7.4-9.2, 11.3-15.2), and even more closely related to that in Diodorus Siculus (25.15), who also has the story that the Saguntines mixed base metal with their gold and silver in order to frustrate Hannibal (see G. De Sanctis, *Storia dei Romani* 3.1 (Torino 1916) p. 423, n. 83). It no doubt comes from the Roman annalistic tradition, and probably owes its origin to Fabius Pictor, with further elaboration to emphasise the greed and cruelty of the Carthaginian. Polybius (3.17) gives a much shorter account, and is more interested in the military consequences of the capture of the town than the details of the actual siege (see Walbank, *Historical Commentary*, 1.327 ff.). Appian gives similar accounts of the ends of sieges: 33.132-6 (Astapa); 96.418-97.420 (Numantia); and in other places elsewhere in his histories (see Leidl, p. 152).

47 **he ... made it a colony of the Carthaginians; and now it is called, I believe, Spartarian Carthage:** Once again Appian's geography is at fault. Having described Saguntum as being north of the Ebro (see above 7.25 and note), he here identifies it with New Carthage (modern Cartagena). He is also wrong, both here and at 75.320, in ascribing the foundation of New Carthage to Hannibal. It was in fact settled by his brother-in-law, Hasdrubal (Polybius 2.13.1, 10.10; Diodorus Siculus 25.12; Strabo 3.4.6). Isidore of Seville (*Orig.* 15.1.67) in the seventh century AD attributes the foundation of the city to the 'Africans' of the period of Hannibal. The name 'Spartaria' is given to New Carthage also by Pliny the Elder (*NH* 31.8.43) in the first century AD and by Isidore. The name derives from the plant called *spartum* by the Romans and *esparto* in Spanish, which was used for making ropes in the ancient world, and is still harvested for paper-making. There was a plain north of New Carthage where a great deal of it grew (Strabo 3.4.9; Pliny, *NH* 19.2.7).

Note that throughout the rest of this book, Appian refers to New Carthage simply as 'Carthage'.

13

48 **The Romans sent ambassadors to Carthage:** This story of the delivery of the ultimatum by the Roman ambassadors appears in both Polybius and Livy, which suggests that it originated with Fabius Pictor (Polybius 3.33.1-4; Livy 21.18.13-14; Walbank, *Historical Commentary* 1.361).

51 **He marched against all the tribes in his vicinity:** Polybius, 3.35.1-4, and Livy, 21.23.1-3, both describe Hannibal as conducting a campaign north of the Ebro, in order to prepare the way for his march to Italy; but only Appian has Hannibal indulge in a campaign of terror against the Iberians at this point, and keep them in ignorance of the reason for assembling the army, once again seeking to show the Carthaginians as excessively cruel and devious.

52 **He sent ambassadors to the Gauls:** The Gauls were not only invaluable to Hannibal in his journey across the Alps but also formed part of his army in Italy (see Lazenby, *Hannibal's War*, pp.14-15). It was probably to avoid such a conjunction that the

Romans had insisted on the Ebro treaty in 226 BC (see above on 7.27). In the long run, the presence of the Gauls with Hannibal's army probably proved a disadvantage to him, in that Rome's Italian allies were more worried about a Gallic invasion than they were afraid of the Romans, especially since Rome had successfully defended Italy against the large-scale invasion by the former in 225 BC.

14

53 **sent Tiberius Sempronius Longus with 160 ships and two legions to Libya:** Longus was one of the consuls of 218 (Polybius 3.40.2 and 41.2-8; Livy 21.17.1 and 5). He reached Sicily, but was recalled when Hannibal arrived in northern Italy and fought alongside Scipio at the battle of the Trebia (Polybius 3.61.7-12, 68.13-74.11; Livy 21.48.7-8, 51.5-7 and 52.1-56.9). It is important to notice that, since the end of the first Punic war, Rome had much more control of the seas than the Carthaginians, which was why Hannibal's invasion had to go by land.

has been recorded in my book on the wars with Carthage: This appears to be a reference to Appian's *Punica*, which in fact contains no mention of Longus. He is mentioned in the *Annibaike*, which describes the war against Hannibal in Italy from 218 to 203, as being present at the Trebia (*Hann.* 6.23). Appian here seems to forget that Longus never reached Africa.

54 **Publius Cornelius Scipio:** Scipio was the other consul of 218, and was assigned the province of Spain (*Hispania*) in order to fight Hannibal there (Polybius 3.10.2; Livy 21.17.1 and 6). As in the case of Longus, the assumptions of the Roman senate were that the war with the Carthaginians could be fought far away from Italy. He was the father of Scipio Africanus, who was the Roman commander in Spain from 210 BC to 206 BC (on the importance of the Scipio family in Appian's work, see above, Introduction, p. 4.

his brother Gnaeus Cornelius Scipio as his legate: Cn. Scipio was the elder brother of Publius, and had already held the consulship in 222 BC, when he had been involved in fighting in northern Italy against the Gauls (Broughton, *MRR* 1.232-3). Although Appian calls him his brother's legate (πρεσβευτής), which is the post that a second-in-command would have held in the late Republic and in the imperial period, it is not clear that he was given any such position or power by the senate before the army left Italy in 218. Gnaeus certainly was in control of the army when his brother he returned to face Hannibal in Italy, and probably held a separate command in 212 and 211 BC (see Richardson, *Hispaniae*, pp. 34-5 and 55-6).

55 **Publius, learning from Massiliote merchants that Hannibal had crossed the Alps into Italy:** As Polybius and Livy make clear, when Publius Scipio arrived at one of the mouths of the river Rhône, while sailing from northern Italy to Spain, he discovered that Hannibal was crossing or had already crossed the Pyrenees, not the Alps. On making further investigations, he learned that the Carthaginian army had in fact crossed the Rhône, and was heading towards the Alpine passes (Polybius 3.41.4-8, 49.1-4; Livy 21.26.3-5, 32.1-5). The Greek colony of Massilia (modern Marseilles) was probably by this time already a friend and ally of the Roman people, and is described as such in an inscription from Lampsacus of c. 196 BC, recording the renewal of an alliance between Rome and Massilia (*SIG*³ 591, ll. 27 and 52-4). Appian seems to believe that Publius

discovered about Hannibal's departure from Spain after he himself arrived there; hence his description of the army that he handed over to his brother as **the army in Iberia**.

handed over to his brother Gnaeus the army in Iberia and sailed in a quinquereme for Etruria: This decision of Publius Scipio to send his brother on to Spain was to be vital not only to the war in Spain and the development of the Hannibalic war as a whole (see note above, before ch.4), but also to the future of the Roman presence in the peninsula. On Gnaeus' position as commander, see above on 14.54. Publius met Hannibal's forces at the battles of the river Ticinus and the river Trebia, and was defeated on both occasions.

56   **are set down in the next book:** This refers to the *Annibaike*, which constitutes the seventh book of Appian's work.

15

57   **Gnaeus on the other hand did nothing worth recording:** Despite Appian's somewhat dismissive account, Gnaeus did succeed in landing at the Massiliote colony of Emporion (modern Empúries, on the Catalan coast, west of Girona) and in establishing a Roman base at Tarraco, and, after establishing friendly relations with some of the local tribes, fought a naval engagement with the Carthaginians at the mouth of the Ebro in late 218 and early 217 (Polybius 3.76.1, 95.1-96.7). Livy also ascribes to him an extraordinary series of military activities throughout Spain, which are almost certainly fictitious (Livy 22.20.3-21.8; cf. Lazenby, *Hannibal's War*, p. 127).

58   **From this time on the two Scipios carried on the war in Iberia:** This clause covers the period of the warfare between the Scipios and the Carthaginians from 217 to 212 BC. On this period, which is dealt with in greater detail but considerable confusion by Livy, see Richardson, *Hispaniae*, pp. 36-40; Leidl, pp. 167-70.

the Carthaginians, under attack from Syphax, ruler of the Numidians, sent for Hasdrubal and part of his army, at which point the Scipios easily overcame the remainder: Livy, 24.48.1-49.6, states that the Scipios actually made contact with Syphax, but this may be an imitation of the younger Scipio's meeting with the Numidian king in 206 (see below 29.115-119). Only Appian has Hasdrubal Barca withdrawn to fight Syphax in Africa, and Livy not only has Hasdrubal in Spain throughout the whole period, but mentions the lack of Carthaginian involvement in the defeat of Syphax, which was achieved by a neighbouring king, Gala, and Gala's son, Massinissa (Livy 24.49.6).

59   **both as generals and as diplomats they were extremely persuasive:** This picture of the Scipios as successful diplomats as well as effective generals is confirmed by both Polybius and Livy, though it needs to be modified by the disaster that befell them in 211. For Appian, it is clearly intended as a counter-poise to his view of the Carthaginians (and especially the Barcids) as terrorising the Iberians. See below on 23.90.

16

60   **two other generals, Mago and another Hasdrubal, the son of Gisgo:** Mago was the youngest of the three sons of Hamilcar Barca to serve in Spain. He was with his brother, Hannibal, at the battle of Cannae in 216, and returned to Carthage to announce

the victory (Livy 23.11-13). In 215, he was sent with reinforcements to support his other brother, Hasdrubal, in Spain (Livy 23.32.5). Hasdrubal, son of Gisgo, the only Carthaginian commander in Spain not known to be a member of the Barca family, was certainly there in 214 (Livy 24.41.5). Polybius and Livy recount stories of the mutual hostility between the three generals, which is said to have prevented them from following up the defeat of the two Scipios in 211 (Polybius 9.11) and to have given the younger Scipio the opportunity to attack New Carthage in 209 (Polybius 10.7; Livy 26.41.20).

61   **Gnaeus wintered at Orso and Publius at Castulo:** This refers to the end of the campaigning season in 212. The fact that the two brothers were in separate winter-quarters, together with an indication in Livy (25.3.6: *Hispaniae P. et C. Corneliis*) that in this year there were two *provinciae* in Spain rather than the single command that had been allocated since 218, suggests that each had his own *imperium* assigned by the senate. This may be because the war had to be fought across a more extended area by now, but it is likely that this division of forces was one of the causes of their defeat in 212/211. See Richardson, *Hispaniae*, pp. 40-1. Of the two places mentioned, Castulo is at the head of the Guadalquivir valley, and it is not unlikely that Publius had succeeded in carrying the war up the valley of the river Segura from the Mediterranean coast-line and across the mountains. Orso, however, should be the Roman Urso (modern Osuna), which is far too far west, and it is probable that Gnaeus was encamped on the river Segura, near Ilorci, which is where the elder Pliny locates the site of his pyre (Pliny, *NH* 3.1.3). Given Appian's carelessness over geographical matters, this is not a good reason for emending the text to read Λόρκωνι here (Schulten, *FHA* 3.92; Scullard, *Scipio*, pp. 264-5, n. 70), particularly because he appears to call the same place Ἰλυργία at 32.128 below (on which, see note). At 65.274, Appian again mentions Orso, and there it appears that it is possible to sail from Orso through the Strait of Gibraltar to Gades, which would suggest that, at least in that context, he thought of the place as being on or close to the Mediterranean coast.

63   **Gnaeus, who knew nothing of this, sent soldiers:** The story of the deaths of the Scipio brothers is given in a different and longer version in Livy (25.32-6), which includes an incident in which Hasdrubal, being adept at the language of the Celtiberians, persuaded some of Gnaeus' forces to desert him. This is confirmed by a remark attributed to the younger Scipio by Polybius, in which he says that the disaster was the result of the division of the forces and the treachery of the Celtiberians (Polybius 10.6.1-7.2).

17

65   **sent to Iberia Marcellus:** Appian here seems to have garbled the account preserved in Livy and some later sources of the events after the death of the Scipios. Immediately after the disaster, Livy states that the Romans were able to regroup, due to the actions of an equestrian officer called L. Marcius, who rallied the forces of the two dead generals and led them back to their base north of the Ebro (Livy 25.37.1-39.18; cf. Val. Max. 1.6.2, 2.7.5, 7.15.11; Frontinus, *Strat.* 2.6.2, 2.10.2; Pliny *NH* 2.111.241). It may be that Appian has confused this man with M. Claudius Marcellus, who in 211 returned from his victory and capture of Syracuse to celebrate two *ovationes* and be elected consul for the fourth time (for sources, see *MRR* 1.273-4 and 277-8). Marcellus was never sent to

Spain. Appian may also be confusing this Marcellus with the consul of 166, 155 and 152, who was in Spain on two occasions, as praetor in 169 and as consul in 152 (see below on 48.198-50.214). Marcius does appear in Appian's account, serving under the younger Scipio in 207 and 206 (below 31.120-126 and 33.132-34.137).

with him Claudius, with ships and one thousand cavalry and ten thousand infantry: According to Livy, the man sent to relieve Marcius was C. Claudius Nero, who had been one of the Roman commanders involved in the capture of Capua in 211, and was sent with six thousand Roman infantry and three hundred cavalry, and a further six thousand infantry and eight hundred cavalry from the Italian allies (Livy 26.17.1-3). This is presumably the origin of Appian's story of this Claudius, who he states was Marcellus' adjutant.

66 **These men achieved nothing remarkable:** Livy (26.4-16) has a story about Nero forcing Hasdrubal Barca into a situation in which he is forced to promise to withdraw Carthaginian forces from Spain, a promise which (with typical Punic deceit) he then breaks. Given the precarious situation of the Romans after the deaths of the Scipios, this is almost certainly false, and Appian's note (wherever it has come from) probably correctly summarises the true position (see H. H. Scullard, *Scipio Africanus in the second Punic War* (Cambridge 1932), p. 55 n. 1).

67 **for fear that the war there might also be transferred to Italy:** The anxiety of the senate in Rome was not, of course, that there might be fighting in Italy, since Hannibal had been there since his arrival in 217 BC; but rather that the Carthaginian armies, currently tied up in the Iberian peninsula, might be able to join with Hannibal (see note before ch. 4 above).

18

68 **Cornelius Scipio, the son of that Publius Cornelius who had perished among the Iberians:** This is the first appearance in Appian's account of P. Scipio, later to acquire the *cognomen* Africanus as a result of his defeat of Hannibal at the battle of Zama in 202, who was to be the major figure in Rome in the latter stages of the Hannibalic war. On Scipio's career and significance, see H. H. Scullard, *Scipio Africanus: soldier and policitian* (London 1970). Appian's version of his election to command in Spain differs from that of Livy (26.18-19), both in that Appian indicates that there was considerable opposition to him from 'the older men' (18.70-71), whereas Livy states that he was not only chosen by every one of the voting units (*centuriae*) in the assembly but by every single individual voter (Livy 26.18.9; though Livy does indicate that there was considerable unease after the vote had been taken: 26.18.10-11); and because Livy represents the meeting of the assembly as a second stage in the process, following a failure by the senate to choose a commander and their passing the choice to the assembly (*comitia centuriata*), whereas Appian moves directly to the meeting of the assembly. It is likely that Appian omitted this first stage because he was not interested in the details of the Roman constitution; but it is probable that there was more opposition than Livy suggests. The senate subsequently appointed a more senior man, M. Iunius Silanus, as his second-in-command, and the period of their holding of the *imperium* was limited in the folowing year to allow the senate to recall them if necessary (Livy 26.19.10, 27.7.17; Richardson, *Hispaniae*, 45-6).

He was only a young man (for he was twenty-four years old): The significance of Scipio's age lies not only in his comparative inexperience (which seems to be the point

Appian is making) but in the fact that he is too young to have been elected to an *imperium*-bearing magistracy. Various dates are given for his age, though Appian and Livy are in agreement here (Livy 26.18.7), and it is probable that his date of birth was 235 or 234 (Walbank, *Historical Commentary*, 2.199). When Scipio's adoptive grandson, Scipio Aemilianus, volunteered to serve in Spain in 151 in circumstances which are presented in Polybius' account as very similar to the situation in 210, he also was remarked on as being young (Polybius 35.4.8; cf. below 53.225). For a parallel with the youthful Hannibal, see above on 6.23 and 8.30.

69 **He spoke fluently and forcefully, as though inspired:** This notion that Scipio was inspired by a god (ἔνθους) is part of the legend of Scipio's relations with the divine, on which see further on 23.88 below. The same word is used by Appian in describing Scipio's attitude towards the invasion of Africa in 205 (*Lib.* 8.30).

he would not only take Iberia but also Libya and Carthage: This is clearly a reference to Scipio's later plans, when consul in 205, to invade Africa to draw Hannibal out of Italy. It is unlikely that he said any such thing when being chosen to fight in Spain in 210. This speech to a reconvened assembly is also given in Livy 26.19 and Zonaras 9.7.3f., in a style similar to that of Appian. On the right of a pro-magistrate to convene such a *contio*, see A. Giovannini, *Consulare imperium* (Basel 1983), pp. 59-63.

72 **set out with ten thousand infantry and five hundred horse:** Livy says he had ten thousand infantry and a thousand horse, and also that he had thirty quinqueremes, as opposed to the twenty-eight ships in Appian's account (Livy 26.19.10-11). Despite Appian's suggestion that this was rather a small number, the additional forces increased the two legions which were there under the two Scipios to four. When Scipio attacked New Carthage in the following year, he had (according to Polybius 10.9.6) twenty-five thousand foot and two thousand five hundred horse, a figure which Livy gives also (Livy 26.42.1). This represents approximately one fifth of the total of Roman forces engaged in the war at this point, when they were also fighting in Italy, Sicily and Greece (for the figures, see P. A. Brunt, *Italian Manpower, 225 BC - AD 14* (Oxford 1971), ch. 23).

19

73 **addressed them also in grandiloquent style:** Livy describes his arrival at Tarraco, which the Scipio brothers had established as their base (see above on 15.57), where he congratulated them, and especially L. Marcius, on having held on in Spain, despite the two disasters that had befallen them (Livy 26.20). The speech is also given in Polybius' account (10.6) though Marcius is omitted (see above on 17.65).

he represented himself as doing everything under the influence of a god: On Scipio and his claims to divine assistance, see below on 23.88.

74 **stationed in four camps, separated from one another by a great distance:** The division of the Carthaginian army into separate sections is mentioned by Polybius (10.7.4-5), and placed by Livy in the speech which he gives to Scipio, addressing his troops before he crosses the river Ebro, having marched south from Tarraco (26.41.20). The reason given by these two writers is the mutual hostility between the three generals, Hasdrubal and Mago Barca and Hasdrubal, son of Gisgo. Appian has the Carthaginian army divided into four, and has one of the four sections placed at New Carthage, under the command of Mago, apparently, since he mentions no one else of that name, Mago

Barca (see above on 16.60). Polybius states that Mago was stationed east of the Pillars of Herakles (10.7.5), and he and Livy have another Mago as the commander of the garrison at New Carthage (Polybius 10.12.2 and 4, 10 15.7, 10.18.1; Livy 26.46.8-9), with (according to Polybius 10.8.4) just one thousand soldiers, rather than the ten thousand that Appian mentions here. Livy mentions that there were wide discrepancies between the various writers he had consulted on this as on other matters, including the name of the Carthaginian commander (Livy 26.49.2 and 5); and he himself later refers to Scipio's victory over four Carthaginian armies and four Carthaginian commanders (28.28.9, 38.3, 43.10; but to three armies at 28.42.5. referring to the time of the attack on New Carthage).

they kept their store of money, corn, armour, weapons, ships, prisoners and hostages from the whole of Iberia: The significance of New Carthage, and the brilliance of Scipio's plan to capture it, lay principally in its use as the main depot of military supplies for the army in Spain, and also as a possible base from which to supply Hannibal's army in Italy. The large quantities of siege-weapons which Scipio seized when he took the town (see below 23.90) were doubtless intended to have followed Hannibal either by sea or land, and would have done so had it not been for Roman control of the seaways of the western Mediterranean and the presence of the army of the two Scipios in northern Spain.

had previously been Saguntum: For this gross error of geography, see above on 7.25.

75   **possessing silver mines:** These mines were later exploited by the Romans, and were described by Polybius in some detail, based on his visit to the area in the mid-second century (Polybius 34.9.8-11, from Strabo 3.2.10; C. Domergue, *Les mines de la péninsule ibérique dans l'antiquité romaine* (Rome1990), pp. 195-6).

20

76   **he led his army through the night against Carthage:** Appian's belief that Scipio marched from Tarraco to New Carthage in one night is completely incredible, and reveals again his lack of knowledge or concern about the geography of Spain. Polybius (10.9.7), followed by Livy (26.42.6), has him arriving on the seventh day from the crossing of the Ebro, and even this is almost certainly too little time, since the distance to be covered is some 460 km. The appearance of the same figure in Livy suggests that the text of Polybius is not corrupt at this point, which indicates that either Polybius is exaggerating or that the distance covered was reckoned from a point nearer to New Carthage. De Sanctis (*Storia dei Romani* 3.2 (Torino 1917), p. 465, n. 35) suggests the ford across the river Sucro (see also Walbank, *Historical Commentary* 2, pp. 204-5; Leidl, pp. 194-6).

The story of the capture of New Carthage, with its combination of brilliant strategy and tactics aided by divine intervention, was irresistible to ancient historians, and Livy mentions the accounts of the Greek historian, Silenus, who was a contemporary and associate of Hannibal, and the Roman annalist, Valerius Antias, writing in the time of Sulla. Polybius' account (10.10-19; see further Walbank, *Historical Commentary* 2, pp. 191-220), which came at least in part from C. Laelius, who was with Scipio at New Carthage (Polybius 10.3.2), appears to be the basis of that of Livy (26.42-51) and of Appian, though both have significant differences of detail. The essential difficulty lies in Scipio's use of a route across a lagoon, of which the water-level dropped in the evening. Polybius clearly states that Scipio knew of this effect before he left Tarraco (10.8.6-7), and Livy indicates that he had heard of it from fishermen at Tarraco (Livy 26.45.7); but if it was entirely predictable that this would happen, it is difficult to imagine why the Carthaginians took so little care of the defences on that side of the city, and to see why Scipio spent so much energy attacking the main gates. Both Livy's account and Appian's suggest that Scipio was taking advantage of an unexpected turn of events: Livy mentions an unusually strong wind springing up from the north, which caused the drop in the level to be much greater than usual (Livy 26.45.8); and though Appian (21.82) wrongly attributes the drop to the normal tides (which are in fact very small in this part of the Mediterranean), he also states that it was only when Scipio saw the tide had turned that he mounted an attack on the sea-wall. It seems likely that Polybius' sources were attempting to emphasise Scipio's foresight rather than his opportunism. For a modern discussion of the attack, see Scullard, *Scipio*, ch. 2; Lazenby, *Hannibal's War*, pp. 134-140, and his plan below.

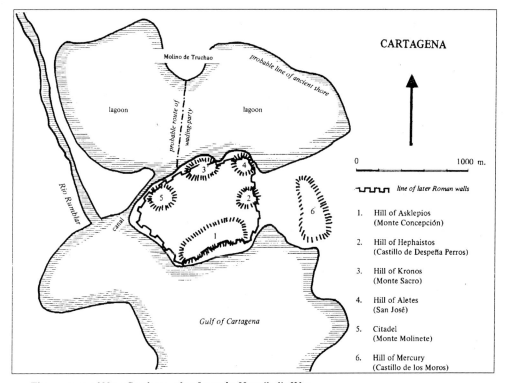

The capture of New Carthage after Lazenby Hannibal's War.

77   **stationed his ships in front of the city's harbour:** Although not previously mentioned by Appian, the fleet had also proceeded south from Tarraco, under the command of his friend, C. Laelius (Polybius 10.9.4-6; Livy 26.42.5). If Polybius is correct in attributing

to Scipio mention, during his speech to his troops before setting out for New Carthage, of a dream in which Poseidon promised him aid in the forthcoming battle, it may be that he was referring to his expectation that the ships would be crucial in the forthcoming siege, rather than that he expected the water-level to drop. The name of the commander of the fleet was another matter on which Livy's sources disagreed (Livy 26.49.4).

21

83 **"Now is the moment, men! Now the god has come to my aid!":** On Appian's view of Scipio's relationship with the gods, see below on 23.88.

22

84 **He was the first to seize one of the ladders, carry it across and was climbing up:** Appian here represents Scipio as in the forefront of the action. This is in contrast to Polybius, who states that at this point Scipio was able to encourage his troops by his words and character (10.14.9-10), and had earlier specifically commented on the fact that he took care that he was not directly involved in the battle, but came as close as he could to the action in order to observe what was happening, protected by three men, covering him with large shields (10.13.1-5), a procedure for which he was commended by Liddell Hart (B. H. Liddell Hart, *Greater than Napoleon: Scipio Africanus* (Edinburgh and London 1926), pp.33-4).

23

88 **he was achieving everything through the influence of a god:** There were already different views about Scipio's relations with the gods in the mid-second century, when Polybius wrote, in his introduction to his description of the capture of New Carthage, that although Scipio was perhaps the most outstanding man of his age, almost all the writers before himself had attributed this to good luck and divine inspiration than to intelligent calculation (Polybius 10.2-5). Polybius portrays Scipio as manipulating such stories, but Appian here follows other writers of the late republic and earlier empire in attributing belief in them to Scipio and in following the historians Polybius criticised in making him the favourite of the gods, and especially Jupiter, even though elsewhere he appears to describe Scipio as manipulating such events for his own purposes (see 18.69, 19.73 and 26.101). According to Gellius (*NA* 6.1.1-5) C. Oppius, an associate of Julius Caesar and Octavian, and Julius Hyginus, writing under Augustus, and various other unnamed writers, recorded that Scipio's mother conceived him after her bed had been visited by a large snake, a story also mentioned by Livy (26.19.6-7), though he remarks that this was also said about Alexander the Great, and that Scipio himself disbelieved it. By the time the *de viris illustribus* was written in the late fourth century AD, it was said that this led to the belief that he was a son of Jupiter. The stories of his consulting Jupiter in the Capitoline temple, mentioned here by Appian (23.89) are earlier, and are probably referred to by Polybius (10.5.5). Livy also has this story (26.19.5), and it is embellished later with the remark that he was the only visitor to the temple at whose approach the guard-dogs did not bark (Gellius, *NA* 6.1.6; *de vir. ill.* 49.2-3). Scipio's image (probably in the form of wax mask) was kept in the temple of Jupiter on the Capitoline, as Appian states (see also Val. Max. 8.15.1), but it is quite uncertain when it was placed there (Walbank, *Historical Commentary* 2.197, points out that this was

almost certainly after the destruction of the temple by fire in 83 BC). On the 'Scipionic legend', see F. W. Walbank, 'The Scipionic legend' *PCPS* n.s. 13 (1967), pp. 54-69; Scullard, *Scipio*, pp. 18-23.

89 **Even now they bring the statue of Scipio alone out of the Capitoline temple during processions:** This probably refers to the funeral processions of the Cornelian family (the *gens Cornelia*), during which the wax-masks of the ancestors were carried (se Val. Max. 8.15.1, who states this in almost the same words).

90 **he took possession there of a store of material for both military and peaceful uses:** The quantities of material captured at New Carthage reinforce the significance of the city as a possible supply base for Hannibal. Livy mentions the widely varying estimates by different authors of the number of captives and the quantity of armaments seized, commenting wryly on the capacity of some historians to produce excessive figures (Livy 26.49.2-6). It is clear from the accounts of both Polybius and Livy that Scipio used the skilled work-force which the Carthaginians had assembled to produce supplies for the Roman army in Spain (Polybius 10.17.9-16 and 10.20; Livy 26.47.2).

he sacrificed to the gods, conducted a triumph, and praised the army: The word here translated as 'conducted a triumph' (ἐθριάμβευε) can be used of a celebratory procession other than a formal Roman triumph, but elsewhere Appian uses this word (and others from the same root) always to mean a Roman triumph (thus in the six other places he uses it in this work: 38.156, 43.179, 57.243, 80.349, 98.424 and 100.436; and in another 51 places elsewhere in his writings). If that is what he means here, he is clearly wrong, since a triumph can only take place in Rome. Livy, 26.48.2-4, describes a ceremony of thanksgiving, but does not call it a triumph. Appian also wrongly attributes a triumph to Scipio on his return to Rome in 206 (below 38.156).

Reminding them of the Scipios, he freed the captives to their own homes: It is clear that Appian is intending to mark a contrast with the policy of the Carthaginians, who took the hostages in the first place, and in particular of Hannibal, who had (according to Appian) subdued the Iberians to a state of terror before starting his invasion of Italy (above 13.51). The same point is made at 15.59. The other sources which mention the return of the captives (Polybius 10.17.7; Livy 26.49.7-9; Diodorus Siculus 26.21) do not include a reference to the Scipios.

91 **He gave rewards to his soldiers:** There are similar stories in Polybius, who comments at length on Roman practices of division of the booty (10.16); and in Livy (26.48), though he states that the reward for climbing the walls was the granting of the decoration of the mural crown, not amounts of cash.

92 **At Rome there was a three-day festival:** Livy recounts that Laelius was sent by Scipio with captives from New Carthage to report the good news, and that as a result a *supplicatio* of one day was ordered by the senate (Livy 26.51.1-2; 27.7.1-4). As elsewhere, Appian (or his source) has made Scipio more impressive by exaggerating the length of the festival.

Iberia and the Phoenicians there: By 'Phoenicians', Appian means the Carthaginians, in reference to the origin of Carthage as a Phoenician colony (see above on 2.5).

24

93 **sending friends to each place, won them over:** Appian is at pains to stress the diplomatic skills of Scipio, as he had been of his father and uncle (see above 15.59 and

23.90). In both Polybius and Livy, there are stories at this point about the voluntary submission to Scipio of several Iberian kings (Polybius 10.34-38; Livy 27.17.1-4). Appian also mentions what was no doubt the case, that Scipio used force where diplomacy failed.

94 **there were two remaining, both called Hasdrubal:** The two Hasdrubals have been distinguished above at 16.60 (see note). However Appian confuses the two in the chapters that follow. According to both Polybius, 10.38.10, and Livy, 27.20.2, Hasdrubal, son of Gisgo, and Mago were still with their armies in places at a distance from Hasdrubal Barca, just as they had been when Scipio launched his attack on New Carthage (see above on 19.74), and it was against Hasdrubal Barca that Scipio launched his attack into southern Spain in 208. There is no other suggestion that Hasdrubal Barca was in the north recruiting mercenaries at this time.

another man called Mago: This Mago was in fact the son of Hamilcar, and brother of Hasdrubal and Hannibal Barca. Appian, having confused him with the commander of the same name who attempted to defend New Carthage against Scipio's attack, has him already killed him by this date, and so has to assume that this is someone else (see above on 16.60 and 17.74).

the territory of Lersa: This place is unknown, and is probably the result of a mistake by Appian or a corruption of the text. In place of Λέρσα γῆν τῶν, Schweighäuser suggested Τυρδιτανῶν ('the Turdetanians', a general name for the people living in the Guadalquivir valley) or Λυσιτανῶν ('the Lusitanians'). Nipperdey suggested Καρπητανῶν, on the basis of their mention at Polybius 10.7.5. Schulten (*FHA* 3.127), followed by Goukowsky, corrects to Λεργητῶν = Ἰλεργητῶν, 'the Ilergetes', a people living in the Ebro valley, whose kings, Indibilis and Mandonius, were among those whom Polybius, 10.35.6-8, and Livy, 27.17.3, record as surrendering to Scipio at this time. However if so, this is an error, since even according to Appian the Hasdrubal who fought Scipio was at this time in the Baetis valley.

95 **Baetyca:** This name, which is the reading in all the manuscripts (Βαιτύκην), is a mistake for Baecula (in Greek Βαίκυλα, cf. Polybius 10.38.7), and probably a confusion with Baetica, the later Roman name of the province within which this battle took place. The exact site is unknown, but is in the general area of Córdoba, which, as Corduba, was to become the capital of the Roman province. Appian's brief description agrees with the much more detailed account in Polybius and Livy (see Walbank, *Historical Commentary* 2, pp. 248-50; Scullard, *Scipio*, pp. 68-85).

One major significance of the battle of Baecula was that, despite being defeated, Hasdrubal Barca managed to elude Scipio, and marched north through Spain, in an attempt to take his army into Italy across the Alps, and thereby to join up with his brother, Hannibal, in Italy. He was successful in reaching the valley of the Po in early 207, but was defeated as he moved south, down the Adriatic coast-line, at the river Metaurus by the consuls, C. Claudius Nero and M. Livius Salinator. Had he succeeded, Scipio, for all the brilliance of his achievements in Spain, would have failed in what had been since 218 the main aim of the Romans in the peninsula, which was to prevent aid reaching Hannibal in Italy. Appian, however, fails to notice this, as he believes that it was Hasdrubal, son of Gisgo, who was defeated at Baecula, and he has Hasdrubal Barca leaving Spain from the north in the following year, after the last major Carthaginian defeat in Spain, at the battle of Ilipa, in 206. See below, 28.113.

25

96   **Hasdrubal gathered together such of the army of the Carthaginians as remained in Iberia at the town of Carmona:** In this chapter and the two which follow, Appian describes the battle which finally destroyed the Carthaginian forces in the peninsula, usually known as the battle of Ilipa. Appian places this immediately after the defeat of Hasdrubal at Baetyca (= Baecula), while Polybius (11.20-24.9) and Livy (28.12.10-16.15) place it in the spring of the following year, 206. Some scholars, following De Sanctis, *Storia dei Romani* 3.2 (Torino 1917), 496-7, n. 84, have believed that Livy's account runs together the events of 207 and 206, and that the battle took place in 207; but Livy's account is in fact reasonably coherent internally and fits with that of Polybius (see Walbank, *Historical Commentary* 2.17-18).

The site of the battle is called *Silipia* by Livy (28.10.14). The manuscripts of Polybius (11.20.1) give the name Ἰλίγγας (Ilinga) or ἠλίγγας (Elinga), which Schweighäuser emended to Ἰλίπας (Ilipa) on the basis of Livy's reading and of the name of a town on the north side of the river Guadalquivir, not far from Italica, given in Strabo 3.2.2 and 3.5.9 (Schweighäuser, *Polybius* 3.350 and 7.38-9). Ilipa is identified with the town of Alcala del Rio, 14 km. north of Seville. V reads καρεώνην here, καρβώνην (altered to ναρβώνην by a subsequent hand) at 109, and καρμένην at 246, which Schweighäuser, in his edition of Appian (1.130 and 3.234-5) emends to Καρμώνην, which is the version of the name followed in this edition. Carmo (the modern Carmona) was an important town in both the pre-Roman and Roman periods, and is situated in the fertile plains on the south side of the Guadalquivir, some 40 km. east of Seville, and an important stronghold of the Carthaginians (see Harrison, *Spain*, pp. 91-2. In some ways this is a more satisfactory site than Ilipa, since both Livy (28.16.2) and Appian (28.110-112) describe the Carthaginians retreating after their defeat towards Gades, which would have been almost impossible from Ilipa, because of the swamps which in ancient times covered the area to the north of the mouth of the river Guadalquivir (Richardson, *Hispaniae*, pp. 50-1; R. Corzo Sanchez, 'La secunda guerra punica en Baetica', *Habis* 6 (1975), pp. 213-40, at 234-40). J. Millán Leon, 'La batalla de Ilipa', *Habis* 17 (1986), pp. 283-303, argues that Ilipa was the correct site.

Appian's account of the battle, though it has some features in common with those in Polybius and Livy (who for the most part follows Polybius), differs considerably from them, and gives a version much less detailed in tactical terms, and with much more emphasis on Scipio's actions and his claims of divine aid. He seems to be relying on sources, probably in the Roman annalist tradition, for whom Scipio was the main focus of interest.

and many Numidians, led by Massinissa: This is the first appearance of Massinissa, son of the Numidian king Gala, and at this point commander of the Numidian cavalry forces with the Carthaginians in Spain. On his subsequent importance, see below on 30.118 and 37.149-50. See further *OCD*[3] s.v. Masinissa. For variant spellings of Massinissa's name both in the manuscripts of Appian and in other sources, see Leidl, p. 225, n. 637. Numidia was renowned in antiquity for the quality of its cavalry, both horses and men (Arrian, *Cyneg.* 24.1).

98   **Laelius:** Here mentioned for the first time in Appian's account, C. Laelius was a close friend of Scipio throughout his life, and an informant of Polybius (Polybius 10.3.2). He had been the only person that Scipio had forewarned of his intention to attack New

Carthage in 209 according to Polybius (10.9.1, followed by Livy 26.42.4) and remained
with him throughout the Spanish campaigns. This story about Laelius does not occur in
any other source. As a *novus homo* without any ancestor who had held the consulship,
he was reliant on the patronage of the Scipios for his political advancement, holding the
consulship in 190 with Scipio's younger brother, Lucius. His son, also called C.
Laelius, was a friend of Scipio Aemilianus, and as such was chosen by Cicero as the
main speaker in his dialogue on friendship (Cic., *de amicitia* 1.4-5). See *OCD³* *s.v.*
Laelius (1), Gaius.

99   **Scipio moved ten *stadia* away:** On the length of the *stadion*, see above on 1.4.

100 **The entire enemy force was seventy thousand infantry, five thousand cavalry and
     thirty-six elephants, while Scipio did not have even a third as many:** The numbers
     on the Carthaginian side which Appian gives are similar to those in Polybius, of 70,000
     foot, 4,000 horse and 32 elephants (11.20.2); but Livy, who discusses variant numbers
     given in his sources, states that there were only 50,000 foot and 4,000 horse (Livy
     28.12.13-14). Polybius' version seems designed to make Scipio's victory the more
     impressive, and probably exaggerates the size of Hasdrubal's army. Scipio's forces
     were some 45,000 foot and 3,000 horse. Appian's assertion that he had less than one
     third as many as his opponents provides a suitable context for the display of the divine
     intervention which enabled him to win, but makes the conduct of the battle
     unintelligible (Walbank, *Historical Commentary* 2.296-7). He uses the immensity of
     the discrepancy in forces in the speech he gives to Scipio after the battle (26.101).

26

101 **Adopting the appearance and the attitude of someone inspired by the gods:** Once
     again Appian presents Scipio as claiming divine inspiration, but apparently doing so as
     a means of influencing others, rather than because he himself believed it (see above on
     18.69, 19.73 and 23.88). No other source has this story. Such use of omens to
     encourage the troops is mentioned as being employed by other generals, and in
     particular Marius, when fighting the Cimbri and the Teutones (eagles: Plutarch, *Marius*,
     17.6-7), and Sertorius in Spain in the 70s (the white doe: Plutarch, *Sertorius*, 11.3-8,
     20.4-5; Appian, *bell. civ.*1.110.514; Polyaen. 8.22; Val. Max. 1.2.4; Pliny, *NH* 8.117;
     Frontinus, *Strat.* 1.11.13; Gellius, *NA* 15.22.3-5. Appian does not mention this story in
     his brief account of Sertorius, below 101.438-441. The observation of birds was one of
     the main forms of divination among the Romans (see *OCD³* *s.v.* birds, sacred).

102 **While he was speaking, he sees some birds flying overhead:** To emphasise the
     dramatic nature of these events, Appian here uses the historic present tense (ὁρᾷ), rather
     than the imperfects which he uses for the rest of the account.

104 **assigning the cavalry to Silanus:** M. Iunius Silanus, first mentioned here by Appian,
     was appointed by the senate as Scipio's second-in-command (*adiutor ad res gerundas*,
     Livy 26.19.10) in 210 (see above on 18.68), and acted in that capacity throughout the
     campaign (see Richardson, *Hispaniae*, pp. 45-54).
     and the infantry to Laelius and Marcius: On Laelius, see above on 25.98; on
     Marcius see above on 17.65.

27

105   **there were only ten *stadia* between them:** On the length of the *stadion*, see above on 1.4.

even though the soldiers had not been fed: This crucial element is found in the accounts of Polybius (11.22) and Livy (28.15.2), but in those authors this is ascribed to Scipio's decision to attack Hasdrubal's camp at day-break, rather than because the Roman troops had been inspired by favourable omens.

107   **he ran out alone just as he was into the space between the armies:** Here again, as in his account of the attack on New Carthage, Appian portrays Scipio as being in the thick of the fighting, and thereby inspiring his soldiers to fight to protect him (see above on 22.84). Once again, the impression given is the opposite of that in Polybius, who shows Scipio as having carefully worked out his tactics for the battle, and pursuing them rigorously (Polybius 11.23).

28

111   **some of them captured a strong place:** This mention of the Carthaginians finding a strong point and being able to put up a temporary resistance to the Romans is also mentioned in Livy (28.16.7-10); but in Livy's account, Scipio leaves to return to the Roman base at Tarraco, and it is there rather than at New Carthage, that Silanus joins up again with Scipio. It appears from his account of the last stages of Scipio's campaigns in Spain that Appian sees New Carthage as being the main Roman base in the peninsula from 209 onwards.

113   **Hasdrubal, the son of Hamilcar, ... was summoned by his brother Hannibal to invade Italy with all speed:** Hasdrubal Barca, according to the account given by Polybius (11.1-3) and Livy (27.20 and 43-51) had left the peninsula in the aftermath of the battle of Baecula in 208, crossed into Italy and was defeated at the river Metaurus in 207 (see above on 24.95). Appian, however, who seems to have confused the two Hasdrubals, has only Hasdrubal, son of Gisgo, at Baecula and Hasdrubal, son of Hamilcar, spending the whole period from 208 to 206 in the northern part of the peninsula on a recruiting mission, and only then departing for Italy.

29

114   **Lucius, however, on his return from Rome:** L. Cornelius Scipio, Publius' brother, is first mentioned here. He was the younger son of the consul of 218, but is not known to have been in Spain before 207. He was consul in 190 when, with his brother, he defeated king Antiochus III of Syria, and took the *cognomen* Asiagenes. See *OCD*[3] *s.v.* Cornelius (*RE* 337) Scipio Asiagenes, Lucius. Livy also tells of Lucius being dispatched to Rome with news of the victory over the Carthaginians (28.17.1), but this happens immediately before Scipio's visit to Syphax, whereas Appian here has him returning from Rome, having made no mention of his going in the first place.

the Romans in the city were considering sending him to Libya as general: In addition to the chronological differences between Appian and Livy, it is worth noticing also that Livy (28.17.2-4) attributes the decision to visit Syphax entirely to Scipio without any new information from Rome, and a fragment of Polybius suggests that he had a similar version (11.24a.1-3). The debate on whether to invade Africa comes (according to Livy) after Scipio's return to Rome, though that does not of course preclude at least some of the senators having thought of it before than.

115 **he sent Laelius with five ships to Libya to king Syphax, taking gifts and reminding Syphax of the friendship of the Scipios towards him:** The story of an earlier contact between Syphax and the Scipio brothers is not in fact part of Appian's account (see above on 15.58), but only in Livy (24.48.1-49.6; mentioned again at 27.4.6), in a passage which has been suspected as a version of the story of this visit in 206. This mention of the earlier friendship suggests however that Appian's sources had also described the contact with the two Scipios.

Syphax was king of the Masaesyli on the coast of North Africa, across the sea from New Carthage, and had been at war with Carthage, and hence a possible ally of the Romans. According to Livy, he had entered into a relationship of *amicitia* with the Romans in 210 and now wished to do so again (Livy 27.4.6; 28.17.8; see Walbank, *Historical Commentary* 2.306; J. Briscoe in *CAH* VIII², pp. 62-3).

30

118 **Having agreed secretly with Scipio and given him pledges of loyalty, Syphax sent him away:** The success of Scipio in his negotiations with Syphax show the importance that both men attached to a possible extension of the war to Africa, but in fact they were of no long term benefit, since the Carthaginians soon won over Syphax again. In the event, however, this led to the desertion of Massinissa from the Carthaginian side, which was of great significance in the defeat of Carthage and for Rome's subsequent position in North Africa (see below 37.149-150). This must in any case have been informal agreement, despite Livy's description of the result as a formal treaty (*foedere icto*, Livy 28.18.12; see Richardson, *Hispaniae*, p. 52).

119 **It is said that Scipio, at a banquet in Syphax' residence, lay on a couch next to Hasdrubal:** The story of the meeting of Scipio and Hasdrubal, son of Gisgo, and of Hasdrubal's opinion of Scipio is also told in Polybius (11.24a.4) and Livy (28.18.6-8).

31

120 **At this time, some of the Celtiberians and Iberians:** This section appears to relate to the account given in Livy, 28.1.1-2.13, of Scipio sending Silanus (rather than Marcius, as in Appian) to fight against Mago and Hanno in Celtiberia in the aftermath of the battle of Ilipa and before the visit to Syphax. In Livy's version however, there is no surrender by the Celtiberians, who are defeated in battle.

121 **under the command of Hanno:** According to Livy (28.1.4), this Hanno was sent to Spain to replace Hasdrubal Barca, following the latter's march across the Pyrenees to the aid of his brother Hannibal in Italy after the battle of Baecula. As often, Appian introduces a new character with no explanation.

122 **They seized Hanno, even though he was their commander:** According to Livy, Hanno was captured in the course of a battle, and sent to Rome with L. Scipio (Livy 28.2.11; 28.4.4. Cf. note on 29.114 above).

125-6 **Mago ... sailed to Gades and, though suffering from lack of supplies, watched to see what would happen next:** Livy also has Mago escape to the Gades region, but by land (Livy 28.2.12). Although 'Celtiberia' is a very unspecific designation, it normally refers to the northern and eastern parts of the central plateau, and thus is not accessible by sea.

32

127 **Silanus was sent by Scipio to bring over the town of Castax:** Livy (28.19-20) describes the attack on two towns, which he calls Castulo and Iliturgi, though he states that it was carried out by Scipio himself, with help from Marcius who brought reinforcements from Tarraco (28.19.4). Appian elsewhere calls Castulo Καστολών (16.61) rather than Κάσταξ as here.

128 **He left his route and attacked the town of Ilyrgia:** Polybius mentioned a town in Spain called Ilurgia ('Ιλούργεια) in his eleventh book, almost certainly in this context (Polybius 11.24.10; cf. Walbank, *Historical Commentary*, 2.305). This town is called Iliturgi by Livy 28.19.1. It used to be though that this was an error, as he sites a town of the same name near the mouth of the river Ebro at 23.49.5. Schulten pointed out ('Iliturgi', *Hermes* 63 (1928), 288-301) that there were in fact two place of the same name, of which one was on the banks of the river Guadalquivir, some 30 km. west of Castulo. However, as in Livy's account Scipio marched from New Carthage to 'Iliturgi' in five days, which would involve covering 200 km. through difficult and mountainous country, and moreover passing Castulo before reaching Iliturgi, it may well be that the town Scipio attacked is in fact Ilurco, which is, according to Pliny, *NH* 3.13, the site of Gnaeus Scipio's pyre. It is clear both in Appian and in Livy (28.19.2 and 7) that Scipio's aim in attacking these two towns was to take revenge on them for the deaths of his father and uncle in 212/11, which probably took place at Castulo and Ilurco (see above 16.61-3 and notes). Appian's reference to 'the elder Scipio' probably refers to Scipio's father, but is slightly surprising, since he might have been expected to write 'the elder Scipios' (thus above, 19.75; 23.90; 29.115).

131 **Scipio ... entrusted the town to one of the Castacians who had a good reputation:** This is probably the man whom Livy calls Cerdubelus (28.20.11-12), who was responsible for surrendering the town to the Romans, despite the presence of Carthaginians there.
He marched to Carthage: As usual in this work, Appian refers to New Carthage as simply 'Carthage'.

33

132 **There was a town called Astapa:** The account given here is substantially the same as that in Livy 28.22-3, and it is clear that a similar account occurred in Polybius (see the fragment at Polybius 11.24.11). The site is not known for certain, but it is thought that it may be at Estepa, 24 km. east of Osuna, of which the name on inscriptions is Ostippo (E. Hübner, *CIL* 2, p. 196).

136 **ensuring that their enemies got no profit from their victory:** This somewhat odd remark suggests that Appian's source included the detail, also found in Livy (28.23.4) and Polybius (11.24.11) but omitted by Appian himself, that the people of Astapa also put their gold and silver into the fire, to prevent the Romans from seizing it. Appian tells a similar story of the Saguntines when under attack by Hannibal in 219 (see above on 12.44-7).

did not do any damage to their houses: Intended as a sign of respect to the courageous dead. Contrast Scipio Aemilianus' destruction of Numantia in 133 BC (below 98.424).

34

137 **After this Scipio fell ill and Marcius took the command of the camp in his place:** The account of the mutiny which Appian gives is closely related to that in Polybius (11.25-30) and Livy (28.24-9); a similar version also occurs in Zonaras (11.10), who was probably using Dio Cassius as his source (cf. Dio 16. fr.57.47). Only Appian, however, has Marcius in command of the camp when the mutiny breaks out. In Polybius and Livy, it is M. Iunius Silanus who is with Scipio, which might lead one to believe that the text here is defective and that Μάρκος should be read for Μάρκιος; but Appian always calls Iunius Silanus Σιλανός elsewhere.

Appian seems particularly interested in mutinies, which he uses elsewhere in his work to illustrate the character of the Roman generals of whom he is writing (see Leidl, pp. 264-5).

rebelled against Marcius and set up camp by themselves: In all the other sources the rebellion takes place not in the camp in which Scipio was present but among another section of troops, stationed, according to Livy at Sucro, in order to guard those people which lived on the near side of the Ebro (28.24.5). Sucro, however, is the Roman name for the river Júcar, which reaches the sea at Cullera, some 25 km. south of Valencia. If this is the site of the camp, it cannot have been for the purpose of controlling the peoples north of the Ebro; and indeed, if the rebellion took place sufficiently far north to be of use for this purpose, it would have been impossible for Scipio to deal with it as he did from New Carthage. Probably the rebellious troops were stationed at or near the mouth of the Júcar, and Appian or his source, failing to realise this but knowing that, for the story of the suppression of the mutiny to work, the rebels had to come into Scipio's camp from some distance away, inserted the decision of the mutineers to remove themselves from the camp at New Carthage. The close proximity of the rebels to Scipio's main camp also allows Appian to present Scipio as being serious ill at the time of the suppression of the mutiny, which is not the impression given in the other sources (see below on 35.143).

138 **some came to them from Mago bringing money:** This is not mentioned by Polybius or Livy, and the latter states that Mago had been driven out of Gades immediately before Scipio fell sick, and had sailed to Africa (Livy 28.23.6-8).

35

141 **Scipio ordered those senators who were with him:** The description of these men as senators is surprising. Polybius (11.26.2) and Livy (28.26.5) describe them as seven military tribunes who had been sent by Scipio beforehand to try to calm the situation in the rebel camp, and who for that reason were likely to be able to convince the ringleaders of their good intentions. It is unlikely that these men were already senators, though probable that they were of senatorial families. Leidl, p. 276-7, suggests that the reference may be to members of Scipio's own *consilium*.

142   **He instructed the military tribunes that each should, without being observed, have his most reliable men equipped with swords:** In the accounts in the other sources, the soldiers who were positioned to deal with the assembly of the mutineers consisted of a detachment which Scipio had pretended to send away to deal with a rebellion by the Ilergetes in the north, thus encouraging the mutineers to believe that they were in control at New Carthage.

143   **they were ashamed to keep their general waiting when he was still sick:** It is an important part of Appian's account that Scipio was still serious ill, unlike the other sources, which represent him as having already recovered (Polybius 11.27.7-8; Livy 128.26.13-14; Zonaras 9.10.6). See above on 34.137.

36

144   **then said that he would attach blame only to the leaders:** In Polybius (11.29.12-13) and Livy (28.29.7-8) this remark occurs at the end of a long speech by Scipio, in which he compares the situation the mutineers would be in if they put their trust in the Iberian leaders, Mandonius and Indibilis (Andobales in Polybius), who had rebelled on hearing of Scipio's illness, an event which Appian does not mention until 37.147. Livy's version of the speech is more elaborate than Polybius', while Appian has reduced it to the brief summary in this section.

37

147   **Indibilis:** This man, with his brother Mandonius, was a chief of the tribe of the Ilergetes, and had been among those who had responded to Gnaeus Scipio's overtures in 218, when he was in command of the army in Spain, before being rejoined by his brother Publius (Polybius 3.76.7; Livy 21.21.61.5. See above on 15.57). They subsequently fought against the Romans (Livy 22.21.2). When the younger Scipio discovered Mandonius' wife among the hostages after the capture of New Carthage and returned her to him, the Ilergetes rejoined the Roman side (Polybius 10.18.7-15; 10.35.6-38.6; 10.40; Livy 26.49.11-16; 27.17.10-17). According to Livy (28.243), it was the revolt stirred up by Mandonius and Indibilis, when they heard the rumour of Scipo's death, which was instrumental in encouraging mutiny among Scipio's troops (see above on 35.142). The Ilergetes were one of the most significant of the tribes in the north-east of the peninsula, and are to be located primarily in the mountainous region on the north side of the lower Ebro valley (see A. Schulten, *RE* 9.999). The account of Scipio's brief campaign against the Ilergetes is also given in Polybius (11.31-33) and Livy (28.31.5-3412). On Indibilis, see further below 38.156 and note).

148   **Scipio demanded money from him in recompense and came to terms with him:** This money was to be used to provide the soldiers' back-pay, according to Livy (28.34.11). This settlement with the leaders of the Ilergetes is significant in two respects: it shows the need for Scipio to conclude his business in Spain as rapidly as possible, in order to get back to Rome, where he hoped to be elected consul for 205; and it illustrates the importance of money gathered from the indigenous tribes for the maintenance of the Roman military presence in Spain (see Richardson, *Hispaniae*, pp. 57-8).

149-150 **Massinissa:** Appian here takes up again the story of Massinissa, which he previously dealt with at 30.118. His change of allegiance was of fundamental importance, since it gave the Romans an ally in north Africa, who in the event was to prove invaluable to them, not only during the Hannibalic war but also thereafter. See P. G. Walsh, 'Massinissa', *JRS* 55 (1965), pp. 149-60.

The part played by Sophonisba, the daughter of Hasdrubal, son of Gisgo, in these events is presented differently in the various sources. Livy, who calls her 'Sophoniba', reports her marriage to Syphax only in 204 (Livy 29.23), when Scipio hears of it at Syracuse, on his way to the invasion of Africa, though he does record a meeting between Massinissa and Scipio before the latter leaves Spain in 206 (28.35). Even then this is seen as linking Syphax with the Carthaginians but not as setting him against Massinissa, since Hasdrubal has to persuade Syphax subsequently to back Massinissa's rival for the kingdom of the Maesuli (29.31). Massinissa's interest in Sophinisba emerges only after Syphax' defeat, when, in a notably romantic passage, she is presented as a potential danger to Massinissa's loyalty to Rome, and commits suicide to avoid falling into the hands of the Romans (30.12-15). In the fragments of Polybius, she is mentioned as the reason why Syphax supported the Carthaginians (14.1.4 and 7.6), and it is likely that his version is behind that of Livy (Walbank, *Historical Commentary*, 2.426). The later writers have a version more like that of Appian, who continues the story at *Lib.* 27.110-28.121, where he names her 'Sophoniba': Dio Cassius, 17, fr. 57.51, (followed by Zonaras 9.11) has Massinissa betrothed to Sophonisba (whom he calls 'Sophonis') in 206, before Scipio leaves Spain, and the marriage to Syphax as the reason for the split between Syphax and Massinissa; and a similar story seems to underlie the abbreviated account in Diodorus Siculus, 27.7. The differences between these writers suggests an increasing interest in the romantic, which continued to fascinate literary audiences. In 1730, James Thomson, the poet who wrote the words for *Rule Britannia*, produced his first play, named *Sophonisba*, at the theatre in Drury Lane.

The modern version of her name, Sophonisba, is found only in the inferior manuscripts of Livy, and it appears that in Punic it was probably 'Saphanabaal' (G. De Sanctis, *Storia dei Romani* 3.2 (Torino 1917), p. 532, n. 137).

151 **The admiral Mago, despairing of the situation in Iberia, sailed to the Ligurians and the Celts:** Mago was Hannibal's brother (see above note before ch. 4). The area in which (according to Appian) he intended to recruit was northern Italy, occupied by Ligurians and Gauls (here called 'Celts': see above on 1.1), but now mostly under Roman control. For Livy's version of Mago's mission, see on 38.152.

38

152 **the Romans took Gades, which he had left:** According to Livy (28.36.1-37.10), Mago had been ordered by the authorities in Carthage to sail to Italy and join Hannibal. He attempted a last attack on New Carthage, trying to emulate Scipio's capture of the city three years previously, and then, not succeeding, returned to Gades, where the inhabitants resisted him. Despite initial success in recapturing the town, he withdrew to the Balearic islands, and the Gaditanes handed over the city to the Romans. This marked the final withdrawal of Carthaginian forces from the peninsula.

The Romans from this time, shortly before the one hundred and forty-fourth Olympiad, began to send praetors annually to those peoples: At this point, Appian is bringing to a close the first section of his account of the Roman conquest of Iberia, as he makes plain below (39.158). For this reason he gives a date, or at least an approximate date, just as he has done at the beginning of this section (see above 4.14). The one hundred and forty-fourth Olympiad begins in 204 BC (see note at 4.14), so that Scipio's departure for Rome in 206, fits well enough with this. What happened in 206 was not, however, quite as straightforward as Appian suggests. It is clear from Livy's detailed account that from 206 to 197 the senate sent a series of commanders who had been given the same power and authority to command (*imperium*) as a consul, but who were not elected magistrates. This was clearly a stop-gap measure, and seems to reflect an uncertainty on the part of the senate as to what their policy should be in the peninsula, especially once the Carthaginians had made peace in 201 (see Richardson, *Hispaniae*, pp. 62-75; and, *contra*, W. V. Harris, in *CAH* VIII², p. 121). It was not until the year 197 that two additional praetors were elected to serve in what were then distinguished as two separate *provinciae* of *Hispania citerior* (nearer Spain) and *Hispania ulterior* (further Spain) (Livy 32.27.6, 28.11; cf. Richardson, *Hispaniae*, pp. 75-9). It is true that the word translated here as 'praetor' (στρατηγός) can also mean 'commander' or 'general', but it is clear from his description of them as 'annual' (στρατηγούς ... ἐτησίους) that he is here referring to the magistracy (T. J. Luce, 'Appian's magisterial terminology', *CP* 56 (1961), pp. 21-8 at 23-4; and, *contra*, Famerie, *Le latin et le grec*, pp. 166-7). He uses the same phrase elsewhere to describe annual magistrates sent to Sicily (*Sic.* 2.6), Africa (*Lib.* 135.641) and Pontus (*Mithr.* 121.596), in each case in connection with the settlement of an area after a war, and he clearly thinks this is what is happening in Spain in 206. This is less surprising, in that the next Roman commanders in Spain that he names are in fact the two praetors sent in 197 (see below 39.159). Appian clearly regards the Iberian peninsula as conquered by the Romans from this time onward, and describes subsequent opposition by the inhabitants in terms of rebellions against the established rule of Rome (see below, 38.157; 39.158; 42.171).

to act as governors and to ensure the peace there: This remark again reflects Appian's expectations rather than the views of the late third century BC. In fact all the commanders who went to Spain for the next thirty years were involved in warfare, and there is no reason to believe that Scipio in 206 imagined that this would not be the case (see Richardson, *The Romans in Spain*, ch. 2).

153 **Scipio left them a small army suitable for peaceful conditions:** This also reflects Appian's own perceptions. As Scipio was hoping to be awarded a triumph by the senate, it is likely that he brought a substantial proportion of his army back with him to Rome, as they would be needed for the celebration; but the commanders to whom Scipio handed over had at least sufficient forces to undertake military exploits worthy of note (see Richardson, *Hispaniae*, pp. 68-73).

established a town for his wounded men, which he named Italica, taking the name from Italy: Appian is the only author who states that Scipio founded Italica, though the biography of the emperor Hadrian in the *Scriptores Historiae Augustae* states (with what authority cannot be known) that the emperor's ancestors settled in Italica in the time of the Scipios (*Hadr.*1.1). Recent excavations at the site (modern Santiponce,

8 km. north of Seville) suggest that the foundation was beside a previously existing Iberian settlement (see Richardson, *The Romans in Spain*, p. 36, n. 90). It is placed to control the route through the Sierra Morena, linking the valleys of the rivers Guadalquivir (the Roman Baetis) and Guadiana (Anas), and looking across the plain on the north side of the Guadalquivir. It appears, however, that it was accorded no official status by the Romans before the time of Caesar, and became a *colonia* only under Hadrian, in whose reign the town was substantially enlarged, probably in honour of his predecessor Trajan (Richardson, *The Romans in Spain*, pp. 222-4). If Appian's account is correct, it suggests that many of the wounded soldiers that Scipio left behind in 206 were of allied Italian origin, rather than Roman citizens.

This is the place of origin of Trajan and Hadrian, who later ruled the Romans as emperors: Both the family of Trajan (the Ulpii) and that of Hadrian (the Aelii) were from Italica, and Trajan certainly was born there (Cassius Dio 68.4.1). Of Hadrian, the majority of the sources suggest the same, though the life in the *Scriptores Historiae Augustae* states that he was born in Rome (*Hadr.*1.3). See R. Syme, 'Hadrian and Italica', *Journal of Roman Studies* 54 (1964), pp. 142-9 (= *Roman Papers* 2 (Oxford 1979), pp. 616- 628).

156 **While Scipio celebrated a triumph amidst all this admiration:** It is clear from Livy's account (28.38.1-4) that Scipio did not in fact celebrate a triumph, because the senate would not permit a commander who had won a victory without holding a magistracy (*sine magistratu*) to celebrate a triumph (see Richardson, *Hispaniae*, pp. 70-1). Appian's assumption, which is a natural one, that Scipio would triumph after such an important series of victories, may also be based on the remark in Polybius that he brought back from Spain a most excellent triumph and victory (κάλλιστον θρίαμβον καὶ κάλλιστην νίκην, 11.33.7). It is possible, though not likely, that Scipio, denied a proper triumph, celebrated a private triumph at the Alban Mount outside Rome, as Marcellus did in 211 (Livy 26.21.4-6; so A. Degrassi, *Inscriptiones Italiae* 13.1 (Rome 1947), p. 551); but, if so, it is surprising that Livy fails to mention it.

Indibilis, once Scipio had gone, again went into revolt: This revolt of the Ilergetes, like that of the previous year which seems to have come about because of the rumour of Scipio's death (above 37.147-8), may have been the result of simple opportunism on the part of Indibilis, but may also be the result of the way in which the connections between the Roman commanders and the local rulers in Spain seem to have been based on personal links rather than international treaties (see Richardson, *Hispaniae*, pp. 58-61).

The praetors in Iberia gathered together the army, which had been left them for a garrison: The two commanders concerned were L. Cornelius Lentulus and L. Manlius Acidinus. They were not praetors (and it may be that Appian here uses the word στρατηγοί to mean simply 'generals'; see above on 38.152); but they were experienced commanders, sent to take over from Scipio with consular *imperium*, without being elected to any magistracy (see above on 38.152). This revolt by Indibilis is described by Livy (29.1.19-3.5), who represents this as an attempt by Indibilis to free his people from the Romans, whom he saw as taking over from the Carthaginians as the dominant power in the peninsula. This is probably anachronistic, since the Ilergetes were not in a part of Spain in which the Carthaginians had been present.

157 **They brought to trial those who were responsible for the uprising:** The language Appian uses here is drawn from the law-courts, and reflects his understanding of the

whole peninsula as a Roman settled province, following the victories of Scipio (see above on 38.152). Livy (29.3.1-5) writes that Mandonius, Indibilis' brother, summoned a council of the Ilergetes after Indibilis' death, and made a formal surrender to the Romans, following which the Ilergetes were required to pay a fine, which amounted to twice the sum they had previous paid as *stipendium* for the upkeep of the army (see above on 37.148) as well as other supplies.

Chs. 39-43: From the Hannibalic war to the settlement of Tiberius Gracchus (201-178 BC)

The period from the end of the Hannibalic war to the settlement of Tiberius Gracchus in 178 BC was one of continuous fighting in Spain. The Roman commanders who succeeded L. Cornelius Lentulus and L. Manlius Acidinus (see above on 38.156) were also not holders of any magistracy, but from 197 BC onwards a pattern was established of sending praetors to the two provinces of Hispania Citerior (Nearer Spain) and Hispania Ulterior (Further Spain) (see below 39.159). These men were given the *imperium* of consuls, in view of the military nature of their task. The only exception to this pattern was the sending of M. Porcius Cato, the consul for 195 BC, in his consular year (see below 39.159 - 41.170). All these commanders were involved in warfare against various tribes, but there is no clear shape to their campaigns, an it appears that one major motive for the fighting was the desire of the commanders for a victory, which would allow then to return to Rome to celebrate a triumph (see Richardson, *The Romans in Spain*, pp 51-59). This came to an end with the successful wars against the Celtiberians conducted by Ti. Sempronius Gracchus, who was praetor in 180 BC, and who established a new relationship between the Romans and at least the Celtiberians by a treaty, which was later regarded as the basic point of reference in subsequent negotiations (see below 43.75-179).

39

158 **These things happened immediately after Scipio left, and at this point the first enterprise of the Romans to Iberia came against an end:** With these words Appian brings to an end the section of his work on the Hannibalic war, which, as in other parts of his overall plan, is seen as a central turning-point in the growth of Roman power. It is noteworthy that the second section, which covers the events from the end of the Hannibalic war to the defeat of Numantia in 133 BC, also ends with the triumph of a Scipio (in that case, of Scipio Aemilianus) and the immediate consequences of the victory (98.424-427).

when the Romans were fighting with the Celts of the Po valley and with Philip the Macedonian: Fighting against the Gallic tribes in the north of Italy had broken out in 201 BC, when the consul, P. Aelius Paetus, attacked the Boii (Livy 30.40 16, 31.2.5-11) and continued sporadically for the next thirty years (see W. V. Harris in *CAH* VIII², pp. 107-118). Philip V of Macedon, who had been an ally of Hannibal during the Hannibalic war, was accused by some Greek states of expansion at their expense, as a result of which Rome declared war on him in 20 BC. He wạs defeated in 197 BC by T. Quinctius Flamininus at the battle of Cynoscephalae (see R. M. Errington in *CAH* VIII², p. 224-274).

taking advantage of the Romans' preoccupations: In fact it would appear from the account in Livy and from the records of the inscribed *Fasti Triumphales* that all the

commanders in the peninsula between the departure of Scipio in 206 and the arrival of
C. Sempronius Tuditanus and M. Helvius in 197 were involved in fighting (Richardson,
Hispaniae, pp. 64-75). As Appian's picture of the area at this time is that it was a
pacified Roman province (see above on 38.152 and 157), he has to explain why the
fighting broke out, and adopts a motif found in other writers, that as Roman power
grew, those under its sway used the opportunities offered by war in other parts of the
world to go into rebellion (see, for instance, Polybius, 3.16, on Demetrius of Pharos in
220).

159   **The generals sent against them from Rome for this war were Sempronius
Tuditanus and Marcus Helvius:** These two men were two of the praetors elected for
197 (Livy 32.27.7), and their election and assignment to the Spanish provinces marks a
major change in the policy of Rome in the peninsula, because it marks the recognition
that the need to send commanders will continue for the foreseeable future. Appian
believes that this change had already taken place in 206 (see above on 38.152). It was
probably also at this time that the two provinces were called Hispania Citerior (Nearer
Spain, comprising the Mediterranean coast and the territory behind it) and Hispania
Ulterior (Further Spain, centred on the valley of the Guadalquivir).

and after them Minucius: Q. Minucius Thermus was praetor in 196 BC, and was
placed in charge of Hispania Citerior. It was as a result of the dangerous situation in
which he found himself that Cato, the consul of 195 BC, was sent out to the province,
though in fact he succeeded in defeating two Spanish chieftains, called Budar and
Baesado by Livy, which considerably reduced anxiety at Rome about the situation there,
even before Cato left (Livy 33.44.4-5). He returned to Rome to celebrate a triumph
(Livy 34.10.5-7).

Cato was sent with larger forces: M. Porcius Cato, a major figure in Roman politics
in the first half of the second century. He was elected consul for 195 BC, and
subsequently held the censorship in 186. His book on agriculture is the earliest piece of
Latin prose to have survived complete, and he also wrote what is probably the first work
of history in Latin, the *Origines*. Despite Appian's assertion of his youth, he was 39
years old at his election. The story of his campaign in Spain is almost certainly based
on his own account, which is also the basis of Livy's longer version (Livy 34.8-9, 11-
21; see A. Astin, *Cato the Censor* (Oxford 1978), pp. 302-7; Richardson, *Hispaniae*, pp.
80-94).

Livy (33.43.2), describing the allocation of provinces for 195, states that the
senators chose Hispania Citerior as one of the consular provinces because they believed
that the situation in Spain under Minucius had deteriorated to such an extent that a
consul with a consular army was required.

because of his speeches the Romans called him Demosthenes: Cato was renowned
for his opposition to Greek culture, but is said by Plutarch to have learned much from
Demosthenes' speeches (*Cato* 2.5).

40

161   **arriving at the place called Emporion:** Emporion was the obvious landing place for
an army sailing from Italy, and had been the land-fall for Cn. Scipio in 218 (see above
15.57). It was Cato's base for much of his period in Hispania Citerior, and the Roman
encampment just outside the Greek city (which subsequently became the site of the

Roman town) has been associated with Cato's tenure. Although Appian describes the enemy as gathering there to meet Cato, the area in which Minucius had been fighting was far to the south (see Richardson, *Hispaniae*, pp. 83-4), which suggests that Cato was attacking tribes which had not previously been giving trouble. Livy, 34.11-16, does not name the enemies whom Cato attacked, but describes them as the opponents of the Ilergetes, who were once again allies of Rome at this date. (on the Ilergetes, see above on 37.147 and 38.157).

162 **Massilia:** The Greek colony on the site of modern Marseilles (see above on 13.55).

41

167 **sent sealed letters to each:** This story is also related by Livy (34.17.5-12) and is almost certainly originally from Cato's own account (see above on 39.159), but he does not connect it to the battle at Emporion but to a later incident.

168 **the authorities in all the towns:** The Iberians in the area certainly lived in towns, of which the best surviving is Ullastret, just to the south-west of Emporion. The ancient writers, however, were sceptical of claims from Spain by Roman commanders that they had captured large numbers of such 'cities', and Strabo records criticism of Polybius' account of Ti. Gracchus' capture of three hundred cities in Celtiberia by Poseidonius, who stated that they were really only towers (Strabo 3.4.13). This sounds like a reference to the hill-forts or *castros*, which were used by the inhabitants of north and north-western parts of the peninsula (see M. Almagro-Gorbea, 'From hillforts to *oppida* in 'Celtic' Iberia', in B. Cunliffe and S. Keay, *Social Complexity and the Development of Towns in Iberia* (London 1995), pp. 175-208).

170 **they remained at peace for a the most part:** Appian is clearly intending to show the situation in Cato's province as peaceful as a result of his clever manoeuvre. The peace, however, in so far as there was any, did not last for more than a few months. Cato's successor in Hispania Citerior, the praetor Sex. Digitius, had to deal with rebellions in the following year (Livy 35.1.1-3; see Richardson, *Hispaniae*, pp.95-6).

42

171 **Four Olympiads later, about the 150th:** The 150th Olympiad began in 180 BC. Appian has left out about fifteen years of continuous warfare, but this is to be expected, given his view of the provinces as being already pacified (see above on 39.158). The tenure of Hispania Citerior by Fulvius Flaccus began in 182: see below on 42.172).

many of the Iberians who had too little land: The motif of land-shortage as the cause of strife among those under Roman control is to be found elsewhere in Appian, notably in the first book of the *Civil Wars* (E. Gabba, *Appiano e la storia delle guerre civili* (Firenze 1956), pp. 34-73), and recurs several times in this work (see below 43.179; 59.249-50;61.257-8; 69.294; 76.321; 100.433-4). There does, none the less, seem to have been a recurrent practice among commanders in Spain to distribute land, witnessed to by other sources than Appian, which indicates that this is not simply a preoccupation of his (see below on 59.247; and Richardson, *The Romans in Spain*, pp. 75-6 and 85).

the Lusones, who lived beside the Ebro, revolted against the Romans: According to Strabo (3.4.13) the Lusones were a Celtiberian people near the source of the river Tagus. This would place them in the eastern section of the *meseta*. There is no indication that they ever lived beside the Ebro, and Livy, who gives the fullest account of Flaccus' campaigns, never mentions them, though he describe Flaccus' opponents as being Celtiberians (Livy 40.16.7-10).

172 **The consul, Fulvius Flaccus, was put in command against them and defeated them in battle:** Flaccus was not consul but praetor when he was sent to Hispania Citerior in 182 (Livy 39.56.5 and 40.1.2).

lived a nomadic existence: This is a strange description of Celtiberians, who were not nomadic, and may well have been applied to the Lusones by Appian out of confusion with the Lusitanians (see below 56.234).

Complega: This name does not appear in any other source, the only city taken by Flaccus in Livy's account being called Uthnica or Utina in the manuscripts, perhaps to be identified with Urbiaca, mentioned in the Antonine Itinerary as being 98 miles south of Zaragoza (Livy 40.16.8; *Itin. Ant.* p. 447-5 (Wess.); cf. Walsh, *Livy XL*, p. 136; Richardson, *Hispaniae*, p. 100, n. 32). However a story very similar to this is told by Diodorus (29.28), relating to a city of the 'Kemeltai'. It may be in the north-east part of the *meseta*, if (as the account in the following chapter suggests) it is close to Caravis (so E. Hübner, *Monumenta Linguae Ibericae* (Berlin 1893), p. 70; in his article on Complega in *RE* 4 (1901) 794-5, Hübner tentatively identifies the site with Complutum, near Madrid).

173 **he would bring them many plaids:** The garment called by Appian and other Greek authors the σάγος (*sagos*) was a hooded cloak, particularly associated with Celtic peoples (as shown in his remarks in 42.174 and 43.176. See also Polybius, 2.28.7, on the Insubres and Boii of Cisalpine Gaul). In its Latin form, *sagum*, it was the name for the war-cloak worn by soldiers in the Roman army (thus Livy 10.30.10; Caesar, *bell. civ.* 1.75.3). Flaccus is here represented as turning the Complegans demand against them, by promising to bring many *saga* and then marching on them with his army.

43

175 **Tiberius Sempronius Gracchus:** Flaccus returned to Rome in 180 BC, but, before doing so, he requested permission from the senate to bring back his army in order to celebrate a triumph. This was opposed by Gracchus, who was one of the praetors for the year and had already been allotted Hispania Citerior. After a debate, Flaccus was allowed to bring back those soldiers who had been in Spain for more than six years (Livy 40.35.3-36.13). Gracchus was the father of Tiberius and Gaius, the tribunes of 133 and 123 BC, and went on to hold the consulship in 177 and 163. On his significance for the development of the Roman provinces in Spain, see Richardson, *Hispaniae*, pp.112-25.

Caravis: This may be the town called Caravi in the Antonine Itinerary (*Itin. Ant.* 443.1 (Wess.)), on the road between Numantia and Caesaraugusta (Zaragoza).

Appian conflates Gracchus' campaigns in Celtiberia, which went on from his arrival in 180 to his departure in 178 (Livy 40.39-40, 47.1-50.5), and involved collaboration with his colleague in Hispania Ulterior, L. Postumius Albinus (see Richardson, *Hispaniae*, pp.101-3). It is in 178 that Livy places the surrender of the Celtiberians (Livy, *ep.* 41; the beginning of book 41 of Livy is lost in the manuscripts); and in the same year, according to the inscribed *Fasti Triumphales*, he celebrated a triumph over the Celtiberi and the Hispani (*Inscr. It.* 13.1.80-1; cf. Livy 41.7.1-3).

178 **Complega:** See above on 42.172.
with olive branches in their hands: A sign of their peaceful intentions. The word used here for an olive branch (ἱκετηρία) means a rod held by a suppliant (see below 58.218).

179 **Those who were poor he settled and distributed land to them:** See above on 42.171.
imposed precise treaties on all: It is clear from references to these treaties in Polybius (35.2.15) and Plutarch (*Ti. Gracchus* 5.2) as well as the important part they play in Appian's account of the resurgence of the Celtiberian wars in 153 BC (below 44.180-3), that they marked a significant change in the relations between Rome and the Celtiberians, and possibly (if the word 'all' in this passage relates to more than just Celtiberia) with wider areas of the peninsula. It appears from this section and the argument which follows between the Segedans and the senate in 153 that the terms were that those who were covered by the treaties were to be friends of the Roman people; were not to found new cities; were to pay specified amounts of tribute; and were to serve with the Roman forces. See further, Richardson, *Hispaniae*, pp. 112-125.
celebrated a magnificent triumph: See above on 43.175.

Chs. 44-55: War against the Cetiberians (153-151 BC)

After Gracchus' tenure of his province, little is know about Roman activity in the peninsula until the outbreak of the Celtiberian wars in 153 BC. The alleged reason for Rome going to war again was the action of the town of Segeda in incorporating other smaller towns into its boundaries; but this seems trivial compared to the Roman response in sending a consul with a consular army of two legions to deal with it, and it seems likely that at least part of the explanation lies in the need of the senate to find somewhere for the consuls to fight in a period of relative peace (see below on 45.183). In the event, fighting the hardy Celtiberians in the harsh mountainous country of the north-eastern *meseta* proved much more difficult than the Romans can have envisaged. The centre of the fighting quickly moved to the city of Numantia (see below on 46.188), which was to prove a rallying point for Celtiberian resistance to Rome until its eventual capture and destruction by Scipio Aemilianus in 133 BC (below 97.419-98.427). Throughout these wars, progress towards a solution of the conflict was made more intractable by the desire of successive Roman commanders to be seen as having successfully ended the fighting, and by the determination of their intended successors and the senate in Rome to continue it. In this first stage, a halt was achieved by the negotiations between the Numantines and M. Claudius Marcellus in 151 BC, but his successor, L. Licinius Lucullus, immediately started another war against the Vaccaei, to satisfy his need for a military campaign (below 49.206-51.215). On Appian's view on the deterioration of Roman standards of behaviour at this time, see above, Introduction pp. 6-7.

44

180 **Segeda is a large and powerful city:** The city of Segeda is probably to be identified with a site 10 km. south-east of Calatayud, on the southern side of the mountains which form the north-eastern edge of the central plateau (*meseta*) of Spain (A. Schulten, 'Segeda' in *Homenagen a Martins Sarmento* (Guimares 1933), pp. 373-5). Diodorus (31.39) calls it Begeda.
Belli: Appian presents this tribe as compelling the Titthi to join with them, and the two subsequently allying themselves with the Arevaci, another Celtiberian tribe (see below

45.184). A fragment of Polybius on the embassies which went to Rome in 152-1 suggests that in his version the Belli and Titthi were allies of the Romans against the Arevaci (Polybius 35.2.1-4.14; see below on 49.206-10).

it was included in Sempronius Gracchus' treaties: On these treaties, see above on 43.179.

183 **the senate, in giving such concessions always adds that they shall be in force for so long as seems good to the senate and the people:** A phrase very similar to that used by Appian here appears on two second century documents from Spain: the edict of L. Aemilius Paullus from Hasta (found at Alcala de los Gazules, 40 km. east of Cadiz), dated to the early 180s (*ILLRP* 514); and the inscription recording the surrender of a people to L. Caesius, dated to 104 BC and found near Alcántara (Cáceres) (R. López Melero et al., *Gerión* 2 (1984), pp. 265-323; Richardson, *Hispaniae*, pp. 199-201), which confirms Appian's view, at least so far as Spain is concerned.

45

184 **Therefore Nobilior was sent as general against them:** Q. Fulvius Nobilior was one of the consuls for 153 BC, and thus only the second consul to have been sent to a Spanish province, the first being Cato in 195 (on whom see above on 39.159). Between 153 and 133, when Numantia is eventually captured, eleven of the thirteen commanders known to have been sent to Hispania Citerior were consuls, the other two being praetors. In order to allow consuls to reach the Spanish provinces in time to campaign during their year of office the beginning of the consular year was changed in 153 from the beginning of March to the beginning of January, which illustrates vividly the importance of this change of policy from praetorian to consular command. It is far from clear, however, why the Romans should have thought the walling of the city of Segeda to have been so crucial. It may be that this was connected less with the significance of the Celtiberians and more with the need to provide the consuls with a war to fight at a time when other parts of the Roman world were relatively quiet (so Richardson, *Hispaniae*, pp. 128-37).

with an army of not far short of thirty thousand men: This was a full consular army, which normally consisted of two legions (totalling about 10,000 citizen infantry), 600 Roman cavalry and a contingent of 10,000 infantry and 1,800 cavalry from the Italian allies. The remainder, about 8,000 men, would probably have been made up of Spanish allied soldiers (see H. Simon, *Roms Kriege*, p. 18; Brunt, *Italian Manpower*, p. 663).

Arevaci: The Arevaci appear as the most powerful of the Celtiberian tribes in the north-eastern *meseta*. By the time of Strabo, writing in the second decade of the first century AD, they included not only the area of the head-waters of the river Durius (Duero), where Numantia is sited (below 46.188) but also the territory to the south near the sources of the river Tagus (Tajo) (Strabo 3.4.13). Strabo also states that Segeda was a city of the Arevaci, which suggests that they had by his time absorbed the Belli and the Titthi.

185 **Carus:** Known only from Appian, though he may be identical with the leader of the Segedans, named Kakyrus in Diodorus' account of the negotiations which led to the outbreak of the war (Diodorus 31.39).

187 **on the day on which the Romans keep the feast of Vulcan:** The Vulcanalia was celebrated on 23 August (see H. H. Scullard, *Festivals and ceremonies of the Roman republic* (London 1981), pp. 178-9.

<h2 style="text-align:center">46</h2>

188 **Numantia, which was a very strong city:** Numantia, which was to be the centre of Celtiberian resistance for the next twenty years, is situated 5 km. north-east of Soria, beside the river Durius (Duero), not far from its headwaters. It is thus on the southern side of the mountains which form the north-eastern edge of the *meseta* and the southern edge of the Ebro valley. The sites of the city and of the Roman encampments surrounding it were excavated with great thoroughness by Adolf Schulten in the early years of the twentieth century, and his results published in four volumes (*Numantia*, vols 1-4 (Munich 1914-1931)). For a general description of the site, see A. Schulten, *Geschichte von Numantia* (Munich 1933), pp. 140-150 and Keay, *Roman Spain*, pp. 36-42. An indication of the strength of this city was not only its fine position on a ridge above the river but its circuit of walls, at points six metres thick. See plan, p. 165.

chose Ambo and Leuco as their generals: As often, these men are unknown apart from this reference.

Nobilior moved against them three days later and encamped twenty four *stadia* away: The site of this camp was identified by Schulten on a hill called La Gran Atalaya at Renieblas, some 6 km. east of Numantia (Appian's twenty four *stadia* would be slightly less than this at c. 4.5 km.: see above on 1.4). The camp is walled with stone, and is one of the earliest surviving sites in the western empire. It shows signs of occupation on a number of occasions, of which Schulten identified the earliest as being that of Cato in 195 and the latest during the wars against Sertorius in the 70s BC (see A. Schulten, *Numantia* 4 (Munich 1929)).

189 **Massinissa:** The king of Numidia, who had been an ally of Scipio Africanus during the Hannibalic war (see above 37.149-159). He died in his nineties in 148 BC. On his involvement with the Romans in this year (153 BC), see further below on 57.240.

190 **never before having seen elephants on the field of battle:** The Romans had had similar reactions when they first met elephants on the battle-field in the armies of Pyrrhus, king of Epirus (Plutarch, *Pyrrhus* 17.6, 21.11). On the use of elephants in the ancient world, see H. H. Scullard, *The Elephant in the Greek and Roman World* (London 1974).

192 **some, because of their untrustworthy nature, call them the common enemy of all:** This view is given by the writer of the Caesarian *de bello Africo*, describing the use of elephants in the battle of Thapsus in 46 BC, who says that they could be a threat both to friend and foe (*bell. Afr.* 27.2). Simon, *Roms Kriege*, p. 28, n. 32, notes that Polybius speaks of the unreliability of elephants at the battle of Panormus in 251 BC in similar terms, and believes that Appian's comment may have come from Polybius.

<h2 style="text-align:center">47</h2>

194 **Axeinion:** This town was identified by Emil Hübner, *Monumenta Linguae Ibericae* (Berlin 1893), p. 244, as Uxama (the present town of El Burgo de Osma, some 70 km.

west of Numantia); but, as Simon, *Roms Kriege*, p. 29, n. 33, points out, this seems to be too far distant from Numantia to make the identification likely.

195 **Biesius:** As Schweighäuser observed (*Appian*, 3.257), this name seems to be corrupt, as it is unlike any Roman or Italian name. The early translators called him 'Blesius', and it may be that the original name was 'Blaesius'.

to a neighbouring tribe to arrange an alliance: Schulten believed that this tribe was the Vaccaei, who were the only neighbouring tribe not already under Roman control (*Numantia* 1.344; cf. below on 51.215).

196 **Ocilis:** Identified with modern Medinaceli, 80 km. south of Numantia in the valley of the river Jalón, which flows into the Ebro 20 km. up river from modern Zaragoza. A major route ran from the Ebro valley and followed the valley of the Jalón up onto the *meseta*, running parallel to the road from Numantia to the Ebro, which roughly coincides with the modern road from Soria to Tudela. This would have made Ocilis a convenient site for supplying his army from his bases on the Catalan coast, at Emporiae and Tarracco. The loss of such a depot would be particularly damaging as winter drew on.

197 **took up winter quarters in his encampment:** This is the first recorded occasion on which a Roman commander in the *meseta* did not return to his base for the winter. It may be that (as Simon suggests, *Roms Kriege*, pp. 29-30) the winter set in rapidly and closed the passes into the Ebro valley. A fragment of Diodorus (31.40) notes that this was a war which not even the onset of winter brought to a close, but although this might refer to Nobilior's difficulties, it appears to be based on a fragmentary passage from Polybius, which states that only the winter brought a pause (35.1).

Nobilior must have extracted his army from the camp at Renieblas (see above on 46.188) the following spring. He is said by Polybius (35.4.1-6) to have given a terrifying account of the experiences of his army on his return to Rome, so much so that it was difficult in 151 to raise an army to fight in Spain.

the heavy falls of snow and the harshness of the frost: The climate on the central *meseta* is not Mediterranean but 'continental', due to the mountain barriers which cut it off from the sea on all sides. Consequently the rainfall is irregular and the range of temperatures much greater than for the coast-lands (R. Way and M. Simmons, *A Geography of Spain and Portugal* (London 1962), pp. 44-59).

48

198 **Claudius Marcellus:** M. Claudius Marcellus was one of the consuls of 152 BC. He had served in Spain when praetor in 169, when he held both the provinces at once, because of the problems caused by the war against Perseus of Macedon (Livy 43.14.2-5, 15.4-5), and had gone on to hold the consulship in 166 and 155. The election of so senior a figure at this indicates the anxiety that was felt at Rome over Nobilior's lack of success.

Ocilis: See above on 47.196.

200 **Nergobriges:** The inhabitants of Nergobriga (below 50.213), no doubt identical with Nertobriga or Nertobrica (so Florus 1.33.10), recorded in the Antonine Itinerary (439.3, cf. 437.3) as being between Bilbilis (Calatayud) and Caesaraugusta (Zaragoza). If so, it will have been on a main route from the *meseta* to the valley of the Ebro. A fragment of Polybius (35.2.2) has Marcellus attacking and taking a town in Lusitania later in the

year, which is named as Ἐρκόβρικα in the source, the *de legationibus gentium* of Constantine Porphyrogenitus, before retiring to winter quarters in Corduba. Schweighäuser (*Appian*, 3.260-261; *Polybius*, 4.659 and 8.124) emended this to Νερκόβρικα and identified it with Nertobriga (near Fregenal de la Sierra, 43 km. southwest of Zafra, in the northern foothills of the Sierra Morena) (Pliny, *NH* 3.14; see Walbank, *Historical Commentary*, 3.643). However as Polybius' town could be anywhere in Lusitania, and the only geographical indication he gives is that Marcellus moved from there to winter quarters in Corduba, it would be prudent not to assume that Schweighäuser's emendation is necessarily correct. The name 'Ercobiga' or 'Ercobica' is the name of a town mentioned by Pliny (*NH* 3.24; cf. *AEArq* 39 (1966), pp.137-8), and is probably identical with 'Ergavica', a town among the Celtiberians which surrendered to Ti. Gracchus in 179 BC (Livy 40.50.1).

The Polybius fragment (35.2.2) presents a larger difficulty, in that it is the only source which states that Marcellus fought in Hispania Citerior and wintered in Corduba. Eutropius, in his abbreviated version of Roman history, wrote that, after the successes of L. Memmius in Lusitania, Marcellus afterwards was successful as consul in the same place (*ibidem*) (Eutropius 4.9); but this may mean no more than that Marcellus fought in · the Iberian peninsula (on Memmius/Mummius, see 56.236ff. below). Another fragment, from the lexicographer Suidas (*s.vv.* κωμάσαι and ἀνδρωνῖτις), which may come from Polybius (fr. 110, cited in the *apparatus criticus* of Büttner-Wobst's edition), appears to say that the general Marcus, freed from the war against the Lusitanians, wanted to change to a softer option, and this has been connected with Marcellus' move into winter-quarters at Corduba (Walbank, *Historical Commentary*, 3.643); but, as Schweighäuser observed (*Polybius*, 8.124), this should be punctuated to give the sense 'freed from the war, he wanted to transfer the fighting to the Lusitanians.' This would then record Marcellus' intention, but not that he actually did it. No other source mentions Marcellus' intervention in Lusitania, even though Appian does describe the campaign of the praetor M. Atilius, who was in charge of Hispania Ulterior in 152-1 (see below 58.243-4). There is no reason, apart from this fragment, to assume that Marcellus ever entered Atilius' province. Although Marcellus is credited with the foundation of Corduba, this might well have happened in 169/8, when he was praetor in charge of both the provinces (Strabo 3.2.1; Livy 43.15.3, 45.4.1). Moreover the similarity of the two names Nergobriga/Nertobrica/Nertobriga and Ergobriga may perhaps be more reasonably explained by an error by the excerptor who compiled the *de legationibus* than by assuming that Marcellus moved from the upper Duero valley to attack a town in the lower part of the valley of the Guadiana before marching across the Sierra Morena in order to winter in Corduba, from which he would have to return to the Duero valley to arrange the surrender of the Numantines early in 151.

204 **a herald, wearing a wolf-skin instead of carrying a herald's staff:** In the Greek and Roman world, the herald, carrying the herald's staff (in Greek κηρύκειον or in Latin *caduceum*) as a sign of peace, was guaranteed his safety (see Cic., *de orat.* 1.202; Pliny, *NH* 29.54; Gellius, *NA* 10.27.3). The use by the Nergobriges of a wolf-skin rather than a herald's staff is perhaps intended to demonstrate their barbarism of practice as opposed to their civilised use of the convention of heralds. For a similar comment of this type, see Polybius 35.2.6 on the Celtiberian ambassadors to Rome in 151.

205 **to go back to the treaties of Gracchus:** See above on 43.179.

49

206 **Marcellus sent the ambassadors from both sides to Rome:** The arrival of the ambassadors and the debate in the senate which followed is given at greater length in the passage of Polybius (35.2-3), preserved in the Byzantine collection, *de legationibus gentium*. Although it is clear from a comparison of the two that Appian's version derives ultimately from Polybius, there are also important differences. The most notable is that in Appian the two sides in the dispute consist of the Arevaci, Belli and Titthi on the one hand and certain unnamed people from the same area on the other, while for Polybius the two sides are the Arevaci, who are fighting against Rome, and the Belli and Titthi, who are Rome's allies. This suggests that Polybius' account of the outbreak of the war was also different, and that according to him either Segeda was from the beginning a town of the Arevaci, or (perhaps more likely) that only some of the Belli and the Titthi had allied themselves to the Arevaci, the remainder staying on the Roman side. See Walbank, *Historical Commentary*, 3.642; Richardson, *Hispaniae*, pp. 141 and 194-8. On the allegiance of the Belli and the Titthi, see further below, 63.268.

privately he sent messages to the senate, urging a cessation of hostilities: According to Polybius (35.3.1-2), there were representatives of Marcellus in Rome at the time of the debate, who wanted peace to be established. It is probable that what Marcellus was proposing was a return to the treaties of Gracchus, as requested by the Celtiberians (48.205), which are referred to explicitly in the speech which Polybius gives to the Arevacan envoys before the senate (35.2.15).

thinking that he would gain a valuable reputation from this also: This remark reveals a trace of the anti-Marcellan bias of Polybius' version, in which Marcellus is twice accused of cowardice in not wishing to fight (35.3.4, 4.3). It is likely that this comes from the influence of Scipio Aemilianus, who was strongly opposed to Marcellus' policy of making peace with the Celtiberians, as is shown by the speech given him by Polybius immediately after the conclusion of the senate debate (35.4.8-14). On Scipio's influence in this passage, see M. Gelzer, *Kleine Schriften* 3 (Wiesbaden 1964), p. 176 and Walbank, *Historical Commentary*, 3.642-3. Cicero's opinion of Marcellus (*Pis.* 44) as a man of the highest courage, duty and military glory stands in marked contrast. It is perhaps not without significance that Marcellus, on his return to Rome, set up memorials to himself, his father and his grandfather in the temples of Honos and Virtus (Asconius, p. 12C).

207 **those from the enemy side took up lodgings, as usual, outside the walls:** In Polybius' account (35.2.4), it is the Arevaci, as Rome's enemies, that are required to remain on the far side of the Tiber (and thus outside the *pomerium*, the sacred boundary of the city), while the Belli and the Titthi are lodged inside the city (Walbank, *Historical Commentary*, 3.644).

208 **The senate ... was offended that they had not surrendered themselves to the Romans:** The language that Appian uses here (ὅτι μή ... Ῥωμαίοις αὐτοὺς ἐπετετρόφεσαν) indicates that what the senate was demanding was a formal surrender (*deditio*), as is also revealed by Marcellus' care to ensure that these conditions were fulfilled subsequently (below 50.211-214). This shows that the senate was determined to continue the war, since it was clear that Celtiberians had not made a *deditio*, nor even been asked to do so; but it is also important to note this first appearance of a demand

which the senate was to make repeatedly in the course of the Celtiberian wars (see Richardson, *Hispaniae*, pp. 140-9).

as Nobilior, Marcellus' predecessor, had demanded of them: There is no record of Nobilior having made such a demand, though the request of the pro-Roman side in Polybius' account for punishment of the Arevaci (35.2.7-10) clearly implied some such humiliation. The fact that they also asked for a consul to be sent each year to Spain (35.2.9) suggests that they had been influenced in their requests by the incoming consuls, who were looking to continue the war for their own prestige.

209 **For the first time they chose an army by lot to serve in Spain, instead of by conscription:** Polybius (35.4.1-14) states that, following the senate's decision to continue the war and to recruit a legion to go out to Spain, there was a wide-spread panic among the population, which was only ended by the young Scipio Aemilianus volunteering himself to serve (it is may well be this which provided the material for the very similar story in Appian (above 18.68) of Scipio Africanus' volunteering in 210 BC). According to the epitome of Livy (*ep.* 48), the tribunes of the plebs intervened on behalf of some of their friends and threw the consuls in gaol, though this may be a mistake, based on the events of 138 BC, when there was similar opposition (Cicero, *de leg.* 3.20, believed that this happened for the first time in 138). There can be no doubt however that recruitment was a major problem at this time and that the Spanish campaigns must have seemed particularly undesirable (see Brunt, *Italian Manpower*, pp. 391-415; Astin, *Scipio Aemilianus*, pp. 42-3 and 167-172). It is probable that what Appian is describing here is not the use of the lot for the selection of individuals for recruitment but to decide who was to go to Spain and who to serve in Italy (Astin, *Scipio Aemilianus*, p. 42).

210 **Licinius Lucullus, the consul:** L. Licinius Lucullus, consul with A. Postumius Albinus in 151 BC. See F. Münzer, Licinius (102) in *RE* 13.1 (1926) 372-5.

Cornelius Scipio, who soon after captured Carthage and later Numantia, as his legate: P. Cornelius Scipio Aemilianus, the son of L. Aemilius Paullus, was adopted by P. Cornelius Scipio, the son of Scipio Africanus. He was elected consul for 147 BC before he was of age, and in 146 captured and sacked the city of Carthage. It is uncertain whether he served as *legatus* under Lucullus (as Appian, and later sources state) or as a tribune of the soldiers (as Livy, *ep.* 48) (see Broughton, *MRR* 1.456, n. 1).

Aemilianus, who was a close associate of the historian Polybius, forms the centre-piece of the later section of Appian's work on the Spanish wars, just as his adoptive grand-father did for the earlier section. On Aemilianus, see especially Astin, *Scipio Aemilianus*.

50

212 **it was suspected at the time ... that he had persuaded them to entrust their affairs to him:** The significance of this would be that if there had been an understanding reached between Marcellus and the Arevaci before he had received their *deditio*, the surrender would have been invalid. See the case of Pompeius in 140/139 BC (below 79.338-345).

213 **five *stadia*:** For the length of the *stadion*, see above on 1.4. Five *stadia* is just under 1 km.

214 **demanded hostages and money from all of them and then let them go free:** The terms which followed a *deditio* were determined entirely by the commander to whom the surrender had been made. An example of the procedure is to be seen on the inscription recording the surrender of a people to L. Caesius, dated to 104 BC and found near Alcántara (Cáceres) (R. López Melero et al., *Gerión* 2 (1984), pp. 265-323; Richardson, *Hispaniae*, pp. 199-201).

51

215 **Lucullus, however, who was keen for glory and needed money because of his lack of it:** Appian's low opinion of Lucullus is very marked throughout the following chapters, and is likely to reflect an antipathy between Lucullus and Scipio Aemilianus (so Astin, *Scipio Aemilianus*, p. 46).
     the Vaccaei, another Celtiberian tribe who were neighbours of the Arevaci: Although Appian insists that the Vaccaei had done no harm to the Romans, they may be the neighbouring tribe who had treacherously attacked 'Biesius' in 152 (see above 46.195). It is also possible that they had been attacking the Carpetani, whose territory in the upper Tagus (Tajo) and Anas (Guadiana) valleys lay to the south of that of the Vaccaei, based on the central section of the Duero (Strabo 3.1.6 and 3.2.3).

216 **Crossing the river called the Tagus:** As Cauca lies north of the Tagus, this implies that Lucullus had moved onto the *meseta* by a more southerly route than was normal, perhaps crossing the river at or near Toletum (modern Toledo), a city of the Carpetani (Livy 39.30.1-2) (so Simon, *Roms Kriege*, pp. 46-7). That would in turn imply that Lucullus had known from the beginning of his tenure of the province that the war against the Numantines was over. It may be, of course, that Appian has misplaced Cauca, and that this is another example of his problems with geography (see Introduction p. XXX).
     Cauca: The modern Coca, some 40 km. north-west of Segovia. Though this is to the south of the main territory of the Vaccaei, it is mentioned as a town of the Vaccaei by Livy in the context of the wars with Sertorius (Livy 91, fr. 22).
     Carpetani: On the Carpetani see above 51.215. The area had been overrun by the Romans in 185 and the Carpetani seem to have been faithful allies of the Romans since that date (Livy 39.30-32).

52

218 **the elders, wearing crowns and carrying olive branches:** The crowns are probably intended to mark the fact that these are the responsible magistrates of the city, and the olive branches that they come as suppliants, to ask for mercy. The word used here for an olive branch (ἱκετηρία) means a rod held by a suppliant. It is probable that this detail was invented by Appian or his source, as Coca is north of the limit of olive-growing (see map in F. Braudel, *The Mediterranean and the Mediterranean World in the Age of Philip II* (second ed., London 1972), p.232).

220 **The Caucaei, calling to witness the gods:** This is the natural dramatic consequence of the emphasis which Appian has laid on the ritual supplication of the Caucaei. It is used to underline the disgraceful nature of Lucullus' behaviour, which is in turn a foil to the courage and generosity of Scipio Aemilianus (see above on 49.210).

53

222 **He travelled through a great tract of desert land and arrived a a town called Intercatia:** Although the exact site of Intercatia is unknown, it is believed to be in the region of Villalpando (Zamora), some 58 km. north-west of Tordesillas and about 110 km. north-west of Coca (see A. Schulten, *RE* 9.1603, 'Intercatia (1)').

224 **one of the barbarians rode out into the space between the lines, splendidly arrayed in armour, and challenged any of the Romans who wished to single combat:** This story of Scipio's duel with the Vaccaean challenger was written up by Polybius, and two tiny fragments of what was evidently a detailed and sensational account survive (Polybius 35.5.1-2). It became a favourite anecdote for historians and moralists (Livy, *ep.* 48; Vell. Pat. 1.12.4; Val. Max. 3.2.6; Pliny, *NH* 37.9; Plutarch, *praec. reip. ger.* 10; Florus 1.33.11 (with inaccurate additions); Oros. 4.21.2; Ps. Victor, *de vir. ill.* 58.2-3; Ampel. 22; cf. Walbank, *Historical Commentary*, 3.648-9).

225 **Scipio, still a young man:** See above on 8.30 for the parallels between Scipio Aemilianus and his adoptive grandfather, Scipio Africanus.

54

227 **the strangeness of the local food:** The wildness of the central areas of the peninsula was legendary, and much commented upon by Strabo. He remarks upon the eating and drinking habits of the inhabitants of the mountains, who eat goat meat, and use beer rather than wine and butter rather than olive oil (Strabo 3.3.7). The prevalence of hares or rabbits is also mentioned (Strabo 3.2.6), and Catullus calls Egnatius, his rival for Lesbia's affections, a 'son of rabbity Celtiberia' (*cuniculosae Celtiberiae fili*: 37.18).

229 **since he was believed because of his high reputation for virtue, he brought the war to an end:** Again, the contrast between Lucullus and Scipio Aemilianus is clear. Note also the implied contrast with Marcellus (see above 49.206).

230 **Lucullus asked for gold and silver, for the sake of which he undertook the war:** Although he was disappointed, Lucullus' expectations were not unreasonable. In the period of the Hannibalic war and the first decades of the second century, the commanders returning from the Spanish provinces brought with them substantial amounts of silver and (to a lesser extent) gold, which they had gathered as booty (see the table compiled by J. J. van Nostrand, in T. Frank, *Economic Survey of Ancient Rome*, vol. 3 (Baltimore 1937), p.129; Richardson, *Hispaniae*, pp. 95-8 and 116-7).
these Celtiberians do not hold it to be of value: Again, Strabo comments on the lack of coined money among the mountain-dwellers, who, he says, used barter or passed pieces of beaten silver amongst themselves in its place (3.3.7). This is another example of Strabo's picture of these peoples as living a simple and uncivilised life. Diodorus specifically mentions the Vaccaei as living a communal life, dividing the produce of the land between themselves after the harvest (5.34.3).

55

231 **Pallantia:** Modern Palencia, on the northern side of the Duero basin and some 80 km. east of Intercatia. See L. de Castro, 'La ubicación de Pallancia prerromana', *Hisp. Ant.* 3 (1973), pp. 416-60.

232 **following him as far as the river Durius:** On the ground, this would be a distance of some 90 km., assuming a direct route.

he went away into the country of the Turdetani to winter: That is, into the valley of the Guadalquivir, and thus into the province of Hispania Ulterior. This is what Marcellus is supposed to have done, on the basis of the fragment of Polybius discussed above (see on 48.200). However in the case of Lucullus, it is clear that he moved into the further province in order to collaborate the following year (150 BC) with the praetor in charge of Hispania Ulterior, Ser. Sulpicius Galba, as is noted by Appian when discussing their joint campaign (see below 59.247-60.255).

233 **Lucullus was not even put on trial because of it:** This is intended to provide a contrast with the cases of Q. Pompeius in 139 BC (below 79.344) and C. Hostilius Mancinus in 136 BC (below 80.348 and 83.358-362). Although neither of these cases was in the proper sense a trial, Appian uses the language of the courts to describe them. On the change in the senate's attitude towards the commanders in Spain during this period, see Richardson, *Hispaniae*, pp.140-9.

Chs. 56-75: War against the Lusitanians (154-139 BC)

Even before the beginnings of the Celtiberian wars, the Romans had been faced with problems in the west of the peninsula with the Lusitanians (on whom, see below on 56.234). The situation there appears to have been of a different type from that in Celtiberia, partly because the Lusitanians were less urbanised than the Celtiberians and because the cause of the difficulties was the raiding activity of the Lusitanians against settled indigenous peoples in the Guadalquivir valley. The fighting was initially entrusted to the praetors who were, as usual, sent out to the province of Hispania Ulterior, and the first occasion on which a consul was involved was in 151 BC, when L. Licinius Lucullus, who had been allotted the province of Hispania Citerior, abandoned his campaigns against the Celtiberian tribes in the northern *meseta* (above 51.215-55.233) in order to assist Ser. Sulpicius Galba, the praetor in Ulterior. The savagery and treachery exhibited by these two, and especially Galba, led to a temporary cessation of the fighting, but also resulted in the emergence of Rome's most formidable adversary among the Lusitanians, Viriathus. This man led a series of campaigns in which the superiority of the Lusitanian cavalry over the Romans became evident, and, because of the deterioration in the situation, the consul of 145 BC, Q. Fabius Maximus Aemilianus was sent to Hispania Ulterior (below 65.273-278). The Roman commanders who followed Maximus were unable to defeat Viriathus, and it was not until Q. Servilius Caepio engineered his assassination in 139 BC that they regained control (below 74.311-75.321). These events were going on at the same time as the wars in Celtiberia, and on at least two occasions, in 153 and (probably) in 146 BC (see 56.237 and 63.268) the Celtiberians were encouraged in their resistance to Rome by the example of the Lusitanians. It is for the Roman commanders involved in this war that Appian reserves his most scornful criticisms (see especially his remarks of Sulpicius Galba, below 60.253-255). Towards the end of his account of the war with the Lusitanians in Hispania Ulterior, Appian inserts a section on the campaigns of D. Iunius Brutus, 71-301-73.310, which is out of place both geographically and chronologically. Appian apologises for this digression at 73.310 (see Introduction, pp. 3-4).

56

234 **Lusitanians:** This is Appian's first mention of the Lusitanians, who were a Celticised, people, living originally in the area north of the river Tagus (see Strabo 3.3.3-6). They are said by Strabo to have been a people of mountaineers, much given to brigandage, and it sounds as though they were a largely nomadic people. They had certainly been causing problems to the peoples in the more settled area of the Guadalquivir valley at least as early as 194, when Livy describes the Roman commander in Hispania Ulterior, P. Scipio Nasica, as defeating them at a battle near Ilipa (Livy 35.1.5-12), and this was probably not the first time they had ventured south to raid the area. Strabo also describes them as the largest of the Iberian nations (3.3.3). On the Lusitanians in general, see A. Tovar, *Iberische Landeskunde* 2.2 *Lusitanien* (Baden-Baden 1976), pp. 196-201; J. de Alarcão, *Roman Portugal*, vol.1 (Warminster 1988), pp. 4-6.

Punicus: This is curious name for a Lusitanian leader, being a Greek transcription of the Latin adjective *Punicus*, meaning a Carthaginian. See also below 236, on Caesaros.

Manilius: This man is probably to be identified with M'. Manilius, who held the consulship in 149, and will have been praetor at about this time. Counting back from the praetorship of Galba in 151 (see below, 58.244), the year is almost certainly 154 (so D. Wilsdorf, *Fasti Hispaniarum provinciarum* (Leipzig 1878), pp. 95-6; see Richardson, *Hispaniae*, p. 185).

Calpurnius Piso: Although Appian does not make it clear, it is probable that Piso was Manilius' successor as praetor in command of Ulterior, and therefore in 154, when both Livy, *ep.* 47, and Obsequens, 17, mention defeats in Spain, Obsequens specifically naming the Lusitanians. His full name was L. Calpurnius Piso Caesoninus, who also succeeded Manilius in the consulship of 148. His quaestor, Terentius Varro, is not otherwise known.

235 **Vettones:** A Celtic people, said by Strabo, 3.1.6, to live between the Tagus and the Durius. The Romans had fought against a coalition consisting of Celiberians, Vaccaei and Vettones near Toletum (modern Toledo) in 193 (Livy 35.7.6-7). For an account of a Vettonian settlement site in the Amblés valley near Ávila, see G. R. Zapatero and J. R. Alvarez-Sanchís, 'Las Cogotas: *oppida* and the roots of urbanism in the Spanish meseta', in B. Cunliffe and S. J. Keay (edd.), *Social Complexity and the Development of Towns in Iberia* (London 1995), pp. 209-35.

the Ocean: As usual, meaning the Atlantic ocean (see, for instance, above 1.2).

Blastophoenicians: These people are unknown in any other author. They may be the people known as the Bastuli, which Strabo (3.1.7; 3.2.1; 3.4.1; 3.4.12) places along the southernmost coast of Spain, on either side of the Strait of Gibraltar, though T. Corey Brennan, *Emerita* 63 (1995), p. 50, n.9, believes that Appian sites the Blastophoenicians on the ocean, and that they are not to be identified with the Bastuli. Ptolemy, *Geogr.*2.4.6, says that they were called 'Punic', and this region was one of settlement and trade by both the Phoenicians and later the Carthaginians from the eighth century BC onwards. It is unlikely therefore that their name, if the identification is correct, had anything to do with Hannibal, but Appian is inclined to ascribe such changes to Hannibal (see below 75.320).

236 **Caesaros:** Although this, like Punicus above (on 56.234) seems an unlikely name for a Lusitanian, it is attested epigraphically in a Celtic context (L. Hernández Guerra,

'Estudio de la antroponomía preromana de Palencia y entorno, I', *Hisp. Ant.* 15 (1991), p. 62).

Mummius: L. Mummius, who as consul in 146 was responsible for the destruction of Corinth. He will have been in Ulterior as praetor in 153. An inscription from Italica (*CIL* 2.1119) has been thought to record the dedication by Mummius of spoils from Corinth, but this may be a dedication by Aemilius Paullus in 167 after the third Macedonian war (A. M. Canto, *La epigrafía romana de Itálica* (Madrid 1985), no. 67).

237 **which the barbarians carried throughout Celtiberia:** Diodorus, 31.52, particularly mentions the Arevaci as having been influenced by this defeat to begin the war against the Romans (see above 44.180-45.187). He also says that Mummius (whom he calls 'Memmius') was defeated just after he had disembarked.

57

239 **Caucaenus:** Not otherwise known. The stem *cauca-* suggests Celtic origin (compare the town of Cauca, on which see above 51.216).

Cunei: A people living in the southern part of modern Portugal, and often identified with the Kynesioi, mentioned by Herodotus, 2.33.3 and 4.49.3, as being the people who lived in the most extreme west, and were neighbours of the Celts (but G. de Sanctis, *Storia dei Romani* 3.2 (Torino 1917), p. 464, n. 34, believes them to be a different people, living in the vicinity of Seville). Polybius, 10.7.5, mentions the Conii (Κονίοι), who lived inside the Pillars of Herakles, though it may be that the text here should read ἐκτὸς ('outside') rather than ἐντὸς ('inside') (see Walbank, *Historical Commentary*, 2.202). On the nature of their settlements, see J. de Alarcão, *Roman Portugal* vol. 1 (Warminster 1988), pp. 2-4; V. Hipólito Correia, 'The Iron Age in Portugal', in B. Cunliffe and S. J. Keay (edd.), *Social Complexity and the Development of Towns in Iberia* (London 1995), pp. 237-62, at p. 248.

Conistorgis: The site of this town is unknown, though Strabo, 3.2.2, states that it belonged to the Celtici, who were the neighbours of the Cunei. Sallust mentions it (*Hist.* 1, fr. 119), probably in the context of the Sertorian war. Appian has Galba wintering there in 151 (below, 58.246).

240 **They crossed the Ocean near the Pillars of Herakles:** The Strait of Gibraltar was frequently crossed by raiding parties, later more often in the opposite direction (see, for instance, Richardson, *The Romans in Spain*, pp. 231-4). Appian records elsewhere (*Lib.* 68.306) an occasion when Massinissa in Numidia in the early years of the second century was troubled by Iberians, though S. Gsell, *Histoire de l'Afrique du Nord* vol.3 (Paris 1921), p. 310, believes that this story belongs to the Lusitanian raid here described by Appian. In either case, it is notable that in this same year Massinissa sent cavalry and elephants to Nobilior at Numantia (see above 46.189).

Ocile: An unknown town in north Africa, identified by S. Gsell, *Histoire de l'Afrique du Nord* vol.3 (Paris 1921), p. 310, n. 8, with Zelis, modern Asilah, some 40 km. south of Tangier on the Atlantic coast.

241 **Mummius however pursued them:** It is clear that, according to Appian, Mummius followed the Lusitanians across the strait into north Africa. On his campaign, see Simon, *Roms Kriege*, pp. 20-25.

242 **burnt the remainder in honour of the gods of war:** The burning of spoils in honour of the gods of war is mentioned by Appian at *Lib.*, 133.632 and *Mith.*, 44.176. Plutarch,

Marius 22.2, describes Marius performing the same rite after his defeat of the Teutones in 102, and Livy, 45.33.1-2, Aemilius Paullus in 167 at the end of the Macedonian war. The emphasis in these examples is on the destruction of weapons, usually after the selection of the best items for reuse or display in a triumph, and this may also have been the case in Appian's source here, since he goes on immediately to mention Mummius' triumph (see J. Rüpke, *Domi militiae, de religiöse Konstruction de Krieges in Rom* (1990), pp. 199-202). It is probably to this success that Eutropius, 4.9.1, refers, when he says of 153 BC that L. Mummius (though all but one of the manuscripts read *Memmius*) fought successfully in Lusitania.

58

243   **celebrated a triumph:** There is no record of this in the inscribed *Fasti Triumphales*, but there is a lacuna at this point in the inscription (A. Degrassi, *Inscr. It.* 13.1.557).
      Marcus Atilius: Not otherwise known, though he may be the father of the moneyer of 148 (Crawford, *RRC*, pp. 254-5), and the brother or uncle of Sex. Atilius Serranus, consul in 136. It is also possible that he is identical with the commander of the fleet in Africa in 147 called 'Serranus' by Appian, *Lib.* 114.543. His year in Ulterior will have been 152.
      Oxthracae: Unknown, despite Appian's description of it as the largest town of the Lusitanians.
      Vettones: See above on 56.235.
244   **Servius Galba:** Praetor in 151, and continued, no doubt with *imperium pro consule*, in 150. Despite the scandal caused by his time in Spain, he became consul in 144. For the sources referring to his tenure, see Broughton, *MRR* 1.455 and 456-7.
      having covered five hundred *stadia* in a day and a night: This, if true, is a remarkable feat, since it would involve marching for over twelve hours continuously at full speed (cf. Vegetius 1.9: see above on 1.4 for the length of the *stadion*; five hundred *stadia* would be almost a hundred km.). As there is no way of telling from the text where he started and where the battle took place, the accuracy of this story may be doubted.
245   **his lack of experience in warfare:** This criticism is conventional rather than historical. He served under L. Aemilius Paullus in Macedonia and was present at the battle of Pydna in 168 (Livy, 45.35-9; Plutarch, *Aem. Paull.*, 30).
246   **Carmona:** Modern Carmona, some 40 km. east of Seville. See above on 25.96.
      advanced into the territory of the Cunei and wintered at Conistorgis: See above on 57.239.

59

247   **Lucullus, who had waged war against the Vaccaei without a vote having been taken:** Here Appian links back to the account of the wars in Citerior, which he had left at 55.232-3. He does not resume his account of the events in the north, however, until after he has completed the war with Viriathus at 76.322.
249   **because of their poverty that they indulged in banditry:** The offer (whether pretended or real) of land to peoples in the peninsula is a recurrent motif not only in Appian (thus Vetilius in 146, 61.259; Q. Fabius Maximus Servilianus in 140, 69.294;

Caepio in 139, 75.231) but also in other writers dealing with the Lusitanian wars (Diodorus Siculus, 33.1.4, on Caepio; Livy, *ep.* 55, on Brutus in 138). This seems to relate also to the policy of Aemilius Paullus, as shown on an inscription from Hasta of 189 (*ILLRP* 514), and that of Ti. Gracchus in 178 (43.179; see Richardson, *The Romans in Spain*, pp. 75-6). With the exception of that of Gracchus, all these instances relate to commanders in Ulterior. Later, Appian mentions similar occasions when offers, both genuine and false, were made to the Celtiberians (100.433-6). See also above on 42.171.

<h1 style="text-align:center">60</h1>

252 **he surrounded them with a trench:** It is not clear what Appian envisages as happening here. Orosius, 4.21.10, simply describes Galba surrounding and then killing the Lusitanians.

killed them all: This is probably rhetorical exaggeration, which Appian himself contradicts at 60.254 and 61.256 below.

253 **Thus he paid back treachery with treachery:** Other sources attribute the outbreak of the war with Viriathus to the treachery of Galba (so Val. Max. 9.6.2, who states that 8,000 were killed; and Suet., *Galba* 3, who numbers the dead at 30,000).

254 **Viriathus:** The first mention of the Lusitanian leader who is depicted by Appian and other ancient writers as the hero of the Lusitanian wars. Livy and the writers that depend on him say that he started life as a shepherd, became a hunter and a bandit and then a great general (Livy, *ep.* 52; Florus 1.33.15; Dio Cassius fr. 73; Eutropius 4.6; Orosius 5.4.1; *de vir. ill.* 71.1). Diodorus, 33.1.1, also says he started life as a shepherd, though he omits the rest of the description, which seems to derive from someone who wished to represent Viriathus as the epitome of all the attributes of the Lusitanians (see above on 56.234). See Simon, *Roms Kriege*, pp. 89-90.

255 **Galba, who was greedier for money than Lucullus:** This remark is intended to show Galba as exceptionally greedy, since Appian has already noted that Lucullus undertook his campaigns chiefly for financial reward (above 51.215 and 54.230).

even though he was already the richest of all the Romans: This remark is not supported elsewhere in the tradition about Galba, and is perhaps simply part of a conventional portrait of a greedy general. Galba was chiefly remembered, apart from this event, as the most celebrated orator of his generation (Cicero, *Brut.* 82; *de or.* 1.58).

Although he was hated and the subject of accusations, he was acquitted because of his wealth: On Galba's return to Rome (according to the account in Livy, *ep.* 49), L. Scribonius Libo, one of the tribunes of the plebs, instituted proceedings against him by introducing a bill (*rogatio*) that the Lusitanians who had surrendered to him and who had been sold into slavery in Gaul, should be set free. This *rogatio* was supported by the aged Cato (on whom see above 39.159-41.170) and opposed by Q. Fulvius Nobilior, who, as consul in 153, had been involved in fighting at Numantia (see above 45.184-48.198). The bill was defeated, but was a *cause célèbre*, commented on by a wide range of authors. Some describe the affair as though it were a trial, as does Appian here (so also Livy 39.40.12; Val. Max. 8.1.2; Gellius, *NA* 1.12.17; Ps.-Ascon. 203 (St.) on Cicero, *div. in Caec.* 20.66), while others (Cicero, *Brut.* 23.89, *de or.* 1.53.227-8; Livy, *ep.* 49; Quintilian 2.15.8) make it clear that the context is legislative rather than judicial. See Simon, *Roms Kriege*, pp. 62-7; Richardson, *Hispaniae*, pp. 138-40. Despite the widespread modern belief that Galba's 'trial' was the reason for the introduction of the first *quaestio de repetundis*, none of the ancient sources makes this connection.

61

257 **Gaius Vetilius:** His period in Ulterior is dated by Livy, *ep.* 52, (who calls him M. Vetilius) and Orosius, 5.4.2, (who calls him Vecilius) to 146 BC, which would fit with Appian's note that this took place 'not long after' the treachery of Lucullus and Galba in 150 (see Richardson, *Hispaniae*, pp. 185-9; *contra* Broughton, *MRR* 1.465, n. 1, and 3.219 who places Vetilius' praetorship in 147).

258 **asking for land on which to settle:** See above on 59.249.

259 **everyone in the army had escaped:** Note that the verb in this sentence is in the first person plural (διαφύγοιμεν), representing the speech of Viriathus himself. See note in Introduction, p. 5.

62

260 **Tribola:** The site of this town is unknown, and it is not mentioned in any other source. Adolf Schulten, 'Viriatus', *Neue Jahrbücher* 39-40 (1917), pp. 209-37 at p. 219, argues that it should not be far from Carteia. The geography of these events, however, is far from clear, and Livy, *ep.* 52, states that Viriathus had over-run the whole of Lusitania. The manoeuvre described here is attributed to Viriathus by Frontinus, *Strat.* 2.13.4.

63

265 **He waged war against the Romans for eight years:** The manuscripts here read ἐς τρία ἔτη ('for three years') which was emended to ἐς ὀκτώ ἔτη ('for eight years') by Schweighäuser (*Appian* 3.277). Goukowsky, *Appien*, pp. LXVI and 57, n. 363, retains the reading of the manuscripts, pointing out that different sources give different periods for the length of Viriathus' command, and associating the peace which he made with Fabius Servilianus (see below 69.294), which Orosius, 5.4.12, thought occurred in 143, with the end of the war (on the different lengths of time in the sources, see Richardson, *Hispaniae*, pp. 186-7). However, Schweighäuser made his emendation on the basis of the figure given by Appian himself at 75.319, which is followed by the end of the section on the war with Viriathus which begins here (76.322). It is difficult to believe that Appian is referring to different periods in these two places, and thus Schweighäuser's emendation is surely correct.

267 **Carpessus:** See above on 2.7. It is often assumed that Appian here means Carteia, on the bay of Algeciras, close to Gibraltar, because other sources erroneously believed that to have been the ancient Tartessus (so E. Hübner, *RE* 3.1619). The name occurs in no other ancient source, apart from a Latin gloss, cited by A. Schulten, *Iberische Landeskunde* 1 (Strasbourg 1955), p. 332, which describes it as a Spanish island, near which the sun sets. It is more likely that Appian found Carpessus in his source, and himself made the identification with Tartessus.
Arganthonius: See above on 2.6.

268 **the Belli and the Titthi:** It is notable that the Belli and Titthi are named as the suppliers of allied forces, given that the war which had been concluded by the peace arranged by Marcellus in 151 had, according to Appian's version, included the Arevaci

as well. The distinction between them at this stage might indicate that the source Appian is using here followed a version of those earlier events more like that which appears in Polybius (see above on 49.206).

64

269 **Carpetania:** On the Carpetani, who lived north of the Sierra Morena in the Tagus valley, with Toledo as one of their main towns, see above on 51.215-7.

Gaius Plautius: If the dating of Livy and Orosius of 146 for the praetorship of Vetilius is accepted (see above on 61.257), Plautius will have been praetor in 145 (see Richardson, *Hispaniae*, p. 186).

271 **called the mountain of Aphrodite:** This has been identified since Schulten, *Viriatus*, p. 220, with the Sierra San Vincente, some 60 km. north-west of Toledo, on the north side of the river Alberche. The name has been associated with a fertility cult there (M. Seguido Aliaga, 'El culto a Venus en el Cerro de San Vincente (Toledo)', *Mem. de Historia Antigua* 10 (1989), pp. 141-50).

went into winter quarters in the middle of summer: This rapid withdrawal may account for the sending of Fabius Aemilianus, the consul of 145, apparently in the same year that Plautius was there as praetor (see Richardson, *Hispaniae*, p. 186). It may also be at this time that the people of Segovia refused to abandon the Roman side, despite Viriathus' capture and torture of their wives and children (Frontinus, *Strat.* 4.5.22).

65

273 **Fabius Maximus Aemilianus, the son of Aemilius Paullus who had defeated Perseus:** Q. Fabius Maximus Aemilianus was the elder brother of Scipio Aemilianus. Their father, L. Aemilius Paullus, had, in his second consulship in 168, defeated Perseus of Macedon at the battle of Pydna. Paullus had four sons, and the two elder, Fabius and Scipio, were adopted into other patrician families. Despite this, the elder sons became his heirs, because both the two youngest died in 167 (Livy 47.40.7). On the families concerned, see Astin, *Scipio Aemilianus*, ch. 2.

Fabius was consul in 145. If the reasoning about the dates of Vetilius and Plautius above are correct, Fabius was sent to Ulterior during the year in which Plautius was praetor. This is quite possible, given the problems that Plautius had faced, and may have been done also in the other province in the same year, with the sending out of the praetor, C. Laelius, perhaps following the defeat of Claudius Unimanus (see Richardson, *Hispaniae*, pp. 186-8). For a different view on the chronology of these commanders, see T. Corey Brennan, 'Notes on the praetors in Spain in the mid-second century BC', *Emerita* 63 (1995), pp. 47-76.

274 **Since the Romans had recently taken Carthage and Greece and had successfully completed the third war in Macedonia:** Scipio Aemilianus had taken Carthage in 146 and Mummius had sacked Corinth in the same year, thus ending the third Macedonian war.

in order to spare those who had returned from these places: There had been trouble in enlisting troops to serve in the Spanish provinces before in 151, and these recurred when D. Iunius Brutus attempted to levy an army to fight there in 138 (see above,

49.209). It is likely that Fabius had the events of 151 in mind when recruiting his army, as also when Scipio Aemilianus drew on volunteers in 134 (see below 84.365).

he arrived at Orso: Orso is usually identified with Urso (modern Osuna) (see above 16.61). However, as is clear from the following sentence, Appian appears to think that Orso is on the coast, or at least close enough to it to make sailing from there to Gades through the straits (which should here mean the Straits of Gibraltar) a natural thing to do. As Urso is located 34 km. south of Ecija in the southern foothills of the middle Guadalquivir valley, this is unlikely. It is not clear, however, whether Appian is wrong about the voyage or whether Orso should in fact be identified with some other place.

275 **to Gades, to sacrifice to Herakles:** See above on 2.9.

276 **When the legate drew them up in order of battle:** It has been suggested (first by E. Kornemann, *Die neue Livius-Epitome aus Oxyrrhynchus* (*Beiträge zur Alten Geschichte* 2, Leipzig 1904), pp. 98-9, and followed by Astin, *Scipio Aemilianus*, p. 344 and T. Corey Brennan, 'Notes on the praetors in Spain in the mid-second century BC', *Emerita* 63 (1995), pp. 47-76 at 65) that this man was C. Nigidius, mentioned in a notice by the fourth century *de viris illustribus*, 71.1. Nigidius (if he existed at all) may, however, have been defeated by Viriathus in Citerior (see Richardson, *Hispaniae*, pp. 188-9).

278 **After the winter:** That is, in 144 BC, Fabius' command having been renewed by the senate for a further year.

he routs Viriathus, though he fought well, being the second to do so: Appian has recorded no previous Roman commander as being successful against Viriathus. The only other person mentioned in any source as defeating him is C. Laelius, who Cicero says overcame the Lusitanian during his praetorship, that is in 145 (Cicero, *Brut.* 84 and *de off.* 2.11.40). Probably Laelius' victory was mentioned in Appian's source, and Appian has failed to notice that he had omitted it when he wrote this remark about Fabius (see Richardson, *Hispaniae*, pp. 187-9; Goukowsky, *Appien*, pp. LXVI-LXVII). This would also explain the mention of Fannius, serving under Fabius Servilianus in 141, as 'son-in-law of Laelius', with no other explanation of who Laelius was (see below 67.287).

Baecor: Schulten, 'Viriatus', *Neue Jahrbücher* 39-40 (1917), pp. 209-37 at 222, argues that this is identical with Baecula, on which see above on 24.95, but it is more probable that the two places are distinct.

Then he went into winter quarters in Corduba: Corduba appears to have become the Roman base in Ulterior, and even (if the fragment of Polybius, 35.2.2, recording Marcellus' use of it in 152, is correct) a place to which commanders in Citerior might retire for the winter.

66

280 **which is called the Numantine war from one of their towns:** This is a somewhat odd remark, given that Appian has already mentioned Numantia as the centre of the resistance to the Romans by the Arevaci, the Belli and the Titthi at 46.188 and 49.210. This probably shows that he was using different sources for the two strands of his account of the wars of the mid-century, one for the Numantine and one for the Lusitanian war.

I shall deal with it as a sequel after Viriathus: This begins at 76.322 below.

281 **Quinctius:** Although there is no known individual called Quinctius who might be identified with this person, Appian's account here seems at first sight clear enough. Having diverted briefly from his account of the war in Ulterior to explain the connection between Viriathus and the Numantine war in Citerior, he returns to the story of Viriathus' activities 'in the other part of Iberia', which should therefore mean 'in Ulterior'. There a commander (or more probably praetor, though the Greek στρατηγός can mean both: see above on 3.10) called Quinctius (the manuscripts call him Κάντιος at this point, though V has Κοίντῳ at 67.283) first was successful, but subsequently was defeated and went into winter quarters at Corduba (66.281-2). He was succeeded in the following year by Fabius Maximus Servilianus, who was consul in 142 (adopting the amendment of Pighius at this point; see below on 67.283).

Two other suggestions have been made with regard to this passage. One, that of Schweighäuser (*Appian* 3.282), is that the short passage at 68.291, which describes Servilianus as returning to Rome and being replaced by Q. Pompeius, son of Aulus, and then goes on to refer to Servilianus' brother, Maximus Aemilianus, and which is clearly out of place where it stands, should be transferred to 65.278. If this were to be done, the 'Quinctius' of the following sections would be Pompeius, and should be read as 'Quintus'. This transposition has found little favour among subsequent scholars, and is rebutted by Simon, *Roms Kriege*, pp. 82-6, in particular on the grounds that Appian is unlikely to have referred to a relatively lesser known person such as Pompeius by his *praenomen* alone: indeed this would be contrary to the practice which Appian himself has set out in his *praefatio*, 13.51-2, that he would call Romans by their most significant (κυριώτατα) names. It is notable that when referring to Pompeius elsewhere in this work, he always calls him 'Pompeius'. The other suggestion is that adopted by Goukowsky, *Appien*, pp. LXVII-LXIX, who believes that Appian's reference to Viriathus' defeat of 'Quinctius' takes place in Citerior ('in the other part of Iberia') and notes that Q. Metellus Macedonicus, who was present as consul in Citerior in 143 and as proconsul in 142, is said by Valerius Maximus, 9.3.7 (nam Q. Metellus, cum utramque Hispaniam consul prius, deinde pro consule paene <to>tam subegisset), to have held command in both provinces. He also associates with this a remark by Charax of Pergamum (*FGH* 103, fr. 27) that a certain Quintus, *polemarchos* in both the Spains, was defeated by Viriathus and made a truce with him. He suggests, therefore, that 'Quintus' in this passage is Metellus Macedonicus. It is true that the Oxyrrhynchus Epitome of Livy (Livy, *ep. Oxy.* 53) says that the consul Metellus (who must be Q. Metellus) was worsted by the Lusitanians, and that we know that Viriathus was active in both provinces, but it does not follow that Q. Metellus is the 'Quinctius' of this passage in Appian. The same arguments are valid in this case as with the identification with Q. Pompeius, with the additional point that Metellus was consul in 143 and is unlikely to be referred to as στρατηγός, which normally would mean praetor. Moreover, even given the carelessness of Appian about such matters (see above on 58.245), it is unlikely that Appian or his source would have described Q. Metellus, the conqueror of Macedonia, as inexperienced in war (below 66.282). For these reasons, it is safest to assume that, at least so far as Appian understood the situation, the successor to Fabius Maximus Aemilianus was an otherwise unknown praetor called Quinctius (so T. Corey Brennan, 'Notes on the praetors in Spain in the mid-second century BC', *Emerita* 63 (1995), pp. 47-76 at 69-72).

the mountain of Aphrodite: See above on 64.271.

282 **Itucca:** This place has been identified with Tucci (the later colonia Augusta Gemella Tucci, recorded by Pliny *NH* 3.12), following Schulten, *Viriatus*, pp. 223-4. However, as Appian calls this place by its later name of Gemella shortly after this at 68.290, it is perhaps preferable to identify Itucca with Ituci, the later colonia Virtus Iulia Ituci, mentioned by Pliny in the same list (so W. Smith (ed.), *A Dictionary of Greek and Roman Geography*, vol. 2 (London 1873), p. 101). Tucci, the modern Martos, is some 20 km. south-west of Jaén, in the upper Guadalquivir valley; Ituci, modern Baena, is some 30 km. south-west of Martos, on the opposite side of the river Guadajoz. Of the other sources, Orosius, 5.4.12, calls this place 'Buccia', while Diodorus, 333.7.5-6, mentions the dealings of Viriathus with the citizens of a town called Tucca (Τύκκη), though it is not clear that Diodorus' story has any connection to that of Appian.

the territory of the Bastitani: These people, also called the Bastuli (see above on 56.235), are recorded by Strabo as occupying the southern coast of Iberia, on either side of Gibraltar (Strabo, *Geogr.* 3.1.7; 3.4.1).

went into winter quarters at Corduba: See above on 65.278.

Gaius Marcius, an Iberian from the town of Italica: The name is undoubtedly Roman or Italian, and this man has been assumed therefore to be a non-indigenous inhabitant of Italica (so J. M. Rodríguez Hidalgo and S. Keay, 'Recent work at Italica', in B. Cunliffe and S. J. Keay (edd.), *Social Complexity and the Development of Towns in Iberia* (London 1995), pp. 395-420, at 399. Appian's insistence that he was an Iberian suggests, however, that he may have been indigenous, in which case he could either have acquired Roman citizenship or, more probably, was using a Roman style of name without it (cf. E. Badian, *Foreign Clientelae (264-70 BC)* (Oxford 1958), pp. 256-7; Richardson, *Hispaniae*, pp. 161-4).

67

283 **Fabius Maximus Servilianus, the brother of Aemilianus:** The manuscripts here read ὁ ἀδελφὸς Αἰμιλιανοῦ, Φάβιος Μάξιμος Αἰμιλιανός ('Fabius Maximus Aemilianus, brother of Aemilianus'), which is clearly an error. The person referred to here, and mentioned below at 67.287 and 68.288 and 290, is Q. Fabius Maximus Servilianus. He was the adoptive brother of Fabius Maximus Aemilianus (on whom see above at 65.273), and had himself been adopted in the family of the Fabii Maximi. He had two natural brothers, Cn. and Q. Servilius Caepio, and the three held the consulship in adjoining years, Servilianus in 142, Cn. Caepio in 141 and Q. Caepio in 140 (see *MRR* 1.474-9 for references).

284 **Micipsa, the king of the Numidians:** The only surviving son of Massinissa, who succeeded to the throne on his father's death in 148 (Sallust, *Iug.* 5.6).

287 **Fannius, the son-in-law of Laelius:** The identification of this man was a matter of debate already by the time of Cicero, since there were two men called C. Fannius in the same period, distinguished from one another by their filiation, one being the son of Gaius and the other the son of Marcus. Laelius' son-in-law was said by Cicero, *de amicit.* 3 and *Brut.* 100, to have been the latter, and it is clear from other evidence that this man was tribune of the plebs in 142 and consul in 122. One of the two was also a historian, but Cicero was, by the time he wrote to Atticus in 45 BC (*ad Att.* 12.5b), uncertain which (see *MRR* 1.519, n. 2; D. R. Shackleton-Bailey, *Cicero's Letters to*

Atticus, vol. 5 (Cambridge 1966), pp. 400-403). On the abrupt mention of Laelius at this point, see above on 65.278.

68

288   **Baeturia:** This name is given by Strabo, *Geogr.* 3.2.3, to the region in the valley of the Anas (the modern river Guadiana), though Pliny, *NH* 3.13, also includes in it the lands north of the Guadalquivir. The fact that Servilianus is pursuing Viriathus into Lusitania at this point, and that he then marches into the territory of the Cunei (see above on 57.239) suggests that he is north of the Sierra Morena in the plains of the Anas at this stage. See L. García Iglesias, 'La Beturia, un problema geográfico de la Hispania antigua', *AEA* 44 (1971), pp. 86-108.

289   **Cunei:** See above on 57.239.

  two bandit chieftains, Curius and Apuleius: These men have evidently Roman or Italian names. They could be Iberians who had taken Roman names (as is probably the case with C. Marcius: see above 66.282); or they could be deserters from the Roman army. Alternatively, they could be the offspring of Roman soldiers and Iberian women, like the group of over 4,000 who applied to the senate in 171 and were settled at Carteia (Livy 43.3.1-4)

290   **Eiskadia, Gemella and Obulcula:** Of these three, Gemella is one of the names given to Tucci when it became a colony in the age of Augustus (Pliny, *NH* 3.12: see above on 66.282); Obulcula is mentioned in the same list by Pliny as a town paying tax to the Romans and is listed in the Antonine Itinerary (*Itin. Ant.* 413 and 414). It is identified with the modern La Monclova, on the road between Carmona and Ecija (the ancient Astigi). Eiskadia is unknown (see A. Tovar, *Iberische Landeskunde* 2.1 (Baden-Baden 1974). p. 138), but, judging by the other two places, should be in the middle Guadalquivir valley.

291   There is clearly something seriously wrong at this point with the text preserved in the manuscripts, which gives an account of Servilianus returning to Rome, being succeeded in the command by Q. Pompeius, son of Aulus, and the introduction into the account of Servilianus brother, Maximus Aemilianus, who could only be Q. Fabius Maximus Aemilianus. Pompeius is not otherwise known to have been present in either of the Spanish provinces before his arrival in Citerior in his consulship in 141 (see below, 76.325-79.344; note the suggestion in Richardson, *Hispaniae*, pp. 189-190, that he may have been the mysterious Quinctius, praetor in Ulterior in 143 and 142, which I would not now wish to defend against the objections of Simon, *Roms Kriege*, pp.85-6); Maximus Aemilianus appears from Appian himself to have been succeeded by Quinctius who was in turn succeeded by Servilianus (above 66.281-67.283). The matter is further complicated by the appearance of the name of Aemilianus in the manuscripts again at 69.293 and 70.296, this last being supported by a quotation of this passage in the Byzantine *Excerpta de legationibus gentium*. Schweighäuser's solution to the problem was to transfer most of the offending passage (from ἐχείμαζε to Μάξιμος Αἰμιλιανὸς) from 68.291 to the end of 65.278, but this creates more problems than it solves (see above on 66.281). The text printed follows Viereck and Roos, who marked the passage transferred by Schweighäuser with brackets, commenting that it does not seem to be by Appian at all (Viereck-Roos, pp. 111 and 113), and emended the

references to Aemilianus at 69.293 and 70.296 to refer to Servilianus. For an alternative approach, see Goukowsky, *Appien* pp. LXIX-LXXI.

he beheaded five hundred and sold the rest: The selling into slavery of prisoners was normal Roman pratice. See below on 98.424.

Connobas: The story of the punishment of the followers of Connobas is also told by Valerius Maximus, 2.7.11, and Frontinus, *Strat.* 4.1.42, both attributing the action to Q. Fabius Maximus and without mentioning Connobas. They also state that the offenders were deserters. Orosius, 5.4.12, also records the story. For a similar instance of brutality, see Scipio's treatment of the young men of the town of Lutia (below 94.411); and M. Popilius Laenas is said to have done the same to some of Viriathus' followers at the end of the abortive negotiations that preceded the renewal of the war with him in 139 (Dio Cassius fr.75; see below on 70.297). The cutting off of both hands was used by Caesar as a punishment after the fall of Uxellodunum in 51 BC (Hirtius, *Bell. Gall.* 8.44.1; Orosius 6.11.29). Strabo, *Geogr.* 3.3.6, says the Lusitanians cut off the right hands of their captives and a story also appears in a late source (*de vir. ill.* 59) that a Numantine father offered his daughter in marriage to the first man to bring him the right hand of an enemy. All this (including the evident embarrassment of Hirtius, *loc. cit.*) shows that this was regarded as an unacceptably barbaric practice.

69

292 **Erisane:** The site of this town is not known.

293 **Servilianus:** See above on 68.291.

294 **the people ratified the agreement:** This is a relatively unusual way of ratifying an international agreement, but does seem to have been used on several occasions, especially in the second century (see Mommsen, *StR* 3.345; A. Lintott, *Imperium Romanum* (London 1993), p. 39, for the normal process). It is interesting to note that in two inscriptions, dealing with agreements made in the Spanish provinces, a standard clause reserving to the Roman state the right to reject an agreement made by a general refers to the *populus senatusque Romanus*, rather than the more normal *senatus populusque Romanus* (see above on 44.183). On the treaty, see also below on 70.296.

Viriathus was to be a friend of the Romans: On the significance of this title, see E. Badian, *Foreign Clientelae (264-70 BC)* (Oxford 1958), pp. 11-12.

that those under his control should all rule over the land which they held: Note once again the importance of land holding in the context of the wars in Iberia (see above on 59.249).

70

296 **Caepio, the brother of Servilianus:** See above on 67.283 and 68.291.

he spoke against the agreement and wrote home, representing it as highly dishonourable to the Romans: The agreement is regarded generally in the sources as having been disgraceful (see Livy, *ep. Oxy.* 54 and *per.* 54; Diodorus 33.1.4; Charax, *FGH* 103, fr. 27). Only Appian comments on the generosity of Viriathus. On the context of this attack on his brother's treaty, see Simon, *Roms Kriege*, pp. 123-5; Richardson, *Hispaniae*, pp. 147-9.

297 **it decided to break the treaty and openly go to war with Viriathus again:** Appian does not mention here an episode that appears in several other writers (Diodorus 33.19; Dio Cassius, fr. 75; *de vir. ill.* 71), in which Viriathus is said to have opened negotiations with M. Popilius Laenas, the consul of 139, who had been sent to Citerior in the wake of Pompeius' attempted treaty with the Numantines (see below, 79.342-345). On this, see Simon, *Roms Kriege*, pp. 127-8; Astin, *Scipio Aemilianus*, pp. 144-5.

298 **Arsa:** This place is mentioned as a town in the judicial district (*conventus*) of Corduba by Pliny, *NH* 3.12 (cf. Ptolemy, *Geogr.* 2.4.10), but the exact location is unknown.

300 **the Vettones and the Callaeci:** The Vettones lived north of the river Tagus (see above on 56.235), and the Callaeci in the north-west, north of the river Durius and close to the Atlantic ocean (Strabo, *Geogr.* 3.3.2; 3.3.7; 3.4.12; 3.4.20). The Vettones had been allies of the Lusitanians (above 56.235 and 58.243). Nothing is known of Caepio's expedition against the Callaeci, who are otherwise not known to have had any military contact with the Romans before the expedition of D. Iunius Brutus, who won the *cognomen* Callaecus as a result of his campaigns there between 138 and 136 (see Strabo, *Geogr.* 3.3.2). It is these campaigns that Appian inserts in his narrative at this point (71.301-73.310), though surprisingly he does not mention the name of the Callaeci in connection with Brutus.

71

301 **Sextus Iunius Brutus:** The man concerned is in fact Decimus Iunius Brutus, the consul of 138. It is not clear whether this error originates with Appian himself (as Goukowsky, *Appien*, p. 65, n. 401) or with a later copyist (as Schweighäuser, *Appian* 3.295). As no reason for the misnaming of Brutus can be identified, it is safer to assume that it was Appian who got it wrong. It is also noteworthy that most of the manuscripts (including the original reading of V) have Ἰούλιος ('Julius') here rather than Ἰούνιος ('Iunius'), but this is a much more common error.

Brutus was Caepio's successor in Ulterior, and his campaigns appear to have covered the years 138 to 136, following the assassination of Viriathus in 139 (see below 74.311-314). His triumph over the Callaeci is linked by Eutropius, 4.19, with that of Scipio Aemilianus, which took place in 132, but the last activities which are attributed to him in his province are his fighting against the Callaeci (Livy, *per.* 54) and his collaboration with Aemilius Lepidus (see below 80.350-82.357), both of which are dated to 136 (see F. Münzer, *RE* 10.1021 ff.; Simon, *Roms Kriege*, p. 160, n. 39; Broughton, *MRR* 1.488, n. 5; Astin, *Scipio Aemilianus*, pp. 146-7).

territory bordered by the Tagus, the Lethes, the Durius and the Baenis: These four are also listed by Strabo, *Geogr.* 3.3.4, and Pliny, *NH* 4.115, as the major rivers which flow westward through the northern part of Iberia into the Atlantic ocean. The river here called Lethes is said by Strabo, *loc. cit.*, to be called the Limaeas by some and by others Belion; Livy, *ep.* 55, also calls it Oblivio, and Pomponius Mela, 3.9, and Pliny, *NH* 4.115, write that its name is Limia or Limaeas and that its *cognomen* is Oblivio, it is probable that Lethes is the Greek translation of the Latin version of a local name (see LSJ, *s.v.* λήθη on the relation between 'Lethe', the place of forgetfulness in the underworld and 'Lethes', the name of the river). The modern name for the river is Lima. The manuscripts read Βαίτης as the name of the fourth river, but, as editors from Schweighäuser, *Appian* 3.295-6, to Goukowsky, *Appien*, p. 65, n. 402, have observed, this must be an error, and as Strabo states that the Baenis was the limit of Brutus' campaigns, it is extremely probable that that is the correct reading here. It is more generally known as Minius (as Strabo states, *loc. cit.*), and is the river Minho. It is not surprising that Pliny, *loc. cit.*, was already complaining that there were mistakes in the accounts of the authors he had read about the famous rivers of this region (*erratum et in amnibus inclutis*).

302 **their towns:** In this case, this must mean the hill-forts, or *castros*, which were the normal type of defensive settlement in this region (see above on 41.168).

303 **the women fighting and dying alongside the men and not uttering a cry:** Strabo, *Geogr.* 3.33.7, comments on the habits of the women of the mountain regions, though not on their fighting alongside the men.
Brutus granted pardon to these when they asked for it, dividing up their property : Compare, however, the story told by Valerius Maximus, 6.4. ext.1, that Brutus refused to allow the Lusitanian town of Cinginnia to pay money to avoid capture, saying that it was by iron not by gold that their ancestors had defended the city.

72

304 **reached the Lethes, being the first Roman to contemplate going across this river:** No previous commander had ventured so far into the north-west, and it was this region that was the last to be conquered by the Romans in the time of Augustus (see below on 102.443). That Brutus reached this far appears to have been a matter of note, to judge by the emphasis placed upon it by the sources (Livy, *per.* 55 and *ep. Oxy.* 55; Florus 1.33.12; Plutarch, *Quaest. Rom.* 34). Strabo, *Geogr.* 3.3.4, however, marks the Minius as the boundary of Brutus' campaign.

305 **Nimis:** This name is unknown, and has been the subject of various suggested emendations (see Schweighäuser, *Appian* 3.297-8; Goukowsky, *Appien* p. 66, n. 405). The most obvious change would be from Νίμιος (the reading of all the manuscripts) to Μινίου, which Goukowsky adopts into his text. However this river is named by Strabo as identical with the Baenis, which is probably what Appian called it at 71.301 above (see note). Unless, as is only too likely, this is another of Appian's geographical confusions, it is perhaps better to think of the smaller river, called the Nebis by Pomponius Mela, 3.10. His description of it as 'another river' (ἑτέρου ποταμοῦ) suggests that it is not a river that he is aware of having mentioned before.
Bracari: One of the tribes in the area generally called Callaecia in the north of modern Portugal, which gave their name to the later *municipium Bracara Augusta* (modern Braga) (see J. de Alarcão, *Roman Portugal*, 1 , (Warminster 1988), pp. 29-32).

73

308 **Talabriga:** The site of this town is unknown, but it has been suggested that it stood on the banks of the river Vouga, which reaches the Atlantic at Aveiro, some 50 km. south of Porto (J. de Alarcão, *Roman Portugal*, 1 (Warminster 1988), p. 9).

309 **took away from them their horses:** This indicates that they were cavalry-based raiders, in the style of Viriathus. Similarly in the surrender-document from Alcántara, dated to 104 BC, the surrendering people were required to give up their captives, their

stallions and their mares (see R. López Melero et al., *Gerión* 2 (1984), pp. 265-323; Richardson, *Hispaniae*, pp. 199-201).

310 **I have brought together these events with the history of Viriathus because they began to be undertaken at the same time by bandits in emulation of him:** This marks the end of the sub-section that Appian has inserted in his account of the war with Viriathus (see above on 70.300 and 71.301). It is clear from this remark that he was aware that he was dealing with these events out of chronological order, though his explanation of this is hardly compelling. It may be that his source included a section on Brutus' campaigns following the mention of the Callaeci (see above 70.300), but in that case it is surprising that Appian does not mention the Callaeci at all in his section on Brutus in Ulterior. It does indicate, however, that Appian's division of his material is not (as it is sometimes described) between the two provinces of Citerior and Ulterior, but (as he himself says) between the wars against Viriathus and against the Numantines (see further, Introduction, pp. 3-4).

74

311 **his most trusted friends, Audax, Ditalco and Minurus:** The story of the betrayal of Viriathus is much reported in the ancient writers (Livy, *per.* 54 and *ep. Oxy.* 54; Diodorus, 33.1.4 and 33.21; Velleius, 2.1.3; Val. Max. 9.6.4; Florus 1.33.17 (who attributes the assassination to Popilius); Eutropius 4.16; *de vir. ill.* 71.3; Orosius 5.4.14; John of Antioch fr. 60). On the relationship of the various sources, see Simon, *Roms Kriege,* pp. 130-8. The names of the betrayers are given in Livy, *ep. Oxy.* 54, in the same form as here, but Diodorus, 33.21, gives them the Hellenised forms of Audas, Dialkes and Nikorontes. Both sets are presumably adaptations of Celtic originals. The story of Viriathus' death has similarities to that of the betrayal of Sertorius (see above 101.441).

75

317 **When the funeral rites were over, they conducted gladiatorial games by the tomb:** The funeral of Viriathus is described in detail also by Diodorus, 33.22, and clearly was also elaborated upon by Livy, to judge from the note in the *periocha* (*per.* 54). Both Appian and Diodorus comment on the use of gladiators, which had been introduced at Rome as part of funeral rites in 264 BC (Livy, *per.* 16; Val. Max. 2.4.6).

318 **who was among the barbarians a leader of outstanding abilities:** This section of praise for Viriathus appears to be part of an *elogium* for the Lusitanian leader, which has left traces in many other authors (thus Livy, *per.* 54; Diodorus 33.1.21; Velleius 2.1.3; Justin 44.2.7; Florus 1.33.15; Eutropius 4.6; Orosius 5.4.14). For analysis of this tradition, see Simon, *Roms Kriege*, 135-8, n. 69; Z. W. Rubinsohn, 'The Viriathic war and its Roman repercussions', *Riv. Stor. dell' Antichità* 11 (1981), p. 163-204, at 190-3.

319 **through the eight years of this war:** See above on 63.265.

320 **Tautalus:** Diodorus, 33.1.4, is the only other author to mention Viriathus' successor by name, and calls him 'Tautamos'.
      Saguntum, which Hannibal founded after his capture of it and called it Carthage: See above on 7.25 and 12.47.

321 **He removed all their weapons from them and gave them enough land:** See above
on 42.171 and 59.249. Diodorus, 33.1.4, also mentions the grant of land.

Chs. 76-98: War against Numantia (143-133 BC)

The Seige of Numantia, after S.J. Keay, Roman Spain *(London 1988).*

The circumstances of the renewal of the war in Celtiberia are far from clear, and Appian says
only that the Vaccaei and the Numantines were stirred up to revolt by the example of
Viriathus (above 76.322). In 143 BC, however, the consul, Q. Caecilius Metellus was sent to
Hispania Citerior to continue the war (see below 76.322), and was succeeded by a string of
consuls: Q. Pompeius in 141 (below 76.325), M. Poplilius Laenas in 139 (below 79.342), C,
Hostlius Mancinus in 137 (below 79.345), who was replaced in the same year by the other
consul, M. Aemilius Lepidus Porcina (below 80.348). At best, these men were ineffective
and at worst (in the case of Pompeius and Mancinus) suffered disastrous and humiliating
defeats. As in the early bout of the war against Numantia (see above, note before ch. 44), the
situation was made more complicated by the desire of the commanders to have the credit of

ending the long conflict, and the insistence of the senate that this should only be done by the total surrender of the Numantines. In 134 BC, after further ineffective action by the consuls of 136 (L. Furius Philus: below 83.361) and of 135 (Q. Calpurnius Piso: below 83.362), P. Scipio Aemilianus, the adoptive grandson of Scipio Africanus (see above on 53.225 and 65.273) was elected consul, and sent to end the war. It is on Scipio's campaign against Numantia that Appian concentrates in this section (below 84.363-98.427), giving far more detail than for any other part of the work, apart from his account of Scipio Africanus' period in Spain during the Hannibalic war (above 18.68-39.158; see Introduction, pp. 3-4).

76

322   **Our account reverts to the war with the Vaccaei and the Numantines:** Since the last point at which Appian wrote about the war in Citerior under Lucullus in 150 (see above, 55.233), six years have passed. The only events recorded in other sources that affected commanders in Citerior during these years all relate to contacts with Viriathus, two of whom (Claudius Unimanus and C. Nigidius) were defeated by him (see Florus 1.33.15 and Orosius 5.4.3 for Claudius; *de vir. ill.* 71.1 fcr Nigidius) and C. Laelius who was successful (see above, on 65.278) On these events see Simon, *Roms Kriege*, pp. 92-7, and Astin, *Scipio Aemilianus*, p. 344.

   Caecilius Metellus: Q. Caecilius Metellus Macedonicus, the consul of 143, had achieved fame as praetor in 148 when he regained control of Macedonia from Andriscus, the pretender to the throne, and celebrated a triumph for this in 146. He was unusual in gaining a triumphal *cognomen* for a triumph obtained before he had reached the consulship. On Macedonicus' career, see Astin, *Scipio Aemilianus*, index *s.v.*; and on his campaigns in Spain, Simon, *Roms Kriege*, pp. 101-8.

   Termantia and Numantia: Termantia is usually identified with the later town of Termes (modern Tiermes), south-west of Soria and not far from Numantia. It would then be the same place which Appian calls Termessus at 99.431, which is there described as having been opposed to Roman rule in the past. Pliny, *NH* 3.27, says that Termes was a town belonging to the Arevaci. On Numantia, see above on 46.188.

323   **Numantia was difficult to reach because of two rivers:** The site of Numantia is on a long low hill in the fork between the river Duero (Roman Durius) and its tributary the river Tera (see map above).

   it had been closed off with ditches and blocks of stone: These fortifications, known as *chevaux de frise*, are typical of Celtic and Celtiberian hill-fort settlements in the northern part of the Iberian peninsula (see M. Almagro-Gorbea, 'From hillforts to *oppida* in 'Celtic' Iberia', in B. Cunliffe and S. J. Keay (edd.), *Social Complexity and the Development of Towns in Iberia* (London 1995), pp. 175-207.

325   **After the winter, Metellus handed over to Quintus Pompeius, son of Aulus:** The chronology of Metellus' campaigns is obscure, but as he was consul in 143 and Pompeius consul in 141, it is probable that he was in his province for two winters (see Simon, *Roms Kriege*, pp. 102-8). On Q. Pompeius, see above on 66.281; and in general, Astin, *Scipio Aemilianus*, index *s.v.*

   who was encamped over against Numantia: Pompeius' camp was identified by Schulten, *Numantia* 3.181, as the Cerro de Castillejo, north of the town.

77

327 **Termantia:** See above on 76.322.

329 **Pompeius attacked the little town of Malia:** This place is called Lagni by Diodorus, 33.17, which may be identified with Almazán, 35 km. south of Soria (see the discussion in Simon, *Roms Kriege*, p. 110, n. 15).

330 **left for Sedetania, which was being ravaged by a bandit-chieftain called Tanginus:** The Sedetani are more usually called the Edetani by Greek writers (so Strabo, *Geogr.* 3.4.1, 12 and 14; Ptolemy, 2.6.15) as also by Pliny (*NH* 3.20, 3.23 and 3.24) and in inscriptions (so *CIL* 2.4251). The form Sedetani and Sedetania are found in Livy (28.24.4, 31.7; 29.1.26; 31.49.7; 31.20.2) and in Silius Italicus (3.372). Its use by Appian may be another instance of his use of Latin name forms. The territory of this people is described by Strabo, *locc. cit.*, as being along the Mediterranean coast, between the Ebro and Carthago Nova, though he also includes Caesaraugusta (Zaragoza) within their region. Tanginus is not known apart from this mention.

78

332 **he diverted a certain river into the plain:** This is probably the river Tera, or the combined stream of the Tera and the river Merdench, which flows on the western side of the hill of Numantia to join with the Duero just south-west of the town (see plan, p. 165). Pompeius' intention was presumably to deprive the Numantines of access to drinking water.

333 **the tribune, Oppius:** Not otherwise known.

334 **At this point, there came to Pompeius from Rome senatorial commissioners:** The arrival of these men suggests that Pompeius had told the senate that he had been much more successful than, to judge by Appian's account, was in fact the case, since this type of commission was normally sent out to assist a victorious commander in the settlement of areas which had been newly conquered (Simon, *Roms Kriege*, p. 113; Richardson, *Hispaniae*, pp. 144-5; on these commissions, see Mommsen, *StR* 2.64-4 and 692-3; B. Schleussner, *Die Legaten der römischen Republik* (Munich 1978), pp. 9-94). This would explain the shame that Pompeius is said to have felt as a result of his failure to achieve an ending of the war (below 78.335).

replacements for his soldiers, who had served six years: This cannot refer to the soldiers who had come out to Citerior with Metellus Macedonicus (above 76.322), but to that part of his army who had been there before Metellus arrived. Six years appears to have been the normal period of service for infantry in Iberia (see Walbank, *Historical Commentary* 1.698 on Polybius 6.19.2), though later the norm was sixteen years. A passage of the satirist Lucilius, writing in the second century BC, suggests that the situation in Spain was regarded as requiring more than usually favourable treatment (Lucilius, 490-1 (M): dum miles Hibera / terras<t> ac meret <hic> ter sex aetat<i> quasi annos. ('while he is a soldier in Iberia, and serves for eighteen years or so at a time')).

336 **suffered sickness in the stomach, and some of them died:** Compare the experience of Fulvius Nobilior's soldiers in 153/2 and of Lucullus' in 151 (above 47.197; 54.227).

337 **Many Romans were killed, both ordinary soldiers and people of distinction:** Orosius, 5.4.13, makes a similar remark about the various social classes involved in Pompeius' losses.

79

338 **Because he was afraid that he would be prosecuted, he secretly undertook negotiations with the Numantines:** Diodorus appears to give a different version of this story, in which Pompeius undertook negotiations with the Termantines as well as with the Numantines, and attributes the breakdown of the process to the unwillingness of the latter to surrender their arms, though it may be that this story relates to Metellus Macedonicus rather than to Pompeius (Astin, *Scipio Aemilianus*, pp.147-8; though see Richardson, *Hispaniae*, p.144, n. 75).

342 **Marcus Popilius Laenas:** Consul in 139, he was assigned to the province of Citerior. Some sources (Diodorus 33.21; Dio Cassius fr. 75) also describe his involvement in negotiations with Viriathus (see above on 70.297), and Florus, 1.33.17, makes him responsible for Viriathus' assassination (see above on 74.311). If there were such negotiations (as seems probable), they are most likely to have taken place in the earlier part of his tenure of the province, while he awaited the outcome of the embassies which went to Rome from Numantia (74.343).

knowing that the agreement was disgraceful: The problem was that the agreement had been made before the surrender had taken place, which made the surrender invalid in the eyes of the senate (see next note). Marcellus in 151 BC had done something rather similar, but had taken care that the public negotiations took place after the surrender (see above on 49.208; and Richardson, *Hispaniae*, pp. 142-7, for a comparison of the two cases).

344 **The trial took place in the senate:** Properly speaking, this was not a trial but a senatorial debate, but here as elsewhere Appian presents such debates as though they were legal proceedings (see above on 55.233 and 60.255). In the debate that followed in the senate, it would appear from other sources (Cicero, *de fin.* 2.54, *de off.* 3.109, *de rep.* 3.28; Livy, *per.* 54; Vell. Pat. 2.1.3; Eutropius 4.17; Orosius 5.4.21; see Richardson, *Hispaniae*, pp. 145-6) that the grounds for the accusation against Pompeius were that he had undertaken negotiations and agreed a peace. This indicates that the problem, so far as the senate was concerned, was that the Numantines had not surrendered (that is, made a formal *deditio*), a process which could not, in principle, be proceeded by negotiations. See above on 49.208; and for the political setting, Astin, *Scipio Aemilianus*, pp. 148-50.

345 **Popilius attacked their neighbours, the Lusones:** On the Lusones, see above on 42.171. Appian is the only source for this campaign. This will have taken place (assuming that Appian is correct) in 138, Popilius' second year in the province. Livy, *per.* 55 and *ep. Oxy.* 55, records that he was worsted by the Numantines.

Hostilius Mancinus: C. Hostilius Mancinus, the consul of 137. On his political associations, see Astin, *Scipio Aemilianus*, pp. 90-1. His departure from Rome was said to have been attended by evil omens, no doubt read back from the disastrous events which followed (Livy, *per.* 55; Obsequens 24; Val. Max. 1.6.7).

80

346 **a remote place where once Nobilior had built a camp:** This is La Gran Atalaya at Renieblas, which Nobilior had occupied in 153 (see above on 46.188).

347 **when the Numantines encircled him and threatened to kill everyone if he did not agree to peace, he made an agreement on equal terms between the Romans and the**

Numantines: The story of Mancinus' surrender and the 'disgraceful' peace that he made following it occurs in many other writers, particularly in contexts which mention the rôle played by Ti. Sempronius Gracchus, son of the praetor of 180 (see above on 43.175) and later tribune of the plebs in 133 (Valerius Antias fr. 57 (in Gellius, *NA* 6.9.12 and Valerius Probus, fr. 100; mentioning Ti. Gracchus); Cic., *de harusp. resp.* 43 (mentioning Ti. Gracchus), *Brutus* 103 (mentioning Ti. Gracchus); Livy, *per.* 55; Vell Pat, 2.1.4 ('foedera ... turpia ac detestablia'), 2.2.1 (mentioning Ti. Gracchus), 2.90.3 ('in illis turpe Q. Pompei foedus turpiusque Mancini'); Val. Max 1.6.7, 2.7.1; Plutarch, *Ti. Gracchus* 5-7; Florus 1.34.4-7 (compares with Pompeius), 2.2.2 (mentioning Ti. Gracchus); Dio Cassius, fr. 83.2; Minucius Felix 26.3 Obsequens 24; *de vir. ill.* 59.4, 64.1; Orosius 5.8.3). It is notable that neither here nor in the section of the *Civil Wars*, which he devotes to the tribunate of Gracchus (*bell. civ.* 1.8-17), does Appian mention his involvement. Plutarch, *loc. cit.*, by contrast, suggests that it was only because of Gracchus' intervention, and the Numanitnes' respect for his father, that the agreement was achieved.

348 **sent the other consul, Aemilius Lepidus, to Iberia:** M. Aemilius Lepidus Porcina, Mancinus' colleague as consul for 137. He is said to have acquired his additional *cognomen*, which means 'pig-meat' (cf. Plautus, *Aul.* 375, *Capt.* 849) because of his obesity (Diodorus 33.27).

summoned Mancinus to trial: As often, Appian uses legal language when describing what was in fact a senatorial debate (see above on 55.233, 60.255 and 79.344). In the case of Mancinus, Cicero, *de off.* 3.109 and *de rep.* 3.28, specifically mentions Mancinus speaking in favour of the legislative bill (*rogatio*) which resulted from the senatorial debate, making it clear that a legislative rather than a judicial process was involved.

349 **for some sought the command for glory or gain or the honour of a triumph, not for the benefit of the city:** Appian is here using the moral criteria by which he marks out 'bad' generals, such as Lucullus (above 51.215 and 54.230) and Galba (above 60.255). On the significance of the triumph to commanders in the mid-second century, see Richardson, *Hispaniae*, pp. 135-6.

falsely alleged that the Vaccaei had provided the Numantines with supplies during the war: Lucullus had also attacked the Vaccaei without authorisation in 151 (51.215). Despite Appian's allegation, it may well be that Lepidus was right to be suspicious of the Vaccaei, since two years later Scipio Aemilianus was to plunder their territory, which is said to have been a source for the provisioning of the Numantines (87.380). Scipio had also served in Lucullus' army in 151 (above 53.225-54.230).

350 **the city of Pallantia, which is the largest city of the Vaccaei:** See above on 55.231.
Brutus, his kinsman by marriage, who had been sent (as I have stated already) to the other part of Iberia: On Brutus, see above 71.301. Precisely how the two were related is not clear. The **other part of Iberia** is the province of Hispania Ulterior (for this usage, see above on 66.81).

81

351 **Ambassadors from Rome, Cinna and Caecilius:** Neither of these men can be identified with certainty, but the former may be L. Cornelius Cinna, consul in 127, and

the latter L. Caecilius Metellus Calvus, the consul of 142 (so, tentatively, Broughton, *MRR* 1.487; G. de Sanctis, *Storia dei Romani* 4.3 (Firenze 1964), p. 253, n. 237).

352 **that the Vaccaei had supplied food, money and troops to the Numantines:** Appian appears to assume here that Lepidus really believed that the Vaccaei had assisted the Numantines (see above 80.349).

353 **Flaccus:** Not otherwise known, though he may be (as Broughton, *MRR* 1.488, n. 6, suggests) either C. Fulvius, the consul of 134, or M. Fulvius, the consul of 125.

82

357 **the Pallantians, turned back by a god, withdrew:** This remark is obscure, but was identified by Schulten, *Numantia* 1.365, n. 2, as the result of an eclipse of the moon which took place on 1 April ¹36.

83

358 **When the Romans heard of it, they r dieved Aemilius of his command and his consulship:** Appian is wrong to say that Lepidus was deprived of his consulship, since he was not consul at the time but holding the *imperium pro consule* following his consulship of the previous year. None the less, the deprivation of consular *imperium* is an amazingly severe action. Although threats of such action had been made before (see Livy 27.20.21 and 29.19.6), it is likely that it had never been carried out, and certainly not in the absence of the commander (Mommsen, *StR* 1.629, n. 4 and 3.1088). On the change in senatorial attitudes to the commanders in Iberia, see Richardson, *Hispaniae*, pp. 149-55.

359 **he transferred the blame for the treaty onto Pompeius:** Several other sources make the comparison between Mancinus and Pompeius (Cic., *de rep.* 3.28; Vell Pat, 2.1.4-5, 2.90.3; Florus 1.34.4-7), invariably to the detriment of the latter. None of them represent Mancinus' argument as a transfer of blame to Pompeius, however. Dio Cassius, fr. 79.2, states that Mancinus' friends argued that what he had done had saved the lives of many Romans and preserved Roman possessions in Iberia.

360 **Pompeius escaped condemnation, on the grounds that he had been tried on these matters already:** See above 79.344. Whatever the argument can have been for not punishing Pompeius, Appian cannot be right in asserting that it was because of a legal problem over double jeopardy, since Pompeius' 'trial' was a senatorial debate, not a judicial hearing.
on the grounds that their ancestors had surrendered twenty officers to the Samnites: The reference is to the aftermath of the disastrous surrender at the Caudine Forks in 321 BC (see T. J. Cornell, *CAH* VII², pp. 370-1; N. M. Horsfall, 'The Caudine Forks: topography and illusion', *PBSR* 50 (1982), pp. 45-52). The same number of officers surrendered is given by Appian, *Samn.* fr. 4.18-19. Cicero, *de off.* 3.109, and Velleius Paterculus, 2.1.5, also draw the parallel between Mancinus' treatment and the events following the Caudine Forks. On the growth of the tradition, see M. H. Crawford, '*Foedus* and *sponsio*', *PBSR* 41 (1973), pp. 1-7.

361 **Furius took Mancinus to Iberia:** L. Furius Philus, consul of 136. He was a friend of Scipio Aemilianus (Astin, *Scipio Aemilianus*, pp. 81-2), and is one of the characters in

Cicero's *de republica*. On his activity in Citerior, see Cicero, *de off.* 3.109; *de rep.* 3.28; Dio Cassius fr. 82).

handed him over naked to the Numantines, who refused to accept him: He was taken to the gates of the city and left there, naked and with his hands tied behind his back, until night-fall (Livy, *per.* 56; Vell. Pat. 2.1.5; Plutarch, *Ti. Gracch.* 7.4; *de vir. ill.* 59; Orosius 5.4.21). The action, or rather inaction, of the Numantines raised the question of the status of Mancinus, once he returned to Rome, since he had properly lost his citizenship as a result of being handed over in this way. The decision reached was that he should retain his citizenship but lost his seat in the senate. Subsequently he is said to have regained it by being elected praetor for a second time (Cic., *Top.* 37; *pro Caec.* 98; *de orat.* 1.181, 1.238, 2.137-8; Pomponius, *D* 50.7.18pr (cf. Modestinus, *D* 49.15.4); *de vir. ill.* 59.4). According to Pliny, *NH* 34.18, there existed a statue of Mancinus, dressed as he had been when handed over to the Numantines; and later tradition, as represented by Cicero (*de off.* 3.109; *de rep.* 3.28; *de or.* 1.181) and Velleius (2.1.5), recognised him as an honourable man (see Simon, *Roms Kriege*, pp. 156-8).

362 **Calpurnius Piso:** Q. Calpurnius Piso, consul of 135. Despite Appian's statement that he did not attack Numantia, Obsequens, 26, records a defeat there in this year.
Carpetania: See above on 51.215-7

84

363 **Cornelius Scipio, who had captured Carthage:** P. Cornelius Scipio Aemilianus Africanus, on whom see above 49.210. He is the hero of the last major section of the work (84.363-99.424). 'Carthage' here means the city in Africa, which Aemilanus had captured and destroyed in 146 BC.

364 **Even at that date he was younger than the age fixed for those holding the consulship:** This had been true when Scipio was elected consul for 147, since he was born in 185 (or possibly 184: see Astin, *Scipio Aemilianus*, pp. 245-7), which meant that he was at least five years too young and, moreover, had not held the prerequisite office of praetor (Astin, *Scipio Aemilianus*, pp. 61-2; R. Develin, *Patterns in office-holding, 366-49 BC* (*Collection Latomus* 161, Brussels 1979), p. 84). In 135, when he was elected consul for 134, neither of these conditions was violated. He was, however, excluded by the rule, introduced after the third consulship of M. Claudius Marcellus in 152, which forbade a second or further consulship (A. E. Astin, *The Lex Annalis before Sulla* (*Collection Latomus* 32, Brussels 1958), pp. 19-20). Livy, *per.* 56, correctly states the position. Other sources (Cic., *de amicit.* 11; Val. Max. 8.15.4) indicate that he was not a candidate, and Cicero, *de rep.* 6.11, that he was not even present.

365 **he did not recruit an army by a levy, since there were many wars going on and many men in Iberia:** This situation is also the setting for a saying of Scipio's ([Plutarch], *apophth. Scip. Min.* 15) where he sets the shortage of citizens against the bravery of the enemy as difficulties in war (see Simon, *Roms Kriege*, pp. 173-6). It is clear that the problems of the wars in Iberia had already led to the use of volunteers before this (see above 49.209 and 65.273).
volunteers, sent to him by cities and kings from personal goodwill: Other sources mention troops sent by Attalus of Pergamum (Cic., *Deiot.* 19 and Schol. Ambros. *ad*

loc. (Stangl, p. 272)), Antiochus of Syria (Livy, *per.* 57) and Micipsa of Numidia (Sallust, *Iug.* 7.2; cf. below 89.387 and above 67.284).

366 **his nephew, Buteo:** The *cognomen* Buteo belongs to the family of the Fabii, and this man has been identified tentatively (see Broughton, *MRR* 1.491) with Q. Fabius Maximus, whom, according to Valerius Maximus, 8.15.4, Scipio was commending to the voters in the elections for the quaestorship when he himself was unexpectedly elected consul. Fabius Maximus was the son of Scipio's adoptive brother, Q. Fabius Maximus Aemilianus, who also served with Scipio at Numantia (see below 90.392).

ὅτι μὴ κρατήσει πολεμίων, πρὶν κατασχεῖν τῶν ἰδίων ἐγκρατῶς: ὅτι μὴ with the indicative in indirect speech is unusual in classical Greek, but more common in later authors (W. W. Goodwin, *The Syntax of Greek Moods and Tenses* (London 1929), section 686).

85

367 **he expelled all the traders, prostitutes, clairvoyants and diviners:** Scipio's measures against bad discipline became legendary, and many of his sayings on the subject were preserved (see Astin, *Scipio Aemilianus*, pp. 259-62, nos. 33-42b). C. Fannius, who served under him during the siege of Carthage, remarked on his use of irony (Cic., *Lucullus* 15; *MRR* 1.464). See also Livy, *per.* 57; Val. Max. 2.7.1; Frontinus, *Strat.* 4.1.1; Polyaenus, *Strat.* 8.16.2.

368 **Their food was limited to boiled and roasted meat:** As it stands, this is an extraordinary statement, since the basic food of a Roman army was grain (thus Polybius 6.39) and Appian has commented already on the problems associated with a diet in which meat played too large a part (54.227; compare Diodorus 24.1.4, on the bad effects of an exclusively meat diet, eaten by Roman and allied soldiers at the siege of Lilybaeum in 250 BC). Appian presumably means that the meat that was eaten had to be plainly cooked (R. W. Davies, *Service in the Roman army* (Edinburgh 1989), p. 203-4)

369 **He forbade them to have beds and was himself the first to take his rest on a straw mattress:** Scipio's setting of a personal example is noted by Frontinus, 4.3.9 (who compares him with Alexander in this). Other sources make similar points (Polyaenus 8.16.2; SHA, *Hadr.* 10.2; [Plutarch], *apophth. Scip. Min.* 16); and it may be that a fragment of Rutilius Rufus, fr. 13 (Peter), about someone who used litter in place of a bed *contra usum imperatorum* also is about Scipio. Rutilius served on Scipio's staff in the Numantine war (see below 88.382), and wrote a book about his own life. Schulten, *Numantia* 3.131f and 196, pointed out that the head-quarters building of Scipio's camp at Castillejo outside Numantia was equipped with a dining area, complete with couches. The same was true of the buildings used by the military tribunes (Schulten, *Numantia* 3.150 ff.), where the story of Scipio's prediction during a dinner party of the coming greatness of C. Marius is set (Val. Max. 8.15.7; Plutarch, *Marius* 3.2-5; Simon, *Roms Kriege*, p. 175).

ἀλείμμασι: This word usually means the oil used during bathing or for rubbing down after exercise, but can also be used for the process of applying the oil, as here (see P. Glare, ed., *Liddell and Scott, Greek-English Lexicon: Revised Suppl.* (Oxford 1996), p. 17).

86

372 **all the plains that were nearest to hand:** The location of these exercises depends on
the view taken of the winter-camp which the Roman army occupied in 135-4, but it is
most likely to have been in the valley of the Ebro if, as Schulten assumed, he used
Tarraco as his base (Schulten, *Numantia* 1.371). If the camp to which Scipio first
directly to the camp was that which had been used by Calpurnius Piso, he may well
have used the area of Carpetania (above 83.362) for his training ground (so Simon,
Roms Kriege, p. 180).

374 **he set up camp:** Polybius, who was a close associate of Scipio Aemilianus and wrote a
monograph on the Numantine war (see above, Introduction, p. 5) was particularly
impressed by the efficiency with which the Romans constructed and guarded both their
permanent and marching camps, and wrote about it at great length in his description of
the Roman army (Polybius 6.27-42; see Walbank, *Historical Commentary*, 1.709-723).

87

375 **he moved closer to the Numantines:** This suggests (so Simon, *Roms Kriege*, pp. 181-
2) that at this point Scipio moved into the vicinity of the town, rather than (as some have
suggested) that he undertook a preliminary expedition through the territory north and
west of Numantia. Hence the care he took not to divide his army.

377 **there was a short way past Numantia to the plains:** Not, as Viereck and Roos, *ad
loc.*, suggest, the plains of the Vaccaei, since Appian separates this foraging expedition
from his attack on their territory (87.380). See Simon, *Roms Kriege*, p. 181.

379 **it is a careless general who fights before it is necessary:** Aulus Gellius records that
the second-century BC historian, Sempronius Asellio, wrote that Scipio attributed a
very similar *bon mot* about not fighting until it was necessary to his father, L. Aemilius
Paullus (Gellius, *NA* 13.3.6 [= Sempronius Asellio fr. 5 (Peter)]). Asellio served under
Scipio as a military tribune at Numantia and is said by Gellius, *NA* 2.13.3, to have
recorded those events at which he was present. Valerius Maximus, 7.2.2, gives a
similar remark to Scipio himself. See Astin, *Scipio Aemilianus*, p. 262.

380 **the territory of the Vaccaei, where the Numantines purchased their food-stuffs:**
See above on 80.349.

88

381 **a plain in the territory of Pallantia called Coplanion:** Schulten, *Numantia* 1.373,
identifies this with the area in the vicinity of Palencia and Burgos, which is a region of
open plains and remains highly productive. The name does not occur elsewhere, and
the precise location is unknown.

382 **Rutilius Rufus, who wrote a history of these exploits and was then a tribune:** P.
Rutilius Rufus, consul in 105. He was eventually convicted in the *quaestio de
repetundis* in 92, following his service as a *legatus* under Q. Mucius Scaevola in the
province of Asia, in a trial which was regarded as having been engineered by his
opponents among the equestrian class because of his protection of the provincials from
the depredations of the Roman tax-farmers in the province. He went into exile in the
province at Smyrna (Dio Cassius fr. 97.2; Cic., *Balb.* 28), and it is assumed that it was
there that he wrote his history, which was described as being *de vita sua* ('about his

life') (the fragments are collected in H. Peter, *Historicorum Romanorum Fragmenta*, vol. 1 (second ed., Leipzig 1914), pp. 187 ff.). The note of Appian suggests that he (or, perhaps more likely, his source) used Rutilius for the events of the Numantine war. On Rutilius at Numantia, see also Cic. *de rep.* 1.17; Suidas, *s.v.* Ῥουτίλιος Ῥοῦφος. See above 85.369.

he ordered his cavalrymen neither to pursue nor to engage: As Simon states, *Roms Kriege*, p. 183 n. 106, this tactic is reminiscent of Viriathus (above 60.262), though, as Goukowsky notes (*Appien*, p. 136, n. 491) Scipio is said by Appian to have used similar tactics himself during the third Punic war (Appian, *Lib.* 103.484).

89

386 **the Caucaei, whose treaty Lucullus had violated:** See above 51.216-52.220. If the identification of Cauca with modern Coca is correct (see above on 51.216), Scipio had marched south from the territory of the Vaccaei and will then have returned to Numantia along the valley of the Durius (Duero).

387 **He reached Numantia and went into winter quarters:** This was the winter of 134-3.
there Jugurtha, the grandson of Massinissa, joined him from Libya: Jugurtha was the son of Mastanabal, one of Massinissa's sons, by a concubine, who had been excluded from the line of succession to the throne of Numidia but had been brought up by Micipsa (on whom see above 67.284) with his own sons, Adherbal and Hiempsal (Sallust, *Iug.* 5.7). Jugurtha's experience of the Romans while he was serving at Numantia is said by Sallust to have sown the seeds for his subsequent take-over of the kingdom of Numidia from his cousins (Sall., *Iug.* 7.2-9.2). C. Marius, who was to defeat Jugurtha and bring him back to Rome, where he was executed in 104 after Marius' triumph, was also serving at Numantia, though it is not clear what his position was (Plutarch, *Marius* 3.2-4 and 13.2).
twelve elephants and the archers and slingers who were marshalled with them in battle: Compare the sending of elephants by Micipsa to help Fabius Aemilianus in 145 (above 67.284). On the deployment of elephants in battle by the Romans in Spain, see H. H. Scullard, *The Elephant in the Roman world* (London 1974), pp. 190-3.

90

392 **he set up two camps very close to Numantia:** On Scipio's siege works at Numantia, the classic work of Schulten, *Numantia* 3 (Die Lager des Scipios) (Munich 1927), remains fundamental.
his brother Maximus: Q. Fabius Maximus Aemilianus, the consul of 145, on whom see above 65.273.

393 **Having set seven forts round it:** See plan, p. 165.
    The manuscripts have a lacuna at this point. The length of the lacuna is uncertain, but it must have contained something about Scipio's decision to requisition troops from his Iberian allies. The supplement here is given *exempli gratia*.

394 **The perimeter of Numantia was twenty-four *stadia*, and that of the fortified wall more than twice that:** Appian's figures here were confirmed by the excavations undertaken by Schulten (see the discussion by Simon, *Roms Kriege*, p. 185 n. 112. A *stadion* is one eighth of a Roman mile and thus approximately 187 m.: see above on 1.4.

The walls of Numantia were approximately 4.5 km. in circumference, and the fortified wall approximately 9 km.

καὶ τοῦτο διῃρεῖτο πᾶν οἱ κατὰ μέρος ἕκαστον: The οἱ here is the dative masculine singular of the third person pronoun, and marks the agent: 'all this was divided up *by him* according to each section.'

396 **Towers were placed round the circuit, one every *plethron*:** A *plethron* is 100 feet.

91

398 **This he was unable to bridge, since it was broad and had a strong current:** In fact Scipio needed to be able to cross the Durius and the other rivers around Numantia in order to maintain contact between his own camps, and Schulten, *Numantia* 3.86 ff., found traces of foot-bridges. The mechanism which Appian describes for preventing the Numantines from travelling along the river, is not recorded in any other source.

92

401 **sharpened missiles and rocks:** Schulten, *Numantia* 3.43 f. and 210 f., found such missiles during the excavation of the siege-lines.

403 **The army, including the indigenous forces, numbered about sixty thousand:** These numbers seem much too large. Scipio had with him a consular army, that is to say two legions and allied auxiliaries, which should have amounted to some 20,000 men (on the size of the legion and the proportion of allies to Romans at this period, see P. A. Brunt, *Italian Manpower 225 BC - AD 14* (Oxford 1971), pp. 671-686) De Sanctis, *Storia dei Romani* 4.3 (Firenze 1964), pp. 266-7, reckons that the true figure would have been less than 25,000, including non-Italians. As to the numbers of Numantines, both Livy, *per.* 55, and Florus, 1.34.2, give the numbers as 4,000 Numantines against 40,000 Romans (Livy is dealing specifically with the case of the surrender of Mancinus); while Appian, 97.491, gives the number as 8,000 before the wars began, as against 60,000 on the Roman side.

93

406 **the whole circuit became extremely formidable to all along the fifty *stadia* of the perimeter:** See above on 90.394.

94

407 **Rhetogenes, a Numantine, surnamed Caraunios:** Florus, 1.34.15, mentions a certain Rhoecogenes, who was leader of the Numantines at the time of the final surrender of the city and who led the mass suicide; Valerius Maximus, 3.2. ext. 7, tells a similar though more detailed story about one Rhoetogenes (Valerius, 5.1.5, has another story about the bravery of a man with the same name during the period of Q. Metellus in Celiberia). These are certainly the same name, probably a Hellenised version of a Celtic name (E. Hübner, *RE* 3.1933, followed by Goukowsky, *Appien*, p. 136 n. 511, suggests *Rectugenos*).

409 **the city of Lutia was wealthy and situated three hundred *stadia* from Numantia:** Identified by Schulten, *Numantia* 1.134, with Cantalucia, 55 km. west of Numantia. If

this is correct, Appian's figure of the distance form Numantia is accurate (see above on 1.4).

411 **He cut off their hands:** This is a punishment used at other times in the Spanish wars, but in other contexts was regarded as peculiarly barbarous. See above on 68.291.

95

412 **Avarus:** This name is given only in Appian, and looks like an adaptation (or invention) by a Roman source.

414 **said that they must hand themselves and their property over to him and surrender their city and their weapons:** Scipio is clearly demanding a full *deditio* from the Numantines (see above on 49.208, 50.214 and 79.344; Richardson, *Hispaniae*, pp. 140-7).

415 **They killed Avarus and the five ambassadors who went with him:** This story is found only in Appian, and is no doubt told as a prelude to the barbarisms of the Numantines in the subsequent events.

96

416 **they boiled and ate human flesh:** This was considered the height of barbarism, but was recognised to happen in times of extreme necessity during sieges (Strabo, *Geogr.* 4.5.4; Thucydides 2.70.1 (Potidaea) Val. Max. 6.7.ext 2 (Numantines) and 3 (Calagurris at end of Sertorian wars) Caesar, *bell. Gall.* 7.77.12 (Gauls, when besieged by the Cimbri and Teutones))

the butchers' shops: The Greek μαγειρεῖον, here translated 'butcher's shop', seems most often to have been used of the work-places of the butchers who prepared the meat which had been used in sacrifices in sanctuaries (see the discussion in Goukowsky, *Appien*, p. 137, n.518). It could, however, be used of non-sacred contexts (as Theophrast., *Chr.* 6.9 where the plural, μαγειρεῖα, means the butchers' stalls in the market place).

97

419 **Although they were only about eight thousand strong in time of peace:** See above on 92.403.

420 **wild animals:** Meaning, of course, the Numantines. Compare Appian's description of them below (97.422-423).

422 **all those who wished to killed themselves:** The stories of communal suicides are found in other authors (Livy, *per.* 59; Seneca, *de ira* 1.11.7; Val. Max 3.2. ext. 7). Florus, 1.34.15, and Orosius, 5.7.17-18, believe that all the Numantines killed themselves, and that as a result none were available for Scipio's triumph (see below 98.424).

98

424 **Scipio chose fifty of them for his triumph:** The triumph took place in 132 (Cic., *Phil.* 11.18; Livy, *ep.* 59; Eutropius 4.19). Although it was not as bereft of spectacle as Florus and Orosius suggested (see on 97.422), Pliny, *NH* 33.141, noted that very little money was distributed to the soldiers. For other references to the triumph, see Cic., *de*

rep. 6.11; Vell. Pat. 2.4.5; Val. Max. 2.7.1 and 4.13.3 (with different views on the wealth displayed); Gellius, *NA* 16.8).

sold the remainder: It was normal Roman practice to sell the captured civilians into slavery, as Fabius Servilianus had done in 141 BC (see above 68.291). For the importance of enslavement in this period, see W. V. Harris, *War and Imperialism in Republican Rome, 327-70 BC* (Oxford 1979), pp. 80-3.

the two cities that had given the most trouble in war: Not surprisingly Scipio's achievement in capturing and destroying Carthage and Numantia became a commonplace, so that Quintilian, writing on oratory in the late first century AD, could cite 'the destroyer of Carthage and Numantia' as an example of *antonomasia*, the use of a description in place of a name (Quint., *Inst.* 8.6.30 and 43). The notion that the Celtiberian war was one of the most dangerous that Rome had ever fought was also common, and is found as early as Cicero, *de off.* 1.38 and *Mur.* 58 (see also Vell. Pat. 2.90.3 and Fronto, *ad M. Ant.* 3.1.3).

425 **Carthage:** Here, as at 84.363, Appian means Carthage in north Africa, which Scipio had captured and destroyed in 146 BC.

426 **the Romans even now call him both Africanus and Numantinus:** He is not so named on the *Fasti Capitolini* (see A. Degrassi, *Inscriptiones Italiae* 13.1 (Rome 1947), pp. 466-9), but the name 'Numantinus' is often found (see Ovid, *Fast.* 1.593; Columella 8.16.5; Pliny, *NH* 8.6.2; Apuleius, *Apol.* 66).

427 **He then divided the territory of the Numantines between those who lived close to them:** It is uncertain who these beneficiaries of Numantine territory were, though they may have included Roman allies among the Belli and the Titthi (see above on 49.207 and 63.268).

Chs. 99-102 From Numantia to the reign of the emperor Augustus, 133 BC - AD 14

Appian concludes his work with three chapters which take the story of the Roman wars in Iberia from Scipio Aemilianus' capture of Numantia down to the time of the emperor Augustus, who, so Appian reckons, left the area in the state it was in in Appian's own period. He deals briefly with the exploits of various Roman commanders in the late second and early first centuries BC, ending with T. Didius, who was in the province of Hispania Citerior from 98 to 93 BC (below 99.431-100.436) and C. Valerius Flaccus, consul in 93, who seems to have commanded in Citerior and later also in southern Gaul down to 81 BC. (below 100.436-437). After that, he writes even more briefly about the impact of the civil wars on the peninsula (especially the Sertorian wars, from 81 to 72 BC), and about the presence of Julius Caesar in Citerior in 61 and 60 BC, ending with a sentence about the re-organisation of the area into three Roman provinces, which took place under Augustus.

99

428 **The Romans, as usual, sent out ten men from the senate:** On these senatorial commissions, see above 78.334.

both those parts which Scipio had taken and those which Brutus before Scipio had made subject or defeated: Appian regards what Scipio had done as adding to Roman territory in some sense. While this was clearly true of Brutus' expedition into the north-west, where no Roman army had previously ventured, it was not the case with Scipio.

This picture of the Roman empire as a territorial entity belongs to Appian's own time, rather than the second century BC.

429 **Calpurnius Piso:** Probably to be identified with L. Calpurnius Piso, whom Cicero, 2 *Verr.* 4.56, describes as being a punctiliously honest governor of Ulterior, who died while in the province. From Appian's account, he was probably there in 113 or 112 BC, since his successor, Galba, was consul in 108 and probably therefore praetor in 111 (Broughton, *MRR* 1.539 and n. 4).

430 **Servius Galba succeeded him:** See previous note. Ser. Sulpicius Galba became consul in 108. He was the son of the praetor of 151, and had been produced by his father in the proceedings in 149 which followed his slaughter of the Lusitanians, in order to win the sympathy of his hearers (Cic. *de or.* 1.228). See above on 58.244 and 60.255.

the Cimbri were invading Italy, and Sicily was also embroiled in the second slave war: The Cimbri were one of the Germanic tribes who were threatening Italy from southern Gaul from 113 BC. This is a rather vague explanation from the chronological point of view, since the Cimbri defeated Cn. Mallius Maximus and Q. Servilius Caepio at the battle of Arausio in 105 and the second Sicilian slave war did not break out until 103. However, Appian's point is that there was much activity at about this time. He could also have mentioned the war against Jugurtha, which lasted from 111 to 105.

they did not send an army to Iberia: On the lack of interest by the senate in affairs in Iberia at this time, see Richardson, *Hispaniae*, pp. 157-8.

431 **Titus Didius came and killed twenty thousand of the Arevaci:** Didius was consul in 98 and held the province of Citerior from that year to 93, when he celebrated a triumph over the Celtiberians (Sallust, *Hist.* 1.88 (M); Livy, *per.* 70; Frontinus 1.8.5 and 2.10.1; Plutarch, *Sert.* 3; Obsequens 47 and 48; Degrassi, *Inscr. It.* 13.1.85 and 562-3). On the longer periods of tenure of commanders in the peninsula at this time, see Richardson, *Hispaniae*, pp. 159-60.

There is some uncertainty as to the name of the people whom Didius attacked, and the manuscripts could be restored to read either 'Arevaci' or 'Vaccaei'. On the assumption that Termessus is the same town as Termantia (above 76.322), it is probable that Schweighäuser is right to suggest that the correct reading is Ἀρουακῶν (Arevaci), since Pliny, *NH* 3.27, states that Termes was a town of the Arevaci.

Termessus, a large city which had always been disinclined to obey the Romans: See above on 76.322.

432 **Colenda:** The identity of this town is not known.

100

433 **Celtiberians, whom Marcus Marius had settled five years earlier, with the agreement of the senate, after they had fought with him against the Lusitanians:** The identity of M. Marius is uncertain, but he is most probably the brother of C. Marius, who adopted his sister's son, M. Marius Gratidianus (Cic., *Brutus* 168, *de leg.* 3.36; see Broughton, *MRR* 1.570 n. 3). Neither his victory over the Lusitanians nor his settlement of his Celtiberian allies is mentioned elsewhere, but it is likely that his tenure of the praetorship was in Ulterior (hence the Lusitanians) and perhaps took place in about 102 or 101 (five years before Didius' period in Citerior; but see below on 100.434). It is noteworthy that in 104 L. Caesius received the surrender of Lusitanians in the region of

Alcántara (see above 44.183) and that in 98 L. Cornelius Dolabella celebrated a triumph over the Lusitanians, probably following a praetorship in 100 (Degrassi, *Inscr. It.* 13.1.85 and 562).

434 **with the agreement of the ten commissioners, who were still present:** Appian evidently believes that these are the same commissioners that he mentioned above at 99.428, which is virtually impossible, since some forty years had elapsed since the departure of Scipio for Rome after the fall of Numantia. It is conceivable, however, that Didius had been sent a commission. If so, it would be expected that this was towards the end of his lengthy period in Citerior (as indeed is suggested by the reference to Didius' triumph at 100.436). If so, his dating of Marius' settlement of the Celtiberians five years earlier is probably in error.

He said to their leaders that he wanted to add the territory of the Colendans to theirs: This story is very like that about Galba's specious offer of land to the Lusitanians (see above 59.249-60.253, and notes thereto). It is quite likely, however, that similar circumstances produced similar events.

436 **For this Didius even celebrated a triumph:** Once again Appian is critical of the triumph-hunting of Roman generals (see above on 80.349).

Flaccus: C. Valerius Flaccus, consul in 93, was in charge of Citerior and subsequently also of Gallia Transalpina (Cic., *Quinct.* 24 and 28), and celebrated a triumph from both provinces in 81 (Granius Licinianus, 35.6 (Flem.): see, on the trustworthiness of this notice, L. A. Curchin, *Roman Spain: conquest and assimilation* (London 1991), p. 42 and Richardson, *The Romans in Spain* (Oxford 1996), p. 86 n. 12). He was the proconsul who issued the legal formula under which the decision on the *Tabula Contrebiensis* was made in 87 (G. Fatás, *Contrebia Belaisca : Tabula Contrebiensis* (Zaragoza 1980); J. S. Richardson, 'The Tabula Contrebiensis' *JRS* 73 (1983), pp. 1-11.

437 **Belgeda:** This is probably identical with modern Belchite, some 40 km. south-southeast of Zaragoza and some 20 km. west of the Iberian settlement at Azaila (see G. Fatás, *Contrebia Belaisca : Tabula Contrebiensis* (Zaragoza 1980), p.114-115). It may also be the same as the place described by Orosius, 5.23.11, as having been captured by Pompey during the Sertorian war, but is probably not the same as Begeda, which is the name Diodorus gives to Segeda, the town of the Belli and Titthi which was the cause of the Celtiberian wars in 153 (see above on 44.180).

101

438 **These are the things worthy of record that I have discovered that the Romans did against the Iberians themselves:** Appian makes the important point, and one which has sometimes eluded more modern writers, that the war with Sertorius was a watershed in the history of the Romans in the peninsula, in that from this time onwards the wars which took place there were between different groups of Romans, supported in different degrees by the people living in the Spanish provinces (see Richardson, *The Romans in Spain*, ch. 3). It is of particular importance for Appian, who makes a distinction in the organisation of his work between wars fought by the Romans with foreign nations and those which they fought between themselves (*praef.* 14.53-15.62).

when Sulla and Cinna were struggling together in Rome: L. Cornelius Sulla, when consul in 88 BC, marched on Rome with an army to secure for himself the command in the war against Mithridates of Pontus in Asia Minor, which had been transferred to his rival, C. Marius. After his departure, L. Cornelius Cinna, one of the consuls of the following year, recalled Marius from exile and seized power in Rome.

439 **Quintus Sertorius:** Q. Sertorius was a praetor in 83 BC, and was assigned the province of Hispania Citerior. He belonged to the Marian side in the struggle with Sulla, and, after Sulla's victory in Rome in 82 BC, a series of commanders was sent out to Spain to deal with him. He was only defeated as a result of his assassination in 72 BC. The history of Sertorius is given in extremely brief form here, since it is not properly part of the wars fought by the Romans against the Iberians (see last note). The main sources for Sertorius are Plutarch's life of him, Appian's somewhat fuller version of his career in *bell. civ.* 1.108.505-115.538 (which he mentions below at 101.441), and the fragments of Sallust's *Historiae*. See P. O. Spann, *Quintus Sertorius and the legacy of Sulla* (Fayetteville 1987); C. F. Konrad, *Plutarch's Sertorius: a historical commentary* (Chapel Hill and London 1994); Richardson, *The Romans in Spain*, pp. 95-104.

440 **Caecilius Metellus:** Q.Caecilius Metellus Pius, consul in 80, and a supporter of Sulla. He was sent to Hispania Ulterior in 79, to deal with the increasing threat posed by Sertorius growing power, but suffered defeats at his hands until joined by Pompeius in 77.

Gnaeus Pompeius: Pompey (who later was to be the great Roman commander in the wars against the pirates and in the east in the 60s BC, and Caesar's opponent in the civil wars from 49 BC to his death in 48 BC, following the battle of Pharsalus) was sent to Spain with *imperium pro consule* in 77 BC

441 **Perperna:** M. Perperna, a supporter of Cinna and Marius, held the praetorship in 82 and was given the province of Sicily. When he was driven out of the island by Pompey, he joined Sertorius in Spain (See Broughton, *MRR* 2.67-8). On the family, see F. Münzer, *Römische Adelsparteien und Adelsfamilien* (Stuttgart 1920), pp. 95-7. The story of Sertorius' betrayal and death in 72 BC has similarities with the death of Viriathus (see above 74.311-316).

The details of this war will be seen in my book about the Civil Wars which deals with Sulla: See on 101.439.

102

442 **Gaius Caesar was chosen to command in Iberia, to fight wherever he needed:** C. Julius Caesar, later dictator, was praetor in 62 and held the province of Ulterior in 61 and 60 (references in Broughton, *MRR* 2.173, 180 and 185). Appian clearly sees this a special command, but in fact it was of the same type as all commanders in the peninsula held at this period (Richardson, *The Romans in Spain*, pp. 106-7). He was sufficiently successful against the Callaeci and the Lusitanians for him to hope for a triumph on his return, but was frustrated by the need to enter Rome to stand for the consulship of 59 (Livy, *ep.* 103; Plutarch, *Caesar* 12; Dio Cassius 37.52-3). It was not possible for him to submit his name as a candidate unless he entered Rome, but, once within the city boundaries, he could not celebrate a triumphal entry. He decided to run for the consulship and succeeded in winning at the elections of 60 for 59 BC, with the help of Pompey and M. Licinius Crassus (often, wrongly, called the 'First Triumvirate'), and this in turn resulted in his ten-year command in Gaul from 58 to 49 BC.

he compelled by force of arms all those Iberians who were still uncertain or were not yet belonging to the Romans into total obedience: This is wild exaggeration, deduced from the assumption that Caesar's command was a special one, and that the Spanish provinces already covered the whole peninsula. See last note. Appian gives a similar account in *bell. civ.* 2.8.

443 **Some, who again went into revolt, were defeated by Julius Caesar, the son of Gaius, surnamed Augustus:** Again, this is a very brief account of Augustus' campaigns in the north-west of Spain, which lasted from 26 to 19 BC, waged against the hitherto unconquered tribes of the Atlantic coastal mountains, the Cantabri and the Astures, under the command of P. Carisius and Augustus' most important general, M. Vipsanius Agrippa (see R. Syme, 'The conquest of north-west Spain', in *Legio VII Gemina* (León 1970), pp. 83-107 and P. Le Roux, *L'armée romaine et l'organisation des provinces ibériques d'Auguste à l'invasion de 409* (Paris 1986), pp. 52-69). Augustus himself was present there in 26 and 25 BC, but the war was finally concluded by Agrippa in 19. This led to the conquest of the last section of the peninsula to come under Roman control.

444 **since that time the Romans have divided Iberia, which they now call Hispania, into three:** Following the wars against the Astures in the north-west, the province of Lusitania was created and the province formerly called Ulterior was thereafter known as Baetica (see Richardson, *The Romans in Spain*, pp. 134-8).

the senate sending two each year and the emperor sending the third : Appian is wrong in thinking that two of the three provinces were senatorial. Strabo, *Geogr.* 3.4.20, and Dio Cassius, 53.12.4-5, rightly state that 'people' (that is, in Appian's terms, the senate) looked after Baetica while the emperor held the other two.

Index

3614468